Physics for Game Programmers

GRANT PALMER

Physics for Game Programmers

Copyright © 2005 by Grant Palmer

ISBN (pbk): 1-59059-472-X

Printed and bound in the United States of America 9 8 7 6 5 4 3 2 1

Lead Editor: Tony Davis
Technical Reviewers: Alan McLeod, Jack Park
Editorial Board: Steve Anglin, Dan Appleman, Ewan Buckingham, Gary Cornell, Tony Davis, Jason Gilmore, Jonathan Hassell, Chris Mills, Dominic Shakeshaft, Jim Sumser
Assistant Publisher: Grace Wong
Project Manager: Laura E. Brown
Copy Manager: Nicole LeClerc
Copy Editor: Ami Knox
Production Manager: Kari Brooks-Copony
Production Editor: Kelly Winquist
Compositor: Susan Glinert
Proofreader: Liz Welch
Indexer: John Collin
Artist: Kinetic Publishing Services, LLC
Cover Designer: Kurt Krames
Manufacturing Manager: Tom Debolski

Distributed to the book trade in the United States by Springer-Verlag New York, Inc., 233 Spring Street, 6th Floor, New York, NY 10013, and outside the United States by Springer-Verlag GmbH & Co. KG, Tiergartenstr. 17, 69112 Heidelberg, Germany.

In the United States: phone 1-800-SPRINGER, fax 201-348-4505, e-mail orders@springer-ny.com, or visit http://www.springer-ny.com. Outside the United States: fax +49 6221 345229, e-mail orders@springer.de, or visit http://www.springer.de.

For information on translations, please contact Apress directly at 2560 Ninth Street, Suite 219, Berkeley, CA 94710. Phone 510-549-5930, fax 510-549-5939, e-mail info@apress.com, or visit http://www.apress.com.

The source code for this book is available to readers at www.apress.com in the Downloads section.

This book is dedicated to my wonderful wife, Lisa.

Contents at a Glance

Contents

About the Author

GRANT PALMER works for the ELORET Corporation, an engineering consulting company under contract to the NASA Ames Research Center in Moffett Field, CA. Grant develops computer programs to simulate the fluid dynamics, thermodynamics, and gas chemistry of spacecraft reentering planetary atmospheres. Grant has authored or coauthored eight books on computer programming, including *Beginning C# Objects* and *Java Programmer's Reference*.

Grant lives in Bothell, WA, with his wife, Lisa, and sons, Jackson and Zachary. He has a dog, Bailey, and cat, Callie, who recently decided that she should start living in Grant's house.

About the Technical Reviewers

ALAN MCLEOD graduated from MIT with a doctorate in materials engineering, having previously gained bachelor and master's degrees in metallurgical engineering from the University of Toronto. He then worked for Alcan International as a materials scientist. After several years in industry, he decided to follow his true passion and is now teaching programming to first- and second-year engineering students as a professor and professional engineer at Queen's University and the Royal Military College in Kingston, Ontario. He also runs his own contract programming company, CA Technical Consulting.

JACK PARK gives pretty good google. To do that, he remains very active developing software in the open source arena. His projects have included NexistWiki, an experimental platform that combines topic maps, issue-based information systems, and storytelling, together with wiki behaviors and weblogs. He produced, with technical editorial help from Sam Hunting, and with authors drawn from all over the planet, the book *XML Topic Maps: Creating and Using Topic Maps for the Web* (Addison-Wesley, 2002). In a former life, he built windmills and solar heaters, and created the book *The Wind Power Book* (Cheshire-Van Nostrand, 1981). He is presently employed as a research scientist with SRI International.

Acknowledgments

As anyone who writes a book knows, a lot of people have to work very hard to bring a book to print. I would like to thank my lead editor, Tony Davis, for always being in my corner during the writing of this book and for helping to formulate the vision for what this book would become. I would also like to thank the project manager, Laura Brown, for keeping this book on track and on schedule and for making sure that things didn't fall through the cracks. The entire production staff at Apress, Ami Knox, Kelly Winquist, and Glenn Munlawin, did a first-rate job throughout this project and always did their best to make the book the way that I wanted it to be.

I would like to thank the two technical reviewers for the book, Alan McLeod and Jack Park. I put them through quite a lot during the course of this book, and I think they both really earned their money on this project. Their insightful, constructive, and sometimes biting comments greatly improved the quality of the final product. Finally, as always, I would like to thank my wife, Lisa, and my sons, Jackson and Zachary, for being patient with me for "living" in my office the past six months while I was writing this book.

Introduction

Welcome to the wonderful world of physics. You may be thinking that "wonderful" and "physics" don't belong in the same sentence. Once you start to learn a little physics, however, you will find that it is a really interesting and rewarding subject because you will begin to gain an understanding of how things work. You will learn, for example, why a golf ball hooks or slices. You will also learn that physics really isn't as hard as you might have thought it was. Just a few basic concepts are pretty much all you need to start adding realistic physics into your game programs.

I've been a computer programmer and aerospace engineer working for NASA for the past 20 years. I really like my job, but one of the things I don't like is when I have to research the physical model for one of the programs I'm writing. Inevitably the references I find are incomplete. Either they don't fully explain things or they "forget" to include key elements of the model. Then I have to try to find another resource to fill in the missing pieces. This process can be very frustrating and time consuming.

What I have tried to do with this book is to spare you as a game programmer from this torturous process. This book is intended to give you all the information you need to install realistic physics into your game programs. This book will be *the* resource that you will turn to for all of your physics needs. For example, if you want to create a car race game, this book will give you not only the basic acceleration equations for a car, but also the drag coefficient for a sportscar and the equations that govern skidding and turning. You won't have to endlessly search the Internet or dig up another book to fill in the missing pieces.

Who This Book Is For

As you probably guessed from the title, this book is focuses on the physics needed by game programmers in order to add realism to their games. You don't need to have any background in physics to make use of this book. You don't need to have an extensive background in math for that matter either. As long as you know basic high-school-level algebra and trigonometry, you will be able to understand the physical models that are presented. This book might have been titled "Basic Physics for Game Programmers" because it focuses on the big picture. You will learn the fundamental physics concepts needed to incorporate physics-based realism into your games with the least amount of pain and suffering on your part. This book does not get bogged down in hopelessly complicated mathematical formulas that would have only a small effect on your game programs.

What This Book Is Not

This book primarily concerns itself with physics and is not a game programming book per se. There will be nothing in this book on game theory or how to render images on the screen. Many other good books on those elements of game programming are available, including *Advanced Java Game Programming* by David Croft (Apress, 2004). This book also focuses on fundamental physics and generally won't go into really advanced topics. For example, equations are presented that will let you create a realistic flight simulator, but advanced subjects like modeling the dynamic stability of an airplane in flight are not covered.

How the Book Is Divided

This book is organized into two main sections. The first six chapters will cover basic concepts, subjects like Newtonian mechanics, kinematics, and collisions. These topics will be applicable to a wide range of game programming situations. The first six chapters will provide you with the tools for your physics toolbelt. Chapters 7 through 15 take the basic concepts and apply them to specific physics models. You will learn how to model cars, planes, boats, and rockets. You will find chapters on developing sports simulations and on how to model explosions, lasers, and projectile penetrations. The later chapters will give you all the information you need to install physics-based realism into your games.

A Note on the Sample Programs

Just about every chapter contains one or more sample games that demonstrate how to code up the physics models presented in the chapter. Because this book focuses on physics, the graphics in the GUIs for the sample games are pretty basic—usually just two-dimensional figures and cartoons. While the graphics are primitive, the physics built into the sample games is real and will realistically depict whatever the game is intended to model.

Game programs can be written in many different programming languages. To keep things consistent throughout the book, the sample programs shown in this book are all written in Java, but the code that implements the physical models should be easily recognizable to anyone with a C, C++, or C# programming background. There are lots of comments throughout the programs, and the code has been made to be as readable as possible. For those of you who prefer to program in C or C#, you can download versions of all of the sample programs written in those languages from the Apress website at www.apress.com.

A Note on the Exercises

Many of the programs include exercises that test the reader's knowledge of the concepts that are covered in the chapter. Usually, the exercises go a little bit beyond the material that is presented in the chapter and are a good way to test your general understanding of the subject matter. The exercises were intended for students who are using this book as part of their course, but other readers are encouraged to try the exercises as well. Answers for the exercises are always provided at the end of the chapter in which they are presented.

Tidbits

Physics really is an interesting subject, and it is one that has been developing over thousands of years. The history of physics is full of many fascinating and quirky characters. Scattered throughout the book are Tidbit sections that provide historical trivia and other interesting information about the subjects being covered in the chapter. Did you ever wonder what they used to make golf balls out of in the old days? Well, there is a tidbit that will tell you.

Contact Me

If you have any questions or comments about the book, you can send me an e-mail at grantepalmer@msn.com. Tell me what you like about the book, or things that you think I could have done better. Also let me know if there are any subjects that you would like to see in future editions of the book.

CHAPTER 1

Adding Realism to Your Games

You're a game programmer. You know how to render complex car chase scenes on the screen. You know about game theory and how to make your games interesting and strategy filled. But physics? Physics is for old guys in white lab coats working in secret laboratories. Game programmers are—well, programmers. Why does a game programmer need to know about physics?

It turns out that a knowledge of physics is crucially important to game programming. It will make your games more fun to play and more realistic. The purpose of this book is to take some of the mystery out of physics and to give you the concepts and tools you will need to add realistic physics to your game programs. Why do you need to know physics? Well, here are just some of the reasons:

Physics Will Keep Your Games from Looking Fake

Game players are pretty sophisticated. They know when something looks or acts fake, and they will slam you for it. Nothing will make a game lose credibility faster than if the physics it uses is incorrect. On the other hand, if you get the physics right, your games will be praised by the gaming community. Look on game bulletin boards and at reviews and you will see many examples of this fact.

Here is an example of a positive review from X-treme Gaming Radio's evaluation of Microsoft's MS Flight Simulator 2004 game:

> *If you're looking for realism in a flight simulator, then this game is the way to go. The experience is breathtaking as you can almost feel the plane's reaction to its surroundings.*

If you read this review, you would probably think, "This game sounds great. I should check it out." The developers got the physics right and people noticed.

On the other hand, if you ignore the proper physics, you might get a review like the one posted on www.gametour.com about the Jet Moto 3 game,

> *Now as much as the series has tried to tout realistic physics and control, I just have to say that there is no physical equation for a hovering jet bike. THEY DO NOT EXIST.*

If someone read a review like this, they might think "Hey, this game sounds cheesy. I don't think I'll buy it."

The point is that physics matters. It is one of the first things reviewers and potential users will look at when they are evaluating your game. Keep in mind when creating games (just like in writing books) that you can't fake it. If you use bogus physics in your games, somebody will notice, and that somebody will write in to the game forums and tell the world how crappy your game is. While if you take the time and effort to get the physics right, your games will get the reputation for being the coolest and most realistic games around.

Adding Physics-Based Realism Is Easier Than You Might Think

Physics has an unfortunate reputation for being really hard. People think of Albert Einstein locked away in his office generating horribly complicated mathematical equations for years and years. In reality, most of the physics models you need as a game programmer, and most of the physics models discussed in this book, are reasonably simple. Ninety-five percent of the mathematical equations you will see in this book will be algebraic equations or simple trigonometry (sines and cosines).

Let's look at a couple of quick examples of the types of mathematical equations you will encounter in this book. A common task for game programmers is to model the trajectory of a projectile—a bullet, cannonball, basketball, and so on. One of the things typically required is to determine the altitude of the projectile at a given time. If the only force acting on the projectile is gravity pulling it towards the earth, the altitude of the projectile is a function of the elapsed time, t, the initial velocity, v_0, the initial altitude, z_0, and the acceleration due to gravity, g.

$$z = z_0 + v_0 t + \frac{1}{2} g t^2 \tag{1.1}$$

Equation (1.1) is a simple algebraic equation, and yet there is real physics in it. In some situations, computing the trajectory of a basketball for instance, Equation (1.1) is the expression you will use in your game programs. An example of when trigonometry is used is the problem of modeling a car resting on a sloped ramp as shown in Figure 1-1.

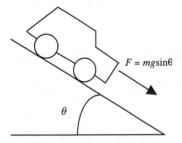

Figure 1-1. *The force acting on the car is a function of the sine of the slope angle.*

The force of gravity will pull on the car down the ramp. The magnitude of the force is equal to the mass of the car, m, the acceleration due to gravity, g, and the sine of the angle of the ramp, θ.

$$F = mg \sin\theta \tag{1.2}$$

Once again, Equation (1.2) is simple, and yet it accurately models the gravitational force acting on the car. You could use Equation (1.2) to determine if the brakes could hold the car on the ramp or to determine the speed of the car if it were to start moving down the ramp.

Now, it's true that some of the equations in the book will be more complicated than Equations (1.1) and (1.2), but as was mentioned before, 95% of the math in this book is algebra and trigonometry. What about the other 5%? There will be times in the book when we will have to make use of things called **differential equations** in our physics models. They may sound a bit scary, but they are really just equations that are used in this book to describe how quantities such as velocity or position change over time. We'll provide you with a handy little program that solves differential equations that you can make use of in your game programs.

So one thing that makes incorporating physics into your game programs easier than you might have thought is that the mathematics for the most part isn't that complicated. Another nice thing about physics is that in most cases you can make your physics models as simple or as complicated as you like or need. For example, the flight of a projectile can be modeled using a simple algebraic equation. If you want, you can add some complexity to the model by including effects such as aerodynamic drag or spin, but these more complicated effects are simply added to the base model. If the simple model is all you need, you can stick with it and leave out the more complicated stuff.

When it comes to adding realistic physics to your games, you get a lot of bang for your buck. Even including a simple physical model in your games will greatly enhance their realism and believability.

Adding Physics Won't Affect Game Performance

Another reason some game programmers are reluctant to add physics-based realism to their games is the perception that "all that complicated math will slow the game down." That might have been true in the dark days when computers boasted "500 kilohertz performance," but modern computer processors are fast enough to zip through anything but the most complicated physics models. Your games will spend a lot more time rendering than they will evaluating whatever physics model you incorporate into them.

The sample games presented in this book demonstrate that physics won't slow down game performance. The car simulator presented in Chapter 8 uses a reasonably complex physics model to simulate the acceleration and gear shifting capabilities of a sports car. The game ran so quickly on a 1.6 GHz Pentium 4 PC (an older, fairly slow computer) that a timer had to be built into the program to actually slow the game down. Otherwise, the user didn't have time to shift gears before the maximum engine speed was reached. The same condition is true for the flight simulator that will be presented in Chapter 10. The physics equations are computed so quickly that the game has to be intentionally slowed down. The physics models in the car and flight simulators would have to be made significantly more complicated for there to be any effect on the execution of the games.

Knowing Some Physics Will Make You a Better Game Programmer

Having a physics-based understanding of how things work will make you a better game programmer in several ways. For one thing, having a physical understanding of what you are trying to simulate gives you the knowledge of what effects to include in your game. For example, let's say you are creating a golf game. You know that golf balls can hook, slice, and draw, but how do you model those effects? If you know the physics behind golf ball flight, you know that it is the spin given to the golf ball that causes these effects. You can then obtain the mathematical equations that describe spin and build realistic spin effects into your golf simulation.

As another example, consider a car simulation where the car has to drive around a curve in the road. If you didn't know anything about physics, you might just have the car go around the curve at whatever speed it was traveling. If you knew the correct physics, however, you would know that when an object travels around a curve, an effect known as **centripetal force** pushes the object outward. If the car is going too fast or if the curve is too sharp, the wheels of the car won't be able to hold on to the road, and the car will slide or spin outwards. Centripetal force can be an interesting and exciting effect to add to your car simulation if you're aware of its existence.

Having knowledge of physics also allows you to know what effects to leave out of your games. A classic example is when a person is shot with a bullet in a computer game and he is thrown backwards through a window or some such thing. In reality, the force caused by a bullet striking an object is relatively small—not enough to drive someone backwards.

Let's Add Some Realism to Your Games

Hopefully by now you're sold on the idea of game programmers learning about physics and are ready to start adding realistic physics models to your game programs. So let's dive right in and get started. The first thing we'll do is to spend some time going over some basic concepts that you will use in all of your physics modeling. We'll accomplish that goal in Chapters 2 through 6. Once we have the basics well in hand, we'll develop physics models for specific applications including sports, cars, boats, planes, rockets, explosions, and lasers. Let's turn the page and start with the basics.

CHAPTER 2

■ ■ ■

Some Basic Concepts

After reading Chapter 1, you're probably anxious to incorporate realistic physics into your game simulations. Before we get into specific physics models to model how airplanes fly or what happens when a bat hits a baseball, you need to have an understanding of some core concepts and definitions that will be used throughout the book. The subjects covered in this chapter are things that can be used in any physics-based model. A lot of this material may be familiar to you, but even if you know most of what is here, it's a good idea to refresh your memory to "set the stage" for the rest of the book.

Physics models are usually expressed mathematically, and as you probably know mathematics is a language all to itself, full of strange symbols and funny-looking letters. In this chapter, we'll review some basic math nomenclature, so you won't be confused when you see the symbols α or Σ later in the book. This chapter will also present some basic mathematical concepts and solution techniques that will be used in developing the physics models in subsequent chapters.

Most of the time when you are putting physics into your games, you will be dealing with a three-dimensional world—how a golf ball flies through the air or how a car drives around a corner. In this chapter, we will discuss how coordinate reference frames are used to position an object in space and about the different types of coordinate reference frames. You will see how certain characteristics, such as velocity, can be expressed three-dimensionally using a mathematical concept known as a **vector**.

Some of the specific subjects we will investigate in this chapter include the following:

- Systems of units

- Scientific notation

- Summation notation

- Greek letters

- Coordinate systems and frames of reference

- Scalars and vectors

- Matrices and matrix multiplication

- Rotation matrices

- Derivatives and differential equations

When you finish this chapter, you will be armed and ready to dive into the wonderful world of physics, so let's get started.

5

Systems of Units

To describe the physical world, we need to measure things. We want to know how heavy something is or how fast it is traveling. In order to measure things, a system of units is required. It would be nice if there were one universal system of units. Unfortunately, there are two widely used systems of units, namely the International System of Units and the English System of Units, and this is a situation that creates the potential for confusion and errors. Both systems of units will be discussed in this section and conversion factors will be provided for moving from one system to another.

The International System of Units, or **SI units**, includes three fundamental units of measure for mass, length, and time. The unit of length in the SI system is the meter, the unit of mass is the kilogram, and the unit of time is the second. The three quantities are usually abbreviated as *m*, *kg*, and *s*. Most other physical quantities, density, pressure, force, and so on, can be expressed in terms of meters, kilograms, and seconds. There are also smaller SI units of measure that we will use from time to time in this book. A gram (*gm*) is 1/1000 or "one one-thousandths" of a kilogram. A centimeter (*cm*) is 1/100 of a meter, and a millimeter (*mm*) is 1/1000 of a meter. The unit of measure for temperature in the SI system is Kelvin (*K*).

An older of system of units known as the **English System** of Units is still widely used in some countries. The unit of mass under the English system is the pound-mass (*lbm*) or the slug. The unit of length is the foot (*ft*). One consistent element between the English and SI systems is that time in both systems is measured in seconds. The English system is still widely used in the United States and (as you might expect) England. Most of the rest of the world uses SI units. Temperature in the English system is expressed in terms of degrees Fahrenheit (*°F*) or Rankine (*R*).

The International System of Units is more logical in that different units of the same quantity are related to each other by factors of ten. There are 100 centimeters in a meter and 1000 meters in a kilometer (*km*). The English system involves more arbitrary conversion factors. There are 12 inches in a foot and 5280 feet in a mile.

This book will tend to lean more to the SI system of units, but equivalent English unit values for equations and constants will sometimes be provided. Table 2-1 shows the units of measure for some common physical quantities, along with conversion factors for moving from the English system to the SI system. If you multiply the value in English units by the conversion factor, you will arrive at the value in SI units. For example, one mile is equal to 1.609 *km*.

Table 2-1. *Units and Conversion Factors*

Quantity	English Units	SI Units	Conversion Factor
Length	foot (*ft*)	meter (*m*)	0.3048
	mile	kilometer (*km*)	1.609
Mass	pound-mass (*lbm*)	kilogram (*kg*)	0.4536
	slug	kilogram (*kg*)	14.593
Force	pound (*lb*)	Newton (*N*)	4.448
Pressure	lb/in^2	N/m^2	6894.7
Density	$slug/ft^3$	kg/m^3	515.379
	lbm/ft^3	kg/m^3	16.018
Temperature	Fahrenheit (*°F*)	Kelvin (*K*)	5/9(F + 459.67)
	Rankine (*R*)	Kelvin (*K*)	5/9

Over the centuries, many other types of units have been devised that you may come across from time to time. In the English system, some of the "other" units can seem a little strange. For example, a grain is a unit of mass in the English system, and there are 7024 *grains* to a pound. The SI system also defines additional units of measure, but these are always defined in terms of the fundamental units. A Newton, for example, is a *kg-m/s²*.

Tidbit The units in the English system of units were developed over many hundreds of years, and some of the origins are interesting. The foot was taken from the measurement of a human foot (the king's according to legend). Zero degrees in the Fahrenheit temperature scale was based on the coldest temperature Dr. Fahrenheit could achieve in his lab.

The key thing about systems of units for game programmers is to make sure to use a consistent system of units. If you mix and match English and SI units, you will not get the right answer. For example, let's say you want to calculate the acceleration of an arrow according to the equation *F=ma*. Let's also say that you want to shoot an arrow whose mass, *m*, is given as 500 *grains* from a bow that can deliver a force, *F*, of 5 *N*. If you want the acceleration, *a*, in units of *m/s²*, you must first convert the mass of the arrow from *grains* to *kg*.

Tidbit A classic case of how mixing and matching units can cause big problems is what happened to the NASA Mars Climate Orbiter mission in 1999. One team of engineers working on the project used English units and another team used SI units. The resulting screwup created an error in the guidance program that caused the spacecraft to enter into the Martian atmosphere at too steep an angle. The billion-dollar space mission failed.

Scientific Notation

In the world of physics, sometimes it is necessary to work with really large or really small numbers. For example, the gravitational constant, a quantity that relates the force two objects exert on each other, is a very small number. Written in standard decimal notation, it is equal to the following:

$$G = 0.0000000000667 \ \frac{N - m^2}{kg^2} \tag{2.1}$$

For small numbers like the gravitational constant, it's pretty inconvenient to have to write out all the zeros. Fortunately, there is something known as **scientific notation** that can be used to express large or small numbers in a more compact form. Under this system, numbers are written as a value between 0 and 10, the letter "e," and a number that represents how many powers of ten are in the value. For example, the gravitational constant could be written more compactly using scientific notation:

$$G = 6.67e - 11 \ \frac{N - m^2}{kg^2} \tag{2.2}$$

For numbers with a magnitude of less than one, the number after the letter "e" is negative. For values with a magnitude greater than one, the number after the letter "e" is positive. The mass of Earth's moon, for instance, is a very large number and would be expressed in scientific notation as 7.3483e+22 *kg*.

An alternative form of scientific notation is to use a "10" raised to the power of the number of zeros in the value. For example, the mass of Earth's moon could be alternatively expressed as 7.3483×10^{22} *kg*. If the magnitude of the number is less than one, the exponent on the power of ten would be negative as in 6.67×10^{-11}.

You will use scientific notation when you incorporate physics into your game programs, for example, when you define constants like the gravitational constant. Most computer languages recognize scientific notation, so you can incorporate it into your game programs. For example, the following snippet of code would be perfectly acceptable in the Java, C, or C# programming languages:

```
double G = 6.67e-11;
```

Summation Notation

Scientific notation is a widely used nomenclature that we will use over and over in this book. Another bit of shorthand employed in mathematical equations is the **summation notation**. There will be a lot of times when you will need to sum up a sequence of numbers. For example, it might be necessary to find the total mass of a collection of five objects. The long and tedious way to write a summation is to write each term in the sum.

$$m_{total} = m_1 + m_2 + m_3 + m_4 + m_5 \tag{2.3}$$

An easier way to indicate a summation is by using summation notation.

$$m_{total} = \sum_{j=1}^{5} m_j \tag{2.4}$$

Equations (2.3) and (2.4) are equivalent, but the summation notation is more compact. It's easy to see that when a large number of terms are involved, you pretty much have to use summation notation when writing the summation. Here is a code snippet that implements the summation shown in Equation (2.4) for the Java, C, or C# programming languages. It is assumed that the mass[] array was declared and initialized somewhere else in the code.

```
massTotal = 0.0;
for(j=0; j<5; ++j) {
  massTotal += mass[j];
}
```

Greek Letters

Mathematics can be thought of as the language of physics, and mathematicians love to use Greek letters in their equations. The reasons are unclear, perhaps it is in honor of the ancient Greek mathematicians, but that's just the way it is. We will follow the same convention in this book. Don't be confused when you see Greek letters in the math equations. Just remember that they are symbols generally used to represent a variable, constant, or mathematical operation. An equation written with Western alphabet letters:

$$d = at^2 + bt + c \tag{2.5}$$

could have been written using Greek letters:

$$\delta = \alpha t^2 + \beta t + \chi \tag{2.6}$$

and the meaning of the two equations would be the same. As a general rule, if you see a symbol in an equation in this book and you don't know what it is, it is probably a Greek letter. Even the summation sign, Σ, is just a Greek capital "S."

Coordinate Systems and Frames of Reference

A fair amount of this book is devoted to developing models that describe the motion of an object. In order to accomplish this task, we need to be able to specify the location of the object in two- or three-dimensional space. Two pieces of information are required to specify the position of an object in two-dimensional space, and three pieces of information are needed to locate an object in three-dimensional space. The manner in which this information is specified defines a **coordinate system**. The coordinate system in turn defines the **frame of reference** for an object. We might say, for example, that the frame of reference of the airplane we are modeling is the Cartesian coordinate system. We will discuss two of the most commonly used coordinate systems in this section—namely the Cartesian and spherical coordinate systems.

The **Cartesian coordinate system** defines the location of an object by specifying the x, y, and z location of the object. The x-, y-, and z-axes of the Cartesian coordinate system, as shown in Figure 2-1, are straight lines that emanate from a common origin. The three axes are perpendicular to each other. The general convention used in this book is that the z-axis will point upwards from the surface of the earth and the x- and y-axes are parallel to the surface of the earth.

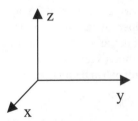

Figure 2-1. *The Cartesian coordinate system*

The Cartesian coordinate system is the one you will most commonly use in your game programming. It is generally the easiest coordinate system to visualize and is useful for describing linear motion. We will use this coordinate system most often in this book.

While the Cartesian coordinate system is the most commonly used, there is nothing unique about it, and the Cartesian coordinate system is not well suited for describing some things, for example, modeling circular motion. Fortunately, many other coordinate systems are available that can be used to describe the position of an object in space. The **spherical coordinate system** defines the position of an object by a distance ρ from an origin and two angles θ and φ as shown in Figure 2-2.

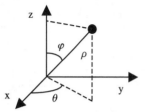

Figure 2-2. *The spherical coordinate system*

The spherical coordinate system is useful for describing circular or rotational motion. There will be times in your game programming when the spherical coordinate will prove easier to use and more appropriate than the Cartesian coordinate system. You would use spherical coordinates, for instance, if you were modeling a satellite in orbit around a planet.

A coordinate system provides a way to locate the position of an object in space. If required, the coordinates in one coordinate system can be converted into another. For example, the coordinates of an object in spherical (ρ, φ, θ) coordinates can be converted into Cartesian (x, y, z) coordinates using the following equations.

$$x = \rho\sin\varphi\cos\theta \tag{2.7a}$$

$$y = \rho\sin\varphi\sin\theta \tag{2.7b}$$

$$z = \rho\cos\varphi \tag{2.7c}$$

There is one other distinction about coordinate systems and frames of reference we need to consider: every coordinate system (and therefore frame of reference) has an origin. The location of the origin is arbitrary. It can be at a fixed point in space, or it can move with the object. If a frame of reference is at rest or moves with a uniform velocity, it is known as an **inertial** frame of reference. If the frame of reference is accelerating, it is known as a **noninertial** frame of reference.

Most of the time in this book, we will be dealing with models that use an inertial frame of reference whereby the origin is at a fixed point in space. In some instances, such as when we are looking at the rotational motion of an object such as the spin of a golf ball in flight, it is more advantageous to use a frame of reference that moves with the object.

Scalars and Vectors

Two types of quantities will go into the mathematical equations we will develop in this book. **Scalar** quantities are those that have a magnitude only. An example of a scalar quantity would be the mass of an object. No matter which way you look at the object, it will have the same mass. A **vector** quantity, on the other hand, has both a magnitude and a direction. An example of a vector quantity would be the velocity of an object. If a baseball player throws a baseball into the air and we want to calculate where it will go, it's not enough to know how fast the baseball is traveling. We would also need to know the direction that the baseball was thrown.

A vector is a way to describe the magnitude and direction of something in two- or three-dimensional space. It is often useful to separate a vector quantity into components that act in each coordinate direction. For example, under the three-dimensional Cartesian coordinate system the velocity of an object could be separated into x-, y-, and z-components.

$$\vec{v} = v_x\vec{x} + v_y\vec{y} + v_z\vec{z} \tag{2.8}$$

The velocity vector, v, is on the left-hand side of Equation (2.8). The arrow symbol on top of the v, x, y, and z terms in Equation (2.8) is used to indicate a vector. The terms v_x, v_y, and v_z are the velocity components in the x-, y-, and z-directions. The separate velocity components are shown graphically in Figure 2-3.

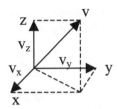

Figure 2-3. *Velocity can be split up into directional components.*

The reason to split a vector quantity such as velocity into its x-, y-, and z-components is that it often makes it easier to model the physical problem. We will perform such "vector separations" quite frequently throughout this book. For example, when we study the motion of a projectile in Chapter 5, the force, acceleration, and velocity of the projectile will be split into x-, y-, and z-components. When we model a collision between two objects in Chapter 6, the collision is modeled based on the directional components of velocity at the moment of impact.

Computing the Magnitude of a Vector

As we have discussed, sometimes a vector is divided into directional components. There are times when you will need to go the other way—you may have the directional components of velocity and need to compute the overall velocity magnitude. The magnitude of a vector is found by taking the square root of the sum of the square of the directional components. For a velocity vector in the Cartesian coordinate system, the velocity magnitude can be found from the square root of the sum of the square of the x-, y-, and z-velocity components.

$$v = \sqrt{v_x^2 + v_y^2 + v_z^2} \tag{2.9}$$

The velocity magnitude of an object is also referred to as the **speed** of the object. You will frequently need to compute vector magnitudes when incorporating physics into your games. For example, aerodynamic drag is a function of the square of the velocity magnitude of an object.

The Unit Vector

In the previous section, you learned how to compute the magnitude of a vector. If the magnitude of a vector is equal to 1, the vector is known as a **unit vector**. Unit vectors are used when splitting a vector into directional components. The x, y, and z terms in Equation (2.8) are unit vectors in the x-, y-, and z-directions. We will use unit vectors several times in this book, for instance, when we calculate the lifting force caused by a spinning golf ball.

Vector Cross Product

Vectors are two- or three-dimensional quantities, but standard mathematical operations can be performed on them. Two vectors can be added to or subtracted from each other. When you are incorporating physics into your game programs, there may be times you will need to find a vector that is normal or perpendicular to one or two other vectors. For example, a spinning object will generate a lifting force—this is a subject we will explore in Chapter 5. The direction of this spin force is perpendicular to the direction the object is traveling and to the axis around which the object is spinning.

There is a special vector operation known as a **vector cross product** that takes two vectors and computes a third vector that is perpendicular to the first two. The x-, y-, and z-components of the perpendicular vector are found from various combinations of the x-, y-, and z-components of the first two vectors. Consider the two vectors shown in Equation (2.10):

$$\vec{a} = a_x \vec{x} + a_y \vec{y} + a_z \vec{z} \tag{2.10a}$$

$$\vec{b} = b_x \vec{x} + b_y \vec{y} + b_z \vec{z} \tag{2.10b}$$

The cross product of the vectors $\vec{a}$ and $\vec{b}$ would be the following:

$$\vec{c} = \left(a_y b_z - b_y a_z\right)\vec{x} + \left(a_z b_x - b_z a_x\right)\vec{y} + \left(a_x b_y - b_x a_y\right)\vec{z} \tag{2.11}$$

Matrices

At times the physics models you incorporate into your games will be simple—one equation with one unknown, for instance. Other times things will be more complicated, and you may have to store a collection of associated data elements. You might have to consider a system of related equations, for example, or you might want to store data for a collection of associated objects.

A mathematical construct known as a **matrix,** also referred to as an **array,** is used to store a set of data in a structured manner. If you have any programming experience at all, you are probably already familiar with the concept of a matrix. A matrix, similar to summation notation, is really just a convenience. You could conceivably store the associated collection of data as separate variables. However, the use of matrices results in more compact, efficient mathematical expressions and computer code. For example, consider a system of three mathematical equations with three unknown variables, x, y, and z.

$$a = 4x + y - 3z \tag{2.12a}$$

$$b = -7x - 2y + 5z \tag{2.12b}$$

$$c = 3x + 3y + z \tag{2.12c}$$

If the three equations are expressed in matrix form, they take the following form:

$$\begin{bmatrix} a \\ b \\ c \end{bmatrix} = \begin{bmatrix} 4 & 1 & -3 \\ -7 & -2 & 5 \\ 3 & 3 & 1 \end{bmatrix} \begin{bmatrix} x \\ y \\ z \end{bmatrix} \tag{2.13}$$

The matrix shown in Equation (2.13) is a two-dimensional matrix with three rows and three columns. Matrices can be of any dimension. In this book, we will use 1-, 2-, and 3-dimensional matrices. Matrices are commonly used in the development of mathematical and physics models. In this book, we will make use of matrices when we model an airplane in flight and when we model collisions between objects.

Matrix Multiplication

Just as with vectors, you can add, subtract, and multiply matrices together. Adding or subtracting matrices involves simply adding or subtracting the individual elements, but the matrices must have the same dimensions. Multiplying matrices is a little more complicated. In this book, we will only concern ourselves with multiplying two-dimensional matrices. In this case, the elements of the final array are found by multiplying each row of the first array with each column of the second array. For example, let's say we want to multiply two two-dimensional arrays, each having three rows and three columns as shown in Equation (2.14).

$$[C] = \begin{bmatrix} a_{11} & a_{12} & a_{13} \\ a_{21} & a_{22} & a_{23} \\ a_{31} & a_{32} & a_{33} \end{bmatrix} \begin{bmatrix} b_{11} & b_{12} & b_{13} \\ b_{21} & b_{22} & b_{23} \\ b_{31} & b_{32} & b_{33} \end{bmatrix} \tag{2.14}$$

The first element of the [C] array is found by multiplying the elements in the first row of the [A] array with the elements in the first column of the [B] array.

$$c_{11} = a_{11}b_{11} + a_{12}b_{21} + a_{13}b_{31} \tag{2.15}$$

The other elements of the [C] array are found in a similar manner. When multiplying two-dimensional arrays, the two arrays don't have to have the same dimensions, but the number of columns of the first matrix must equal the number of rows of the second matrix.

Matrix multiplication is a common feature to many mathematics and physics models. In this book, we'll use matrix multiplication when we create an airplane flight simulator in Chapter 10.

Rotation Matrices

Previously in this chapter we discussed how a coordinate system is required to specify the location of an object in two- or three-dimensional space. The orientation of the coordinate axes is arbitrary; one orientation is equally as valid as any other. Most of the time in this book when we are using the Cartesian frame of reference, the x- and y-coordinate axes will be oriented such that they are parallel to the earth's surface, and the z-axis will be in the vertical direction, perpendicular to the earth. This orientation works well when analyzing the motion of projectiles, cars, boats, basketballs, and so on.

There are times, however, when you will need to temporarily rotate the coordinate axes to perform a calculation. This is required, for example, when modeling the collision of a golf club head and a golf ball. Coordinate axes rotations are typically performed two-dimensionally. The axis of rotation is taken to be one of the original coordinate axes, and the other two axes are rotated a given angle from their nominal setting. In Figure 2-4, the x- and y-axes are rotated by an angle θ with the z-axis serving as the axis of rotation.

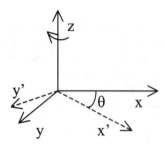

Figure 2-4. *A coordinate axes rotation about the z-axis*

A vector quantity such as location or velocity in the original xyz coordinate system can be expressed in terms of the rotated coordinate system using the sine and cosine of the rotation angle.

$$\begin{bmatrix} v'_x \\ v'_y \\ v'_z \end{bmatrix} = \begin{bmatrix} \cos\theta & \sin\theta & 0 \\ -\sin\theta & \cos\theta & 0 \\ 0 & 0 & 1 \end{bmatrix} \begin{bmatrix} v_x \\ v_y \\ v_z \end{bmatrix} \tag{2.16}$$

The matrix shown in Equation (2.16) is called a **rotation matrix**. The rotation angle is also referred to as an **Euler angle** after the famous mathematician. Based on what we know about matrix multiplication, the rotated velocity components can also be written in equation form.

$$v'_x = v_x \cos\theta + v_y \sin\theta \tag{2.17a}$$

$$v'_y = -v_x \sin\theta + v_y \cos\theta \tag{2.17b}$$

$$v'_z = v_z \tag{2.17c}$$

Since the rotation was about the z-axis, the rotated z-component of velocity is unchanged. Similar rotation matrices exist for rotations about the x- and y-axes. What is shown in Equation (2.16) is a two-dimensional coordinate axis rotation. A three-dimensional coordinate axis rotation is a much more complicated problem and is usually achieved by performing three successive two-dimensional rotations. The final rotation matrix will be the result of multiplying three two-dimensional rotation matrices together, and the matrix elements will be a function of three separate Euler (rotation) angles.

We won't go into the problem of developing and displaying a three-dimensional rotation matrix here, but instead will defer that problem to Chapter 10, where we will use a three-dimensional rotation matrix to build an airplane flight simulator. We will use two-dimensional rotation matrices when we model collisions in Chapters 6 and 7.

Derivatives

A popular misconception about physics is it involves a lot of really hard math. In some cases that is true. If you are a nuclear physicist, you will work with some really scary-looking equations. For game programmers, however, it is not true. Probably 95% of the math you will need to add realistic physics to your game programs will be basic algebra and trigonometry. Part of the other 5% will involve working with things called **derivatives**.

Derivatives sound complex, but the idea behind them is quite simple. A derivative is simply a ratio that defines how one thing changes when another thing changes. If a baseball player throws a baseball, a derivative might be used to describe how the location of the baseball changes with time. If a laser beam is fired into a metal plate, a derivative could be used to characterize how the temperature of the metal changes with increasing distance of the laser from the surface of the plate. Countless other examples of derivatives are used in physical modeling.

Let's look at a theoretical example: in Figure 2-5, a snowboarder doesn't look where he's going and inadvertently skis off a cliff. We're watching him do this from the safety of the ski lodge and want to model the change in his altitude as a function of time as he plummets towards the earth.

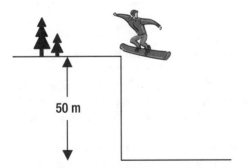

Figure 2-5. *Don't let this happen to you.*

You know that the cliff is 50 *m* high and notice that it takes the snowboarder about 3.3 seconds to hit the ground. If you were to make a plot of this altitude, *z*, over time, *t*, it would look something like the curve shown in Figure 2-6. When the snowboarder first flies off the cliff, his rate of descent is small. As gravity takes hold of the snowboarder, he accelerates and the rate at which he falls increases over time and is the greatest when he hits the ground (unfortunately for him).

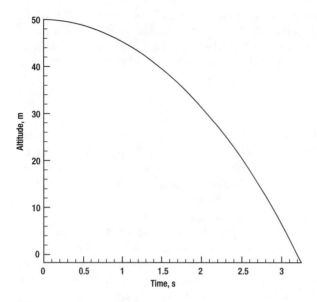

Figure 2-6. *The altitude of the snowboarder as a function of time*

You might think of modeling the rate of change of altitude of the snowboarder over time by simply subtracting the final altitude and time from the initial altitude and time.

$$\frac{\Delta z}{\Delta t} = \frac{z_{final} - z_{initial}}{t_{final} - t_{initial}} \tag{2.18}$$

Using the Δ form shown in Equation (2.18) is the equivalent of drawing a straight line from the endpoints of the curve shown in Figure 2-6. Equation (2.18) provides the average rate of change of altitude with time. However, as shown in Figure 2-7, it fails to accurately calculate the rate of fall at a given time, because, unlike the curve shown in Figure 2-6, this result is linear. At first the snowboarder's rate of fall is small. When he hits the ground, his rate of fall is much larger. The Δ expression shown in Equation (2.18) only correctly predicts the altitude of the snowboarder at the beginning and end of his fall.

A derivative, on the other hand, provides an *instantaneous* rate of change. In the case of the snowboarder, it's the rate of change in altitude at any time during the fall of the snowboarder. Instead of using the Δ symbol, derivatives are represented using the letter d. A derivative that represents the change in altitude over time would be written as the following:

$$\frac{dz}{dt} \tag{2.19}$$

The variable on top of the derivative, z in this case, is known as the **dependent variable**, because its value depends on changes to the variable on the bottom of the derivative known as the **independent variable**. The derivative shown in Equation (2.19) would be referred to as "the derivative of z with respect to t."

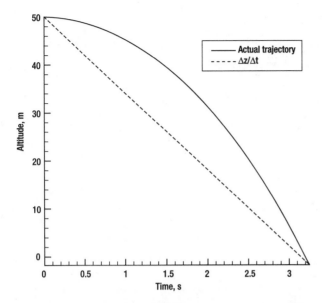

Figure 2-7. *Δz/Δt does not accurately predict the rate of fall at a given time.*

The derivative *dz/dt* can also be thought of as the slope of the curve shown in Figure 2-6, and its value will change over time. When the snowboarder starts his fall, the slope of the altitude vs. time curve is shallow, and the value of the derivative is a small negative number (it's negative because his altitude is decreasing with time). At the end of his fall, the rate of descent is large and so are the slope of the curve and the value of the derivative.

The derivative shown in Equation (2.19) represents the rate of change of one scalar quantity to another scalar quantity. This type of derivative is known as a **first-order derivative**. It's possible to take a derivative of another derivative. A derivative of a derivative is called a **second-order derivative** and is indicated by using the number 2 as superscripts in the derivative expression. For example, the z-component of velocity is defined as the derivative of altitude with respect to time.

$$v_z = \frac{dz}{dt} \tag{2.20}$$

Acceleration is defined as the derivative of velocity with respect to time, but acceleration can also be written as the second derivative of altitude with respect to time.

$$a_z = \frac{dv_z}{dt} = \frac{d}{dt}\left(\frac{dz}{dt}\right) = \frac{d^2z}{dt^2} \tag{2.21}$$

To see graphically the relationship between first and second derivatives, the altitude, velocity, and acceleration of the unfortunate snowboarder are shown as a function of time in Figure 2-8. The acceleration and velocity values are really negative, but they are shown as positive values in Figure 2-8 to make the figure more compact.

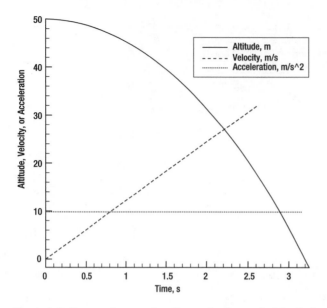

Figure 2-8. *Comparing acceleration, velocity, and altitude for the snowboarder*

The acceleration due to gravity is constant, so the acceleration line in Figure 2-8 is horizontal. The derivative of velocity with respect to time is equal to the acceleration. Since acceleration is constant, the velocity of the snowboarder increases linearly with time and the velocity curve in Figure 2-8 is a straight diagonal line. The derivative of altitude with respect to time is equal to the velocity. As velocity increases, the value of the altitude derivative becomes a larger and larger negative number and the altitude curve becomes steeper and steeper.

In this section, we used derivatives to describe the motion of a snowboarder as he plummeted to Earth. We will also use derivatives throughout this book to model the motion of other objects including springs, cannonballs, golf balls, cars, boats, bullets, and airplanes.

Differential Equations

In the previous section, the concept of a derivative was introduced as a ratio of how the value of one quantity changes when the value of another quantity changes. A mathematical equation that includes derivatives is called, as one might expect, a **differential equation**. A differential equation that has only one dependent variable is known as an **ordinary differential equation** or ODE. When we work with differential equations in this book, we will be dealing with ODEs.

A differential equation can also have more than one dependent variable, in which case it is known as a **partial differential equation**, or PDE. A typical PDE is shown in Equation (2.22).

$$\frac{\partial u}{\partial x} + \frac{\partial v}{\partial y} = 0 \qquad (2.22)$$

Partial differential equations are used for such things as modeling the fluid dynamic conservation of mass, momentum, and energy equations. An in-depth discussion of partial differential equations and how to solve them is beyond the scope of this book.

An example of an ODE is shown in Equation (2.23). It models the motion of a spring and includes both first- and second-order derivatives. The quantity x represents the displacement of the spring from its resting position and m is the mass of a weight attached to the end of the spring. The μ parameter models the damping forces that cause the spring to slow down over time and k is the spring constant that represents how stiff the spring is.

$$m\frac{d^2x}{dt^2} + \mu\frac{dx}{dt} + kx = 0 \tag{2.23}$$

When modeling the motion of a spring, we want to determine the x-position of the spring as a function of time. To accomplish this task, we need to solve the ODE shown in Equation (2.23). To avoid filling your brain with too much math this early in the book, a discussion of how to solve ODEs will be deferred to when we study kinematics in Chapter 4. A typical solution to the spring ODE is shown in Figure 2-9. The spring is initially stretched 0.2 m and then released. The spring oscillates back and forth, and the oscillations gradually die out over time.

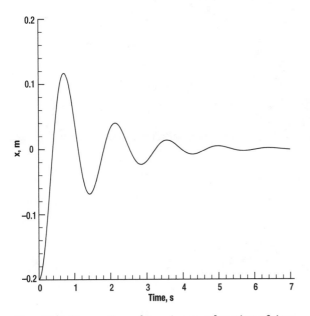

Figure 2-9. *The motion of a spring as a function of time*

Summary

This chapter provided a brief look at some basic concepts that we will use throughout this book. The subjects covered in this chapter will be the tools that we will use to build our physics models. You learned about the English and SI system of units and how scientific and summation notation can be used to make equations more readable and compact. The Cartesian and spherical coordinate systems were introduced. The differences between scalars and vectors were presented. We discussed matrices—how to multiply them together and how rotation matrices can be used to rotate coordinate systems. We also looked at derivatives and differential equations.

Some of the specific points to remember from this chapter include the following:

- It is important to be consistent with units when implementing physics models.

- It is a standard convention to use Greek letters in physics equations.

- Most programming languages recognize scientific notation.

- We can use the vector cross product to find a vector that is perpendicular to two other vectors.

- Derivatives are used to model the motion of objects.

Now that you've seen some of the basics, let's learn some physics!

■ ■ ■

Basic Newtonian Mechanics

People have been interested in the science of how objects move for thousands of years. The ancient Greeks, men like Aristotle, were responsible for many of the early theories on the causes of motion. Unfortunately, the ancient Greeks made a lot of mistakes. For instance, they thought that if two objects were dropped from a height that the heavier object would reach the ground first.

During the Renaissance period, scientists like Galileo and Newton reformulated the basic laws of motion. Using experiments and observations, they developed improved physical models for predicting the motion of objects. They came up with the basic relationships that model the interaction of force, mass, and acceleration. From these Sir Isaac Newton derived his famous three laws of motion, and it's because of contributions such as this that the subject is sometimes referred to as **Newtonian mechanics**.

In this chapter, you will learn about the basic laws of motion. We will explore the relationship between force, mass, and acceleration. You will learn about some different types of forces and about the concepts of work, energy, and power. Newtonian mechanics will form the foundation of nearly every physical model you will use in your game programming. For example, the trajectory of a bullet depends on the forces that act upon the bullet during its flight. The way in which two objects bounce off of each other after a collision or whether a car can drive around a curve without sliding off the road are typical problems that are described by Newtonian mechanics.

Specifically, this chapter will cover the following topics:

- A short biography of Sir Isaac Newton

- Newton's three laws of motion

- Some special types of forces—gravitational, friction, centripetal, and spring

- The concept of a force vector

- Force balances and force diagrams

- Work

- Energy

- Power

A Short Biography of Sir Isaac Newton

Before we delve into the subject of Newtonian mechanics, let's learn a little bit about the man behind them. Sir Isaac Newton (1642–1727) was an English mathematician, physicist, chemist, and one of the most brilliant men who ever walked the face of the earth. Newton developed the basic laws of motion and the law of universal gravitation that are the cornerstones of many scientific disciplines. In contrast to the breadth of his scientific achievements, he was born into rather unacademic circumstances. He was born in 1642 the son of a farmer. His father, who died before Isaac was born, was completely uneducated and was unable to even sign his own name.

Newton attended grammar school as a boy, where his teachers described him as "idle" and "inattentive." His mother pulled him out of school at the age of 14 to manage the family estates, but it quickly became apparent that he had neither the talent nor the inclination to be a farmer. He was allowed to return to grammar school in 1660. This time he lodged with the headmaster of the school and began to show some considerable academic promise.

Newton entered university at Trinity College, Cambridge, when he was 18. His original intention was to pursue a law degree, but during his studies he became interested in the works on astronomy written by Galileo and Johannes Kepler. His interests broadened into the fields of mathematics and optics. He gained his degree in 1665, and then had to return home when Cambridge was closed because of an outbreak of the plague.

When he was at home, still younger than 25 years old, he began a remarkable two-year stretch where he made revolutionary advances in the fields of mathematics, optics, physics, and astronomy, including the invention of differential and integral calculus. Newton returned to Cambridge in 1667, where he continued making a dazzling series of inventions and advancements in multiple academic fields.

Newton's most famous written work is a book titled *Philosophiae Naturalis Principia Mathematica* (*The Mathematical Principles of Natural Philosophy*), written in 1687 and considered one of the most important single works in the history of science. Included in this work were the descriptions and mathematical formulas that comprised Newton's famous three laws of motion—subjects that the next three sections of this chapter will briefly describe.

■**Tidbit** Would you like to own a copy of Newton's *Principia*? You'd better start saving your money. A first edition copy in good condition can fetch upwards of $350,000.

Newton's First Law of Motion: Inertia

The basis of Newton's first law of motion was experimental observations of balls rolling on inclined and flat planes performed by Galileo. It had been conventional wisdom in Galileo's time that an external force was required to keep an object moving. Based on his observations, Galileo concluded that an external force was necessary to change the velocity of an object, but in the absence of an external force the velocity would remain constant. Newton formalized Galileo's observations in his *Principia* as his first law of motion:

> *Every body preserves in its state of rest, or of uniform in a right line, unless it is compelled to change that state by forces impressed thereon.*

In other words, a body at rest will stay at rest unless acted upon by an external force. Similarly, a body traveling in a straight line, what Newton called a "right line," will maintain a constant velocity unless acted upon by an external force. The ability of an object to resist a change in its motion is called the **inertia** of the object. Newton determined that the inertia of an object is proportional to its mass. This observation is pretty obvious if you think about it. It's a lot easier to stop a skateboard than it is to stop a car because the car has a greater mass and therefore more inertia than the skateboard.

Newton's Second Law of Motion: Force, Mass, and Acceleration

The best known of Newton's laws of motion is his second law, which relates a force applied to an object to the resulting acceleration of the object. An acceleration represents a change in velocity, so a net applied force changes the velocity of an object. In the *Principia* Newton wrote

> *The alteration of motion is ever proportional to the motive force impressed: and is made in the direction of the right line in which that force is impressed.*

Newton's second law says that an acceleration of an object is due to a net external force applied to the object. Force, therefore, is proportional to acceleration. The inertia of the object, which is proportional to the mass of the object, resists the acceleration, so the force required to achieve a given acceleration is proportional to the mass of the object as well. Stated mathematically, Newton's second law takes a very simple and familiar form:

$$F = ma \tag{3.1}$$

We can see from Equation (3.1) that a force applied to an object is proportional to the acceleration of the object. The amount of acceleration due to an applied force depends on the object's mass. If the same force is applied, a bowling ball with a mass of 5 *kg* will accelerate twice as fast as one with a mass of 10 *kg*. It is also important to remember that the force term that appears in Newton's second law is the net force on an object. If equal forces are applied to an object in opposite directions, the net force on the object, and therefore its acceleration, is equal to zero.

The units of force are *pounds* in the English System of Units and (appropriately) *Newtons* in the International System of Units. These units are often abbreviated as *lb* and *N*. As we saw in Chapter 2, a Newton is equivalent to a $kg\text{-}m/s^2$. The units for mass are *kg* in the SI system and *slugs* or *pound-mass* in the English system. Acceleration has units of ft/s^2 in the English system and m/s^2 in the SI system. For the most part in this book, the SI system of units will be used. SI units are more consistent and easier to work with, and are the standard for scientific endeavors. If you really want to use English units, you can use the conversion factors given in Chapter 2.

We will use Newton's second law in most of the physics models we will develop throughout this book—everything from the motion of bullets to basketballs to boats can be modeled with the help of Newton's second law.

Weight and Mass

Before we leave the discussion of Newton's second law, let's spend a little time talking about the distinction between weight and mass. Mass is what is known as an **intrinsic property** of an object, meaning it is a property that is essential to the object and doesn't change. For example, a rock will have a certain mass, and the mass of the rock is the same whether the rock is on the surface of the earth or on Jupiter.

Weight, on the other hand, is the force of gravity that acts upon an object. It is equal to the mass of the object, m, times the gravitational acceleration, g.

$$w = mg \tag{3.2}$$

Weight is not an intrinsic property because it depends on gravitational acceleration, which can vary from place to place. A rock will weigh less on Earth than it will on Jupiter because the gravitational acceleration on Earth is less than that of Jupiter. A rock that is floating in outer space is weightless, but it will still have a mass.

For the most part in this book, we will be working with mass rather than weight. As was mentioned in Chapter 1, the unit of mass in the SI system is the kilogram or *kg*.

Newton's Third Law of Motion: Equal and Opposite Forces

When people think about forces, it is common to think of one object exerting a force upon another object. For example, we might think of a baseball bat exerting a force on a baseball when it strikes the ball. Newton's third law of motion states that there is no such thing as an isolated force. When a bat exerts a force on the baseball, the baseball exerts an equal and opposite force on the bat. In his *Principia* he wrote

> *To every action there is always opposed an equal reaction: or the mutual actions of two bodies upon each other are always equal, and directed to contrary parts.*

The more commonly used way to express this concept is "for every action there is an equal and opposite reaction." There are a lot of everyday examples of Newton's third law in action—the recoil of a gun, a swimmer pushing off the wall of a pool, and so on. An easy way to test Newton's third law is to have two people sit in rolling chairs on a hard floor. If one person pushes on the other chair, both chairs will begin to move in opposite directions. The first person exerted a force on the second person's chair, but the chair exerted an equal an opposite force on the person who did the pushing.

Force Vector

Force is a vector quantity in that a force has both a magnitude and a direction. The result of the force depends on the direction, or **line of action**, of the force. If a gun is shot straight up in the air, the motion of the bullet due to that force will obviously be different than if the gun is fired horizontally. When creating physics models that involve forces, it is usually beneficial to split the overall force vector into directional components. The effect of each directional force can be evaluated independently of the others, and this approach often simplifies the overall problem.

A force vector is split into directional components according to whatever frame of reference is being used. If the frame of reference is Cartesian, the force is split into components that act in the x-, y-, and z-directions.

$$F_x = ma_x \tag{3.3a}$$

$$F_y = ma_y \tag{3.3b}$$

$$F_z = ma_z \tag{3.3c}$$

In Equation (3.3a), the quantity a_x is the acceleration in the x-direction. Dividing a force into directional components allows for a more refined analysis of the effects of the given force on an object. If the force is directed in the x-direction, the acceleration will be in the x-direction as well, and there will be no change in velocity in the y- or z-direction.

Sometimes you will have directional components of a force and will need to compute the overall magnitude of the force. The magnitude of a force vector is equal to the square root of the sum of the square of the directional components.

$$F = \sqrt{F_x^2 + F_y^2 + F_z^2} \tag{3.4}$$

Most of the time in this book we will use the Cartesian frame of reference with the x- and y-directions parallel to the surface of the earth and the z-direction normal to it. The Cartesian frame of reference is the best choice for problems involving linear motion. If a model involves circular or rotational motion, like modeling the spin of a golf ball for instance, it usually makes more sense to use either the spherical or cylindrical coordinate systems where a vector is split into angular components.

Types of Forces

In very simplistic terms, a force is something that pushes or pulls on an object with the potential to change the motion of the object. When a baseball player hits a baseball, the bat imparts a force to the ball. When a gun is fired, the gunpowder charge imparts a force to the bullet. In this section, we will discuss in more detail four special types of forces that will be a part of many of the physical models you will use as a game developer—gravitational, friction, spring, and centripetal force.

Gravitational Force

One of the many disciplines that Newton applied himself to was a study of the motion of celestial objects. It was known at that time that the moon traveled in a nearly circular orbit around the earth. From his first law of motion, Newton knew that the only way the moon could circle the earth is if there was a force directed toward the earth acting on the moon. Without the presence of such a force, the moon would fly off into space.

Newton eventually came to the conclusion that there was a **gravitational force** between the earth and the moon. He then generalized this finding to say that there was a gravitational force, F_G, between any two objects that was proportional to the masses of the objects, m_1 and m_2, and inversely proportional to the square of the distance between them, r.

$$F_G = \frac{Gm_1m_2}{r^2} \tag{3.5}$$

The parameter *G* in Equation (3.5) is a constant value known as the **gravitational constant**. It has a value of 6.674e-11 *N-m²/kg²*. The gravitational constant is referred to as a fundamental physical constant because its value can be used to compute the gravitational force between any two objects.

The distance *r* in Equation (3.5) is the distance between the centers of the two objects being considered. The gravitational force acts along the line connecting the centers of the two objects, meaning that the second object is pulled towards the center of the first object and vice versa. When a skydiver jumps out of an airplane, she falls downwards because the gravitational force due to the earth is pulling her towards the center of the earth. The magnitude of the gravitational force depends on the masses of the objects involved. You exert a small gravitational force on your car, but the earth exerts a much more significant gravitational force on you.

The magnitude of the gravitational force between two objects can be determined from Equation (3.5). The acceleration of an object due to gravitational force can be calculated by equating the gravitational force equation to Newton's second law.

$$F_G = \frac{Gm_1m_2}{r^2} = m_1a \tag{3.6}$$

In Equation (3.6), m_1 is the mass of the object being considered and *a* is the acceleration of the object. The quantity m_1 is on both sides of the equation and cancels out.

$$a = \frac{Gm_2}{r^2} \tag{3.7}$$

We can see from Equation (3.7) that the acceleration of an object due to gravity is equal to the gravitational constant multiplied by the mass of the other object divided by the square of the distance between the centers of the objects. Because the mass of the object being considered cancels out of the equation, we reach a very important conclusion. *The acceleration of an object due to gravitational force is independent of the mass of the object.* If a bowling ball with a mass of 5 *kg* is dropped from an airplane, it will experience the same gravitational acceleration as would a marble with a mass of 0.1 *kg*.

■**Tidbit** Proving that the gravitational acceleration was constant irrespective of an object's mass was shown rather dramatically by Galileo almost 400 years ago when he dropped cannon balls of different masses from the Leaning Tower of Pisa. Sure enough, the cannon balls underwent the same acceleration and hit the ground at the same time.

When incorporating gravitational effects into game programming applications, we will usually be working with the acceleration due to Earth's gravity. The magnitude of Earth's gravitational acceleration can be computed from Equation (3.7). The mass of Earth is 5.9736e+24 *kg* and the average radius of Earth is 6375 *km* or 6.375e+6 *m*.

$$a = \frac{6.674e-11 * 5.9736e+24}{\left(6.375e+6\right)^2} = 9.81 \ \frac{m}{s^2} \tag{3.8}$$

Gravitational acceleration is typically represented by a lowercase *g*, and we will use that convention throughout this book.

One characteristic of gravitational force is that it is always "turned on." Every object on Earth is always subject to Earth's gravitational force. Gravitational force and its corresponding acceleration will be a part of almost every physical model that we will develop in this book and that you will use in your game programming. Gravitational force determines the trajectories of projectiles and is a major influence in the motion and performance of cars, boats, airplanes, and rockets.

The Gravity Game

Throughout this book, we will develop sample games that will demonstrate how to code up the various physical models being discussed. Since we just learned about gravitational force, the first game we will write will be the Gravity Game. Like all of the games in this book, the Gravity Game is written in Java, but much of the syntax should be familiar to someone who programs in C, C++, or C#. The full source code for all of the games presented in the book can be downloaded from the Apress website at www.apress.com. You will find C and C# versions of all the games at the Apress website as well.

The Gravity Game, as the name would suggest, is intended to demonstrate the effects of gravity. A sample screen shot of the game is shown in Figure 3-1. The objective of the game is to release a ball at just the right time so it falls into a rectangular box that is sliding across the ground. The box begins at the left-hand side of the display. When the Start button is pressed, the box begins to move to the right. The ball starts at a height of 120 *m* above the ground. When the Drop button is pressed, the ball is released and begins to fall to the ground. If the ball falls into the box, the message "You Win" appears in the Results text field. If you miss the box, the message "Try Again" appears.

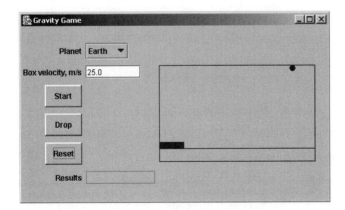

Figure 3-1. *Gravity Game screen shot*

There are two user inputs that can be adjusted. The first is the speed that the box will move across the ground. The user can also select the planet where the simulation will take place. The choices are "Earth," "Moon," or "Jupiter." The gravitational acceleration will be different depending on which planet is selected. The ball will fall faster on Jupiter than it will on the moon.

The Gravity Game is implemented in a class called GravityGame. Most of the program involves setting up the GUI elements of the game. We won't cover the GUI aspects of the code in any detail. The first thing the program does is to declare the fields used in the class. The first group of fields declared in the class are the GUI components.

```
import javax.swing.*;
import java.awt.*;
import javax.swing.border.BevelBorder;
import java.awt.event.*;
import java.util.Random;
import javax.swing.Timer;

public class GravityGame extends JFrame implements ActionListener
{
    private JTextField resultsTextField;
    private JTextField velocityTextField;

    private JComboBox planetComboBox;

    private JLabel planetLabel;
    private JLabel velocityLabel;
    private JLabel resultsLabel;

    private JButton startButton;
    private JButton dropButton;
    private JButton resetButton;
    private JPanel drawingPanel;
    private GridBagConstraints gbc;
```

Additional fields are declared that describe the position and characteristics of the box and ball.

```
private double boxLocation;   //  horizontal location of box
    private double boxVelocity;
    private int boxWidth;         // width of box in pixels
    private double ballAltitude;  // vertical location of ball
    private double ballLocation;  //  horizontal location of ball
    private double initialAltitude;  // initial ball altitude
    private double g;             //  gravitational acceleration
    private double time;          // time since box begins to move
    private double dropTime;      // time since ball was dropped
    private boolean dropped;      // true if the ball has been dropped
```

As mentioned in Chapter 1, in many cases the physics models are computed so quickly that the games actually have to be slowed down so they will simulate more or less real-time behavior. Since the program has been artificially slowed down, the time it will take the ball to drop 120 m on the screen is close to the time it would actually take. If the program was allowed to run at full speed, then the ball would appear to drop in a fraction of a second. This kind of behavior would not convince anyone using the game that it was simulating reality! In the

Gravity Game, a Timer object is used to slow the game down. The GameUpdater class is a user-defined class that declares a method that the Timer object will call. We'll discuss this method in more detail in a little bit.

```
// These elements are used to control the execution
  // speed of the game. Without them, the game would
  // run too quickly.
  private GameUpdater gameUpdater;
  private Timer gameTimer;
```

The GravityGame constructor initializes the box and ball fields, creates and initializes the Timer object, and creates and initializes the GUI components. The GUI initialization code isn't shown.

```
public GravityGame() {

    // Set box, ball, and time parameters.
    boxLocation = 0.0;
    boxWidth = 40;
    initialAltitude = 120.0;
    ballAltitude = initialAltitude;
    ballLocation = 210.0;
    time = 0.0;
    dropTime = 0.0;
    dropped = false;

    // Create a Timer object that will be used
    // to slow the action down and an ActionListener
    // that the Timer will call. The timeDelay variable
    // is the time delay in milliseconds.
    gameUpdater = new GameUpdater();
    int timeDelay = 50;
    gameTimer = new Timer(timeDelay, gameUpdater);

    // GUI initialization code not shown …
```

The GravityGame class declares a method called actionPerformed that is called when the Start button is pressed. The method obtains the box velocity and planet selection values from the GUI components. The value of the gravitational acceleration is set according to which planet is selected. The start method is then called on the Timer object to start the simulation.

```
// The actionPerformed() method is called when
  // the "Start" button is pressed.
  public void actionPerformed(ActionEvent event) {

    // Get the box velocity from the textfield
    boxVelocity = Double.parseDouble(velocityTextField.getText());
```

```
    // Determine which planet is selected and set
    // the gravitational acceleration accordingly.
    String planet = (String)planetComboBox.getSelectedItem();

    if ( planet.equals("Earth") ) {
      g = 9.81;
    }
    else if ( planet.equals("Moon") ) {
      g = 1.624;
    }
    else {
      g = 24.8;  // Jupiter
    }

    // Start the box sliding using a Timer object
    // to slow down the action.
    gameTimer.start();
  }
```

The Timer object itself calls an actionPerformed method that is declared inside the GameUpdater class (an inner class of the GravityGame class). The Timer object is set up to call this method every 0.05 seconds. This actionPerformed method updates the location of the box and ball. The box moves to the right by a constant amount every time the method is called. If the ball has been dropped, it begins to accelerate due to gravity. Because the velocity of the ball increases over time, it will drop further and further each time the actionPerformed method is called. When the ball hits the ground, the method determines if it landed inside the box or not and displays the appropriate message.

```
class GameUpdater implements ActionListener {
    public void actionPerformed(ActionEvent event) {

        // Update the time and compute the new position
        // of the box and ball.
        double timeIncrement = 0.05;
        time += timeIncrement;
        boxLocation = boxVelocity*time;

        if ( dropped ) {
          dropTime += timeIncrement;
          ballAltitude =
              initialAltitude - 0.5*g*dropTime*dropTime;
        }

        // Update the display
        updateDisplay();
```

```
  //  If the ball hits the ground, stop the simulation
  //  and determine if it landed in the box.
  if ( ballAltitude <= 0.0 ) {
    gameTimer.stop();

    if ( ballLocation >= boxLocation &&
         ballLocation <= boxLocation + boxWidth - 10 ) {
      resultsTextField.setText("You Win!");
    }
    else {
      resultsTextField.setText("Try again");
    }
  }
 }
}
```

Play around with the Gravity Game. The Reset button resets the display. If the box and ball don't appear for any reason, press the Reset button to redraw the GUI. Also remember that the ball won't start to drop until the Drop button is pressed. Try switching the planet from "Earth" to "Moon" or "Jupiter" and see what happens. Don't forget that you can also adjust the velocity at which the box will travel.

You'll notice that the ball travels very slowly just after it is dropped but gains speed steadily with each passing second. This effect is a characteristic of gravity in that it provides a constant acceleration. The longer an object falls, the faster it will go.

■**Note** When an object travels through an atmosphere, gravity won't continue to accelerate the object forever because an effect known as **aerodynamic drag** will limit how fast the object can travel. We'll learn about aerodynamic drag when we study projectiles in Chapter 5.

Exercise

1. Compute the gravitational acceleration on the surface of Earth's moon. The radius of the moon is $1.7374e+6$ m, and the mass of the moon is $7.3483e+22$ kg.

Friction

Friction is the force that resists motion between two contacting surfaces. When you pick up a glass of water, it is friction between your hand and the glass that allows you to lift the glass to your mouth. When a car drives around a curve in the road, it is friction between the tires and the road that keeps the car from sliding off the road. Friction occurs between all types of matter—solids, liquids, and gases—and is an important component in many physical models.

One of the consequences of friction is heat. When objects rub against each other, heat is generated. Rockets reentering a planetary atmosphere will heat up due to friction between the surface of the rocket and the colliding gas particles of the atmosphere. One reason your car engine needs a cooling system is the heat generated due to friction between the various moving parts of the engine.

Friction will be important to many game programming physical models. Obviously any game that involves something sliding over a surface, hockey or shuffleboard, for example, will have to include frictional effects. The friction between the golf ball and club head causes the golf ball to spin and can cause the ball to hook or slice. Friction between the tires and the road is what propels a car forward and keeps the car on the road when it drives around a curve.

In developing a mathematical relation to describe frictional force, we start with some general observations about friction. For one thing, the amount of friction between two objects depends on what the materials of the two objects are. The friction force between a metal box sliding on a sheet of glass is less than that of the same box sliding on a piece of sandpaper.

Another general observation about friction is that it is proportional to the **normal force** between the contacting surfaces. The normal force exerted by an object is the component of the force vector normal, that is, perpendicular, to the surface that is in contact with the object. To compute the normal force between objects, we can make use of Newton's third law of motion. If a box is resting flat on the ground, as shown in Figure 3-2, the normal force will be equal and opposite to the gravitational force applied to the object.

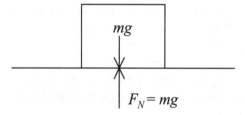

mg

$F_N = mg$

Figure 3-2. *Normal force on a box resting on the flat ground*

The situation is a little different if the box is placed on a ramp inclined at an angle θ as shown in Figure 3-3. The normal force exerted on the box by the ramp is now perpendicular to the surface of the ramp and has a value of $mg\cos\theta$. Since friction is proportional to normal force, we can conclude that friction will be less for a box on an inclined ramp than it will be if the ramp were placed flat on the ground. In addition, the friction force will decrease as the angle of the ramp increases.

In addition to the magnitude of the normal force, friction force is also a function of the material properties of the two objects in contact with each other. The material property effects are characterized by a quantity called the **coefficient of friction**. The value of the friction force, F_F, is equal to the coefficient of friction, μ, multiplied by the normal force, F_N.

$$F_F = \mu F_N \tag{3.9}$$

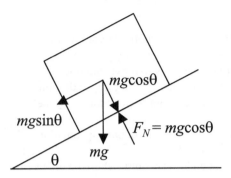

Figure 3-3. *Normal force on a box resting on an inclined ramp*

■Tidbit Did you ever wonder why snails and slugs emit their disgusting slime? Among other reasons, the slime helps the snail move by reducing the coefficient of friction between the snail and the ground.

There are some other interesting characteristics about frictional force. The direction of the force of friction an object experiences is always in the opposite direction to any net external force applied to the object. In Figure 3-4, if a box resting on the ground is pulled to the left, the friction force will counterbalance this force by acting towards the right. If the box is on an inclined ramp, gravity will pull the box down the ramp, but friction will resist this motion by exerting a force up the ramp.

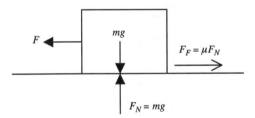

Figure 3-4. *The friction force, F_F, acts in the opposite direction of an applied force, F.*

Another interesting thing about friction is that, in a sense, it is a *variable magnitude* force. Friction will counterbalance an externally applied force up to a maximum possible level defined by μF_N. Let's say the box in Figure 3-4 has a mass of 10 *kg* and that the coefficient of friction between the box and the flat surface it rests on has a value of 0.5. The box will remain motionless for any horizontally applied force less than $\mu F_N = 0.5*9.81*10 = 49.05\ N$. If a 5 *N* force is applied to the box, friction will counterbalance the applied force with a 5 *N* force in the opposite direction. If a 40 *N* force is applied, the counterbalancing friction force will be 40 *N*. If the applied force exceeds the maximum frictional force value of μF_N, friction is no longer able to counterbalance the applied force and the box begins to move.

The Coefficient of Friction

The value of frictional force between two objects depends on the coefficient of friction, μ, between the contacting surfaces. If you've ever removed a cork from a bottle, you may have noticed that initially you have to exert a lot of force to get the cork to move, but once the cork begins to move it becomes easier to pull it out the rest of the way. Another way to demonstrate this effect is to push a heavy box across the floor. It becomes easier to push the box once it begins to move.

These observations highlight another characteristic about friction, namely that objects in motion generally have a lower coefficient of friction than do objects at rest. When modeling the effects of friction, two coefficients of friction must be taken into account. When the objects are motionless, the coefficient of static friction, μ_s, governs the frictional force. When the objects begin to slide, the friction between them usually decreases, and the frictional force is defined by the coefficient of kinetic friction, μ_k. The values of static and kinetic coefficients of friction for some material pairs are shown in Table 3-1. Unless otherwise noted, the coefficients are for dry materials.

Table 3-1. *Friction Coefficients for Some Common Surface Interactions*

Materials	μ_s	μ_k
Steel—steel	0.7–0.74	0.57–0.6
Steel—steel (lubricated)	0.12	0.07
Aluminum—steel	0.61	0.47
Copper—steel	0.53	0.36
Cast iron—cast iron	1.1	0.15
Teflon—Teflon	0.04	0.04
Glass—glass	0.94	0.4
Wood—wood	0.25–0.5	0.2–0.3
Rubber—concrete	1.0	0.8
Rubber—concrete (wet)	0.7	0.5
Ice—ice	0.1	0.03
Waxed ski—snow	0.1–0.14	0.05–0.1

* Source: RoyMech, www.roymech.co.uk

* Raymond Serway and John Jewitt, Physics for Scientists and Engineers, Sixth Edition (Brooks-Cole, 2003)

* www.physlink.com/Reference/FrictionCoefficients.cfm

* Encarta.msn.com

Shuffleboard Game

To demonstrate the effects of friction, let's create a simple Shuffleboard Game simulation. The game is implemented in a class named Shuffleboard. A typical screen shot for the game is shown in Figure 3-5. When the Start button is pressed, a black disk slides across the surface of the board with an initial velocity that is determined by the user. A friction force between the disk and the board resists the motion of the disk. When the disk comes to rest, the user is awarded the score according to the section of the board that the disk occupies. The user can specify the mass of the disk and the coefficient of friction between the disk and the surface of the board. The Reset button is used to reset the display.

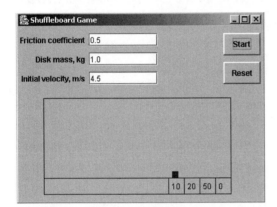

Figure 3-5. *Shuffleboard Game screen shot*

The GUI setup of the Shuffleboard Game is very similar to the Gravity Game, so we won't spend much time going over the GUI aspects of the code. As with the Gravity Game, the Shuffleboard class makes use of a Timer object to slow the action of the game down. When the Start button is pressed, the actionPerformed method that is declared in the Shuffleboard class is called. The actionPerformed method extracts the values of the friction coefficient, disk mass, and initial disk velocity from the values inside the text fields. The time and disk location values are reset to zero and the start method is called on the Timer object to start the disk moving.

```
public void actionPerformed(ActionEvent event) {

    //  Extract initial data from the text fields.
    mu = Double.parseDouble(muTextField.getText());
    mass = Double.parseDouble(massTextField.getText());
    initialVelocity = Double.parseDouble(velocityTextField.getText());

    //  Set the time and the initial x-location of the disk
    time = 0.0;
    xLocation = 0.0;

    //  Start the disk sliding using a Timer object
    //  to slow down the action.
    gameTimer.start();
}
```

The Timer is set up to call the actionPerformed method declared in the GameUpdater class (an inner class of the Shuffleboard class) every 0.05 seconds. Inside the method, the time, disk velocity, and disk location are updated. The display is then redrawn using the updateDisplay method to show the new location of the disk.

Friction force resists the motion of an object, but it won't reverse the motion of an object. The most friction will do is to bring the disk to a stop. If the computed velocity of the disk is less than or equal to zero or if the disk hits the end of the board, the Timer is stopped, which ends the movement of the disk.

```
//  This ActionListener is called by the Timer
class GameUpdater implements ActionListener {
  public void actionPerformed(ActionEvent event) {

    //  Update the time and compute the new position
    //  of the disk.
    time += 0.05;

    //  Compute the current velocity of the disk.
    double velocity = initialVelocity - mu*G*time;

    //  Update the position of the disk.
    xLocation = initialVelocity*time - 0.5*mu*G*time*time;

    //  Update the display
    updateDisplay();

    //  If the disk stops moving or if it reaches
    //  the end of the board, stop the simulation
    if ( velocity <= 0.0 || xLocation > 2.9) {
      gameTimer.stop();
    }

  }
}
```

Play around with the Shuffleboard Game. As with the Gravity Game, if for some reason the entire display isn't rendered, press the Reset button to redraw the GUI. Change the values of friction coefficient and initial velocity and try to get the disk to come to reset in the "50" zone.

Try changing the mass of the disk and see what happens. You will find that nothing changes. The acceleration of the disk is determined by the equation $\mu mg = ma$. The mass is on both sides of the equation and cancels out, meaning that the acceleration of the disk due to friction is independent of the mass of the disk. The only things that will affect the distance that the disk will travel are the initial velocity of the disk and the coefficient of friction.

Exercise

2. An aluminum box with a mass of 2 *kg* is placed on a steel plate that is initially placed on a flat, level surface. One edge of the plate is lifted such that the plate is now at an inclined angle. If the edge of the plate is continually lifted thereby increasing the inclined angle, at what angle will the aluminum box begin to slide down the plate?

Springs

Gravity and friction are forces that you will deal with all the time in your game programming physics models. Less commonly used, but still important in some circumstances, is the force generated by springs. Typically, we think of a spring as a metal or plastic coil, but objects with other shapes can exhibit spring-like behavior. In an archery simulation, the bow acts like a spring. A diving board acts like a spring; so does a catapult.

■**Tidbit** Metal springs have been around since the Bronze age. The development of precision springs occurred in the Renaissance period and was driven by a need to build precision timepieces for celestial navigation.

A typical coiled spring that is attached to a wall and resting on the ground is shown in Figure 3-6. When no force is applied to either end of the spring, it has an equilibrium length l_0. If the spring is deflected from its equilibrium position to a new location l, a force is exerted by the spring on whatever is connected at the two ends. If the spring is attached to a wall and you pull on it with your finger, the spring will exert an equal and opposite force on both your finger and the wall. A relation known as **Hooke's Law** describes the force, F_S, exerted at either end of the spring.

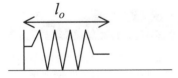

Figure 3-6. *A typical spring*

$$F_S = -k\left(l - l_0\right) \tag{3.10}$$

The spring constant, k, in Equation (3.10) is a material and structural property of the spring that characterizes the stiffness of the spring. A stiffer spring will have a larger spring constant. Hooke's Law can also be used to determine the force necessary to achieve a specified deflection for a given spring. For example, to deflect a spring with a spring constant value of 400 *N/m* a distance of 0.01 *m* from its equilibrium position would require a force of 4 *N*.

There are a couple of interesting things to note about spring forces. First of all, a spring exerts a restoring force, one that acts to restore the spring to its equilibrium position. If the spring at its equilibrium position is pulled to the right to a new length l, as shown in Figure 3-7, the spring force on the object doing the pulling will be directed to the left. The restoring nature of the force is the reason for the negative sign in Equation (3.10).

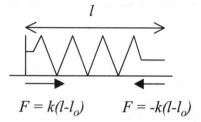

$$F = k(l-l_o) \qquad F = -k(l-l_o)$$

Figure 3-7. *A spring exerts an equal and opposite restoring force when deflected.*

Another interesting thing about springs is that they exert a variable force in that the spring force increases with increasing deflection of the spring from its equilibrium position. As the spring moves back towards its equilibrium position, the force exerted on either end of the spring steadily decreases.

The final topic we will discuss about springs is the damping force associated with them. According to Hooke's Law, if a spring with a weight on the end of it is extended and released, it will oscillate forever about its equilibrium location. Of course, in reality this perpetual motion doesn't occur and the spring motion gradually decreases until the spring comes to a rest. The gradual decrease in motion is due to a damping force that is proportional to the difference in velocity of the two ends of the spring.

$$F_d = k_d\left(v_2 - v_1\right) \tag{3.11}$$

The damping force, F_d, serves to reduce the acceleration of the spring. We'll revisit Hooke's Law and damping forces in Chapter 4 when we discuss spring motion.

Exercise

3. A spring with a spring constant of 325 *N/m* hangs vertically from a ceiling. If a 1 *kg* mass is attached to the end of the spring, how much lower will the end of the spring be when it reaches its new equilibrium position?

Centripetal Force

Force, acceleration, and velocity are vectors and have a direction as well as a magnitude. We have also learned that a force is required for a change in velocity to occur. These two facts lead to an interesting situation that occurs when an object is traveling at a constant velocity v around a circle with a radius r as shown in Figure 3-8.

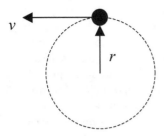

Figure 3-8. *An object traveling in circular motion has continually changing velocity vector.*

Even though the velocity magnitude of the object may be constant, the directional components of velocity are continually changing. If we consider the circular motion in a two-dimensional Cartesian coordinate system, when the object is at the top of the circle, all of the velocity is in the x-direction and there is no velocity in the y-direction. When the object travels 90 degrees around the circle, all the velocity will now be in the y-direction.

The only way the velocity components can continually change in this manner is if there is a continuous acceleration of the object and therefore a continuous force upon the object. This force is known as a **centripetal force**. The centripetal force, F_C, is a function of the mass of the object, m, the square of the velocity magnitude (that is, speed) of the object, v, and the radius of the circle, r.

$$F_C = \frac{mv^2}{r} \qquad\qquad (3.12)$$

The direction of centripetal force is towards the center of the circle. Centripetal force is not limited to objects traveling along circular trajectories. You will encounter centripetal force in your game programming whenever you model an object traveling along a curved path. When a car drives around a curve in the road, the friction generated between the tires and the road must balance the centripetal force generated by the car traveling around the curve. The centripetal force is an inverse function of the radius of curvature, which is why it is harder to drive around a sharp curve than a gentle one. Centripetal force is also a function of the square of velocity, so when you approach a sharp curve it's a good idea to slow down.

Exercise

4. A satellite is able to orbit a planet because the centripetal force generated by the motion of the satellite balances the gravitational pull on the satellite from the planet. Using what you know about centripetal and gravitational force, compute the radius of the moon's orbit. The mass of Earth is 5.974e+24 *kg* and the mean orbital velocity of the moon is 1023 *m/s*.

Force Balances and Force Diagrams

You have learned that when a net external force is applied to an object that the object will accelerate in direction of the applied force. However, when calculating how a body will react to an applied force, the important thing to determine is the net force on the body. An object may have more than one force acting on it. We have seen multiple force situations already in this chapter in the schematics of the box on the inclined plane and in our discussion of springs.

When analyzing the forces at work in a physical model, it is often useful to draw a force diagram. This diagram is simply a schematic of the objects in the model and the magnitude and directions of the forces acting on those objects. A force diagram can be tailored according to the level of complexity you want to include in the physical model. For instance, a force diagram can help to evaluate what would happen if you ignored the effects of air resistance or surface friction in the physical model.

To demonstrate the process for developing a force diagram, consider the situation shown in Figure 3-9. A box is sliding down a ramp that is at an incline angle of θ. One end of the box is attached to a spring that has been stretched beyond its equilibrium position. The other end of the spring is attached to a fixed wall. The box is subject to multiple forces. The problem is to express all of the forces mathematically and draw the resulting force diagram.

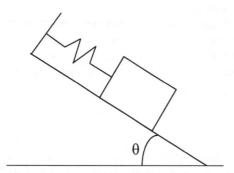

Figure 3-9. *A box subject to multiple forces*

Let's start with the spring, which will exert a force on both the box and the wall to which it is attached. The magnitude of the spring force is equal to $-k\Delta x$ where Δx is the amount the spring is stretched from its equilibrium position. The box is subject to the force of gravity. Gravity will act in the vertical direction, but because the box is on the ramp, it will be useful to split the gravity force into components that are normal and parallel to the ramp. The gravitational force on the box normal to the ramp is equal to $mg\cos\theta$. The ramp exerts an equal and opposite force on the box. The gravitational force parallel to the ramp is equal to $mg\sin\theta$. Finally, because the box is sliding, there will be a friction force between the box and the ramp. The friction force is equal to μF_N where F_N is the normal gravitational force. A force diagram that incorporates these results is shown in Figure 3-10.

One use for force diagrams is they make it easier to visualize and evaluate the net force on an object. For example, looking at the force diagram shown in Figure 3-10, we can see that the net force on the box parallel to the ramp, F_P, is equal to the sum of the gravitational, frictional, and spring force components.

$$F_P = mg\sin\theta - k\Delta x - \mu mg\cos\theta \qquad (3.13)$$

The negative signs in Equation (3.13) are used to indicate that the spring and friction forces act in the opposite direction of the gravitational force.

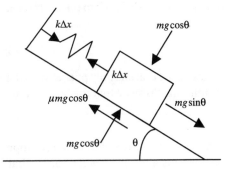

Figure 3-10. *The force diagram for the box on a ramp*

Work

So far in this chapter, we have introduced the concept of a force and how a force is characterized by Newton's three laws of motion. In the remaining sections of this chapter, we will look at some other fundamental physical concepts that are related to the concept of force. The first topic we will introduce is that of **work**. In terms of physics, work is performed when a force, F, is applied to an object over a distance, d.

$$W = Fd \tag{3.14}$$

The physics definition of work may seem a bit strange because an object has to move for work to be performed. If a person lifts a barbell over her head, she is performing work. If she holds the barbell over her head without moving it, it may seem like work to her but in a physics sense no work is performed. The amount of work performed is equal to the force component in the direction that the object moves.

For an example of a work calculation, consider the situation shown in Figure 3-11 where there is a box with a mass of 10 *kg* sitting on the ground. The coefficient of friction between the box and ground is equal to 0.5. There is also a cow and it is the cow's job to push the box horizontally across the ground a distance, $d = 2.0\ m$.

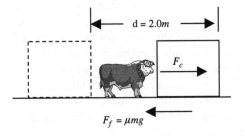

Figure 3-11. *This is a mooving example.*

For the box to move, the cow must push with a horizontal force, F_C, equal to the coefficient of friction multiplied by the weight of the box.

$$F_C = \mu mg = 49.05 \ N \tag{3.15}$$

The work that the cow has done in moving the box, assuming that she only pushes with the minimum required force, is equal to the applied force times the distance that the box moved.

$$W = F_c d = 98.1 \ N\text{-}m \tag{3.16}$$

Now let's consider a second example, shown in Figure 3-12, where the cow pulls on a rope that is attached to the same box. She still must pull the box a distance of 2.0 m. The angle that the rope makes with the ground is equal to $\theta = 30 \ degrees$. To overcome the friction force, the cow must apply a horizontal force of 49.05 N. If she pulls on the rope with a force, F_C, the horizontal component of that force will be equal to $F_C \cos 30$. The force that the cow will have to exert on the rope to move the box is equal to the friction force divided by cos30.

$$F_C = \frac{\mu mg}{\cos 30} = 56.6 \ N \tag{3.17}$$

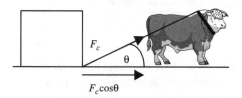

Figure 3-12. *More force is needed to move the box if the force is applied at an angle.*

Comparing the situations shown in Figures 3-11 and 3-12, in both cases the cow is performing the same amount of work. The same horizontal force is applied to move the box the same 2.0 m distance. However, in the second example the cow has to exert a greater force to perform the work. Because the rope is at an angle, there is a vertical component to the force the cow exerts that is wasted in terms of doing horizontal work.

If a force is applied in the direction perpendicular to the motion of an object, then no work is performed. In Figure 3-12, the vertical component of force exerted by the cow pulling on the rope does no work because the box does not move in the vertical direction. Another example of when this situation occurs is with centripetal force. When an object travels in a circle, the resulting centripetal force is directed inwards perpendicular to the flight path, and because it is perpendicular to the motion of the object, centripetal force performs no work on the object.

Because work is a force multiplied by a distance, in the SI system of units work will have units of $N\text{-}m$. An $N\text{-}m$ is also referred to as a *Joule* or *J* for short. A Joule is a unit of energy, and work and energy are closely related, as we will learn in the next section.

Energy

Energy is defined as the capacity for doing work. Energy is a **state variable**, meaning that it is used to characterize the physical state of an object. Energy, work, and force are closely related. We learned in the last section that it requires a force to perform work. Since energy is the capacity for doing work, the source of a force that performs work must possess a certain level of energy. Objects can store energy. When the object work is performed, part or all of the stored energy of an object is converted to work. Work and energy are both scalar quantities.

There are several different forms that energy can take. **Kinetic energy** is related to the motion of an object. **Potential energy** can be thought of as stored energy and is related to the position of an object. If work is performed to move an object from one location to another, part or all of that work might be stored in the object as potential energy. Taken together, the kinetic and potential energies of an object are also referred to as the **mechanical energy** of the object.

In addition to the mechanical energy components, there are also what are called internal energy types that relate to how individual molecules and atoms store energy. The internal energy type you are probably most familiar with is **thermal energy**, which is related to the temperature of an object. Objects can also store **chemical energy**. When chemical energy is released rapidly, the result can be an explosion—a topic we will explore in Chapter 13.

One of the characteristics of energy is that it can be converted from one form into another. For example, the kinetic energy of an object can be converted into work that in turn is converted into potential or thermal energy. For example, when a meteorite hits the ground, the kinetic energy of the meteorite is very rapidly converted to heat and and/or work that is performed, pushing the ground away from the point of impact. The SI units of energy are the same as those of work, namely $N\text{-}m$ or J.

Kinetic Energy

Kinetic energy is the energy of motion. The kinetic energy of an object, E_K, is proportional to the mass of the object, m, and the square of the velocity of the object, v.

$$E_K = \frac{1}{2}mv^2 \tag{3.18}$$

Because kinetic energy is a scalar quantity, the velocity term in Equation (3.18) is the velocity magnitude, or speed, of the object.

We know from Newton's second law that a force is required to change the velocity of an object. According to something known as the **work-energy theorem**, the work done by a net force on an object is equal to the change in the kinetic energy of an object.

$$W = \frac{1}{2}m\left(v_f^2 - v_0^2\right) \tag{3.19}$$

In Equation (3.19), v_0 is the initial velocity of the object and v_f is the final velocity. We can use the work-energy theorem to determine the height that a projectile that is shot straight up into the air will reach. The projectile will have an initial kinetic energy equal to one half its mass multiplied by its velocity magnitude squared. Work is performed on the projectile as it travels upwards. When the projectile reaches its highest point, its velocity is zero, meaning that all of its kinetic energy has been converted to work. The height, h, that the projectile will reach can be found by equating its original kinetic energy to the work performed on it.

$$\frac{1}{2}mv^2 = mgh \tag{3.20}$$

$$h = \frac{v^2}{2g} \tag{3.21}$$

Potential Energy

Kinetic energy is the energy of an object due to its motion. Potential energy is the energy of an object due to its location. We saw earlier in this chapter that work is required to change the location of an object. The work that is performed can be stored in the object as potential energy. Potential energy can take several forms. For example, it takes work to compress a spring. The work is converted to potential energy that is stored in the compressed spring. The magnitude of the potential energy, P_E, is equal to one half the spring constant, k, multiplied by the square of the distance, Δx, that the spring was compressed.

$$E_P = \frac{1}{2}k\Delta x^2 \tag{3.22}$$

If the compressed spring is released, the potential energy stored in the spring is released as well and will typically be converted into either kinetic energy or work.

Another important form of potential energy is **gravitational potential energy**. If a person lifts a ball over his head, he is performing work on the ball. The ball has been given potential energy because it has been moved to a location farther away from the center of the earth. If the person then drops the ball, the potential energy is converted into kinetic energy as the ball falls towards the earth. The amount of gravitational potential energy an object has is equal to the weight of the object, mg, multiplied by the height of the object, h, above some reference height location (typically the ground).

$$E_p = mgh \tag{3.23}$$

If you look back at the problem at the end of the "Kinetic Energy" section, the term mgh appears in Equation (3.20) indicating that when the projectile reaches its maximum height its initial kinetic energy has been completely converted to gravitational potential energy.

Other Forms of Energy

Kinetic and potential energy are known as mechanical energy because they are based on external factors such as velocity and location. Energy can also be stored internally inside the molecules and atoms that make up an object. One form of internal energy is thermal energy or heat. One mechanism that can transfer thermal energy to an object is friction. Try rubbing your hands together quickly, and the palms of your hands will heat up. Another energy type is chemical energy, which is the energy stored in the chemical bonds of molecules. When chemical energy is rapidly released, an explosion can occur, a subject that will be covered in Chapter 13.

Conservation of Energy

We have already talked about how energy can be converted from one form into another. This concept can be expanded into one of the fundamental concepts of physics—**conservation of energy**, which states that energy can neither be created nor destroyed, only converted from one form into another.

There are times when you can use the conservation of energy principle to model the motion of an object. For example, let's say that a ball of mass m is held motionless at a height h_0 above the earth. If the ball is released, it will fall to the earth. As the ball falls, some of its initial potential energy is converted into kinetic energy. If only kinetic and potential energy is being considered, the velocity of the ball, v, at any height, h, during its fall could be obtained from the conservation of energy equation.

$$\frac{1}{2}mv^2 + mgh = mgh_0 \tag{3.24}$$

A common mistake that is made is to assume that conservation of energy applies only to kinetic and potential energy—that the sum of kinetic and potential energy for a given system is constant. This statement is only true if there are no other energy modes (thermal, chemical, etc.) that are available. If there is some other way that energy can be stored, into thermal energy for instance, then the sum of kinetic and potential energy may not be constant.

For example, let's say that there is a box resting on top of a ramp at an initial height, h_0, as shown in Figure 3-13. At some point the box is released and slides to the bottom of the ramp. If only kinetic and potential energy were being considered, you might think to compute the velocity of the box when it reaches the bottom of the ramp by Equation (3.24). However, the actual velocity of the box will be less than the value predicted by Equation (3.24). The reason is that there will be friction between the box and the ramp and some of the initial potential energy of the box will be converted to thermal energy. The bottom of the box and the surface of the ramp will heat up by a small amount. The overall energy of the system is still conserved, but the sum of the potential and kinetic energy is not.

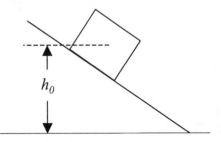

Figure 3-13. *A box sliding down a ramp will generate some heat.*

Power

You have learned that work is performed when a force is applied to an object over a certain distance. But nowhere in the definition of work is the concept of how long it took to perform the work. The concept of **power** is used to characterize the rate at which work is being performed. Power is defined as the amount of work performed per unit time. It has units of J/s, which is also known as a *watt* or *W* for short. A commonly used unit of power in the English system of units is the *horsepower* or *hp*. One *hp* is equal to 745.7 *W*.

Power is also used to describe the performance of engines. We will use the concept of power when we simulate cars in Chapter 8, boats in Chapter 9, and airplanes in Chapter 10.

Summary

In this chapter, you learned about basic Newtonian mechanics—the study of forces and how they affect the acceleration of objects. Newton's three laws of motion were introduced. Newton's three laws will form the basis for every physical model we develop in this book. Some of the other things we discussed in this chapter include the following:

- Force is a vector quantity that has both a magnitude and a direction.

- Gravitational force is exerted by every object on every other object and is a function of masses of the two objects and an inverse function of the square of the distance between them.

- Frictional force is the resistance of one object sliding over another. It is proportional to the normal force exerted on the object and a constant known as the coefficient of friction.

- Spring force is a variable force that is a function of the distance the spring has been displaced from its equilibrium position.

- A centripetal force is required for an object to travel around a curve. Centripetal force is proportional to the square of the velocity of the object and is inversely proportional to the radius of curvature of the object's trajectory.

- How to develop force diagrams as an aid to physical modeling.

- How mechanical work is a force exerted on an object over a certain distance.

- About energy and some of the different types of energy including kinetic, potential, and thermal energy.

- How power is equal to an amount of work done per unit time.

Answers to Exercises

1. Using the gravitational force equation and Newton's second law, the acceleration at the surface of the moon is equal to

$$a = \frac{Gm_{moon}}{r_{moon}^2} = \frac{6.67e-11 * 7.3483e+22}{\left(1.7374e+6\right)^2} = 1.624 \frac{m}{s^2}$$

From this result, we see that the acceleration due to gravity on the moon is about 1/6 that found on Earth.

2. Referring to the schematic diagram shown in Figure 3-2 earlier in this chapter, the box will begin to slide when the force on the box parallel to the ramp is equal to the maximum static friction force.

$$mg \sin\theta = \mu_s mg \cos\theta$$

The angle at which the box begins to slide is therefore equal to the following:

$$\tan\theta = \mu_s = 0.61 \quad \text{or} \quad \theta = 31.4$$

An interesting thing to note about this problem is that the angle at which sliding begins is independent of the mass of the box. A 10 kg box will begin to slide at the same angle as a 2 kg box. This is an experiment you can easily try out on your own. If you don't have a steel plate or aluminum box, use some other combination of materials listed in Table 3-1.

3. As shown in Figure 3-14, the spring will reach its new equilibrium position when upward force due to the extended spring balances the downward force due to the 1 kg mass. If the spring deflection is taken to be in the z-direction, the equation becomes

$$k\Delta z = mg$$

$$\Delta z = \frac{mg}{k} = \frac{9.81}{325} = 0.0302$$

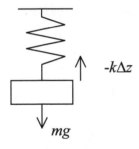

$$-k\Delta z$$

$$mg$$

Figure 3-14. *The location of the spring is where the spring and gravity forces balance.*

The spring will end up 3.02 cm from its original equilibrium position.

4. The radius of the moon's orbit will be at a value where the gravitational force between the earth and moon equals the centripetal force required to keep the moon in that orbit.

$$\frac{Gm_m m_e}{r^2} = \frac{m_m v^2}{r}$$

$$r = \frac{Gm_e}{v^2} = \frac{6.67e-11 * 5.974e+24}{1023^2} = 3.81e+8 \ m$$

CHAPTER 4

Basic Kinematics

The previous chapter introduced Newtonian mechanics and the subjects of force, work, energy, and power. We encountered Newton's three laws of motion, which characterize the behavior of forces and relate a force applied to an object to the resulting acceleration of the object. In this chapter, we will expand the discussion of Newton's laws of motion to explore the field of kinematics—the study of motion. This chapter will provide you with the basic models and equations that govern the motion of all objects.

Understanding the laws of motion is critically important to game programming. Pretty much every live-action game will involve things flying through the air, driving along the ground, moving through water, and so on. A good understanding of kinematics will give your games realism. You will apply the concepts you learn in this chapter to just about every live-action game you will program.

To cover the subject of basic kinematics, this chapter will explore the following topics:

- The equations that govern acceleration, velocity, and location in translational motion

- Solving the translational equations of motion

- The equations that govern rotational motion

- The concepts of torque, moment of inertia, and center of mass

- Rigid body motion

Translational Motion

The first topic this chapter covers is the development of the equations that describe the linear, or translational, motion of an object. Translational motion describes the movement of an object through space. You will have to model translational motion all the time in your game programming—modeling the flight of a golf ball, simulating an airplane flying through the air, or modeling a car driving around a curve are just a few of the many types of translational motion that a game programmer might have to simulate.

The mathematical description of translational motion begins with Newton's second law, $F = ma$. Once the net external forces on an object have been evaluated, the acceleration of the object can be determined. Knowing the acceleration allows the determination of the velocity and location of the object at any point in time. Let's start our discussion of translational motion by talking about the relationship between force, acceleration, velocity, and location.

The Relationship Between Force, Acceleration, Velocity, and Location

Newton's second law, which was introduced in Chapter 3, relates the net external force on an object, F, to the mass and acceleration of the object.

$$\vec{F} = m\vec{a} \tag{4.1}$$

The arrows above the force and acceleration terms in Equation (4.1) indicate that they are vector quantities having both a magnitude and a direction. The force and acceleration vectors can be divided into components that act in the individual coordinate directions. For example, in the Cartesian reference frame, force and the resulting accelerations can be divided into x-, y-, and z-components.

$$F_x = ma_x \qquad F_y = ma_y \qquad F_z = ma_z \tag{4.2}$$

One of the motivations for splitting the force and acceleration vectors into directional components is that the directional components can be analyzed independently of each other. A force in the x-direction will have no effect on acceleration in the y-direction. If the net force acts in only one direction, it can simplify the modeling of a problem in that the other two directions can oftentimes be ignored.

Once the accelerations are known, the velocity of the object can be determined. Acceleration is the time rate of change of velocity. Recall from Chapter 1 that a time rate of change of something can be expressed as a derivative. Acceleration can be represented as the derivative of velocity, v, with respect to time.

$$\vec{a} = \frac{d\vec{v}}{dt} \tag{4.3}$$

As indicated in Equation (4.3), velocity is a vector quantity and can be split into directional components. In the Cartesian frame of reference, the relationship between acceleration and velocity derivative could be divided into x-, y-, and z-components.

$$a_x = \frac{dv_x}{dt} \qquad a_y = \frac{dv_y}{dt} \qquad a_z = \frac{dv_z}{dt} \tag{4.4}$$

While velocity can be expressed in terms of its three directional components, there are times when the velocity magnitude, or speed, is required. Velocity magnitude, v, can be found by obtaining the square root of the sum of the square of the directional components.

$$v = \sqrt{v_x^2 + v_y^2 + v_z^2} \tag{4.5}$$

If you have taken geometry, you may recognize Equation (4.5) as the Pythagorean theorem.

Once the velocity of an object has been determined, the location of an object can be computed from the velocity components. Velocity is the rate of change of location, s, with respect to time.

$$\vec{v} = \frac{d\vec{s}}{dt} \tag{4.6}$$

The location of an object is a vector quantity, and Equation (4.6) can be divided into directional components. In the Cartesian frame of reference, Equation (4.6) would be split into x-, y-, and z-direction components.

$$v_x = \frac{dx}{dt} \qquad v_y = \frac{dy}{dt} \qquad v_z = \frac{dz}{dt} \qquad (4.7)$$

Since acceleration is the derivative of velocity with respect to time and velocity is the derivative of location with respect to time, it follows that acceleration is the second derivative (the derivative of the derivative) of location with respect to time.

$$a_x = \frac{d}{dt}\left(\frac{dx}{dt}\right) = \frac{d^2x}{dt^2} \qquad (4.8)$$

It is helpful to look at the relationship between acceleration, velocity, and location visually. Figure 4-1 shows the acceleration, velocity, and location (altitude in this case) when an object is dropped (or skis off a cliff) and falls vertically towards the ground. The acceleration due to gravity is constant. Because the acceleration is constant, the velocity increases linearly with time. Since the speed of the object is continually increasing, location of the object decreases along a parabolic-shaped curve.

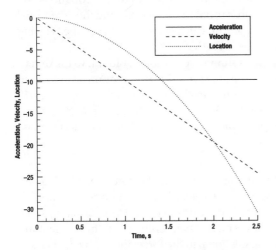

Figure 4-1. *The acceleration, velocity, and location curves of a falling object*

Recall from Chapter 1 that a derivative can be thought of as the slope of a curve. The slope of the location curve at a given time is equal to the velocity. The slope of the velocity curve at a given time is equal to the acceleration.

Solving the Translational Equations of Motion

Newton's second law and the derivatives presented in the previous section provide the basic equations needed to solve for the acceleration, velocity, and location of an object as a function of time. To obtain the velocity and location requires the solution of the corresponding differential equations. For example, consider the relationship between the z-location of an object and the z-component of velocity.

$$v_z = \frac{dz}{dt} \tag{4.9}$$

To determine the z-location at a given time, it is necessary to **integrate** the differential equation shown in Equation (4.9). Integration is a way to determine the value of a variable from its derivative. In the case of Equation (4.9), the corresponding integral equation would be the following:

$$z - z_0 = \int v_z dt \tag{4.10}$$

The $\int$ symbol in Equation (4.10) is the integral symbol and the quantity z_0 is the initial value of the z. For example, if an object was dropped from an altitude of 50 m, the initial value of z would be $z_0 = 50$.

This book won't go into the subject of integration in any detail, but it will provide you with enough information to solve the basic equations of motion. If the initial differential equation is relatively simple, it can be solved directly, giving what is called a **closed-form solution**. Closed-form solutions can sometimes be simple algebraic equations. If the differential equations are more complicated, however, a closed-form solution is usually not possible, and the differential equations must be solved using other techniques, one of which we will discuss in the "Solving Ordinary Differential Equations" section a little later in the chapter.

If the forces acting on an object are constant, a simple closed-form solution to the differential equations can usually be obtained. For example, the force due to gravity on an object can usually be assumed to be constant (if minor changes due to changing altitude are ignored). If gravity is the only force acting on an object, the net external force on the object in the vertical direction is equal to the mass of the object, m, multiplied by the gravitational acceleration, g.

$$F_z = -mg \tag{4.11}$$

Since gravity force acts in the vertical, or z-, direction, the x- and y-components of force will be zero. Recall from Chapter 3 that the gravitational acceleration on the surface of the earth is 9.81 m/s^2. The negative sign in Equation (4.11) indicates that the gravity force is acting in the downward direction towards the ground. If the mass of the object is constant, the acceleration on the object in the z-direction is also constant and is equal to the force divided by the mass of the object.

$$a_z = -g \tag{4.12}$$

The derivative of the z-component of velocity with respect to time is equal to the z-component of acceleration. The z-component of velocity at any given time can be found by integrating Equation (4.4).

$$a_z = -g = \frac{dv_z}{dt} \tag{4.13}$$

$$v_z = v_{z0} + \int a_z dt = v_{z0} - \int g dt = v_{z0} - gt \tag{4.14}$$

The quantity v_{z0} in Equation (4.14) is the initial velocity in the z-direction of the object at time $t = 0$. The z-location of the object as a function of time can be computed from Equations (4.14) and (4.7).

$$v_z = v_{z0} + at = v_{z0} - gt = \frac{dz}{dt}$$ (4.15)

$$z = z_0 + \int (v_{z0} - gt)dt = z_0 + v_{z0}t - \frac{1}{2}gt^2$$ (4.16)

The quantity z_0 in Equation (4.16) is the initial z-location of the object at time $t = 0$. Equations (4.14) and (4.16) show that when an object is subject to a constant force, the velocity and location of the object at any time can be determined from simple algebraic equations. The equations that determine acceleration, velocity, and location for an object subjected to a constant vertical force are summarized in Table 4-1. Acceleration is not characterized with a differential equation but rather by Newton's second law, $F = ma$.

Table 4-1. The Equations of Motion for an Object Subject to a Constant Gravitational Force

Quantity	Differential Equation	Solution
Acceleration	None	$a_z = \dfrac{F}{m} = -g$
Velocity	$\dfrac{dv_z}{dt} = a_z = -g$	$v_z = v_{z0} - gt$
Location	$\dfrac{dz}{dt} = v_z = v_{z0} - gt$	$z = z_0 + v_{z0}t - \dfrac{1}{2}gt^2$

Beanbag Game

Let's use the constant-force equations of motion and create a beanbag game. The goal of the game is to throw a beanbag onto a square several meters away. A score is awarded depending on what square the beanbag lands on. A sample GUI screen shot for the game is shown in Figure 4-2. You will probably notice that it looks a lot like the shuffleboard game developed in the previous chapter. There are two text fields on the left-hand side of the GUI that allow the user to specify the initial horizontal and vertical velocity components. When the Fire button is pressed, the beanbag is thrown. The Reset button resets the display.

The Beanbag Game makes use of the constant-force equations of motion that were developed in the previous section. When the beanbag is released, it experiences no force in the x-direction. The horizontal location of the beanbag at any time is a function only of the initial x-location and x-velocity component.

$$x = x_0 + v_{x0}t$$ (4.17)

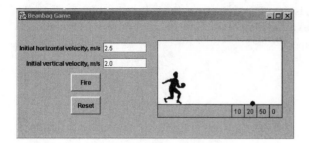

Figure 4-2. *A sample Beanbag Game screen shot*

In the vertical direction, the beanbag will be subject to gravitational acceleration. The vertical location of the beanbag at any point in time is a function of the gravitational acceleration, the initial vertical location, and the initial z-velocity component.

$$z = z_0 + v_{z0}t - \frac{1}{2}gt^2 \tag{4.18}$$

The Beanbag Game is implemented in a class named BeanBag. The development of the class is very similar to the games that were written in the previous chapter, so we won't go over the entire code listing in detail, but we will focus on the elements that are used to compute the motion of the beanbag. In addition to GUI component declarations, the BeanBag class also declares fields that represent the initial and current horizontal and vertical locations and velocities of the beanbag.

```
public class BeanBag extends JFrame implements ActionListener
{
  private JTextField vxTextField;
  private JTextField vzTextField;

  private JLabel vxLabel;
  private JLabel vzLabel;

  private JButton fireButton;
  private JButton resetButton;
  private JPanel drawingPanel;
  private GridBagConstraints gbc;

  private double z;      // altitude of beanbag
  private double z0;     // initial altitude of beanbag
  private double vz0;    // initial vertical velocity
  private double x;      // horizontal location
  private double x0;     // initial horizontal location
  private double vx0;    // initial horizontal velocity
  private double time;
```

As with the previous games, the BeanBag class makes use of a Timer object to control the execution of the game. The Timer object is set up to call the actionPerformed method every 0.05 seconds to compute the current position of the beanbag and to update the display.

The `actionPerformed` method itself is quite simple. The current time is incremented, and then the x- and z-locations of the beanbag are computed according to Equations (4.17) and (4.18). The display is then updated. If the beanbag has hit the ground, the simulation is stopped. The ground in this game is defined at a height of 1.4 m because the line that indicates the ground in the GUI is drawn 140 pixels below the top of the display panel.

```
// This ActionListener is called by the Timer
  class GameUpdater implements ActionListener {
    public void actionPerformed(ActionEvent event) {

      // Update the time and compute the new position
      // of the beanbag.
      double timeIncrement = 0.05;
      time += timeIncrement;

      // There is no force in the x-direction, so the
      // new x location is the initial x location plus
      // the product of the horizontal velocity and time.
      x = x0 + vx0*time;

      // The z-location is influenced by the acceleration
      // due to gravity.
      double g = -9.81;
      z = z0 + vz0*time + 0.5*g*time*time;

      // Update the display
      updateDisplay();

      // If the beanbag hits the ground, stop
      // the simulation.
      if ( z <= 1.4 ) {
        gameTimer.stop();
      }
    }
  }
```

When you play around with the Beanbag Game, try adjusting the initial horizontal and vertical velocities and see what happens. The beanbag is our first attempt at modeling the flight of a projectile, a subject we'll cover in much more detail in the next chapter.

Solving Ordinary Differential Equations

In the beginning of this section we learned that if the forces applied to an object are constant, the velocity and location of the object at any time can be computed from simple algebraic equations. Many times the forces acting on an object will not be constant but instead will vary depending on the velocity or location of the object. For example, if a projectile is flying through the air, it will be subject to the force of aerodynamic drag, which is a function of the square of the velocity of the object. The forces on the projectile will vary during its flight, and the resulting equations of motion cannot be directly solved.

Fortunately, a number of techniques can be used to solve differential equations when a closed-form solution is not possible. In the next section, a program called a **Runge-Kutta ODE solver** will be presented that you can use to solve the differential equations that you will encounter in your game programming. The Runge-Kutta ODE solver is versatile, dependable, and applicable to a wide range of problems.

Fourth-Order Runge-Kutta ODE Solver

Many techniques have been developed over the years for solving ordinary differential equations. The one presented in this chapter and used throughout this book is called the **fourth-order Runge-Kutta method**. This method is one of a family of step-wise integration methods, meaning that from a set of initial conditions, the ODE is solved at discrete increments of the independent variable. For the equations of motion, the independent variable will be time. The fourth-order Runge-Kutta method is not the most efficient ODE solver available, but it is simple and dependable, and will give good results as long as very high accuracy is not required.

■**Tidbit** Carl Runge and Martin Kutta were German mathematicians who, among other things, developed methods to solve ordinary differential equations. The Runge-Kutta method, first presented in 1901, has really stood the test of time. Despite the fact that they are over 100 years old, Runge-Kutta methods are still widely used today.

Runge-Kutta methods are designed to work on first-order ODEs. If you recall from Chapter 1, a first-order ODE is an equation with one dependent variable where the highest-order derivative appearing in the equation is a first derivative. For example, an equation relating the derivative of z-location with respect to time to the z-component of velocity would be a first-order ODE.

$$\frac{dz}{dt} = v_z(z,t) \tag{4.19}$$

The z-component of velocity, v_z, in Equation (4.19) does not have to be a constant, but instead is expressed as a general function of z and t. For example, consider the curve shown in Figure 4-3 that displays z-location as a function of time. The shape of the curve indicates that the z-location is a nonlinear function of time. The slope of the curve at any time, t, is equal to the velocity, $v_z(z,t)$.

Let's say that the z-location and velocity, z_n and v_{zn}, are known at a given time, t_n. We want to determine the z-location at a future time, $t_n+\Delta t$, where Δt is a certain time increment. For small enough increments in the independent variable, t, the derivative in Equation (4.19) can be replaced with its delta form.

$$\frac{dz}{dt} \approx \frac{\Delta z}{\Delta t} = v_z(z,t) \tag{4.20}$$

The value of the z-location, z_{n+1}, at the future time $t_n+\Delta t$ can be determined from Equation (4.20).

$$\Delta z = z_{n+1} - z_n = v_z(z,t)\Delta t \tag{4.21}$$

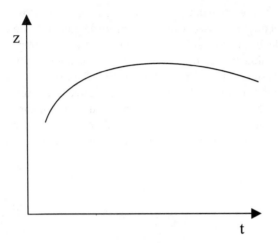

Figure 4-3. *A general z-location vs. time curve*

The issue that remains is where should the velocity, $v_z(z,t)$, be evaluated. A natural choice would be to evaluate the velocity at the known conditions, z_n and t_n.

$$\Delta z = z_{n+1} - z_n = v_z\left(z_n, t_n\right)\Delta t \tag{4.22}$$

This approach is known as **Euler's method**. Unfortunately, Euler's method is not accurate unless the slope of the velocity curve is more or less constant between times t_n and $t_n + \Delta t$. If the slope of the velocity curve changes significantly between the two time levels, errors will be introduced into the solution. To see how this happens, let's look at a close-up view of one part of the velocity curve shown in Figure 4-3. In Figure 4-4, the dashed line shows the value of z_{n+1} computed by Euler's method, which computes the z-location based on the velocity at time t_n. Because the slope of the velocity curve decreases over time, Euler's method overpredicts what the z-location will be at time $t_n + \Delta t$.

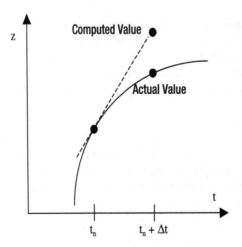

Figure 4-4. *Euler's method is inaccurate if the curve is not linear.*

Clearly, a better way is needed to estimate the value of z_{n+1}, and that's where the fourth-order Runge-Kutta method comes into the picture. The essence of the fourth-order Runge-Kutta scheme is that a series of estimates are made for the z-location at the new time by evaluating the velocity at different values of x and t. An initial estimate is made for z_{n+1} using the velocity at x_n and t_n (that is, Euler's method). A second estimate is computed by evaluating the velocity at a point halfway between the known conditions and the results of the first estimate. Two more estimates are made in a similar manner, and the final value for z_{n+1} is obtained from a linear combination of the four estimates. The five mathematical equations that form the fourth-order Runge-Kutta scheme when it is applied to solve Equation (4.19) are shown in Equation (4.23).

$$\Delta z_1 = v(z_n, t_n)\Delta t \tag{4.23a}$$

$$\Delta z_2 = v(z_n + \frac{1}{2}\Delta z_1, t_n + \frac{1}{2}\Delta t)\Delta t \tag{4.23b}$$

$$\Delta z_3 = v(z_n + \frac{1}{2}\Delta z_2, t_n + \frac{1}{2}\Delta t)\Delta t \tag{4.23c}$$

$$\Delta z_4 = v(z_n + \Delta z_3, t_n + \Delta t)\Delta t \tag{4.23d}$$

$$z_{n+1} = z_n + \frac{\Delta z_1}{6} + \frac{\Delta z_2}{3} + \frac{\Delta z_3}{3} + \frac{\Delta z_4}{6} \tag{4.23e}$$

Naturally, the Runge-Kutta method is not restricted to solving the ODE shown in Equation (4.19). It can be applied to solve any first-order ODE. As long as a derivative can be expressed as a function of the dependent and independent variables, the Runge-Kutta method can be used to solve for the value of the dependent variable.

This section has provided a very brief introduction to Runge-Kutta ODE solution techniques. If the theory behind Runge-Kutta solvers is still a bit unclear to you, don't worry. A little later in this chapter, we will develop a Runge-Kutta code that you can use in your game programming.

Solving Higher-Order ODEs

As was mentioned before, the Runge-Kutta technique is designed for solving first-order ODEs. So what do you do to solve higher-order ODEs? The answer is to expand the higher-order derivatives into a series of first-order ODEs. The Runge-Kutta solver is then applied to each first-order ODE. For example, let's say we want to model the motion of a spring. The location of a mass, m, at the end of a spring as a function of time is described by a second-order differential equation.

$$m\frac{d^2 x}{dt^2} + \mu\frac{dx}{dt} + kx = 0 \tag{4.24}$$

In Equation (4.24), k is the spring constant that defines how stiff the spring is, and μ is the damping coefficient that characterizes how quickly the spring motion will die out. Knowing that $v_x = dx/dt$, the equation of motion for a spring shown in Equation (4.24) can be rewritten as two first-order differential equations.

$$m\frac{dv_x}{dt} = -\mu v_x - kx \qquad\qquad\qquad (4.25)$$

$$\frac{dx}{dt} = v_x \qquad\qquad\qquad (4.26)$$

In Equation (4.25), the derivative of v_x is a function of v_x and x. In Equation (4.26), the derivative of x is a function of v_x. Because the solution of v_x as a function of time depends on x and the solution of x as a function of time depends on v_x, the two equations are said to be **coupled** and must be solved simultaneously by the ODE solver. The ODE solver will compute the velocity, v_x, and the location, x, at discrete time increments.

Most of the ODEs that we will solve in this book will be higher-order ODEs that will first be expanded into a set of first-order ODEs before they are solved.

Boundary Conditions

Solving an ODE requires more than just knowing the form of the differential equation. Also required are things called **boundary conditions**, values of the dependent variables either at the beginning or end of whatever range the ODE is being solved over. For example, if the flight of a bullet is being modeled, boundary conditions might include the initial velocity and location of the bullet as it leaves the gun barrel. Generally speaking, an ODE has an infinite number of possible solutions. Specifying boundary conditions "pins down" the solution to the one that we want.

An ODE where initial conditions for all the dependent variables are defined is called an **initial value problem**. The Runge-Kutta solver solves this type of ODE by successively incrementing the independent variable, a process known as "marching," updating the values of the dependent variables every step of the way. All of the ODEs that we will encounter in this book will be initial value problems.

Sometimes initial values are not available for all of the dependent variables. Instead, the values of some dependent variables may be defined at the end of the range of interest. For example, you might want to specify the location of an object at one time and the velocity of the object at a later time. This situation is referred to as a **two-point boundary problem** and is generally more difficult to solve than an initial value problem.

One way to solve a two-point boundary problem is to make guesses for the initial values of those dependent variables for which initial conditions aren't available. The ODE is integrated and then it is determined whether the boundary conditions at the end of the range of interest are met. If they aren't, another guess is made for the initial conditions, and the procedure repeats itself over and over until the boundary conditions at the end of the range of interest are satisfied. This technique is known as **shooting**.

Programming the Fourth-Order Runge-Kutta Solver

We now have all the information we need to write a program that will implement a fourth-order Runge-Kutta ODE solver that will solve initial value problem-type ODEs. The solver will be written as general as possible so that it will be able to solve any number of coupled first-order ODEs. Two classes are needed to implement the ODE solver—the solver itself and a class that represents the ODE to be solved.

The ODE Class

We'll start with the class that represents the ODE to be solved, which will be called the ODE class. This class will represent a generic ordinary differential equation. Classes to represent specific types of ODEs, to model spring or projectile motion for instance, will be written as subclasses of the ODE class. The ODE class declares three fields that represent the number of first-order ODEs to be solved, an array containing the dependent variable values, and the value of the independent variable. The constructor initializes the numEqns variable and sizes the q[ ] array that will store the dependent variable values.

```java
public abstract class ODE
{
  // Declare fields used by the class
  private int numEqns;  // number of equations to solve
  private double q[];   // array of dependent variables
  private double s;     // independent variable

  // Constructor
  public ODE(int numEqns) {
    this.numEqns = numEqns;
    q = new double[numEqns];
  }
```

The ODE class declares a standard series of get/set methods to return or change the values of the fields declared in the class.

```java
// These methods return the number of equations or
//  the value of the dependent or independent variables.
public int getNumEqns() {
  return numEqns;
}

public double getS() {
  return s;
}

public double getQ(int index) {
  return q[index];
}

public double[] getAllQ() {
  return q;
}
```

```
//  These methods change the value of the dependent
//  or independent variables.
public void setS(double value) {
  s = value;
  return;
}

public void setQ(double value, int index) {
  q[index] = value;
  return;
}
```

The final thing the ODE class does is to declare a method called getRightHandSide. To solve an ODE equation, the right-hand side of the differential equation must be evaluated. For example, to solve the spring motion problem characterized by Equations (4.25) and (4.26), the getRightHandSide method would compute and return the expressions $(-\mu v_x - kx)/m$ and v_x. Since the method is declared to be abstract, subclasses of ODE will have to provide their own implementation of the getRightHandSide method tailored to whatever set of equations needs to be solved.

```
//  This method returns the right-hand side of the
//  ODEs. It is declared abstract to force subclasses
//  to implement their own version of the method.
public abstract double[] getRightHandSide(double s,
     double q[],double deltaQ[], double ds, double qScale);
```

A little later in this section, a subclass of the ODE class will be written to model the motion of a spring.

The ODESolver Class

Now that a class that represents an ODE has been written, we can turn our attention towards implementing the fourth-order Runge-Kutta solver. The solver is implemented in a method called rungeKutta4 that is declared inside the ODESolver class. Since many programs will have a need for an ODE solver, the rungeKutta4 method is declared to be public and static, allowing the method to be accessed by any other program. The rungeKutta4 method takes two arguments, an ODE object representing the equation to be solved and an increment to the independent variable ds.

The objective of the rungeKutta4 method is to implement the five steps of the fourth-order Runge-Kutta solution process shown in Equations (4.23a) through (4.23e). The first thing done in the method is the declaration of some convenience variables and four arrays, dq1[] through dq4[], that will store the intermediate updates to the dependent variables. The method then uses the ODE object to obtain the current values of the independent and dependent variables. The independent variable is called s, and the dependent variables are stored in an array named q[].

```
public class ODESolver
{
  // Fourth-order Runge-Kutta ODE solver.
  public static void rungeKutta4(ODE ode, double ds) {

    // Define some convenience variables to make the
    // code more readable
    int j;
    int numEqns = ode.getNumEqns();
    double s;
    double q[];
    double dq1[] = new double[numEqns];
    double dq2[] = new double[numEqns];
    double dq3[] = new double[numEqns];
    double dq4[] = new double[numEqns];


    // Retrieve the current values of the dependent
    // and independent variables.
    s = ode.getS();      // independent variable
    q = ode.getAllQ(); // dependent variables
```

The method computes the four estimates for Δq according to Equations (4.23a) through (4.23d) by calling the getRightHandSide method on the ODE object. The arguments to the getRightHandSide method define where the dependent and independent variables are evaluated for each step ($q_n + 1/2\Delta q_1$, for example).

```
// Compute the four Runge-Kutta steps. The return
    // value of getRightHandSide method is an array of
    // delta-q values for each of the four steps.
    dq1 = ode.getRightHandSide(s, q, q, ds, 0.0);
    dq2 = ode.getRightHandSide(s+0.5*ds, q, dq1, ds, 0.5);
    dq3 = ode.getRightHandSide(s+0.5*ds, q, dq2, ds, 0.5);
    dq4 = ode.getRightHandSide(s+ds, q, dq3, ds, 1.0);
```

Once the four estimates for Δq have been computed, the update to the dependent variables can be calculated according to Equation (4.23e). The value of the independent variable, s, is incremented to its new value.

```
// Update the dependent and independent variable values
    // at the new dependent variable location and store the
    // values in the ODE object arrays.
    ode.setS(s+ds);
```

```
    for(j=0; j<numEqns; ++j) {
      q[j] = q[j] + (dq1[j] + 2.0*dq2[j] + 2.0*dq3[j] + dq4[j])/6.0;
      ode.setQ(q[j], j);
    }

    return;
  }
}
```

The rungeKutta4 method is quite simple and takes only 38 lines of code including comment statements. To apply the Runge-Kutta solver to a specific problem requires one more step—an ODE subclass must be written that models the equations to be solved. We'll look at an example of that in the next section where the Runge-Kutta solver will be used to model the motion of a spring.

Example: Spring Motion

Let's demonstrate the Runge-Kutta ODE solver by applying it to the problem of predicting the motion of a spring. The equations that describe the change in the location and velocity as a function of time for the spring are shown in Equations (4.25) and (4.26). They consist of two first-order ODEs. The spring problem is a good test case for the ODE solver because there is an exact solution to the governing equations that can be compared against the values predicted by the ODE solver.

In order to compute the motion of the spring, it is necessary to write a class that represents the spring motion ODEs. The class, called SpringODE, is written as a subclass of ODE so the code written in the ODE class can be reused. The first thing the SpringODE class does is to declare fields that represent spring-specific data such as the spring constant and damping coefficient. Since the motion of the spring will be computed as a function of time, the independent variable for this problem is time.

```
public class SpringODE extends ODE
{
  private double mass;  //  mass at end of spring
  private double mu;    //  damping coefficient
  private double k;     //  spring constant
  private double x0;    //  initial spring deflection
  private double time;  //  independent variable
```

The SpringODE class declares a constructor that is used to define the initial state of the spring. The first thing the constructor does is to call the ODE class constructor to initialize the values of the fields declared in the ODE class. The fields declared in the SpringODE class are then initialized according to the arguments passed to the SpringODE constructor. The last thing the constructor does is to set the initial conditions for the spring. The initial velocity of the spring is set to zero and the initial location of the spring is set according to the $x0$ argument passed to the constructor.

```
//  SpringODE constructor.
  public SpringODE(double mass, double mu, double k,
                   double x0) {
    //  Call the ODE constructor indicating that there
    //  will be two coupled first-order ODEs.
    super(2);

    //  Initialize fields declared in the class.
    this.mass = mass;
    this.mu = mu;
    this.k = k;
    this.x0 = x0;
    time = 0.0;

    //  Set the initial conditions of the dependent
    //  variables.
    //   q[0] = vx
    //   q[1] = x;
    setQ(0.0, 0);
    setQ(x0, 1);
  }
```

The SpringODE class declares a series of get/set methods to return or change the value of the fields declared in the class. Not all of the get/set methods are shown here.

```
//  These methods return field values
  public double getMass() {
    return mass;
  }

  //  Other get methods not shown…

  //  These methods change field values
  public void setMass(double value) {
    mass = value;
    return;
  }

  //  Other set methods not shown …
```

Methods are declared that return the location and velocity of the spring as computed by the ODE solver, as well as the current time value.

```
//  These methods return the spring location
  //   and velocity as computed by the ODE solver.
  public double getVx() {
    return getQ(0);
  }
```

```
public double getX() {
  return getQ(1);
}

public double getTime() {
  return getS();
}
```

The ODE solver will be used to update the location and velocity of the spring as a function of time. The SpringODE class declares a method called updatePositionAndVelocity that calls the Runge-Kutta solver.

```
//  This method updates the velocity and position
  //  of the spring using a 4th order Runge-Kutta
  //  solver to integrate the equations of motion.
  public void updatePositionAndVelocity(double dt) {
    ODESolver.rungeKutta4(this, dt);
  }
```

The final method declared in the SpringODE class is an implementation of the getRightHandSide method first declared in the ODE class. The getRightHandSide method computes the right-hand side of the two spring motion ODEs according to the Runge-Kutta method relations shown in Equations (4.23a) through (4.23d). Which of the four relations is computed (Δq_1, Δq_2, Δq_3, or Δq_4) depends on the arguments sent to the method.

```
//  sides of the two first-order damped spring ODEs
  //   q[0] = vx
  //   q[1] = x
  //   dq[0] = d(vx) = dt*(-mu*dxdt - k*x)/mass
  //   dq[1] = d(x) = dt*(v)
  public double[] getRightHandSide(double s, double q[],
            double deltaQ[], double ds, double qScale) {

    double dq[] = new double[4];    // right-hand side values
    double newQ[] = new double[4]; // intermediate dependent
                                   // variable values.

    //  Compute the intermediate values of the
    //  dependent variables.
    for(int i=0; i<2; ++i) {
      newQ[i] = q[i] + qScale*deltaQ[i];
    }

    //  Compute right-hand side values.
    dq[0] = -ds*(mu*newQ[0] + k*newQ[1])/mass;
    dq[1] = ds*(newQ[0]);

    return dq;
  }
}
```

The only thing that remains to be done is to write a driver program that will create a
SpringODE object and compute its motion using the Runge-Kutta solver. The driver class is
called RK4Spring, and it really is quite simple. Values for mass, damping coefficient, spring
constant, and initial location are defined and a SpringODE object is created based on those
values. The spring ODEs are then integrated over a 7-second interval and the computed locations
and velocities are printed to the screen.

```
public class RK4Spring
{
  public static void main(String args[]) {

    //  Create a SpringODE object that represents
    //  a 1.0 kg spring with a spring constant of
    //  20 N/m and a damping coefficient of 1.5 N-s/m
    double mass = 1.0;
    double mu = 1.5;
    double k = 20.0;
    double x0 = -0.2;

    SpringODE ode = new SpringODE(mass, mu, k, x0);

    //  Solve the ODE over a range of 7 seconds
    //  using a 0.1 second time increment.
    double dt = 0.1;

    System.out.println("t   x   v");
    System.out.println(""+ode.getTime()+"  "+(float)ode.getX()+
                       "  "+(float)ode.getVx());

    while ( ode.getTime() <= 7.0 ) {
      ode.updatePositionAndVelocity(dt);
      System.out.println(""+ode.getTime()+"  "+(float)ode.getX()+
                         "  "+(float)ode.getVx());
    }

    return;
  }
}
```

A plot showing the results of the RK4Spring program is shown in Figure 4-5. The plot shows
the location of the end of the spring computed by the ODE solver as a function of time. The
spring oscillates back and forth, and the oscillations die out over time. Also shown in Figure 4-5
is the exact solution of the spring equations for these conditions. The ODE solver does an excellent
job of reproducing the exact solution.

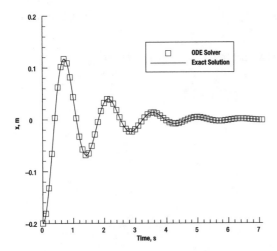

Figure 4-5. *Spring location as a function of time*

One great thing about the ODE solver as we have written it is that it is completely general to virtually any time of initial boundary value ODE. You never have to change the code in the ODE or ODESolver classes. Whenever you have a need to solve an ODE in your game programming, simply write the appropriate ODE subclass and invoke the solver in the game code.

Spring Motion Simulator

Let's write a simple program that simulates the motion of a spring and demonstrates how easy it is to incorporate an ODE subclass object into a simulation. A typical screen shot of the Spring Simulator is shown in Figure 4-6. A spring with a mass hanging on one end is displayed in the right-hand side of the GUI. There are text fields to input the mass, spring constant, damping coefficient, and initial location of the spring. The initial location is the distance the spring is stretched from its equilibrium position. A Start button starts the spring moving and a Reset button stops the simulation and returns the spring to its initial position.

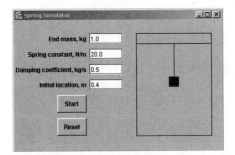

Figure 4-6. *Spring Simulator screen shot*

The Spring Simulator is implemented by the SpringSimulator class. The GUI elements of the class are very similar to the previous games presented in this book and won't be discussed in detail. As always, the full code listing can be downloaded from the Apress website. In addition to fields representing the GUI components, the SpringSimulator class declares a SpringODE object as one of its fields.

```
public class SpringSimulator extends JFrame implements ActionListener
{
  private JTextField massTextField;
  private JTextField muTextField;
  private JTextField kTextField;
  private JTextField x0TextField;

  private JLabel massLabel;
  private JLabel muLabel;
  private JLabel kLabel;
  private JLabel x0Label;

  private JButton startButton;
  private JButton resetButton;
  private JPanel drawingPanel;
  private GridBagConstraints gbc;

  SpringODE spring;
```

When the Start button is pressed, the actionPerformed method declared in the SpringSimulator class is called. Initial values for the mass, damping coefficient, spring constant, and initial location are obtained from the values inside the text fields. A SpringODE object is created based on these initial values. As with the other games created in this book, a Timer object is used to control the execution of the simulation. When the start method is called on the Timer object, the simulation begins and the spring starts to move.

```
// The actionPerformed() method is called when
//  the "Start" button is pressed.
  public void actionPerformed(ActionEvent event) {

    //  Get the initial values from the text field
    double mass = Double.parseDouble(massTextField.getText());
    double mu = Double.parseDouble(muTextField.getText());
    double k = Double.parseDouble(kTextField.getText());
    double x0 = Double.parseDouble(x0TextField.getText());

    //  Create a SpringODE object
    spring = new SpringODE(mass, mu, k, x0);

    //  Start the spring moving using a Timer object
    //  to slow down the action.
    gameTimer.start();
  }
```

The Timer object is set up to call the actionPerformed method declared in the GameUpdater class (an inner class of the SpringSimulator class) every 0.05 seconds. The method is very simple, consisting of only three lines of executable code. Every time the method is called, the updatePositionAndVelocity method is called on the SpringODE object to update the velocity and location of the spring. The update is performed using the Runge-Kutta ODE solver. Once the new values of velocity and location are obtained, the display is updated to show the new position of the spring.

```
class GameUpdater implements ActionListener {
    public void actionPerformed(ActionEvent event) {

        //  Use the ODE solver to update the location of
        //  the spring.
        double dt = 0.05;
        spring.updatePositionAndVelocity(dt);

        //  Update the display
        updateDisplay();
    }
}
```

As we can see from this example, once the SpringODE class is written, it's a simple process to incorporate a spring into a game simulation. Play around with the Spring Simulator. Change the values of the mass, spring constant, damping coefficient, and initial location and see what happens to the motion of the spring.

Exercises

1. A bullet is shot horizontally from a rifle at the same time a ball is released from a person's hand towards the ground. The bullet and ball start at the same vertical distance from the ground. If the only force acting on the ball and bullet is due to gravity, which object will strike the ground first?

2. A soccer player is standing 5 meters straight in front of the opponent's goal when she shoots the ball. The initial velocity of the ball is 12 *m/s* and the ball is initially directed upward at a 45-degree angle. The top of the goal is 2.44 *m* (8 *ft*) high. Assuming that the only external force on the ball is due to gravity, will the ball sail over the goal?

3. The SpringODE class written in this section does not model the force of gravity, but the Spring Simulator uses a spring that hangs vertically where gravity would be a factor. Modify the SpringODE class to include gravity in the equations of motion.

Rotational Motion

The first part of this chapter dealt with translational motion where an object moves linearly through the air, on the ground, or under water. There is another general type of motion known as **rotational motion**, which is the motion of spinning objects. Rotational motion is very important to game programming. A golfer can use spin to increase the distance a golf shot travels or to make a ball "stick" on the green. A car engine uses the rotational motion of the driveshaft and gearbox to transmit power to the wheels. These are just two of the many examples where you will have to model rotational motion in your game programming.

Let's start our exploration of rotational motion by discussing some terminology. Consider a flat disk rotating in the counterclockwise direction as shown in Figure 4-7. The origin of the frame of reference is taken to be the center of the disk. The y-axis is perpendicular to the face of the disk pointing into the page. The location of a point P on the outside of the disk is specified by the radius of the disk and an angle θ measured counterclockwise from the x-axis.

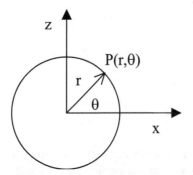

Figure 4-7. *A schematic of rotational motion*

The rate at which the disk is rotating can be expressed in several ways. One way to describe the rate of rotation is by the frequency, f, of rotation, which is the number of revolutions the disk completes per second. Another way to express the rate of rotation is by the rate at which the angle θ changes as a function of time. This quantity is known as the **angular velocity**, ω.

$$\omega = \frac{d\theta}{dt} \tag{4.27}$$

Angular velocity can be expressed in units of *degrees/s* but more commonly is characterized in units of *radians/s*, sometimes abbreviated as *rad/s*. There are 2π *radians* in one revolution, so 2π *radians* is equal to 360 *degrees*. The angular velocity, ω, is related to the frequency of rotation, f, by a factor of 2π.

$$\omega = 2\pi f \tag{4.28}$$

Just as translational acceleration is the time rate of change of translational velocity, the angular acceleration, α, is defined as the time rate of change of angular velocity.

$$\alpha = \frac{d\omega}{dt} \tag{4.29}$$

The angular acceleration will have units of *rad/s²*. The tangential velocity, v_r, of any point on the disk is equal to the angular velocity, ω, multiplied by the distance, r, from the origin to the point.

$$v_r = \omega r \tag{4.30}$$

The tangential velocity will have units of *m/s* and will be in a direction perpendicular to the line drawn from the origin to the point.

A rotating object will have an **axis of rotation**, a line about which the object is spinning. In Figure 4-7, the axis of rotation is the y-axis. The axis of rotation won't always conveniently line up along one of the coordinate axes, but in general it can be defined by any vector in three-dimensional space.

Torque

According to Newton's second law, a net external force on an object causes a translational acceleration of the object. The rotational counterpart of force is **torque**, which causes a rotational acceleration of an object. Torque is defined as a force applied to an object at a certain distance from an axis of rotation.

$$\tau = Fr \tag{4.31}$$

Torque has units of *N-m*. The distance, r, from the center of rotation to the applied force is called the **moment arm** of the torque. To get a feeling for torque, consider the situation shown in Figure 4-8, where a wrench is applied to a nut. If a force of 10 *N* is applied at a distance of 0.12 *m* from the center of the nut, a torque of 1.2 *N-m* will be applied to the center of the nut.

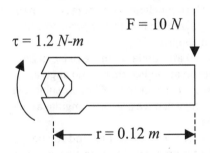

Figure 4-8. *Force applied at a distance from an axis of rotation generates a torque.*

When computing torque, it is the force component perpendicular to the moment arm that is used in the calculation. In Figure 4-8 the force vector and moment arm are perpendicular to each other, so the full force value of 10 *N* is used in the calculation. If the wrench were at an angle of 30 degrees, as shown in Figure 4-9, and the force was still applied vertically, the force vector and moment arm would no longer be perpendicular to each other. The perpendicular force component, $F_p = F\cos30$, would be used in the torque calculation so the torque applied to the nut would be equal to $Fr\cos30 = 1.04$ *N-m*.

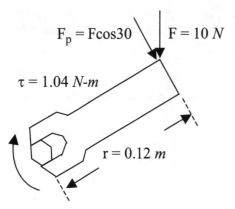

$F_p = F\cos 30$ $F = 10\ N$

$\tau = 1.04\ N\text{-}m$

$r = 0.12\ m$

Figure 4-9. *If force is applied at an angle to the moment arm, torque is reduced.*

Torque and Angular Acceleration

Newton's second law relates a net external force to a translational acceleration by the equation $F = ma$. There is a corresponding equation in rotational motion that relates a net torque, τ, on an object to a resulting angular acceleration, α.

$$\tau = I\alpha \qquad\qquad\qquad (4.32)$$

The quantity, I, in Equation (4.32) is known as the **moment of inertia**. Just as mass is a physical quantity that resists a change in translational motion, moment of inertia is a physical quantity that resists a change in rotational motion. Mass is a material property. The mass of an object depends on what material the object is made of and how much material there is. Moment of inertia is both a material and a geometrical property. The moment of inertia of an object depends on the mass of the object and on the shape of the object.

The conclusions that can be taken from Equation (4.32) are similar to those that can be taken from Newton's second law. If there is no net torque on an object, there is no angular acceleration, and the angular velocity of the object is either zero or a constant. If they are subjected to the same torque, an object with a large moment of inertia will have a smaller angular acceleration than an object that has a small moment of inertia.

Torque, moment of inertia, and angular acceleration are vector quantities and can be divided into components acting about the three axes of rotation defined by a particular frame of reference. The value of the moment of inertia will depend on which axis of rotation is being considered, the shape of the object, and the distribution of mass within the object. Moments of inertia for some common objects are shown in Table 4-2. The m term in the moment of inertia expressions is the mass of the object.

Table 4-2. *Moments of Inertia for Some Common Objects*

Object	Axis of Rotation	Moment of Inertia
Solid sphere of radius r	Through the center of the sphere	$\frac{2}{5}mr^2$
Spherical shell of radius r	Through the center of the sphere	$\frac{2}{3}mr^2$
Cylinder of radius r and length l	Through the ends of the cylinder	$\frac{1}{2}mr^2$
Cylinder of radius r and length l	Through the middle of the cylinder	$\frac{1}{12}ml^2 + \frac{1}{4}mr^2$
Ring of radius r	Perpendicular axis through the center of the ring	mr^2
Ring of radius r	Through the diameter of the ring	$\frac{1}{2}mr^2$

Rigid Body Motion

So far in this chapter, we have looked at translational and rotational motion separately. It's time now to put the two together to describe what is known as **rigid body motion**—the general motion of an object that is traveling through space and rotating at the same time. Combined rotational and translational motion will happen quite frequently in game programming situations. When a pitcher throws a baseball, it will be spinning as it flies towards the catcher (unless it is a knuckleball). Golf balls, tennis balls, footballs, and hockey pucks will usually be tumbling or spinning as they travel through the air.

Fortunately, while the overall motion of an object, like the flight of a curveball, can seem quite complicated, for modeling purposes the overall motion can be separated into translational and rotational components, and the two components can be analyzed independently. To separate the translational and rotational motion components, we need to be familiar with a concept known as the **center of mass**, discussed next.

Center of Mass

According to Newton's second law, the acceleration of an object is a function of the mass of the object and the external forces applied to the object. The size of the object does not enter into the equation. The acceleration of a basketball will be the same as that of a marble if the two objects have the same mass and are subject to the same net external force.

Because "size doesn't matter" when it comes to Newton's second law, the translational motion that results from an external force on an object can be modeled as if the object were shrunk to an infinitesimally small particle located at a point known as the **center of mass** of the object. For symmetrical objects made from a uniform distribution of material, the center of mass will be located at the center of the object. For example, the center of mass for a solid copper sphere would be located at the center of the sphere. The center of mass is also sometimes referred to as the **center of gravity**, because the force of gravity will always act through the center of mass.

The concept of the center of mass is useful for separating the linear motion of an object from its rotational motion. When computing the linear motion of an object, Newton's second law, and the resulting acceleration and velocity, can be applied to the center of mass of the object. Even if an object is rotating, its center of mass moves as if it were a particle. This can be very handy when modeling the motion of an object that is rotating in that it allows the separation of the linear motion computations from the rotational motion computations. For example, consider the case of a knife being thrown towards a target as shown in Figure 4-10. Even though the knife may be spinning through the air in what looks like a very complicated motion, if you could follow the path of the center of mass, you would see that it follows a smooth, parabolic trajectory.

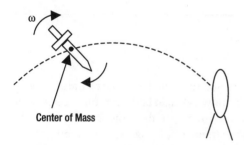

Figure 4-10. *The center of mass of the knife travels in a smooth curve.*

Computing the center of mass for nice, simple, symmetrical objects is quite easy, but what about more complicated shapes like an airplane? One way to think of the center of mass is that it is the point of zero net torque. It is this point at which an object will be perfectly balanced in space. Sometimes the center of mass for a complicated object can be computed analytically or sometimes it can be found experimentally. An interesting characteristic about the center of mass is that, depending on the geometry and composition of an object, it's possible for the center of mass to lie outside of the object. For example, the center of mass of the L-shaped figure shown in Figure 4-11 is in the empty space between the two legs.

Determination of the center of mass is complicated even further if the object has a nonuniform distribution of mass or can change its orientation. The center of mass for a person, for example, will change if the person bends over or raises her leg. Center of mass considerations can also be applied to systems of objects. When computing the center of mass of a boat, for example, it is important to include the contributions due to any passengers who might be on the boat. If the passengers on the boat move around the deck, the center of mass of the boat (and possibly the stability of the boat) will change as well.

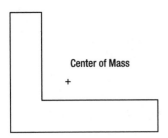

Figure 4-11. *The center of mass can lie outside of an object.*

Rigid Body Motion Coordinate Axes

The translational motion of an object can be modeled by treating the object as a particle located at the center of mass of the object. Any external forces on the object are assumed to act through the center of mass. The rotational motion of the object can be modeled by assuming that every part of the object moves in a circular motion about the axis of rotation.

Because the translational and rotational motions are treated independently, it is often convenient to use two sets of coordinate axis, one to describe the translational motion and one to characterize the rotational motion. Figure 4-12 shows a football flying through the air. The translational motion of the object is typically evaluated relative to a fixed point in space, and the xyz coordinate axes for translational motion originate from this fixed point. The rotational motion is usually described using coordinate axes x′y′z′ that move with the body as it flies through the air. The rotational coordinate axes are generally taken to originate at the center of mass of the object.

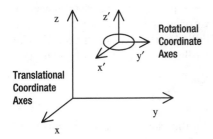

Figure 4-12. *The six coordinate axes for analyzing rigid body motion*

Rolling Motion

To demonstrate the process of analyzing rigid body kinematics, let's look at two typical problems. A common problem in rigid body motion is to characterize the translational and rotational motion of an object that is rolling on a surface. Consider a solid object rolling down a ramp as shown in Figure 4-13. The figure shown is a cylinder, but let's consider the general case of any rolling object.

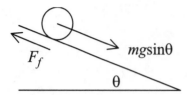

Figure 4-13. *An object rolling down a ramp has both translational and rotational motion.*

As the object rolls down the ramp, it experiences both translational and rotational motion. If the object is symmetrical and has a uniform material distribution, the center of mass will be located in the center of the object, and as the object rolls down the ramp, the center of mass moves in a straight line parallel to the face of the ramp. As the object rolls down the ramp, every part of the object is rotating about an axis of rotation that extends lengthwise through the object and passes through the center of mass. There is a gravitational force that pulls the center of mass down the ramp, and there is a frictional force where the surfaces of the object and the ramp meet that acts in the opposite direction.

If the object rolls without slipping, the center of mass will move a distance of $2\pi r$, where r is the radius of the object for every rotation of the object. If the angular velocity of the object is ω, the time it takes to complete one revolution is equal to $2\pi/\omega$. Therefore, the velocity of the center of mass of the object as it rolls down the ramp is equal to the distance traveled per rotation divided by the time to complete one rotation.

$$v = \frac{2\pi r}{\left(\frac{2\pi}{\omega}\right)} = \omega r$$

(4.33)

The expression shown in Equation (4.33) is the same as Equation (4.30) derived earlier in this chapter. It states that the velocity of the center of mass of an object that is rolling without slipping is equal to the angular velocity of the object multiplied by the radius of the object. The angular and translational accelerations for a nonslipping, rolling object can be related by a similar expression.

$$a = r\alpha$$

(4.34)

Now let's turn our attention to deriving expressions for the translational and angular velocity of a rolling object. The component of gravitational force that acts parallel to the ramp is equal to $mg\sin\theta$. There will also be a force due to friction acting in the opposite direction to the parallel component of the gravitational force. Because the friction force acts on the outer surface of the object, it creates a torque about the axis of rotation with a value of $\tau = F_f r$. This torque causes the object to rotate according to Equation (4.32).

When the object begins to roll down the ramp, the center of mass of the object undergoes a translational acceleration that is proportional to the net force on the object in the direction parallel to the face of the ramp.

$$mg\sin\theta - F_f = ma$$

(4.35)

Equations (4.32) and (4.35) can be combined to express the rotational acceleration, α, as a function of the friction force.

$$\tau = F_f r = (mg\sin\theta - ma)r = I\alpha \tag{4.36}$$

Because the object is rolling without slipping, the translational acceleration can be related to the angular acceleration by the expression $a = r\alpha$. Replacing a with $r\alpha$ in Equation (4.36), an expression for the angular acceleration of the object can be obtained.

$$\alpha = \frac{rmg\sin\theta}{I + mr^2} \tag{4.37}$$

The translational acceleration can be determined from Equation (4.37) once again using the expression $a = r\alpha$.

$$a = r\alpha = \frac{r^2 mg\sin\theta}{I + mr^2} \tag{4.38}$$

If the ramp angle, θ, is constant, then the translational and rotational accelerations of the object as it rolls down the ramp are constant as well. Expressions for the rotational and translational velocity of the object rolling down the ramp can be obtained by integrating Equations (4.37) and (4.38).

$$\omega = \frac{rmg\sin\theta}{I + mr^2}t + \omega_0 \tag{4.39}$$

$$v = \frac{r^2 mg\sin\theta}{I + mr^2}t + v_0 \tag{4.40}$$

The quantities w_0 and v_0 are the initial angular and translational velocities of the object. To apply Equations (4.39) and (4.40) to any object, the mass, radius, and moment of inertia of the object must be determined.

Exercise

4. A cylinder and a sphere of equal diameter and mass are released at the top of a ramp at the same time. Assuming that both objects roll without slipping, which object will reach the bottom of the ramp first?

Bowling Ball Kinematics

If you have ever been bowling, you know that if you throw the ball hard enough it will start off sliding down the lane. As the ball slows down, it begins to roll rather than slide. The second problem we will look at to demonstrate the rigid body kinematic analysis process is to analyze the motion of a bowling ball as it travels down the lane. The information that we want to determine is how long the bowling ball will slide and what will be the translational and rotational velocity of the ball when it begins to roll without sliding.

As was done with the previous problem, the analysis of this problem begins with a force diagram, shown in Figure 4-14. The bowling ball is sliding down the lane with a translational velocity, v_x. The surface is horizontal, so the normal force, F_N, between the ball and the lane is equal to the gravitational force, mg. A frictional force, F_f, resists the sliding motion and is equal to the coefficient of friction, μ, between the ball and the lane multiplied by the normal force.

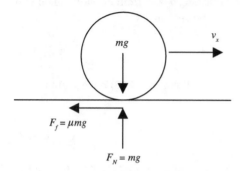

Figure 4-14. *Force diagram of a sliding bowling ball*

As with the object rolling down a ramp, the friction force acting on the outer surface of the bowling ball creates a torque about the center of mass of the ball. According to Equation (4.30), the torque results in an angular acceleration of the ball.

$$\tau = F_f r = \mu mgr = I\alpha \tag{4.41}$$

The torque applied to the ball causes it to rotate. The angular velocity, ω, of the ball continues to increase until the ball is rolling without sliding. When the ball is no longer sliding, there is no sliding friction, and the friction force goes to zero. The point at which the ball rolls without sliding is when the translational velocity, v_x, is equal to the angular velocity multiplied by the radius of the bowling ball.

$$v_x = r\omega \tag{4.42}$$

The key to solving the bowling ball problem is to determine when the condition shown in Equation (4.42) occurs. Let's start by determining an equation for angular velocity as a function of time. As the ball slides down the lane, the angular velocity, ω, increases according to Equation (4.41).

$$\alpha = \frac{d\omega}{dt} = \frac{\mu mgr}{I} \tag{4.43}$$

An equation for ω as a function of time can be found by integrating Equation (4.43).

$$\omega = \frac{\mu mgr}{I}t + \omega_0 \tag{4.44}$$

Since the bowling ball is initially sliding without rolling, the initial angular velocity, ω_0, is equal to zero. The moment of inertia for the ball can be found earlier in Table 4-2.

$$I = \frac{2}{5}mr^2 \tag{4.45}$$

Inserting Equation (4.45) into Equation (4.44) results in an equation for angular velocity of the bowling ball at any time, t.

$$\omega = \frac{5}{2}\frac{\mu gt}{r} \tag{4.46}$$

The next step in the analysis process is to determine an equation for the translational velocity, v_x, of the ball as a function of time. The ball begins with an initial translational velocity equal to v_0. As the ball slides down the lane, the friction force slows the ball down according to Equation (4.15).

$$v_x = v_0 + at = v_0 - \frac{F_f}{m}t = v_0 - \mu gt \tag{4.47}$$

The time at which the bowling ball begins to roll without sliding can be found by multiplying Equation (4.46) by the radius, r, and setting it equal to Equation (4.47).

$$v_0 - \mu gt = \frac{5}{2}\mu gt \tag{4.48}$$

$$t = \frac{2}{7}\frac{v_0}{\mu g} \tag{4.49}$$

The time at which the bowling ball rolls without sliding is proportional to the initial translational velocity of the ball and the coefficient of friction between the ball and the lane. The translational velocity of the bowling ball when it begins to roll without sliding can be calculating by inserting the results from Equation (4.49) into Equation (4.47).

$$v_x = v_0 - \mu g\frac{2}{7}\frac{v_0}{\mu g} = \frac{5}{7}v_0 \tag{4.50}$$

In looking at the results of Equation (4.50), an interesting conclusion appears. The velocity at which the bowling ball begins to roll without sliding is independent of the coefficient of friction between the ball and the lane. Whether the ball is sliding on a bowling lane or a slab of concrete, it will begin to roll without sliding when the translational velocity decreases to 5/7 of its original value. The time it takes the ball to roll without sliding, however, is a function of the coefficient of friction. A ball traveling on a slippery surface, where the coefficient of friction is low, will slide longer than will a ball traveling on a rough surface.

Summary

A lot of ground was covered in this chapter. You are now armed with the basic equations that can be used to compute the translational and rotational motion of objects. These basic kinematic relations will form the basis of almost every physical model we develop in the rest of the book.

Whether it's modeling arrows, cars, boats, or airplanes, every physical model that describes a body in motion will use the basic kinematic relations.

The chapter began with an examination of translational motion. If the forces acting upon an object can be determined, the acceleration, velocity, and position of the object can be computed as a function of time. If the net external force is constant, the equations of motion can sometimes by solved directly into simple algebraic equations. In more complicated cases, an ODE solver can be used to solve the equations of motion. We developed a general-purpose fourth-order Runge-Kutta solver in this chapter that can be applied to many different game programming situations.

The next section of the chapter dealt with rotational motion. The concepts of torque and moment of inertia were introduced as well as equations that related torque to angular acceleration and velocity. The subject of rigid body motion, the combined translational and rotational motion of an object, was discussed. We looked at two real-world examples of rigid body analysis—an object rolling down a ramp and a bowling ball traveling down the lane.

Answers to Exercises

1. Because velocity and acceleration are vectors that can be divided into directional components, the vertical velocity is independent of the horizontal velocity. If the only force considered is gravitational and the bullet and ball start with the same initial vertical location and velocity, they will strike the ground at the same time.

2. Assume that the x-direction is parallel to the ground and the z-direction is vertical. The soccer ball starts with an initial horizontal velocity of $v_x = 12\cos(45) = 8.49$ *m/s*. Assuming no changes to the horizontal velocity, the soccer ball will reach the plane of the goal in $t = 5/8.49 = 0.59$ *s*.

   The soccer ball will have an initial vertical velocity of $v_y = 12\sin(45) = 8.49$ *m/s*. Assuming that the only force on the ball is due to gravity, the height of the ball at 0.59 *s* will be

   $$z(t) = -\frac{1}{2}gt^2 + v_o t + z_o = -\frac{1}{2}(9.8)(0.59)^2 + 8.49*0.59 = 3.3\ m$$

   The ball will sail over the goal, and the crowd will moan "Awwwwww."

3. The acceleration due to gravity needs to be added to the expression for dq[0] in the getRightHandSide method of the SpringODE class. Here is the modified code included the gravity term.

```
public double[] getRightHandSide(double s, double q[],
            double deltaQ[], double ds, double qScale) {

    double dq[] = new double[4];    // right-hand side values
    double newQ[] = new double[4]; // intermediate dependent
                                   // variable values.
```

```
// Compute the intermediate values of the
// dependent variables.
for(int i=0; i<2; ++i) {
  newQ[i] = q[i] + qScale*deltaQ[i];
}

// Compute right-hand side values.
double G = -9.81;
dq[0] = ds*G - ds*(mu*newQ[0] + k*newQ[1])/mass;
dq[1] = ds*(newQ[0]);

return dq;
}
```

Recompile the Spring Simulator with the gravity term included. See how the behavior of the spring changes.

4. The angular acceleration of an object rolling down a ramp without slipping is given by the following equation:

$$\alpha = \frac{rmg \sin\theta}{I + mr^2}$$

The moment of inertia for a solid cylinder is $1/2mr^2$. The moment of inertia for a sphere is $2/5\ mr^2$. The angular accelerations experienced by the cylinder and sphere are therefore

$$\alpha_{cylinder} = \frac{rmg \sin\theta}{\frac{1}{2}mr^2 + mr^2} = \frac{2}{3}\frac{g}{r}\sin\theta$$

$$\alpha_{sphere} = \frac{rmg \sin\theta}{\frac{2}{5}mr^2 + mr^2} = \frac{5}{7}\frac{g}{r}\sin\theta$$

Since the sphere has the lower moment of inertia, it will have the higher angular acceleration and will reach the bottom of the ramp first.

CHAPTER 5

■ ■ ■

Projectiles

The previous two chapters explored the subjects of Newtonian mechanics and kinematics, and presented the basic equations that govern linear and rotational motion. It's time now to apply those basic relations to a more specific problem, namely modeling the flight of a projectile. You will probably work with projectiles quite a lot in your game programming. There are, of course, obvious things like bullets and cannonballs, but other objects such as golf balls or tennis balls are essentially projectiles as well. The good news is that this book has already covered almost everything you need to know to model a projectile in flight. For the most part, projectile physics are straightforward application of Newtonian mechanics and kinematics.

This chapter will take a building-block approach to modeling projectile motion. We'll start with a quick-and-dirty model in which the only external force on an object is due to gravity. This is the least accurate model, but also the easiest one to program and the fastest one to compute. As the chapter progresses, we'll add more and more physics to the model including the effects of aerodynamic drag, wind, and spin effects. The differences between laminar and turbulent flow will be explored. You'll learn about things called lift and drag coefficients and how they are used to characterize the forces experienced by a projectile in flight. In the latter part of the chapter, we will discuss specific modeling issues for specific types of projectiles.

The topics that will be covered in this chapter include the following:

- The basic concepts that apply to all projectile trajectory models

- The gravity-only model

- Aerodynamic drag

- Laminar and turbulent flow

- Wind effects

- Spin effects

- Details on specific types of projectiles including bullets, cannonballs, and arrows

You may have noticed from the previous list that some important projectile topics are missing. A football can certainly be considered a projectile as can a missile fired from an airplane. Modeling the balls used in sporting events will be covered in Chapter 7. Rockets and missiles are discussed in Chapter 11.

Basic Concepts

The fundamental relations that govern projectile flight can be found in Newton's laws of motion and basic kinematics. To determine the linear motion of a projectile requires an evaluation of the forces acting on the projectile. Generally speaking, projectiles will rotate as they fly through the air, so the projectile motion will include both translational and rotational components. Here are some general concepts to keep in mind that apply to all types of projectiles:

- The translational acceleration of a projectile is determined from computing the net external force on the object and applying Newton's second law, $F = ma$.

- The translational velocity, v, and location, s, of a projectile as a function of time, t, can be calculated from the differential equations for translational motion.

$$\frac{d\vec{v}}{dt} = \vec{a} \tag{5.1}$$

$$\frac{d\vec{s}}{dt} = \vec{v} \tag{5.2}$$

- The rotational acceleration of the projectile, α, is determined by computing the net torque on the projectile, τ, the moment of inertia, I, and applying the equation $\tau = I\alpha$.

- The equations of motion are separated into directional components. We will use the Cartesian reference frame, so the force, acceleration, velocity, and position vectors will be separated into x-, y-, and z-components.

In this chapter, we will use the convention that the z-axis is in the vertical direction with the positive z-direction pointing upward from the surface of the ground. The x- and y-axes are parallel to the ground. The coordinate system and frame of reference that will be used in this chapter is shown in Figure 5-1.

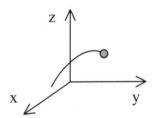

Figure 5-1. *The projectile trajectory frame of reference*

The Gravity-Only Model

The simplest projectile trajectory model is the **gravity-only** model in which the only force acting on the projectile is due to gravity. This model is appropriate for projectiles that don't travel very fast, don't spin rapidly, and aren't exposed to strong winds. For example, modeling the flight of a basketball in an indoor gym would be an appropriate time to use the gravity-only model. A force diagram for the gravity-only model is shown in Figure 5-2. The force of gravity, F_g, always acts in the vertical direction regardless of the direction of the velocity vector.

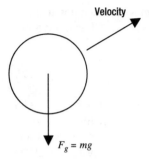

Figure 5-2. *Force diagram for the gravity-only model*

The advantage of the gravity-only model is its simplicity. As we saw in Chapter 4, if the force applied to an object is constant, then the velocity and location of the object as a function of time are described by simple algebraic equations. There is no need to use an ODE solver with the gravity-only model. The disadvantage of the gravity-only model is that it's only accurate for a limited number of situations because it leaves out the effects of aerodynamic drag, wind, and spin.

Force and Acceleration Equations

As seen in Figure 5-2, the only force in the gravity-only model is due to gravity. The force of gravity acts in the vertical, or z-, direction. There are no forces acting on the projectile in the x- or y-directions. The force equations for the gravity-only model are shown in Equation (5.3).

$$F_x = 0 \tag{5.3a}$$

$$F_y = 0 \tag{5.3b}$$

$$F_z = -mg \tag{5.3c}$$

The negative sign on the F_z force component in Equation (5.3c) indicates that gravity acts downwards towards the ground. The gravity-only model assumes there is no net torque on the projectile and that whatever rotation the projectile has does not affect its trajectory. Therefore, the equations of rotational motion are not included in the gravity-only model.

The acceleration equations are obtained from the force equations and Newton's second law. If the mass of the projectile is constant, which it will be in most situations, the acceleration equations are found by simply dividing the force equations by the mass, m, of the projectile. The acceleration equations for the gravity-only model are shown in Equation (5.4).

$$a_x = 0 \tag{5.4a}$$

$$a_y = 0 \tag{5.4b}$$

$$a_z = -g \tag{5.4c}$$

As shown in Equation (5.1) the derivative of velocity with respect to time is equal to acceleration. As we saw in Chapter 4, if an expression for the acceleration is known, then the velocity of the projectile can be found by integrating Equation (5.1).

$$v - v_0 = \int a dt \tag{5.5}$$

The quantity v_0 is the initial velocity of the projectile. If the acceleration is zero, as it is for the x- and y-directions, then the integral shown on the right-hand side of Equation (5.5) is equal to zero. If the acceleration is constant, the integral is equal to the constant acceleration multiplied by time. From these two facts, the equations for the velocity of the projectile under the gravity-only model can be determined and are shown in Equation (5.6).

$$v_x = v_{x0} \tag{5.6a}$$

$$v_y = v_{y0} \tag{5.6b}$$

$$v_z = v_{z0} - gt \tag{5.6c}$$

The quantities v_{x0}, v_{y0}, and v_{z0} in Equations (5.6a) through (5.6c) are the initial velocities in the x-, y-, and z-directions at time $t = 0$. The x- and y-velocity components are constant at all time under the gravity-only model. This situation reflects Newton's first law of motion, which states that the velocity of an object will remain constant unless acted upon by an external force, and there are no x- or y-direction forces in the gravity-only model. The z-component of velocity will change over time, its value becoming increasing negative as gravity pulls the projectile towards the ground.

Location Equations

The location of the projectile at any time can be computed if the velocity of the projectile is known because the derivative of location with respect to time is equal to the velocity. The location as a function of time can be computed by integrating Equation (5.2).

$$s - s_0 = \int v dt \tag{5.7}$$

The expressions that determine the x-, y-, and z-locations of a projectile according to the gravity-only model are shown in Equation (5.8). The x_0, y_0, and z_0 parameters are the initial x-, y-, and z-locations of the projectile at time $t = 0$.

$$x = x_0 + v_{x0}t \tag{5.8a}$$

$$y = y_0 + y_{x0}t \tag{5.8b}$$

$$z = z_0 + v_{z0}t - \frac{1}{2}gt^2 \tag{5.8c}$$

Because the x- and y-velocities are constant, the x- and y-locations of the projectile change at a constant rate. The equation for the z-location shown in Equation (5.8c) is what is known as **a quadratic equation**. The rate of change of z-location is constantly increasing as the projectile accelerates towards the ground.

Let's see what a typical trajectory under the gravity-only model looks like. We'll assume that the y-components of motion are zero, so the trajectory will be restricted to the x-z plane. Here are the initial conditions that will be used:

$$x_0 = 0 \ m \qquad z_0 = 0 \ m \qquad v_{x0} = 15 \ m/s \qquad v_{z0} = 20 \ m/s$$

The x- and z-locations as a function of time are computed using Equations (5.8a) and (5.8c). The resulting trajectory profile is shown in Figure 5-3.

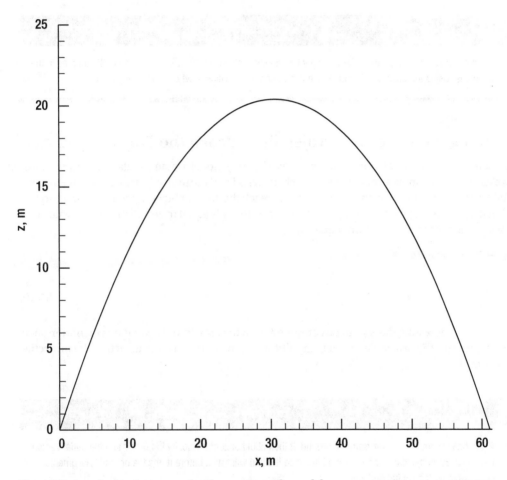

Figure 5-3. *A typical trajectory under the gravity-only model*

You might recognize the shape of the curve shown in Figure 5-3 as a parabola. One characteristic of the gravity-only model is that it will always generate a parabolic-shaped trajectory. The gravity-only trajectory is symmetrical in many ways. If the projectile is fired from a flat surface, the amount of time the projectile takes going up is the same as the amount of time it will take coming back down. The horizontal distance the projectile travels on the way up is the same as the horizontal distance it travels on the way down.

If you look at the expressions in Equations (5.6) and (5.8), you will see that the location and velocity in each coordinate direction is independent of the other directions. For example, there are no x- or y-components in the z-direction equations of motion. Another important point to note about the equations of motion under the gravity-only model is that there is nothing in the equations about the mass or shape of the projectile. Under the gravity-only model, a 5 *kg* cannonball and a 400 *kg* cow would have the same trajectory if they were launched from the same spot with the same initial velocity.

Exercise

1. A projectile starts its flight from the ground with an initial velocity of 20 *m/s* at an angle of 30 degrees in the x-z plane. Using the gravity-only model, what is the projectile velocity when it hits the ground?

Finding the Time for a Projectile to Reach the Trajectory Apex

Because the equations of motion under the gravity-only model are simple algebraic expressions, we can easily manipulate them to discover characteristics of the projectile trajectory. For example, let's calculate the time it takes for a projectile to reach the apex, or highest point, of its trajectory. When the projectile reaches its apex, its vertical velocity is equal to zero. The time at which this event occurs can be found from Equation (5.6c).

$$v_z = 0 = v_{z0} - gt \tag{5.9}$$

$$t = \frac{v_{z0}}{g} \tag{5.10}$$

Other interesting things can be computed from the gravity-only equations of motion such as the time for the projectile to reach any altitude or the horizontal distance that the projectile will travel.

Exercise

2. A golf ball is shot into the air from the ground. If the initial horizontal velocity is 20 *m/s* and the initial vertical velocity is 30 *m/s*, what is the horizontal distance the ball will travel before it hits the ground? Assume that the golf course surface is flat and level.

The SimpleProjectile Class

Let's implement a projectile that travels under the gravity-only model in a class called `SimpleProjectile`. The class will maintain the state of the projectile—its location and velocity as a function of time. It will also implement code that will update the location and velocity of the projectile.

When designing the SimpleProjectile class, we need to think a little bit about the future. One of the central goals of object-oriented programming in a language such as Java is to reuse as much code as possible. The equations of motion for the gravity-only model can be solved directly using simple algebraic equations. However, later in this chapter when we add effects like aerodynamic drag and spin to the projectile model, the equations of motion will have to be solved with an ODE solver. At the same time, when we build the more complicated models, we will want to reuse as much code as possible from the SimpleProjectile class.

The answer to satisfying these objectives is to make the SimpleProjectile class a subclass of ODE. The ODE class, if you remember from Chapter 4, defines the data structure and methods needed to use the rungeKutta4 ODE solver method declared in the ODESolver class. Any subclass of ODE will inherit this data structure and can therefore make use of the ODE solver. When more sophisticated effects are added to the projectile model, those classes will be written as subclasses of SimpleProjectile. By setting up this type of class hierarchy, the sophisticated projectile classes will have access to all of the code from the SimpleProjectile class and the data structure from the ODE class and will be able to use the ODE solver without any further modifications. The SimpleProjectile class may seem more complicated than it needs to be, but creating it in this manner will make things much easier when we code up the more complicated projectile classes a little later in the chapter. As a reminder, the ODE class code listing is shown in its entirety in Chapter 4.

The SimpleProjectile class only declares one field representing the gravitational acceleration. The class will make use of the fields declared in the ODE class to store the location and velocity of the projectile. The SimpleProjectile class constructor calls the ODE constructor and then loads the initial values of time, location, and velocity into the s field and q[] array of the ODE class using the setS and setQ methods.

```java
public class SimpleProjectile extends ODE
{
  // Gravitational acceleration.
  public final static double G = -9.81;

  public SimpleProjectile(double x0, double y0, double z0,
                          double vx0, double vy0, double vz0,
                          double time) {
    // Call the ODE class constructor.
    super(6);

    // Load the initial position, velocity, and time
    // values into the s field and q array from the
    // ODE class.
    setS(time);
    setQ(vx0,0);
    setQ(x0, 1);
    setQ(vy0,2);
    setQ(y0, 3);
    setQ(vz0,4);
    setQ(z0, 5);
  }
```

The `SimpleProjectile` class declares a series of methods to return the current location, velocity, and time values for the projectile. Since these quantities are stored in the s field and q[ ] array of the `ODE` class, the get methods in the `SimpleProjectile` class simply call the getS or getQ methods from the `ODE` class.

```
// These methods return the location, velocity,
// and time values.
public double getVx() {
  return getQ(0);
}

public double getVy() {
  return getQ(2);
}

public double getVz() {
  return getQ(4);
}

public double getX() {
  return getQ(1);
}

public double getY() {
  return getQ(3);
}

public double getZ() {
  return getQ(5);
}

public double getTime() {
  return getS();
}
```

The `updateLocationAndVelocity` method is called to update the location and velocity of the projectile according to the equations of motion in the gravity-only model. The first thing the method does is to acquire the current location and velocity of the projectile. It then updates the location and velocity at the new time increment according to the expressions in Equations (5.6) and (5.8). The time value is updated, and then the new time, location, and velocity values are loaded into the s and q[ ] arrays using the setS and setQ methods of the `ODE` class.

```
// This method updates the velocity and position
// of the projectile according to the gravity-only model.
public void updateLocationAndVelocity(double dt) {
  // Get current location, velocity, and time values
  // from the values stored in the ODE class.
```

```
    double time = getS();
    double vx0 = getQ(0);
    double x0 = getQ(1);
    double vy0 = getQ(2);
    double y0 = getQ(3);
    double vz0 = getQ(4);
    double z0 = getQ(5);

    // Update the xyz locations and the z-component
    // of velocity. The x- and y-velocities don't change.
    double x = x0 + vx0*dt;
    double y = y0 + vy0*dt;
    double vz = vz0 + G*dt;
    double z = z0 + vz0*dt + 0.5*G*dt*dt;

    // Update time;
    time = time + dt;

    // Load new values into ODE arrays and fields.
    setS(time);
    setQ(x, 1);
    setQ(y, 3);
    setQ(vz,4);
    setQ(z, 5);
  }
```

Because the SimpleProjectile class is a subclass of ODE, it has to provide an implementation of the getRightHandSide method. If you remember from the previous chapter, this method is used to compute the right-hand side of the ODEs that will be solved. The SimpleProjectile class doesn't solve any ODEs, so the method is written to return a dummy array.

```
// Because SimpleProjectile extends the ODE class,
  // it must implement the getRightHandSide method.
  // In this case, the method returns a dummy array.
  public double[] getRightHandSide(double s, double Q[],
             double deltaQ[], double ds, double qScale) {
    return new double[1];
  }
}
```

In the next section, the SimpleProjectile class will be used to create a golf game.

The Golf Game

Let's use the SimpleProjectile class to create a golf game. The objective of the game is to hit a golf ball onto the green. A sample screen shot for the Golf Game is shown in Figure 5-4. Like the other games in this book, the Golf Game is based on a simple Java GUI. The graphics in the game are a bit primitive, but the physics in the game is real. The GUI consists of text field components that are used to input the initial velocity components of the golf ball. These values can be changed to adjust the trajectory of the ball. Another text field adjusts the distance from the tee to the flag, and a combo box lets the user select either a side or top-down view.

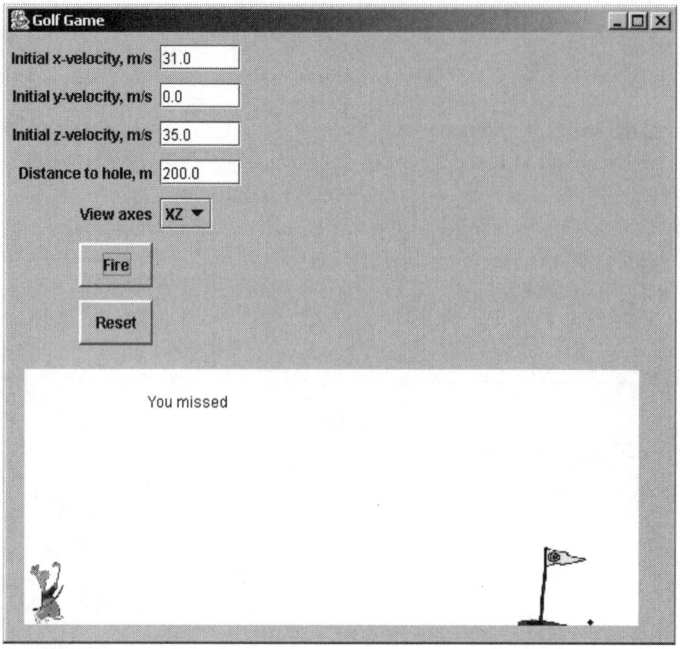

Figure 5-4. *A sample Golf Game screen shot*

A Fire button fires the golf ball, and a Reset button is used to stop the simulation and return the golf ball to the tee. Below the buttons and text fields is a white drawing area that displays the ball as it flies through the air. If you get the ball to within 10 *m* of the flag, it is considered to be "on the green" and you win.

The Golf Game makes use of the SimpleProjectile class that was developed in the previous section to model the flight of the golf ball. The GUI elements of the game are contained in a class called GolfGame. As with the previous games in this book, the code that sets up the GUI components will not be shown in detail, but instead the focus will be on the projectile modeling elements of the code.

Along with fields representing the GUI components of the game, the GolfGame class declares a SimpleProjectile object that will represent the golf ball. Additional fields store the value of the distance from the tee to the hole and encapsulate some images that are used in the game. A Timer object is created that will be used to control how quickly the simulation runs.

```
import javax.swing.*;
import java.awt.*;
import javax.swing.border.BevelBorder;
import java.awt.event.*;
import javax.swing.Timer;
```

```
public class GolfGame extends JFrame implements ActionListener
{
  private JTextField vxTextField;
  private JTextField vyTextField;
  private JTextField vzTextField;
  private JTextField distanceTextField;

  private JLabel vxLabel;
  private JLabel vyLabel;
  private JLabel vzLabel;
  private JLabel distanceLabel;

  private JComboBox axesComboBox;

  private JButton fireButton;
  private JButton resetButton;
  private JPanel drawingPanel;
  private GridBagConstraints gbc;

  // The golf ball is a SimpleProjectile.
  private SimpleProjectile golfball;

  // The player can control the distance to the hole.
  private double distanceToHole;

  // These fields are for the images used in the game.
  private ImageIcon golferIcon;
  private ImageIcon flagIcon;
  private int golferWidth;
  private int golferHeight;
  private int flagWidth;
  private int flagHeight;

  // These elements are used to control the execution
  // speed of the game. Without them, the game would
  // run too quickly.
  private GameUpdater gameUpdater;
  private Timer gameTimer;
```

Like all constructors, the GolfGame constructor is used to initialize the fields declared in the class. A SimpleProjectile object is created to represent the golf ball that is fired from the tee. The velocities of the golf ball are initially set to zero, but their values will be updated based on the text in the text fields when the Fire button is pressed. The initial x-, y-, and z-coordinates of the golf ball are all set to zero. The distanceToHole field is initially set to be 200 m.

```
public GolfGame() {

    // Create a SimpleProjectile object.
    golfball =
        new SimpleProjectile(0.0, 0.0, 0.0, 0.0, 0.0, 0.0, 0.0);

    // Initialize the distanceToHole field.
    distanceToHole = 200.0;

    // Create a Timer object that will be used
    // to slow the action down and an ActionListener
    // that the Timer will call. The timeDelay variable
    // is the time delay in milliseconds.
    gameUpdater = new GameUpdater();
    int timeDelay = 50;
    gameTimer = new Timer(timeDelay, gameUpdater);

    // Set up some images and determine their dimensions.
    golferIcon = new ImageIcon("Golfer.jpg");
    golferWidth = golferIcon.getIconWidth();
    golferHeight = golferIcon.getIconHeight();

    flagIcon = new ImageIcon("Hole_Cartoon.jpg");
    flagWidth = flagIcon.getIconWidth();
    flagHeight = flagIcon.getIconHeight();

    // GUI component initialization not shown.
```

When the Fire button is pressed for the first time, the golf ball is struck and starts to fly through the air. Values for the initial golf ball velocity components are obtained from the text that is inside the text fields. These initial values are used to create a SimpleProjectile object that will represent the golf ball. The distanceToHole field value is set, and the display is updated to show the golf flag in its current location. A Timer object is used to control the game flow. When the start method is called on the Timer object, the simulation begins.

```
// The actionPerformed() method is called when
  // the Fire button is pressed.
  public void actionPerformed(ActionEvent event) {

    // Get the initial velocities and distance-to-hole
    // from the text fields.
    double vx0 = Double.parseDouble(vxTextField.getText());
    double vy0 = Double.parseDouble(vyTextField.getText());
    double vz0 = Double.parseDouble(vzTextField.getText());
    distanceToHole = Double.parseDouble(distanceTextField.getText());
```

```
// Create a SimpleProjectile object.
golfball = new SimpleProjectile(0.0, 0.0, 0.0,
    vx0, vy0, vz0, 0.0);

// Update the display.
updateDisplay();

// Start the box sliding using a Timer object
// to slow down the action.
gameTimer.start();
}
```

The GolfGame class declares an inner class named GameUpdater that declares an actionPerformed method. The Timer object calls this method to update the velocities and location of the golf ball by calling the updateLocationAndVelocity method of the SimpleProjectile class. Recall from the previous section of this chapter that the updateLocationAndVelocity method solves the gravity-only equations of motion.

```
// This ActionListener is called by the Timer.
  class GameUpdater implements ActionListener {
    public void actionPerformed(ActionEvent event) {

      // Update the time and compute the new position
      // of the golfball.
      double timeIncrement = 0.07;
      golfball.updateLocationAndVelocity(timeIncrement);

      // Update the display.
      updateDisplay();
```

If the z-location of the golf ball is zero, it means that the ball has hit the ground. The simulation is stopped. If the ball lands within 10 *m* of the hole, it is considered to be on the green, and the triumphant "You're on the green" message is displayed on the screen. Otherwise, the disappointing "You missed" message is displayed.

```
// Access the Graphics object of the drawing panel.
    Graphics g = drawingPanel.getGraphics();

    // When the golfball hits the ground, stop the simulation
    // and see where ball has landed.
    if ( golfball.getZ() <= 0.0 ) {

      // Stop the simulation.
      gameTimer.stop();
```

```
    // Determine if ball is on the green.
    if ( golfball.getX() > distanceToHole - 10.0 &&
         golfball.getX() < distanceToHole + 10.0 &&
         golfball.getY() < 10.0) {
      g.drawString("You're on the green", 100, 30);

    }
    else {
      drawingPanel.getGraphics().drawString("You missed", 100, 30);
    }
   }
  }
 }
}
```

Because the SimpleProjectile class is a subclass of ODE, the Java compiler will have to have access to the ODE class source file or class file when the GolfGame class is compiled. Play around with the Golf Game. You will find that it takes some fairly small adjustments to get the ball to land within 10 *m* of the green. If the view axes are changed to "XY", the result is a bird's-eye view of the hole as shown in Figure 5-5. The display now tracks the horizontal components of the golf ball trajectory. The green is shown as a circle with a radius of 10 *m*. Try giving the golf ball an initial y-velocity component and see what happens.

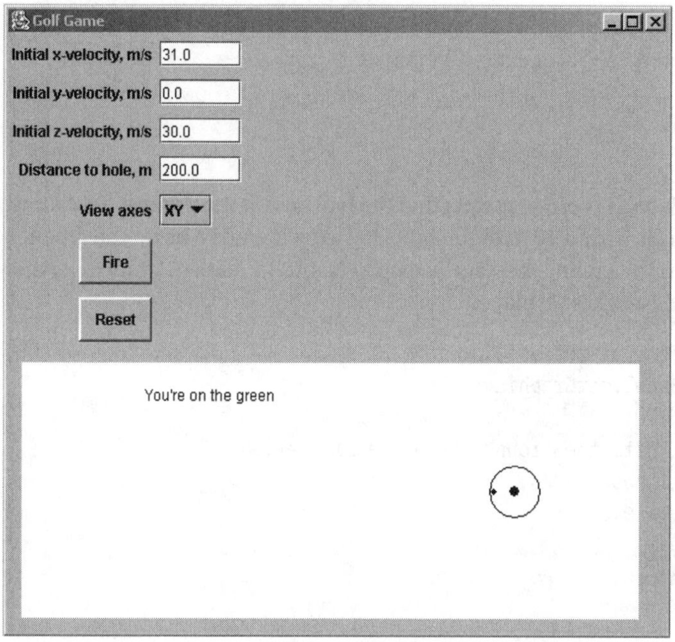

Figure 5-5. *A bird's-eye view of the Golf Game*

Summary: Gravity-Only Projectile Trajectory Model

A very simple projectile model that we call the gravity-only model can be formulated if it is assumed that the only net force on the projectile is due to gravity. Here are some of the key outcomes of the gravity-only model:

- The only force on the projectile is due to gravity, which acts in the vertical, or z-, direction. The horizontal velocity components in the x- and y-directions will remain constant at whatever the initial velocities in those directions are.

- The motion in the three coordinate directions is independent. What happens in the y-direction, for instance, has no effect on what happens in the x- or z-directions.

- The projectile trajectory is independent of mass and projectile geometry.

- The velocity in the x- and y-directions is constant over the entire trajectory and is equal to the initial velocities in the x- and y-direction.

- The shape of the projectile trajectory will be a parabola.

The advantage of the gravity only model is that it is easy to formulate and minimizes the computer time required to solve the equations of motion. Closed-form expressions can be obtained for the velocity and location of the projectile as a function of time. The disadvantage, as you probably could guess, is that it ignores some potentially important effects, such as aerodynamic drag and wind effects. The gravity-only model cannot be applied to all projectile trajectory problems, but it gives a reasonably accurate representation of projectile motion if the projectile is not traveling too quickly, spinning too rapidly, or exposed to a strong wind.

A summary of the equations of motion for the gravity-only projectile trajectory model is shown in Table 5-1.

Table 5-1. *Summary of Equations of Motion for the Gravity-Only Projectile Model*

	x-Direction	y-Direction	z-Direction
Force	0	0	$-mg$
Acceleration	0	0	$-g$
Velocity	v_{x0}	v_{y0}	$v_{z0} - gt$
Location	$v_{x0}t + x_0$	$y_0 + v_{y0}t$	$z_0 + v_{z0}t - \frac{1}{2}gt^2$

Aerodynamic Drag

Aerodynamic drag is the resistance that air or any other type of gas exerts on a body traveling through it. If you stick your hand out of the window of a moving car or try to ride your bicycle into the wind, you can feel the drag force on your body. Drag is an important physical effect, particularly for high-speed projectiles such as bullets, golf balls, or even parachutists. The next level of complexity we will add to our projectile model will be to account for aerodynamic drag forces and model how they affect the trajectory of a projectile.

Basic Concepts

Drag is a force that resists motion through a fluid medium. Like frictional force, drag force acts in the opposite direction to the velocity vector of an object. If a projectile is moving to the right, the drag force on the body will be directed towards the left. For purposes of analyzing projectile motion, there are two components to the total drag force on a projectile. The first drag component is due to pressure. The surface pressure on the front of an object traveling through the fluid will be greater than the pressure on the back of the object. This pressure difference creates a net force, or **pressure drag**, on the object.

The second component of drag on a projectile is due to the friction. In Chapter 3, you learned how friction is a force that resists the motion of two objects sliding against each other. With a projectile in flight, a frictional force develops between the surface of the projectile and the air or other fluid that is sliding past it. This frictional force is commonly referred to as **friction drag** or **skin drag**.

The total drag on a projectile is the sum of the pressure and friction drag components.

$$F_D = F_{D,pressure} + F_{D,friction} \tag{5.11}$$

It turns out there are other components of drag that become important in modeling the flight of an airplane, but we'll defer discussion of that topic until Chapter 10.

The magnitude of the drag force on an object is a function of the geometry of the object, the density of the fluid, ρ, in which it is traveling, and the square of the velocity, v. Drag force is usually expressed as a function of these terms and a quantity known as a **drag coefficient**, C_D.

$$F_D = \frac{1}{2}\rho v^2 A C_D \tag{5.12}$$

In Equation (5.12) the quantity A is a characteristic body area. Its definition will differ depending on the body geometry. For most objects, the characteristic area is taken to be the frontal area. For a sphere, the frontal area would be the cross-sectional area, πr^2. Density is a measure of how heavy the fluid is and is defined as the mass of a fluid per unit volume. Water, for example, will have a greater density than air. In SI units, density will have units of kg/m^3, velocity will have units of m/s, and area will have units of m^2. In the English system of units, density will have units of $slug/ft^3$, velocity will be in ft/s, and area will have units of ft^2.

Drag Coefficient

The drag coefficient, C_D, is a nondimensional number that is used to evaluate drag force. Being nondimensional means that drag coefficient has no units, it's just a number. Generally speaking, the drag coefficient for an object will not be a constant, but will be a function of the density of the fluid, the velocity at which the object is traveling, and the size of the object. Based on a lot of experimental and theoretical research, it was found that the drag coefficient of an object could be expressed in terms of a quantity known as **Reynolds number**, *Re*.

$$C_D = C_D \left(\text{Re} \right) \tag{5.13}$$

Reynolds number is another nondimensional quantity that is used to characterize the nature of a fluid flow. It is defined as the ratio of the fluid density, ρ, object velocity, v, and characteristic length of the object, L, divided by the viscosity of the fluid, μ.

$$\text{Re} = \frac{\rho v L}{\mu} \tag{5.14}$$

As was the case with the characteristic area in Equation (5.12), the definition of characteristic length can vary depending on the situation, but it is commonly taken to be the body length parallel to the direction of the fluid flow. For a sphere, the characteristic length would be the diameter of the sphere. The viscosity of a fluid is a measure of how "thick" a fluid is. Maple syrup, for example, would have a higher viscosity than would air. The value of Reynolds number can vary widely from numbers less than one to numbers in the tens of millions. As an example, a 0.1 m cannonball traveling at 100 km/hr at sea level would have a Reynolds number of about 194,000.

As an example of how drag coefficient can vary with Reynolds number, Figure 5-6 shows a plot of the drag coefficient of a sphere. At low Reynolds numbers (low densities, low velocities, and/or small objects), the drag coefficient decreases with increasing Reynolds number. Over a range of Re = 1000 to Re = 250,000, the drag coefficient is more or less constant. A sharp drop in drag coefficient at around Re = 250,000 occurs due to the transition from laminar to turbulent flow, a topic we will discuss in the next section.

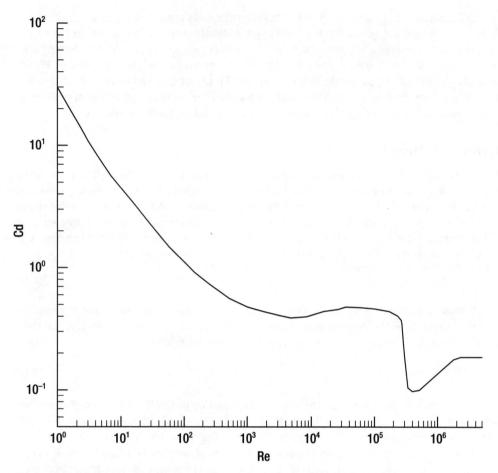

Figure 5-6. *The drag coefficient of a sphere as a function of Reynolds number*

In addition to Reynolds number, the drag coefficient is strongly influenced by the geometry and orientation of an object. Table 5-2 shows the drag coefficient of some basic two-dimensional shapes in air at a Reynolds number of 1.0e+5. The drag coefficient values are based on the frontal area of the object. The arrows indicate the direction of the air flow.

Table 5-2. *Drag Coefficients of Simple Two-Dimensional Shapes (Re = 1.0e+5)*

Shape	Picture	C_D
Flat plate		2.0
Square cylinder		2.1
Rotated square cylinder		1.6
Solid half-cylinder		1.7
Solid half-cylinder		1.2
Circular cylinder		1.2
2:1 Elliptical cylinder		0.6
Hollow half-cylinder		2.3
Hollow half-cylinder		1.2

Drag coefficient is also influenced by whether a shape is two- or three-dimensional. Table 5-3 shows drag coefficients for a Reynolds number of 1.0e+5 for some typical three-dimensional shapes. The drag coefficient for a three-dimensional shape is less than that for the corresponding two-dimensional shape. For example, the drag coefficient for a three-dimensional hollow half-sphere with the concave side facing the air flow is 1.4, whereas the drag coefficient for the corresponding two-dimensional hollow half-cylinder is 2.3.

Table 5-3. *Drag Coefficients of Three-Dimensional Shapes (Re = 1.0e+5)*

Shape	Picture	C_D
Square flat plate		1.17
Cube		1.05–1.07
Rotated cube		0.8–0.81
Solid hemisphere		0.42
60-degree cone		0.5
Sphere		0.4–0.47
2:1 Ellipsoid		0.27
Hollow hemisphere		1.4
Hollow hemisphere		0.38–0.4

We have seen that the value of the drag coefficient is a function of Reynolds number. It would simplify the implementation of drag effects into the projectile trajectory model, however, if the drag coefficient could be assumed to be a constant. For a certain range of Reynolds number, the drag coefficient for a sphere is more or less constant. Depending on how much accuracy you want to build into your game programming projectile simulation, it might be reasonable to assume that the drag coefficient for a projectile is constant. You could also take the more rigorous approach and build a variable drag coefficient into your projectile model. As a game programmer, you will have to decide whether it is necessary to add this extra complexity to your simulation.

Altitude Effects on Density

It would simplify the drag model even further if the drag force could be considered to be a function of velocity only—that is to say, if density could be considered to be constant as well as the drag coefficient. The density of air is a function of altitude, but unless the altitude changes by several miles over the course of the trajectory, it is reasonable to assume that density is constant during the flight of the projectile. That being said, there will be altitude effects on the trajectory of a projectile. Drag effects will be less at Denver, Colorado, than they will be at sea level because the atmospheric density will be lower in Denver. While assuming that density is constant over the course of a projectile trajectory is probably okay, the density value should be adjusted according to the local altitude. Table 5-4 shows the value of air density at several altitudes in both SI and English units.

Table 5-4. *Values of Air Density As a Function of Altitude*

Altitude (*m*)	Altitude (*ft*)	Density (*kg/m³*)	Density (*slug/ft³*)
0.0	0.0	1.225	0.00238
305	1000	1.189	0.00231
610	2000	1.154	0.00224
914	3000	1.121	0.00218
1219	4000	1.088	0.00211
1524	5000	1.055	0.00205
2134	7000	0.992	0.00192
3048	10,000	0.905	0.00176

A situation where the assumption of density would not be valid would be in modeling the trajectory of a rocket or missile because the air density at the upper extent of the earth's atmosphere is orders of magnitude less than at sea level. We'll look into modeling rocket and missile trajectories in Chapter 11.

Laminar and Turbulent Flow

So far in this chapter, we have discussed the physics of a projectile flying through a fluid such as air. In the previous section, we introduced the concept of drag as the resistance a fluid exerts on an object traveling through it. It turns out there are two general ways that air or any other fluid can travel over an object. The fluid can travel smoothly and steadily over the object. This is known as **laminar** flow. Typically, low Reynolds number flows will be laminar. As the Reynolds

number is increased, there is a point where the smooth laminar flow over the object transitions
to an agitated, chaotic condition known as **turbulent** flow.

Modeling the physics of turbulent flow and the transition from laminar to turbulent flow
is a very complex subject. Even today, there is no generally applicable model for turbulent or
transitional flow. Fortunately, as a game programmer, all you need to know about turbulence
with regards to projectile trajectory modeling is that turbulence reduces the drag coefficient of
a projectile.

This fact may seem a little counterintuitive, because you might think that smooth, laminar
flow would generate less drag than chaotic, turbulent flow. If you recall at the beginning of the
section on drag, we discussed pressure drag, which is caused by a pressure difference between
the forward and rearward facing surfaces of an object. Under turbulent flow conditions, the
pressure difference is less than under laminar flow conditions, and the pressure drag component is
lower. Table 5-5 compares the laminar and turbulent drag coefficients for some common shapes.

Table 5-5. *Laminar and Turbulent Drag Coefficients*

Shape	Laminar C_D	Turbulent C_D
Sphere	0.4–0.47	0.2
2:1 Ellipsoid	0.27	0.13
Circular cylinder	1.2	0.3
2:1 Elliptical cylinder	0.6	0.2

Whether the flow around an object is laminar or turbulent depends on the Reynolds number,
surface roughness, and other geometrical considerations. Generally speaking, low Reynolds
number flows are laminar, and high Reynolds number flows are turbulent. For a sphere, the
transition from laminar to turbulent flow occurs at a Reynolds number of about 250,000. For
game programming purposes, it might be enough to simply carry around two sets of drag
coefficients. If the Reynolds number is below a laminar-to-turbulent transition value, the
laminar coefficient would be used. If the Reynolds number is above the threshold, the turbulent
drag coefficient is applied.

Adding Drag Effects to the Equations of Motion

We are now ready to add drag effects to the projectile trajectory model. The force balance
diagram when drag is added to the gravity-only model is shown in Figure 5-7. There are now
two forces acting on the projectile—gravity that acts in the vertical direction and drag that acts
in a direction opposite to the velocity vector.

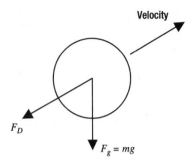

Figure 5-7. *The force diagram with gravity and drag effects*

The value of drag force for a given object can be computed from Equation (5.12). What is required to evaluate that expression is the density of the fluid, a characteristic area, the velocity magnitude of the object, and the drag coefficient. The velocity magnitude, or speed, of an object can be found by taking the square root of the sum of the square of the velocity components.

$$v = \sqrt{v_x^2 + v_y^2 + v_z^2} \tag{5.15}$$

To include aerodynamic drag in the projectile equations of motion, the overall drag force, F_D, determined from Equation (5.12), is split into directional components. Because drag acts in the opposite direction of velocity, the x-, y-, and z-components of drag force will be in the same proportion relative to each other as will the x-, y-, and z-components of velocity, but the signs will be reversed. As shown in Equation (5.16), the drag force in any coordinate direction will be equal to the overall drag force multiplied by the ratio of the directional velocity component divided by the velocity magnitude.

$$F_{Dx} = -F_D \frac{v_x}{v} \qquad F_{Dy} = -F_D \frac{v_y}{v} \qquad F_{Dz} = -F_D \frac{v_z}{v} \tag{5.16}$$

The negative signs in Equation (5.16) indicate that drag force acts in the opposite direction to velocity. The drag force component equations as shown in Equation (5.16) can be added to the projectile equations of motion to include the effects of aerodynamic drag.

Force and Acceleration Equations

One of the big changes when aerodynamic drag forces are added to the equations of motion is that the horizontal force components in the x- and y-directions are no longer zero. Instead aerodynamic drag forces will act in the x- and y-directions, and they will be proportional to the x- and y-components of velocity. The force acting on the projectile in the vertical direction will include both gravitational and drag components. The force equations in the x-, y-, and z-directions including aerodynamic drag effects are shown in Equation (5.17)

$$F_x = -F_D \frac{v_x}{v} \tag{5.17a}$$

$$F_y = -F_D \frac{v_y}{v} \tag{5.17b}$$

$$F_z = -mg - F_D \frac{v_z}{v} \tag{5.17c}$$

$$F_D = \frac{1}{2}\rho v^2 A C_D \tag{5.17d}$$

Since drag force acts in the opposite direction to velocity, the general effect of drag is that it reduces the projectile velocity. Looking at the z-direction force equation shown in Equation (5.17c), when the projectile is climbing, drag will slow down the rate of climb. When the projectile is falling back down to Earth, drag will slow the rate of fall.

The acceleration equations for the trajectory model with gravity and drag are obtained by dividing the force equations in Equation (5.17) by the projectile mass, m. The acceleration equations are shown in Equation (5.18).

$$a_x = -\frac{F_D v_x}{mv} \tag{5.18a}$$

$$a_y = -\frac{F_D v_y}{mv} \tag{5.18b}$$

$$a_z = -g - \frac{F_D v_z}{mv} \tag{5.18c}$$

Another significant difference between the gravity-only model and the equations of motion when aerodynamic drag is included is that the accelerations are now a function of the projectile mass. Specifically, the acceleration due to aerodynamic drag is inversely proportional to the mass of the projectile. All other things being equal, a cannonball with a mass of 5 kg will experience twice the acceleration due to drag than will a cannonball with a mass of 10 kg.

Velocity Equations

In determining the velocity components for a projectile when aerodynamic drag is included in the model, we start once again with the differential equations that relate a velocity derivative with respect to time to an acceleration. Using the acceleration equations shown in Equation (5.18), the differential velocity equations for the projectile are as follows:

$$\frac{dv_x}{dt} = a_x = -\frac{F_D v_x}{mv} \tag{5.19a}$$

$$\frac{dv_y}{dt} = a_y = -\frac{F_D v_y}{mv} \tag{5.19b}$$

$$\frac{dv_z}{dt} = a_z = -g - \frac{F_D v_z}{mv} \tag{5.19c}$$

To determine the velocity components as a function of time, the differential equations shown in Equation (5.19) must be integrated. For the gravity-only model, the velocity differential equations were simple enough to be solved directly into simple algebraic equations. Unfortunately, this simplicity is not the case when aerodynamic drag is added to the model. In looking at Equation (5.19a), the derivative of x-velocity with respect to time is a function of the x-velocity and velocity magnitude, which is a function of all three velocity components. The equations cannot be solved independently of each other and there are no simple, closed-form solutions to the differential equations.

Luckily for us, the ODE solver that was developed in Chapter 4 will save the day. The ODE solver will solve the velocity differential equations for us and will automatically update the velocity of the projectile as a function of time. Having access to the ODE solver was the reason why the SimpleProjectile class was written as a subclass of the ODE class. When we write the DragProjectile class to model drag effects a bit later in the chapter, it will be written as a subclass of SimpleProjectile (which itself is a subclass of the ODE class), so the DragProjectile class will have access to all of the data structure and methods defined in the ODE class that are needed to run the ODE solver.

Keep in mind that the accelerations due to aerodynamic drag will change over the course of the trajectory. Drag force is a function of velocity. When the velocity increases, the acceleration due to drag increases with the square of velocity. Because of the "velocity squared" nature of drag, it will often be a limiting factor in the maximum velocity a projectile can attain. When a parachutist jumps out of an airplane, she doesn't accelerate forever (luckily for her). Instead, she accelerates until the drag force on the parachute is equal to the force of gravity.

Location Equations

The inclusion of drag effects similarly complicates the equations that determine the location of the projectile as a function of time. As shown in Equation (5.20), the derivatives of the x-, y-, or z-location with respect to time are equal to the x-, y-, or z-velocities.

$$\frac{dx}{dt} = v_x \tag{5.20a}$$

$$\frac{dy}{dt} = v_y \tag{5.20b}$$

$$\frac{dz}{dt} = v_z \tag{5.20c}$$

The problem in trying to solve for x, y, or z as a function of time is that the velocities cannot be expressed in terms of simple algebraic equations. Luckily, the ODE solver comes to the rescue once again, because it can solve the velocity and location differential equations simultaneously. Once we have written the code that defines the differential equations, the ODE solver takes over and does all the rest of the work. The output from the ODE solver is the location and velocity values for the projectile at any time.

Terminal Velocity

Before we start to code up aerodynamic drag effects, let's take a little detour to discuss an interesting feature of aerodynamic drag. As we have seen, aerodynamic drag resists the motion of an object through the air and is proportional to the square of the velocity of the object. Because aerodynamic drag increases with the square of the velocity, drag will oftentimes be a limiting factor in how fast an object can travel.

Returning to our parachuting example, when the parachutist jumps out of the airplane the velocity of the parachutist increases over time, as does the drag force, until a point is reached where the aerodynamic drag exactly balances the force of gravity. At this point, there is no net force on the parachutist, and velocity of the parachutist remains constant. The velocity at which drag is equal to gravity is called the **terminal velocity**.

It isn't necessary to use an ODE solver to compute terminal velocity; a simple force balance will suffice. Terminal velocity occurs when the force of gravity on an object is equal to the drag force.

$$mg = \frac{1}{2}\rho v^2 A C_D \qquad (5.21)$$

Equation (5.21) can be rearranged in terms of the velocity where the force balance occurs.

$$v = \sqrt{\frac{2mg}{\rho A C_D}} \qquad (5.22)$$

In order to minimize terminal velocity, you want to either minimize mass or maximize density, area, or drag coefficient. When a parachute is opened, it increases the characteristic area, A, and the drag coefficient, C_D, that is experienced by the parachutist and allows her to float gently down to Earth.

Programming Drag Effects into the Projectile Trajectory Model

It's time to write a class called DragProjectile that will represent a projectile that is subject to the forces of gravity and aerodynamic drag. Adding drag effects to the projectile trajectory model is actually quite simple because we can reuse much of the code from the SimpleProjectile and ODE classes by making the DragProjectile class a subclass of SimpleProjectile. The DragProjectile class will have access to the methods declared in the SimpleProjectile and ODE classes and only needs to declare fields for the projectile mass, air density, characteristic area, and drag coefficient that will be used in the drag force equation.

```
public class DragProjectile extends SimpleProjectile
{
  private double mass;
  private double area;
  private double density;
  private double Cd;
```

The DragProjectile constructor is quite simple. It calls the SimpleProjectile constructor, passing it initial values for the location and velocity components of the projectile. It then initializes the values of the fields declared in the DragProjectile class.

```
public DragProjectile(double x0, double y0, double z0,
            double vx0, double vy0, double vz0, double time,
            double mass, double area, double density, double Cd) {
    // Call the SimpleProjectile class constructor.
    super(x0, y0, z0, vx0, vy0, vz0, time);

    // Initialize variables declared in the DragProjectile class.
    this.mass = mass;
    this.area = area;
    this.density = density;
    this.Cd = Cd;
}
```

A series of get methods are declared to return the values of the fields declared in the class.

```
// These methods return the value of the fields
//   declared in this class.
public double getMass() {
    return mass;
}

public double getArea() {
    return area;
}

public double getDensity() {
    return density;
}

public double getCd() {
    return Cd;
}
```

The updateLocationAndVelocity method is used to update the location and velocity of the projectile at the next time increment. In the SimpleProjectile class, this method solved the gravity-only equations of motion. In the DragProjectile class, the equations of motion are solved by calling the fourth-order Runge-Kutta ODE solver.

```
// This method updates the velocity and location
//   of the projectile using a 4th order Runge-Kutta
//   solver to integrate the equations of motion.
public void updateLocationAndVelocity(double dt) {
    ODESolver.rungeKutta4(this, dt);
}
```

The real "meat" of the DragProjectile class is its implementation of the getRightHandSide method that calculates the right-hand sides of the six differential equations that determine the motion of the projectile. If you recall from Chapter 4, the ODE solver updates the location and velocity components by making four intermediate guesses for the values. The final answer is a combination of the four guesses. The first thing the getRightHandSide method does is to compute the intermediate values of location, velocity, and time.

```
//  The getRightHandSide() method returns the right-hand
  //   sides of the six first-order projectile ODEs
  //   q[0] = vx = dxdt
  //   q[1] = x
  //   q[2] = vy = dydt
  //   q[3] = y
  //   q[4] = vz = dzdt
  //   q[5] = z
  public double[] getRightHandSide(double s, double q[],
                               double deltaQ[], double ds,
                               double qScale) {
    double dQ[] = new double[6];
    double newQ[] = new double[6];

    //  Compute the intermediate values of the
    //  dependent variables.
    for(int i=0; i<6; ++i) {
      newQ[i] = q[i] + qScale*deltaQ[i];
    }
```

The directional velocity components and overall velocity magnitude are determined. The method then computes the overall drag force according to Equation (5.12). Once the overall drag force is calculated, it is split into directional components according to Equation (5.16). The drag force components are then added to the right-hand sides of the ODEs.

```
//  Declare some convenience variables representing
    //   the intermediate values of velocity.
    double vx = newQ[0];
    double vy = newQ[2];
    double vz = newQ[4];

    //  Compute the velocity magnitude. The 1.0e-8 term
    //   ensures there won't be a divide by zero later on
    //   if all of the velocity components are zero.
    double v = Math.sqrt(vx*vx + vy*vy + vz*vz) + 1.0e-8;

    //  Compute the total drag force.
    double Fd = 0.5*density*area*Cd*v*v;

    //  Compute the right-hand sides of the six ODEs.
    dQ[0] = -ds*Fd*vx/(mass*v);
    dQ[1] = ds*vx;
    dQ[2] = -ds*Fd*vy/(mass*v);
```

```
    dQ[3] = ds*vy;
    dQ[4] = ds*(G - Fd*vz/(mass*v));
    dQ[5] = ds*vz;

    return dQ;
  }
}
```

Because it can reuse so much code from the SimpleProjectile and ODE classes, the DragProjectile class is quite short, only requiring 90 lines of code including comment statements. In the next section, the DragProjectile class will be incorporated into a new version of the Golf Game that will include drag effects.

Golf Game Version 2

Version 2 of the Golf Game uses the DragProjectile class to include drag effects in the simulation. The class that implements the GUI is called GolfGame2. A sample screen shot of the GUI display is shown in Figure 5-8. In addition to the velocity and distance-to-hole text fields, there are now text fields to input the mass, area, drag coefficient, and density. These parameters are used to compute the drag force on the golf ball. Everything else about Golf Game version 2 is the same as with the original Golf Game. The objective is to hit the ball so it lands within 10 m of the flag.

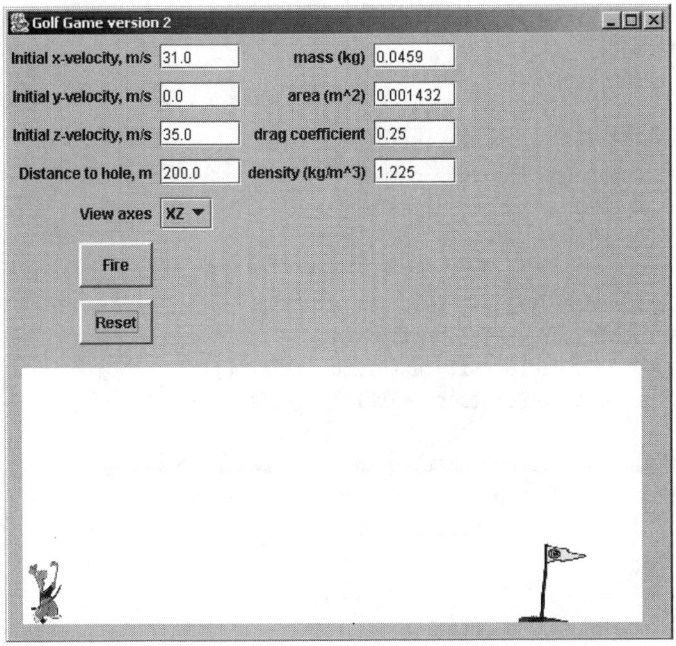

Figure 5-8. *A typical Golf Game version 2 display*

The GolfGame2 class is quite similar to the GolfGame class, so rather than discuss the entire code, we'll only focus on the differences. As always, the entire code listing can be downloaded from the Apress website. In addition to declaring fields for the four new text fields, the GolfGame2 class also declares a DragProjectile object that will represent the golf ball.

```
import javax.swing.*;
import java.awt.*;
import javax.swing.border.BevelBorder;
import java.awt.event.*;
import javax.swing.Timer;

public class GolfGame2 extends JFrame implements ActionListener
{
  // GUI component declarations not shown ...

  // The golf ball is a DragProjectile.
  private DragProjectile golfball;
```

As was the case with the games developed previously, when the Fire button is pressed, the actionPerformed method declared in the GolfGame2 class is called. The method goes through a similar process as in the original Golf Game. The values from the text fields are obtained, and from these values a DragProjectile object representing the golf ball is created. The start method is then called on the Timer to start the simulation.

```
// The actionPerformed() method is called when
  // the Fire button is pressed.
  public void actionPerformed(ActionEvent event) {

    // Get the initial quantities from the text fields.
    double vx0 = Double.parseDouble(vxTextField.getText());
    double vy0 = Double.parseDouble(vyTextField.getText());
    double vz0 = Double.parseDouble(vzTextField.getText());
    double mass = Double.parseDouble(massTextField.getText());
    double area = Double.parseDouble(areaTextField.getText());
    double cd = Double.parseDouble(cdTextField.getText());
    double density = Double.parseDouble(densityTextField.getText());
    distanceToHole = Double.parseDouble(distanceTextField.getText());

    // Create a DragProjectile object representing the golf ball.
    golfball = new DragProjectile(0.0, 0.0, 0.0,
        vx0, vy0, vz0, 0.0, mass, area, density, cd);

    // Update the display.
    updateDisplay();

    // Start the box sliding using a Timer object
    // to slow down the action.
    gameTimer.start();
  }
```

The `actionPerformed` method called by the `Timer` is exactly the same as the version in the original Golf Game. Because the projectile trajectory classes have been created sequentially using a common data structure, no changes need to be made to this method. Play around with the Golf Game version 2 by adjusting the variables that influence drag. As always, if for some reason the entire GUI is not displayed, pressing the Reset button will redraw the display.

Drag effects make a big difference when it comes to the flight of a golf ball as the Golf Game version 2 can demonstrate. Figure 5-9 shows two trajectories that use the same initial velocities, mass, density, and area values. The first trajectory uses a drag coefficient of 0.25, which is a typical value for a golf ball. For the second trajectory, drag effects are turned off by setting the drag coefficient value to zero. Without drag, the golf ball travels 221 m. When drag is included in the simulation, the same golf ball only travels 126 m. Clearly when it comes to projectiles such as golf balls, drag must be included in the model.

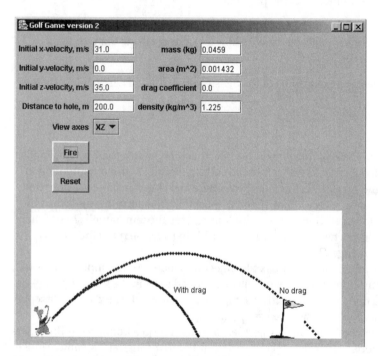

Figure 5-9. *The effect of drag on the flight of a golf ball*

Also notice in Figure 5-9 that when drag effects are included, the shape of the trajectory is not a perfect parabola. Instead, the downward part of the trajectory is steeper because drag is slowing the golf ball down.

Summary: Adding Drag to the Projectile Trajectory Model

In this section, we have added a key element to the projectile trajectory model—aerodynamic drag force. Drag is the resistance a fluid such as air exerts on an object traveling through it. Drag is an important effect for many projectile simulations. We saw the effect drag has on the flight of a golf ball in this section. Drag will also be important when modeling such things as bullets, cannonballs, and baseballs. The inclusion of drag effects complicates the projectile trajectory model. Simple closed-form solutions to the equations of motion are no longer possible, but the equations can be solved using an ODE solver.

Some of the key points of the projectile trajectory model with drag effects are as follows:

- Drag force acts in the opposite direction to the velocity. The magnitude of the drag force is proportional to the square of the velocity.

- The three components of motion are coupled when drag is taken into account. The x-component of drag force will depend on the y- and z-velocity components and so on. The x-, y-, and z-components of velocity and position can no longer be computed separately.

- The drag force is a function of the projectile geometry and is proportional to both the frontal area and drag coefficient of the projectile.

- The acceleration due to drag is inversely proportional to the mass of the projectile. Other things being equal, a heavier projectile will show fewer drag effects than a lighter projectile.

- The drag on an object is proportional to the density of the fluid in which it is traveling.

Wind Effects

When we developed the aerodynamic drag model previously in this chapter, there was an implicit assumption that the projectile was traveling through still air. Now let's turn our attention to modeling the effect of wind on a projectile trajectory. There are a lot of instances when wind will affect the trajectory of a projectile. Sharpshooters must take into account wind when they aim their rifles towards the target. Golfers must similarly change the aim of their shots if there is a crosswind. Baseball players have a much easier time hitting a home run if the wind is blowing out than if it is blowing in.

When wind is incorporated into our projectile trajectory model, some simplifications will be made. The velocity components of the wind will be assumed to be in the x-y plane only—in other words, it is assumed that there is no vertical component to the wind. The x- and y-direction wind velocity components will be designated as v_{wx} and v_{wy}.

To understand the effect of wind on a projectile, consider this question: what is the difference in the drag force experienced by an object traveling at 10 m/s through still air and a similar object at rest experiencing a 10 m/s headwind? The answer is that the two drag force values will be the same, because the **apparent velocity** seen by the two objects is the same.

■**Tidbit** The concept of apparent velocity is used to test new airplane concepts. A scale model of the plane is built and placed into a facility known as a **wind tunnel**. The model is fixed in place and large fans blow air over the stationary model to evaluate how the airplane would perform in flight. The largest wind tunnel in the United States is at the NASA Ames Research Center in Moffett Field, California. The test section is 80 feet wide and 40 feet high, and can test full-sized airplanes.

The presence of wind changes the apparent velocity seen by a projectile. In Figure 5-10, a projectile travels with a velocity, v. There is a wind present with a velocity, v_w. The apparent velocity, v_a, seen by the projectile is the vector sum of the projectile and wind velocities. The directional components of apparent velocity are found by subtracting the wind velocity components from the translational velocity components.

$$v_{ax} = v_x - v_{wx} \tag{5.23a}$$

$$v_{ay} = v_y - v_{wy} \tag{5.23b}$$

$$v_{az} = v_z - v_{wz} \tag{5.23c}$$

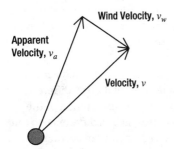

Wind Velocity, v_w

Apparent Velocity, v_a

Velocity, v

Figure 5-10. *Apparent velocity is the vector sum of the projectile velocity and wind velocity.*

The wind velocities are subtracted from the projectile velocities in Equation (5.23) because a positive wind velocity in the x- or y-direction will decrease the apparent velocity in the x- or y-direction.

The presence of wind alters the aerodynamic drag experienced by the projectile. In the presence of wind, the total drag force and directional drag force components are computed using the apparent velocities experienced by the projectile.

$$F_D = \frac{1}{2}\rho A C_D v_a^2 \tag{5.24}$$

$$F_{Dx} = -F_D \frac{v_{xa}}{v_a} \tag{5.25a}$$

$$F_{Dy} = -F_D \frac{v_{ya}}{v_a} \tag{5.25b}$$

$$F_{Dz} = -F_D \frac{v_{za}}{v_a} \tag{5.25c}$$

$$v_a = \sqrt{v_{xa}^2 + v_{ya}^2 + v_{za}^2} \tag{5.26}$$

The equations of motion when wind effects are included are solved in exactly the same way as when only drag was included. The only difference is that the apparent velocity is used to compute the drag force. The acceleration components would be equal to the force components divided by the projectile mass, and the velocity and position components would be found by integrating the acceleration and velocity equations.

An interesting thing to note about Equation (5.25c) is that while there is no wind velocity component in the z-direction, the drag force in the z-direction is affected by wind, because the z-component of drag force is now a function of the apparent velocity magnitude. The presence of wind changes the apparent velocity of the projectile, which alters the overall drag on the projectile. A projectile will reach a different height in the presence of a crosswind than it would if there was no wind.

There are some problems with this approach to modeling wind effects. The basic drag force expression shown in Equation (5.24) is based on the frontal area of the projectile. When wind is taken into account, the apparent velocity vector no longer lines up with the inertial velocity vector. The wind doesn't act solely on the frontal area of the projectile but on some combination of the frontal and lateral areas. The same situation exists for the drag coefficient. It is based on the object having a certain orientation with respect to the velocity vector. When wind is included in the model, the apparent velocity may have a different orientation, and the drag coefficient may no longer have the same value.

This is another case when you, as a game developer, need to evaluate how much accuracy you want to build into your models. For a spherical projectile, it doesn't make any difference. The frontal area and drag coefficient will be the same no matter what the orientation of the apparent velocity vector. If the projectile shape is asymmetrical, there will be a difference to the frontal area and drag coefficient, but then the question becomes whether you can accurately model the differences. It may be difficult to determine what the proper area term should be, and drag coefficient data may not be available for different velocity-geometry orientations. For the rest of this section, we will take the easy way out and assume that the same frontal area and drag coefficient can be used when wind effects are added to the model.

Programming Wind Effects into the Projectile Trajectory Model

Adding wind effects to our projectile trajectory modeling code is really quite simple, because we did most of the work when we wrote the DragProjectile class. We will call the class that represents a projectile under the influence of wind and drag the WindProjectile class. To reuse as much of the previous code as possible, we will make the WindProjectile class a subclass of DragProjectile. The WindProjectile class declares two fields that represent the x- and y-velocity components of the wind.

```
public class WindProjectil e extends DragProjectile
{
  private double windVx;
  private double windVy;
```

The WindProjectile constructor calls the DragProjectile constructor to initialize the fields declared in the DragProjectile, SimpleProjectile, and ODE classes. The windVx and windVy fields are then given initial values.

```
public DragProjectile(double x0, double y0, double z0,
            double vx0, double vy0, double vz0, double time,
            double mass, double area, double density, double Cd,
            double windVx, double windVy) {
  // Call the DragProjectile class constructor.
  super(x0, y0, z0, vx0, vy0, vz0, time, mass, area, density, Cd);

  // Initialize variables declared in the DragProjectile class.
  this.windVx = windVx;
  this.windVy = windVy;
}
```

Two get methods are declared that return the values of the windVx and windVy fields.

```
// These methods return the value of the fields
  //  declared in this class.
  public double getWindVx() {
    return windVx;
  }

  public double getWindVy() {
    return windVy;
  }
```

Just as it did for the DragProjectile class, the updateLocationAndVelocity method of the WindProjectile class solves the equations of motion by invoking the Runge-Kutta ODE solver.

```
// This method updates the velocity and location
  // of the projectile using a 4th order Runge-Kutta
  // solver to integrate the equations of motion.
  public void updateLocationAndVelocity(double dt) {
    ODESolver.rungeKutta4(this, dt);
  }
```

The getRightHandSide method in the WindProjectile class is exactly the same as the getRightHandSide method in the DragProjectile class with two exceptions. When the intermediate values of the x-, y-, and z-velocity components are obtained, they are converted into apparent velocities by subtracting the wind velocity components. The apparent velocities are then used to compute the drag force terms. The other difference is because the mass, density, area, and Cd fields were given private access in the DragProjectile class, we must use the getMass, getDensity, getArea, and getCd methods to access their values in the WindProjectile class.

```
// The getRightHandSide() method returns the right-hand
  //  sides of the six first-order projectile ODEs.
  //  q[0] = vx = dxdt
  //  q[1] = x
  //  q[2] = vy = dydt
  //  q[3] = y
  //  q[4] = vz = dzdt
  //  q[5] = z
```

```
      public double[] getRightHandSide(double s, double q[],
                                double deltaQ[], double ds,
                                double qScale) {
    double dQ[] = new double[6];
    double newQ[] = new double[6];

    //  Compute the intermediate values of the
    //  dependent variables.
    for(int i=0; i<6; ++i) {
      newQ[i] = q[i] + qScale*deltaQ[i];
    }

    //  Declare some convenience variables representing
    //  the intermediate values of velocity.
    double vx = newQ[0];
    double vy = newQ[2];
    double vz = newQ[4];

    //  Compute the apparent velocities by subtracting
    //  the wind velocity components from the projectile
    //  velocity components.
    double vax = vx - windVx;
    double vay = vy - windVy;
    double vaz = vz;

    //  Compute the apparent velocity magnitude. The 1.0e-8 term
    //  ensures there won't be a divide by zero later on
    //  if all of the velocity components are zero.
    double va = Math.sqrt(vax*vax + vay*vay + vaz*vaz) + 1.0e-8;

    //  Compute the total drag force.
    double Fd = 0.5*getDensity()*getArea()*getCd()*va*va;

    //  Compute the right-hand sides of the six ODEs.
    dQ[0] = -ds*Fd*vax/(getMass()*va);
    dQ[1] = ds*vx;
    dQ[2] = -ds*Fd*vay/(getMass()*va);
    dQ[3] = ds*vy;
    dQ[4] = ds*(G - Fd*vaz/(getMass()*va));
    dQ[5] = ds*vz;

    return dQ;
  }
}
```

All-in-all, the changes required to write the WindProjectile class from the DragProjectile class were pretty minor. As you may have guessed, we're now going to use the WindProjectile class to create a new version of the Golf Game—version 3 with wind effects.

Golf Game Version 3

With the WindProjectile class available to us, we can modify the Golf Game to incorporate wind effects. The class that will implement the new version of the game is called GolfGame3. A typical screen shot for the game is shown in Figure 5-11. Two new text fields have been added to the GUI that allow the x- and y-components of wind velocity to be specified. Everything else about the GUI is the same as in version 2 of the Golf Game. A negative x-component of wind velocity indicates a headwind. If the x-component of wind velocity is positive, then there is a tailwind. A positive y-component of wind velocity indicates a right-to-left crosswind.

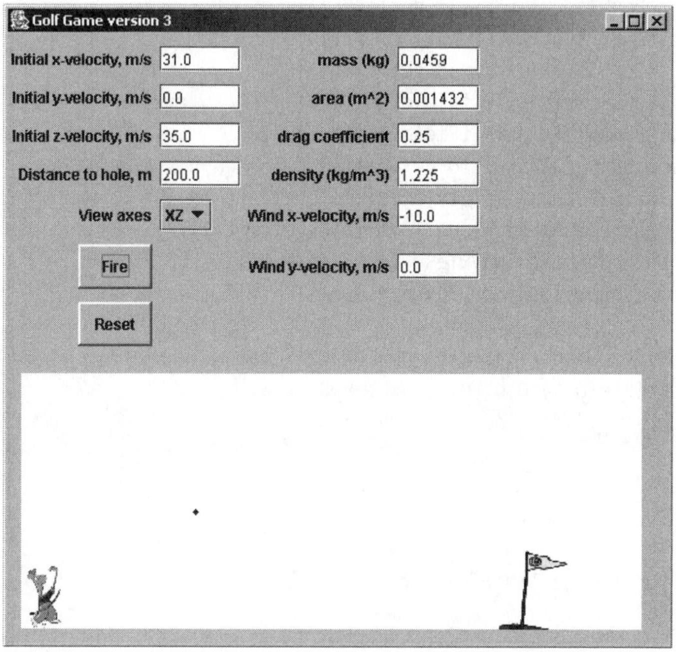

Figure 5-11. *A typical Golf Game version 3 screen shot*

Very few changes had to be made to the GolfGame2 class to produce the GolfGame3 class. A WindProjectile field is declared that will represent the golf ball.

```
import javax.swing.*;
import java.awt.*;
import javax.swing.border.BevelBorder;
import java.awt.event.*;
import javax.swing.Timer;

public class GolfGame3 extends JFrame implements ActionListener
{
  // GUI component declarations not shown ...

  // The golf ball is a WindProjectile.
  private WindProjectile golfball;
```

The actionPerformed method that is called when the Fire button is pressed extracts the input values from all of the text fields including the input values for the x- and y-components of wind velocity. A WindProjectile object is created and initialized with the input values. The start method is called to begin the simulation.

```
//  The actionPerformed() method is called when
  //  the Fire button is pressed.
  public void actionPerformed(ActionEvent event) {

    //  Get the initial quantities from the text fields.
    double vx0 = Double.parseDouble(vxTextField.getText());
    double vy0 = Double.parseDouble(vyTextField.getText());
    double vz0 = Double.parseDouble(vzTextField.getText());
    double mass = Double.parseDouble(massTextField.getText());
    double area = Double.parseDouble(areaTextField.getText());
    double cd = Double.parseDouble(cdTextField.getText());
    double density = Double.parseDouble(densityTextField.getText());
    distanceToHole = Double.parseDouble(distanceTextField.getText());
    double windVx = Double.parseDouble(windVxTextField.getText());
    double windVy = Double.parseDouble(windVyTextField.getText());

    //  Create a WindProjectile object representing the golf ball.
    golfball = new WindProjectile(0.0, 0.0, 0.0, vx0, vy0, vz0,
        0.0, mass, area, density, cd, windVx, windVy);

    //  Update the display.
    updateDisplay();

    //  Start the box sliding using a Timer object
    //  to slow down the action.
    gameTimer.start();
  }
```

The actionPerformed method that the Timer object calls in the GolfGame3 class is exactly the same as the actionPerformed method that the Timer called in the GolfGame2 class (which was exactly the same as the actionPerformed method in the GolfGame class).

Play around with Golf Game version 3 and you will discover that wind has a strong effect on the flight of a golf ball. Figure 5-12 shows the trajectory of a golf ball under a 10 *m/s* (36 *km/hr*) headwind, a 10 *m/s* tailwind, and under a zero wind condition. If there is no wind, the golf ball travels 126 *m*. In the presence of a 10 *m/s* headwind, the ball only travels 95 *m*. If the golfer is lucky enough to have a 10 *m/s* tailwind, his ball will travel 154 *m*.

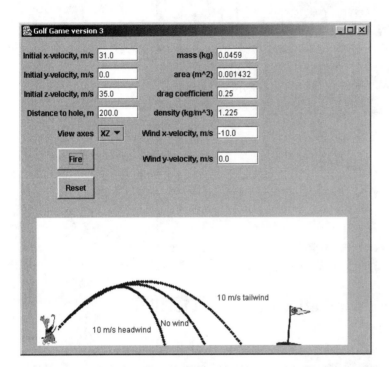

Figure 5-12. *The effects of headwind or tailwind on a golf ball trajectory*

Another interesting thing to look at with the new Golf Game is the effect of crosswind. The presence of a crosswind will make the ball turn away from its original flight path. For example, Figure 5-13 shows the trajectory of a golf ball under a 10 *m/s* crosswind. The wind pushes the ball to the left during its flight. In order to get the ball to land on the green, the golfer would have to initially aim the ball to the right (giving it a negative initial y-component of velocity).

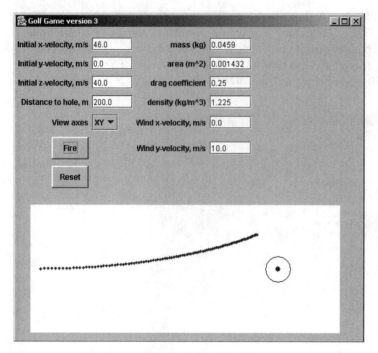

Figure 5-13. *The effect of crosswind on golf ball flight*

Summary: Adding Wind Effects to the Projectile Trajectory Model

Adding wind effects to the projectile trajectory model required changing the way the drag force components were evaluated. To account for the effects of wind, the apparent velocities, rather than the translational velocities, were used to evaluate the drag force and accelerations in the x-, y-, and z-directions. The apparent velocities were the vector difference of the translational and wind velocities. There were some assumptions made for this model—namely that the drag coefficient and characteristic area were the same as they would be if no wind was present.

Here are a couple of key points about the wind model that we implemented in this section:

- The presence of wind changes the apparent velocity seen by the projectile in flight. A headwind will increase the apparent velocity. A tailwind will decrease it.

- The wind velocity affects the drag force in all three coordinate directions even if the wind velocities themselves are only in the x- and z-planes.

Spin Effects

The final subject we will cover with regards to projectile trajectory modeling concerns the effects of spin. It is quite common for projectiles to spin as they fly through the air. A bullet spins as it leaves the gun. A golf ball spins after impact with the golf club face. A spinning object does a very curious thing as it travels through the air—it generates a force perpendicular to the flow velocity and spin axis.

Before we can come up with an equation that describes the force due to spinning, we need to back up a bit and talk about an expression known as **Bernoulli's equation**. It is an equation that relates the pressure, p, of a fluid to the kinetic and potential energy of the fluid.

$$p + \frac{1}{2}\rho v^2 + \rho gz = \text{constant} \tag{5.27}$$

In Equation (5.27), ρ is the fluid density, v is the velocity, g is gravitational acceleration, and z is the altitude of the fluid relative to some reference altitude (sea level, for instance).

Bernoulli's equation is useful for many different applications from flow rate meters to airfoil design. One of the results that comes out of Bernoulli's equation is that if the altitude is constant and the fluid velocity increases, the pressure will decrease. In Chapter 10, you will learn that airplane wings generate lift because the fluid velocity is faster over the top surface of the wing than it is over the bottom surface. The velocity difference between the top and bottom surfaces causes a pressure difference that generates a lifting force on the wing.

Now let's apply Bernoulli's equation to the problem of an object that is spinning while traveling through a fluid such as the soccer ball shown in Figure 5-14. The soccer ball is traveling through with a velocity, v, and it is spinning counterclockwise with an angular velocity, ω. When a fluid travels over the surface of an object, the fluid that is right next to the surface sticks to the surface. If the object is spinning, the fluid that is stuck to the surface of the object is pulled along with the object in the direction of the spin. In the region close to the surface of the object, the spin therefore adds to or subtracts from the fluid velocity. In Figure 5-14, the soccer ball is spinning in the counterclockwise direction. The spin will increase the fluid velocity along the top surface of the ball and decrease it along the bottom surface. Because the fluid velocity along the top surface is greater than it is along the bottom, according to Bernoulli's equation the pressure along the top surface of the soccer ball will be less than along the bottom. This pressure difference will generate a positive lifting force.

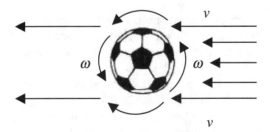

Figure 5-14. *A spinning object generates lift.*

Magnus Force

The phenomenon of a spinning object generating lift is known as the **Magnus effect**, sometimes also referred to as **Robin's effect**, and has been studied analytically and experimentally since the 18th century. The direction of the force depends on the direction of the spin. If an object is given backspin, the Magnus force will be in the positive vertical direction and will lift the object up. If an object is given topspin, the resulting force will be in the opposite direction and will push the object down.

■**Tidbit** In 1672, Sir Isaac Newton was the first to note in writing that the flight of a tennis ball was affected by its spin. Apparently even when he was exercising, Newton's mind was on physics.

The size of the Magnus force exerted on an object depends on the characteristics of the fluid, the geometry of the object, and the speed at which the object is traveling. To characterize Magnus force, or any other lifting force for that matter, an equation very similar to that used for drag in Equation (5.12) is typically used. The Magnus force, F_M, is expressed as a function of the fluid density, ρ, the velocity magnitude, v, a characteristic area, A, and a nondimensional number known as a lift coefficient, C_L.

$$F_M = \frac{1}{2} C_L \rho v^2 A \qquad (5.28)$$

Determining the Magnus force lift coefficient for an arbitrarily shaped object is a difficult problem. If certain simplifying assumptions are made, analytical relations are possible for some simple shapes. For example, according to Bernoulli's equation, the Magnus force lift coefficient for a sphere is the product of the sphere radius, r, and angular velocity, ω, divided by the translational velocity magnitude, v.

$$C_L = \frac{r\omega}{v} \qquad (5.29)$$

The ratio in Equation (5.29) is also known as the **rotational spin ratio**. The Magnus lift coefficient equation for a cylinder rotating about the long axis of the cylinder is given in Equation (5.30).

$$C_L = \frac{2\pi r\omega}{v} \qquad (5.30)$$

The direction of Magnus force will always be perpendicular to both the velocity vector and the spin axis. One way to determine the direction of Magnus force is to take the vector cross product of the velocity and spin axis vectors. An equation for the cross product of two vectors was presented in Chapter 2 in Equation (2.11).

The force diagram for a projectile subject to gravity, aerodynamic drag, and Magnus force is shown in Figure 5-15. Also shown in Figure 5-15 is the direction that the object is spinning. If the object has backspin, as it does in Figure 5-15, the Magnus force will be directed upward and will lift the object. In this case, the Magnus force will counteract the downward force of gravity and allow a projectile to stay in the air longer than it normally would. If the rotation of the object was in the opposite direction (that is, topspin), the direction of the Magnus force vector would be directed downward and would cause the object to fall faster.

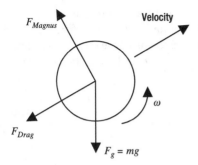

Figure 5-15. *The projectile force diagram including gravity, drag, and Magnus force*

The Magnus force effect is very important in the sporting world. Golfers make use of back-spin to increase the length of their golf shots. Putting the proper spin on a baseball is what makes curveballs curve and sliders slide. Tennis players, on other hand, make use of topspin to cause the tennis ball to "drop" into their opponent's court. We'll revisit some of these phenomena in Chapter 7 when we take up the subject of sports.

▮**Tidbit** In the early 1920s, a German engineer named Anton Flettner proposed a sailing ship that instead of using sails would generate propulsion from two large spinning cylinders placed vertically on the deck. The idea worked, but the propulsive force generated by the cylinders was less than if the motor spinning the cylinders had been connected to a standard propeller.

Programming Spin Effects into the Projectile Trajectory Model

Adding spin effects to the projectile trajectory model is a bit tricky because the equations for Magnus force are geometry dependent. You have to know beforehand if you are dealing with a sphere or cylinder, for example. Another complication lies in the fact that the Magnus force vector is perpendicular to both the axis of rotation and the velocity vector, so the axis of rotation must be precisely defined. The direction of the Magnus force vector can be obtained by taking the cross product of the velocity and spin-axis vectors. Using the cross product relation developed in Chapter 2, the directional components of Magnus force are shown in Equation (5.31).

$$F_{Mx} = \left(\frac{v_y}{v} r_z - \frac{v_z}{v} r_y \right) F_M \tag{5.31a}$$

$$F_{My} = -\left(\frac{v_x}{v} r_z - \frac{v_z}{v} r_x \right) F_M \tag{5.31b}$$

$$F_{Mz} = \left(\frac{v_x}{v} r_y - \frac{v_y}{v} r_x \right) F_M \tag{5.31c}$$

In Equation (5.31), r_x, r_y, and r_z are unit vectors that define the axis of rotation. Equation (5.31) is the general equation for the Cartesian components of Magnus force. The equations simplify considerably if the axis of rotation is parallel to one of the coordinate axes. For a sphere with an axis of rotation parallel to the y-axis, $r_x = 0$, $r_y = 1$, and $r_z = 0$, the x-, y-, and z-components of Magnus force become the following:

$$F_{Mx} = -\frac{v_z}{v} r_y F_M \tag{5.32a}$$

$$F_{My} = 0 \tag{5.32b}$$

$$F_{Mz} = \frac{v_x}{v} r_y F_M \tag{5.32c}$$

At first the Magnus force equations shown in Equation (5.32) may look a bit strange because the x-component of force is a function of the z-component of velocity, but keep in mind that Magnus force acts perpendicular to velocity vector. The y-component of force is zero in Equation (5.32b) because we assumed the axis of rotation was parallel to the y-axis and the direction of Magnus force is always perpendicular to the spin axis.

Now that we have expressions for the x-, y-, and z-components of Magnus force, spin effects can be incorporated into our projectile trajectory code. The process we will follow is the same as we used when including wind effects. A class named SpinProjectile will be written that will be a subclass of WindProjectile. In this way the SpinProjectile class can use the code declared in the ODE, SimpleProjectile, DragProjectile, and WindProjectile classes. The SpinProjectile class starts off by declaring the fields that will be used to calculate Magnus force, namely the angular velocity, radius, and spin axis.

```
public class SpinProjectile extends WindProjectile
{
    private double rx;      //  spin axis vector component
    private double ry;      //  spin axis vector component
    private double rz;      //  spin axis vector component
    private double omega;   //  angular velocity, m/s
    private double radius;  //  sphere radius, m
```

The SpinProjectile constructor calls the WindProjectile constructor to initialize the fields declared in the WindProjectile, DragProjectile, SimpleProjectile, and ODE classes. It then provides initial values to the omega, radius, rx, ry, and rz fields.

```
public SpinProjectile(double x0, double y0, double z0,
            double vx0, double vy0, double vz0, double time,
            double mass, double area, double density, double Cd,
            double windVx, double windVy, double rx, double ry,
            double rz, double omega, double radius) {
    //  Call the WindProjectile class constructor.
    super(x0, y0, z0, vx0, vy0, vz0, time, mass, area,
          density, Cd, windVx, windVy);
```

```
  //  Initialize variables declared in the SpinProjectile class.
  this.rx = rx;
  this.ry = ry;
  this.rz = rz;
  this.omega = omega;
  this.radius = radius;
}
```

A series of get methods are declared to return the values of the fields declared in the SpinProjectile class. The updateLocationAndPosition method is exactly the same as it was before. It simply invokes the Runge-Kutta ODE solver to solve the equations of motion.

```
//  These methods return the value of the fields
  //  declared in this class.
  public double getRx() {
    return rx;
  }

  public double getRy() {
    return ry;
  }

  public double getRz() {
    return rz;
  }

  public double getOmega() {
    return omega;
  }

  public double getRadius() {
    return radius;
  }

  //  This method updates the velocity and location
  //  of the projectile using a 4th order Runge-Kutta
  //  solver to integrate the equations of motion.
  public void updateLocationAndVelocity(double dt) {
    ODESolver.rungeKutta4(this, dt);
  }
```

The getRightHandSide method declared in the SpinProjectile class includes the equations to compute the Magnus force terms. The first part of the method is the same. Intermediate values of the location and velocity components are computed as apparent velocity seen by the projectile.

```
//  The getRightHandSide() method returns the right-hand
  //   sides of the six first-order projectile ODEs.
  //   q[0] = vx = dxdt
  //   q[1] = x
  //   q[2] = vy = dydt
  //   q[3] = y
  //   q[4] = vz = dzdt
  //   q[5] = z
  public double[] getRightHandSide(double s, double q[],
                                   double deltaQ[], double ds,
                                   double qScale) {
    double dQ[] = new double[6];
    double newQ[] = new double[6];

    //  Compute the intermediate values of the
    //   dependent variables.
    for(int i=0; i<6; ++i) {
      newQ[i] = q[i] + qScale*deltaQ[i];
    }

    //  Declare some convenience variables representing
    //   the intermediate values of velocity.
    double vx = newQ[0];
    double vy = newQ[2];
    double vz = newQ[4];

    //  Compute the apparent velocities by subtracting
    //   the wind velocity components from the projectile
    //   velocity components.
    double vax = vx - getWindVx();
    double vay = vy - getWindVy();
    double vaz = vz;

    //  Compute the apparent velocity magnitude. The 1.0e-8 term
    //   ensures there won't be a divide by zero later on
    //   if all of the velocity components are zero.
    double va = Math.sqrt(vax*vax + vay*vay + vaz*vaz) + 1.0e-8;
```

The directional components of drag force are computed separately, which will clean up the right-hand-side code a little later in the method.

```
//  Compute the total drag force and the dirctional
    //   drag components.
    double Fd = 0.5*getDensity()*getArea()*getCd()*va*va;
    double Fdx = -Fd*vax/va;
    double Fdy = -Fd*vay/va;
    double Fdz = -Fd*vaz/va;
```

The method now turns to the computation of the Magnus force. The velocity magnitude is computed and the overall Magnus force is computed from Equation (5.28). The lift coefficient is calculated from Equation (5.29). This particular lift coefficient equation is valid only for a sphere. If the shape of the projectile being modeled is not spherical, the line of code that computes C_L would have to be changed. Based on the total Magnus force, the directional components of Magnus force are determined from Equation (5.31).

```
// Compute the velocity magnitude.
  double v = Math.sqrt(vx*vx + vy*vy + vz*vz) + 1.0e-8;

  // Evaluate the Magnus force terms.
  double Cl = radius*omega/v;
  double Fm = 0.5*getDensity()*getArea()*Cl*v*v;
  double Fmx =  (vy*rz - ry*vz)*Fm/v;
  double Fmy = -(vx*rz - rx*vz)*Fm/v;
  double Fmz =  (vx*ry - rx*vy)*Fm/v;
```

The gravitational, drag, and Magnus force terms are added to the right-hand sides of the ODEs that describe the equations of motion.

```
// Compute the right-hand sides of the six ODEs.
  dQ[0] = ds*(Fdx + Fmx)/getMass();
  dQ[1] = ds*vx;
  dQ[2] = ds*(Fdy + Fmy)/getMass();
  dQ[3] = ds*vy;
  dQ[4] = ds*(G + (Fdz + Fmz)/getMass());
  dQ[5] = ds*vz;

  return dQ;
 }
}
```

Well, we've done it. The SpinProjectile class models the general motion of a projectile under the influence of gravity, aerodynamic drag, wind, and spin. The SpinProjectile, WindProjectile, DragProjectile, and SimpleProjectile classes can be used to model the motion of just about any projectile that you will come across in your game programming. In the next section, we'll create one last version of the Golf Game that will include spin effects on the flight of the golf ball.

Golf Game Version 4

Using the SpinProjectile class, one final version of the Golf Game will be created that will model the flight of a golf ball under the forces of gravity, drag, wind, and spin. Because the SpinProjectile class uses the same data structure as the previous projectile classes, very little has to be done to the GUI class to incorporate SpinProjectile objects. The GUI class is named GolfGame4, and a typical screen shot of the game is shown in Figure 5-16. There are five new text fields allowing the user to specify the angular velocity of the golf ball, the golf ball radius, and the vectors that define the spin axis. The default setting is for the ball to spin about the y-axis.

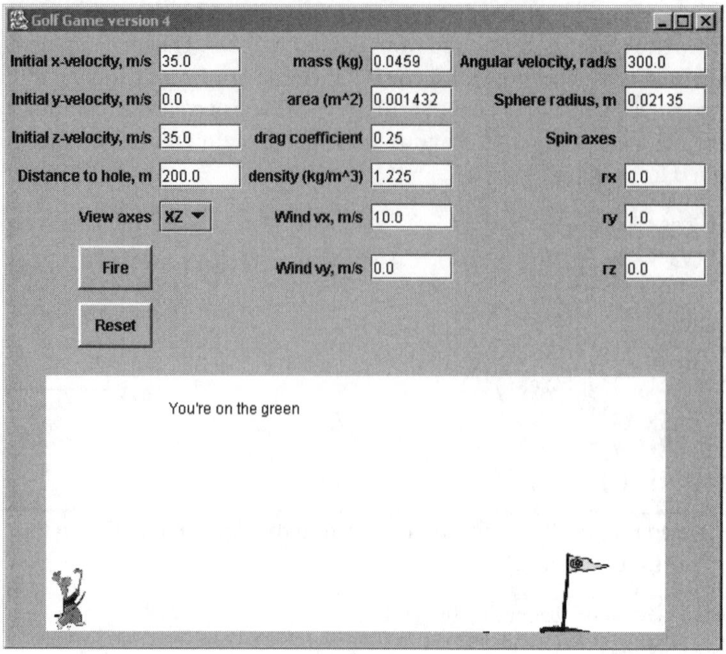

Figure 5-16. *A typical Golf Game version 4 screen shot*

Since much of the GolfGame4 code is the same as the previous versions of the Golf Game, only a couple of aspects of the code will be discussed. A SpinProjectile object is declared as a field of the GolfGame4 class and will be used to model the golf ball.

```
import javax.swing.*;
import java.awt.*;
import javax.swing.border.BevelBorder;
import java.awt.event.*;
import javax.swing.Timer;

public class GolfGame4 extends JFrame implements ActionListener
{
  // GUI component declarations not shown ...

  //  The golf ball is a SpinProjectile.
  private SpinProjectile golfball;
```

When the Fire button is pressed, the actionPerformed method declared in the GolfGame4 class is called. The method extracts the values in the text fields and creates a SpinProjectile object based on these initial values.

```
// The actionPerformed() method is called when
  // the Fire button is pressed.
  public void actionPerformed(ActionEvent event) {

    // Get the initial quantities from the text fields.
    double vx0 = Double.parseDouble(vxTextField.getText());
    double vy0 = Double.parseDouble(vyTextField.getText());
    double vz0 = Double.parseDouble(vzTextField.getText());
    double mass = Double.parseDouble(massTextField.getText());
    double area = Double.parseDouble(areaTextField.getText());
    double cd = Double.parseDouble(cdTextField.getText());
    double density = Double.parseDouble(densityTextField.getText());
    distanceToHole = Double.parseDouble(distanceTextField.getText());
    double windVx = Double.parseDouble(windVxTextField.getText());
    double windVy = Double.parseDouble(windVyTextField.getText());
    double rx = Double.parseDouble(rxTextField.getText());
    double ry = Double.parseDouble(ryTextField.getText());
    double rz = Double.parseDouble(rzTextField.getText());
    double omega = Double.parseDouble(omegaTextField.getText());
    double radius = Double.parseDouble(radiusTextField.getText());

    // Create a SpinProjectile object representing the golf ball.
    golfball = new SpinProjectile(0.0, 0.0, 0.0, vx0, vy0, vz0,
        0.0, mass, area, density, cd, windVx, windVy,
        rx, ry, rz, omega, radius);

    // Update the display.
    updateDisplay();

    // Start the box sliding using a Timer object
    // to slow down the action.
    gameTimer.start();
  }
```

Just as was the case with drag and wind, spin can have a significant effect on the flight of a golf ball. Two golf ball trajectories are shown in Figure 5-17. The first trajectory is computed for a golf ball with a 300 *rad/s* backspin. The golf ball travels a distance of 170.5 *m*. The second golf ball has identical input parameters as the first except that the spin is set to zero. Without the lift caused by the backspin, the ball only travels 154.3 *m*. Since distance per shot is an important element of golf, you can see why putting the proper spin on the ball is very important.

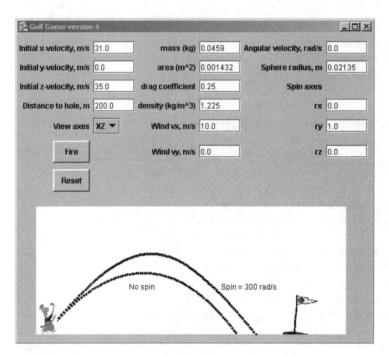

Figure 5-17. *The effect of spin on golf ball flight*

Another interesting effect that spin can have on a golf ball is if the spin axis is tilted so that it isn't parallel to one of the coordinate axes. When the axis is tilted, there will be Magnus force components in all three directions, and the golf ball trajectory will curve in the horizontal direction. To see an example of this effect, look at the trajectory shown in Figure 5-18. The view has been switched to the x-y plane, so we are looking at the trajectory from above. The spin axis in this case was tilted at a 45-degree angle in the y-z plane. Even though the initial y-velocity was zero, the ball begins to curve to the right in what is called in the golf world a "slice." If the spin axis had been tilted a negative 45 degrees in the y-z plane, the golf ball would have curved to the left in a shot known as a "hook."

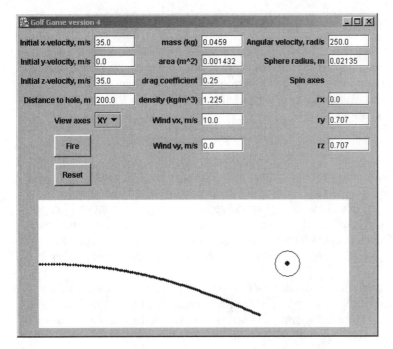

Figure 5-18. *A tilt in the spin axis causes the ball to curve.*

Summary: Adding Spin Effects to the Projectile Trajectory Model

In this section, you learned that a spinning object develops a lifting force known as Magnus force. The magnitude of Magnus force is proportional to the rate at which the object is spinning, and the direction of Magnus force is perpendicular to the flow velocity and spin axis. A general expression for the Magnus force generated by an arbitrarily shaped object is difficult to derive, but force expressions have been developed for cylindrical and spherical objects if certain modeling simplifications are made. Here are some general concepts to keep in mind about the effects of spin:

- An object given backspin will generate a lifting force. An object given topspin will generate a force that will push the object downwards.

- The acceleration that results from Magnus force is inversely proportional to mass. A heavier object will experience less acceleration than a similar, lighter object.

- The magnitude of Magnus force depends on the geometry. All other things being equal, larger objects will generate a larger Magnus force than will smaller objects.

Details on Specific Types of Projectiles

So far in this chapter, the discussion has focused on the general physics of projectile trajectories. The equations that we explored to model drag, wind, and spin can be applied to any type of projectile. In the last main section of this chapter, we will turn our attention to the specific modeling issues associated with some specific types of projectiles that are commonly used in game programming applications.

Bullets

Guns and bullets are common features in combat and adventure game applications. Bullets are small, relatively heavy (for their size) projectiles that travel initially at high speeds. The forces that act upon a bullet in flight include gravity, drag, and wind, forces that we have previously discussed. Bullets are generally given a spin as they leave the muzzle to enhance the stability of the bullet in fight. The spin is about the longitudinal axis of the bullet, parallel to the direction of flight, so the Magnus force that results from bullet spin is small and can generally be ignored.

When bullets fly through the air, the nose of the bullet will usually not point precisely in the same direction that the bullet is traveling. As shown in Figure 5-19, the angle, δ, between where the nose of the bullet is pointing and its velocity vector is called a **yaw** angle. The value of yaw for most bullets is relatively small, on the order of a few degrees.

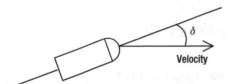

Figure 5-19. *Bullets usually have a yaw angle during flight.*

If the yaw angle becomes large, the bullet will become unstable and will begin to tumble in flight. To counteract the effect of yaw, modern gun barrels are **rifled**—spiral grooves are cut into the barrel. Rifling imparts a spin to the bullet as it travels down the barrel. The spin helps to stabilize the bullet during flight and helps to keep the yaw angle down to a stable value.

Unless you are programming a super-accurate bullet simulation, you can probably ignore the effects of yaw and spin on the flight of the bullet. For general game programming applications, it is probably acceptable to focus on gravity, drag, and wind as the forces that will act upon the bullet in flight. Therefore, factors that will influence a bullet in flight are the following:

- The initial velocity of the bullet

- The angle at which the bullet is fired

- The initial height of the bullet

- The drag coefficient of the bullet

- The mass of the bullet

- The density of the air in which the bullet is fired

- The direction and velocity of the wind

There are many types of bullets in the world today, and they vary in terms of mass, diameter, and muzzle velocity. Table 5-6 lists specifications for some representative types of bullets. The abbreviation FMJ stands for Full Metal Jacket and indicates a bullet with a lead core covered with a copper-zinc alloy jacket. The last three bullets in the table are military bullets used by NATO countries.

Table 5-6. *Characteristics of Some Representative Bullets*

Bullet	Muzzle Velocity (*m/s*)	Mass (*gm*)	Diameter (*mm*)
.22 Long rifle round nose	330	2.6	5.6
.32 ACP FMJ round nose	262	4.7	7.84
.357 Magnum	506	7.3	9
.38 ACP FMJ round nose	322	6.2	9.7
9 *mm* FMJ	341–373	8.0	9
9 *mm* FMJ high velocity	436	8.2	9
.44 Magnum	436	15.6	11.2
M74 (5.45 *mm*)	917	3.44	5.64
M80 (7.62 *mm* FMJ)	877	9.5	7.82
M2 .30 armor piercing	869	10.8	7.7

The drag coefficient for bullets varies with Reynolds number and therefore depends on the velocity and length of the bullet. For the M80 bullet, the drag coefficient at the muzzle velocity of 877 *m/s* is about 0.3. As the velocity decreases, the drag coefficient increases until the speed of the velocity of the bullet reaches the speed of sound (about 340 *m/s*) at which point the drag coefficient is about 0.45. At subsonic velocities, the coefficient of drag for the M80 bullet drops below 0.2. If you want to use a constant coefficient of drag for the bullets used in your game programming, a value of 0.3 is a fairly representative value.

Cannonballs

Modeling a cannonball in flight is fairly straightforward since you can assume that a cannonball is a solid sphere. Depending on the Reynolds number, the drag coefficient can be assumed to be 0.4 (for laminar flow) or 0.2 (for turbulent flow). A cannonball in flight will be subject to the forces of gravity, wind, and aerodynamic drag. Depending on the spin given to the cannonball, Magnus force effects may also have to be considered.

■**Tidbit** Cannons have been used in warfare since the early 14th century. Early cannons fired hand-cut stone balls because it was too expensive to smelt iron cannonballs. Cannons were used to fire large arrows as well as cannonballs. As they became more sophisticated and reliable, cannons revolutionized warfare on land and sea, making it possible to easily destroy castle walls and other fortifications.

In your game programming simulations, you can make the size and mass of the cannon-ball whatever you like. Early stone cannonballs sometimes weighed as much as 400 pounds. The English and French typically used cannonballs weighing 4, 8, 12, 16, and 24 pounds. The muzzle velocity of a cannonball was a function of the size of the cannonball and how much gunpowder was used to fire the cannon. The English culverin (a midsized cannon) would fire its ball with a muzzle velocity of about 260 *m/s* (865 *ft/s*). An upper end to the muzzle velocity for a cannonball is the speed of sound. At a temperature of 21 °C (70 °F) the speed of sound is 344 *m/s* (1129 *ft/s*).

Arrows

When an archer pulls back on a bowstring, he is performing work that is converted to potential energy and stored in the elastically deformed bow (also called a bowstave). When the bowstring is released, the potential energy stored in the bow is converted into kinetic energy as the bow snaps back to its undeformed position. If an arrow is in contact with the bowstring when it is released, some of the potential energy is transferred to the arrow, causing it to fly away.

A bow is essentially a type of spring. The potential energy, E_P, stored in the bow is a function of the force, F, required to draw the bowstring back and the distance, x, that the bowstring was pulled.

$$E_P = \frac{1}{2} eFx \tag{5.33}$$

The e term in Equation (5.33) is an efficiency coefficient that accounts for the fact that the bow does not behave exactly like an idealized spring, meaning that not all of the work done on the bow by bending it will be stored as potential energy. Wood bows typically have an efficiency factor of about 0.9, whereas modern composite bows can have an efficiency factor greater than one.

When the bow is released, the arrow flies off and acquires a certain kinetic energy. As the bow is also moving back to its original position, it acquires a certain kinetic energy as well. The potential energy in the deformed bow therefore is transferred to the kinetic energy of both the arrow and the bow.

$$\frac{1}{2} eFx = \frac{1}{2} m_a v_a^2 + k \frac{1}{2} m_b v_a^2 \tag{5.34}$$

In Equation (5.34), m_a is the mass of the arrow, v_a is the velocity of the arrow, m_b is the mass of the bow, and k is a scaling factor that accounts for the fact that different parts of the bow move at different velocities when the bow is released. The value of k depends on the geometry and material properties of the bow. Typical values of k for wood bows range from 0.03 to 0.07.

Using Equation (5.34), an expression can be derived for the initial velocity, v_a, of an arrow when the bow is released.

$$v_a = \sqrt{\frac{eFx}{m_a + km_b}} \qquad (5.35)$$

Arrows are long, fairly light objects, and as such the flight of an arrow will be strongly influenced by wind and drag effects. The drag experienced by an arrow in flight has been measured experimentally, and the drag was found to be a function of the velocity of the arrow squared multiplied by a constant, c, that depended on the geometry of the arrow.

$$F_D = cv^2 \qquad (5.36)$$

For a typical medieval war arrow, the value of c would be 0.0001 $N\text{-}s^2/m^2$.

Tidbit An experienced medieval archer could aim and fire 10 arrows a minute. The English King Henry V won the battle of Agincourt in 1415 even though he was outnumbered at least 4 to 1 because his 6000 archers armed with longbows rained 60,000 arrows a minute upon the advancing French army.

Exercise

3. If it takes 700 N (154 *lbs*) of force to draw a longbow back a distance of 0.5 m, compute the initial velocity imparted to a 0.06 kg arrow when the bow is released. Assume that the longbow weighs 1 kg, has an efficiency factor of 0.9, and has a scaling factor $k = 0.05$.

Summary

We certainly have come a long way in this chapter. Starting with basic Newtonian mechanics and kinematics, we developed a series of projectile trajectory models of increasing complexity. We started with the gravity-only model, which as the name implies only considers the effects of gravity on the projectile. The concept of aerodynamic drag was introduced. A formula was presented that relates drag to the fluid density, object velocity, a characteristic area, and a drag coefficient.

Wind effects were incorporated by having wind change the apparent velocity seen by the projectile. Drag forces were then computed using the apparent wind velocities. The phenomenon known as Magnus force was introduced whereby a lifting force is generated by a spinning object. The value of Magnus force can be expressed as a function of a lift coefficient that has an analytical form for simple shapes such as a sphere or cylinder.

The final part of the chapter gave details on some common types of projectiles—bullets, cannonballs, and arrows. These sections gave the mass, velocity, and size data you can use to simulate the flight of these projectiles.

Answers to Exercises

1. The time of impact is the time when the vertical or z-position of the projectile will be zero. The time of impact can be determined from Equation (5.8c).

$$-\frac{1}{2}gt^2 + v_{z0}t = 0 \quad \text{so} \quad t = \frac{2v_{z0}}{g}$$

The z-component of velocity at the time of impact can be found from Equation (5.8b).

$$v_z = -gt + v_{z0} = -g\frac{2v_{z0}}{g} + v_{z0} = -v_{z0}$$

The x-component of velocity using the gravity-only model is constant throughout the trajectory. Therefore, the velocity of the projectile at impact is equal to the following:

$$v = \sqrt{v_x^2 + v_z^2} = \sqrt{v_{xo}^2 + \left(-v_{z0}\right)^2} = v_0$$

The velocity at impact under the gravity-only model is equal to the initial velocity of the projectile.

2. The golf ball will continue to travel through the air until gravity brings it back down to the ground. Under the gravity-only model, the vertical location of the ball as a function of time is given by Equation (5.8c).

$$z = z_0 + v_{z0}t - \frac{1}{2}gt^2$$

Since the ground is flat and level, z and z_0 are equal to each other. The time it takes the golf ball to return the ground is equal to

$$t = \frac{2v_{z0}}{g} \tag{5.37}$$

The horizontal distance the ball will travel before it hits the ground can be computed from Equation (5.8a) using the expression for time from Equation (5.37) and the fact that $v_{x0} = 30$ and $v_{z0} = 20$.

$$\Delta x = x - x_0 = v_{x0}t = \frac{2v_{x0}v_{z0}}{g} = 122.4\ m$$

3. The initial velocity of the arrow can be calculated from Equation (29).

$$v = \sqrt{\frac{eFx}{m+kM}} = 53.5\ \frac{m}{s}$$

CHAPTER 6

■■■

Collisions

In Chapter 5, you learned how to model a projectile flying through the air. Eventually all projectiles, whether they are bullets or baseballs, are going to hit something. An important aspect of physics modeling for games is what happens when two objects collide. Do they bounce off each other or stick and travel together? If the objects do bounce off each other, what direction do they travel after the collision and what speed do they travel? This chapter will answer some of these questions by developing models used to describe object collisions.

This chapter will introduce the concept of momentum, both linear and angular, and describe how momentum is used to model collisions. We'll see how and why momentum is conserved. A couple of sample games will be developed that will demonstrate some aspects of collisions and allow you to play a stirring game of Pong. Some of the specific topics covered in this chapter include the following:

- **Linear momentum and impulse**: How these concepts can be used to describe the collision of objects that are moving linearly, like the collision of a golf club head with a golf ball.

- **Conservation of linear momentum**: This concept allows you to compute the post-collision velocities of two objects.

- **Two-body linear collisions**: We'll develop the mathematical equations that describe the collision of two objects.

- **Elastic and inelastic collisions**: An important distinction that defines the extent to which objects will rebound after a collision.

- **Determining when a collision occurs**: A crucial step in collision analysis.

- **Angular momentum and impulse**: In addition, we'll also see how these concepts can be used to model the collision of rotating objects.

- **Conservation of angular momentum**: This concept allows the determination of the post-collision angular velocity (that is, spin) of two objects.

- **General two-body collisions**: How to model the collisions of objects that are in translational motion and spinning at the same time.

139

Linear Momentum and Impulse

In Chapter 2, you learned about force, mass, acceleration, and velocity and used these concepts to model the motion of an object. In modeling a collision between two objects, another physical quantity needs to be introduced—**momentum**. Momentum is another way to characterize the state of an object in motion.

The linear momentum, p, of an object is simply the mass of the object, m, multiplied by its velocity, v.

$$\vec{p} = m\vec{v} \tag{6.1}$$

As introduced in Chapter 2, the arrow symbols in Equation (6.1) indicate vector quantities. Linear momentum has units of *kg-m/s* in the SI system of units or *slug-ft/s* under the English system. Since velocity is a vector quantity, momentum is as well. Under the Cartesian coordinate system, the overall linear momentum of an object can be separated into x-, y-, and z-components.

$$p_x = mv_x \tag{6.2a}$$

$$p_y = mv_y \tag{6.2b}$$

$$p_z = mv_z \tag{6.2c}$$

In Chapter 3, Newton's second law of motion was introduced, which relates the net external force on an object to a resulting acceleration of the object. As shown in Equation (6.3), Newton's second law can also be written in terms of a velocity derivative.

$$\vec{F} = m\vec{a} = m\frac{d\vec{v}}{dt} \tag{6.3}$$

If the mass of an object is constant, it can be moved into the derivative term, and Newton's second law can be written in terms of momentum.

$$\vec{F} = \frac{dm\vec{v}}{dt} = \frac{d\vec{p}}{dt} \tag{6.4}$$

Equation (6.4) states that the change of the momentum with respect to time is equal to the net external force applied to the object. If the net force on the object is zero, then the derivative of momentum with respect to time is zero—which means that momentum is constant. To determine the change in momentum caused by an applied force, the left- and right-hand sides of Equation (6.4) can be integrated with respect to time.

$$\vec{p}_1 - \vec{p}_0 = \int \vec{F}dt \tag{6.5}$$

In Equation (6.5), p_0 is the initial value of linear momentum and p_1 is the momentum at the end of the time interval being considered. Equation (6.5) indicates that a change in momentum of an object is equal to the integral of the net external force on the object as a function of time. The integration of the force with respect to time is known as the **linear impulse** of force.

$$\hat{F} = \int \vec{F}dt \tag{6.6}$$

Combining Equations (6.5) and (6.6) results in an equation relating a linear impulse of force to the resulting change in linear momentum.

$$\hat{F} = \vec{p}_1 - \vec{p}_0 = m\left(\vec{v}_1 - \vec{v}_0\right) \tag{6.7}$$

Let's apply Equation (6.7) to the collision of a moving object with something solid such as a wall. When the object strikes the wall, it will change the direction of its flight and therefore its velocity components will change as well. According to Equation (6.7), this change in velocity is the result of a linear impulse of force acting on the object due to the collision. The time of the collision, or dt, is generally very small, so according to Equation (6.6), in order for the impulse to be large enough to significantly change the momentum of the object, the force acting on the object must be very large. The force due to collision is known as an **impulsive force**. The magnitude of the impulsive force is usually so much larger than any other forces (gravity, drag, etc.) acting on the object during the collision, that all other forces can be ignored during the collision.

An important feature of impulsive force and linear impulse of force is that they act normal to the point of impact. As we shall see in a little while, the change in velocity due to a collision occurs normal to the point of impact as well. Newton's third law applies to linear impulses. If one object exerts a linear impulse on another, the second object will exert an equal and opposite impulse on the first object.

Conservation of Linear Momentum

According to the momentum version of Newton's second law shown in Equation (6.4), if there is no net force applied to an object, its momentum will remain constant. In other words, if there is no net force, momentum is conserved. It is also clear from Equation (6.5) that if there is no net force applied to an object over a certain time interval, the momentum of the object remains constant over that time interval.

What is true for a single object is also true for two or more objects being analyzed as a group, also called a **system of objects**. For instance, if the system under consideration consists of two objects and if no net forces are applied to the objects, then the linear momentum of the system of objects will remain constant.

$$m_1\vec{v}_1 + m_2\vec{v}_2 = C \tag{6.8}$$

The C parameter in Equation (6.8) is some constant value. Equation (6.8) states that the overall linear momentum of the two-body system is constant if no external forces are acting on the objects, but linear momentum conservation also applies to the directional components of momentum. If there are no net forces in the x-, y-, and z-directions, then linear momentum is conserved in the x-, y-, and z-directions.

$$m_1 v_{x1} + m_2 v_{x2} = C_x \tag{6.9a}$$

$$m_1 v_{y1} + m_2 v_{y2} = C_y \tag{6.9b}$$

$$m_1 v_{z1} + m_2 v_{z2} = C_z \tag{6.9c}$$

One area where the principle of conservation of linear momentum of a system of objects appears is in the analysis of two-body linear collisions—a subject we will explore a little later in the chapter.

Elastic and Inelastic Collisions

An analysis of the collision between two objects depends on the momentum of the objects, but collisions can also be analyzed in terms of energy. Consider the sphere falling to the ground in Figure 6-1. Just before the sphere collides with the ground, it has a velocity, v. The kinetic energy of the sphere as it hits the ground is equal to $1/2mv^2$.

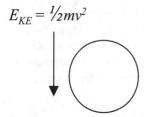

$$E_{KE} = \tfrac{1}{2}mv^2$$

Figure 6-1. *An elastic collision conserves kinetic energy.*

If the sphere bounces off the ground with the same velocity magnitude (in the opposite direction) as the impact velocity, then the kinetic energy of the sphere will be the same before and after the collision. A collision in which kinetic energy is conserved is called an **elastic collision**.

On the other hand, if a ball of string is dropped to the ground, it may only bounce a little. Because the post-collision velocity of the ball of string is less than the pre-collision velocity, kinetic energy is not conserved in this instance. A collision in which part or all of the kinetic energy is lost is called an **inelastic collision**. If you're wondering where the kinetic energy goes in an inelastic collision, the answer is work. Inelastic collisions usually involve the deformation of one or both colliding objects. When the force of collision moves part of an object a certain distance, work is performed.

If both colliding objects are moving at the time of collision, the element to look at when evaluating the collision is the relative velocity between the two objects. Figure 6-2 shows two objects just before they collide. The relative velocity between the two objects just before the collision is equal to $v_2 - v_1$. If the magnitude of the relative velocity between the objects is the same after the collision as it is before the collision, then kinetic energy is conserved and the collision is elastic.

Generally speaking, the harder the objects are that collide, the closer the collision will be to being elastic. The collision of two marbles, for instance, will be a nearly elastic collision. On the other hand, the collision of a beanbag on the floor will be an inelastic collision.

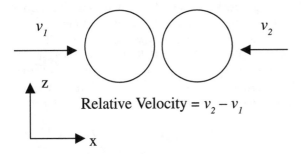

Figure 6-2. *If the relative pre- and post-collision velocities are equal, the collision is elastic.*

Two-Body Linear Collisions

Let's apply what you have learned about the impulse of force and the conservation of linear momentum to the problem of analyzing a two-body linear collision. We will start with a simplified problem by assuming that the two objects are spheres and that their motion is restricted to the x-y plane. Figure 6-3 shows a general two-body collision in the x-y plane. The objects have some initial velocities v_1 and v_2 and masses m_1 and m_2.

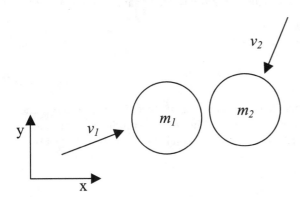

Figure 6-3. *Schematic of a two-body linear collision*

When they collide, the two objects will experience an impulse of force due to the collision. The magnitude of the impulse will be equal for both objects but will act in opposing directions. The geometric line along which the impulse acts is called the **line of action** for the collision. The line of action of the collision is a line drawn normal, or perpendicular, to the tangential plane at the point of collision. For the collision of the two spheres shown in Figure 6-4, the line of action is a line drawn through the center of the spheres that goes through the point of contact.

To develop the equations that determine post-collision velocity, we will consider the collision of two spheres such that the line of action of the collision is parallel to the x-axis as shown in Figure 6-4. We will also assume that the impulsive force is significantly greater than all other forces acting on the colliding objects. For the duration of the collision, all other forces acting on the objects can be ignored. There is also assumed to be no friction between the two objects.

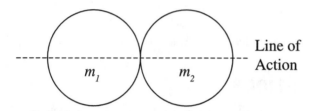

Figure 6-4. *A collision causes an impulse of force to act along the line of action.*

The linear impulse of force caused by the collision changes the velocity of the objects. The post-collision velocity components for the first object can be determined from Equation (6.7). Since the line of action for the collision is parallel to the x-axis, the linear impulse in the y-direction is equal to zero.

$$\hat{F}_x = m_1\left(v'_{1x} - v_{1x}\right) \tag{6.10a}$$

$$0 = m_1\left(v'_{1y} - v_{1y}\right) \tag{6.10b}$$

In Equation (6.10), the pre-collision velocity components of object 1 are v_{1x} and v_{1y}, and the post-collision velocity components are v'_{1x} and v'_{1y}. The collision produces an equal-but-opposite linear impulse applied to object 2. The post-collision velocities for object 2 can also be determined from Equation (6.7)

$$-\hat{F}_x = m_2\left(v'_{2x} - v_{2x}\right) \tag{6.11a}$$

$$0 = m_2\left(v'_{2y} - v_{2y}\right) \tag{6.11b}$$

Because the same linear impulse, $\hat{F}_x$, acts on objects 1 and 2, the right-hand side of Equations (6.10a) and (6.11a) can be set equal to each other. If this operation is performed and the two expressions shown in Equations (6.10b) and (6.11b) are simplified, the result is three equations that define the post-collision velocities of the two objects.

$$m_1(v'_{1x} - v_{1x}) + m_2(v'_{2x} - v_{2x}) = 0 \tag{6.12a}$$

$$v'_{1y} = v_{1y} \tag{6.12b}$$

$$v'_{2y} = v_{2y} \tag{6.12c}$$

If you look at Equation (6.12), you will see that momentum is conserved in both the x- and y-directions, but only the velocities in the x-direction change as a result of the collision. If you recall, the line of action for this analysis was taken to be parallel to the x-axis. This observation highlights a general rule about linear collision analysis: *a linear collision will only change the velocities in the direction of the line of action of the collision.* The velocity components normal to the line of action of a collision will be unchanged by the collision. Strictly speaking, these conclusions are only valid if there is no friction between the colliding objects, but that is currently the assumption for our analysis.

Looking more closely at the velocity expressions in Equation (6.12), there is still a problem. There are four unknowns, $v'_{1x}, v'_{1y}, v'_{2x}, v'_{2y}$, but only three equations. In order to solve for the post-collision velocities, an additional equation is introduced that relates the relative pre- and post-collision velocities of the two spheres along the line of action of the collision.

$$e(v_{1x} - v_{2x}) = -(v'_{1x} - v'_{2x}) \tag{6.13}$$

The coefficient, e, is known as the **coefficient of restitution** and has a value between 0 and 1. The coefficient of restitution relates back to the earlier discussion on elastic and inelastic collisions. If $e = 1$, the pre- and post-collision relative velocities are equal, meaning that the collision is elastic. On the other hand, if $e = 0$, the post-collision relative velocity is zero (meaning that the objects are stuck together) and the collision is completely inelastic. As you might expect, in most situations the coefficient of restitution will have a value between 0 and 1.

Combining Equations (6.12a) and (6.13), expressions can be obtained for the post-collision velocities along the line of action.

$$v'_{1x} = \frac{m_1 - em_2}{m_1 + m_2} v_{1x} + \frac{(1+e)m_2}{m_1 + m_2} v_{2x} \tag{6.14a}$$

$$v'_{2x} = \frac{(1+e)m_1}{m_1 + m_2} v_{1x} + \frac{m_2 - em_1}{m_1 + m_2} v_{2x} \tag{6.14b}$$

We can see from Equation (6.14) that the post-collision velocities along the line of action of the collision are a function of the pre-collision velocities along the line of action, the masses of the two objects, and the coefficient of restitution. The velocities in the y-direction, perpendicular to the line of action of the collision, are unaffected by the collision.

The development in this section has assumed a two-body collision in which the line of action of the collision is parallel to the x-axis. Of course, this situation will not always be the case. In general, the vector that defines the line of action for a collision can have any orientation. You'll learn how to handle general, two-, and three-dimensional collisions a little later in the chapter.

1. A solid sphere with a mass of 1 *kg* and with velocity components $v_{1x} = 20$ *m/s* and $v_{1y} = 4$ *m/s* strikes a second sphere with a mass of 9 *kg* and velocity components of $v_{2x} = 5$ *m/s* and $v_{2y} = -3$ *m/s*. Assuming that the line of action for the impact is parallel to the x-axis and that the coefficient of restitution is 0.9, determine the post-collision velocity components.

Collisions with Immovable Objects

In the previous section, equations were derived to compute the post-collision velocities of two objects. How would the equations be applied to the situation where one of the objects is immovable? This situation would occur frequently in game programming applications—a baseball could hit a foul pole or a golf ball could hit a tree, for example. Equation (6.14a) can be used to determine the velocity of an object after it collides with an immovable object if two assumptions are made. The first assumption is obvious—the velocity of the second object is assumed to be zero. The second assumption that is made is that the mass of the second object is infinite, so that the impulse applied to the immovable object does not change its (zero) momentum. Under these assumptions, Equation (6.14a) takes a very simple form.

$$v'_{1x} = -ev_{1x} \tag{6.15}$$

We can see from Equation (6.15) that when an object strikes an immovable object, it bounces off the immovable object in the opposite direction to its initial motion. The post-collision velocity is determined by the coefficient of restitution. If $e = 0$, the post-collision velocity of the moving object is zero (the moving object would stick to the immovable object). If $e = 1$, the pre- and post-collision velocities have the same magnitude but the opposite directions.

2. An object with a mass of 1 *kg* is dropped from a height of 2 meters. If the object strikes a concrete slab and the coefficient of restitution for the collision is 0.9, determine the height to which the object will bounce.

Linear Collision Simulator

Let's write a simple linear collision simulator that will demonstrate some of the factors that affect linear collisions. The class that implements the simulator is called `SphereCollision`, and a sample screen shot of the simulator is shown in Figure 6-5. The simulator consists of two spheres that move in the horizontal direction. The mass and initial velocities of the spheres are defined by the values inside text fields. Another text field allows the user to change the coefficient of restitution between the spheres. A Start button starts the spheres moving and a Reset button stops the simulation and resets the spheres to their original positions.

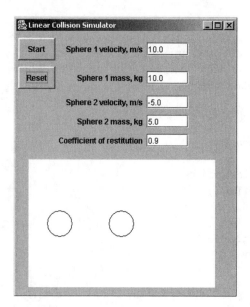

Figure 6-5. *A typical screen shot for the Linear Collision Simulator*

The spheres are modeled such that they are not subject to gravity or any other force. In addition to fields representing the GUI components, the SphereCollision class declares fields that represent the location, velocity, and mass of the spheres and the coefficient of restitution between them. The x-locations represent the locations of the center of each sphere.

```java
import javax.swing.*;
import java.awt.*;
import javax.swing.border.BevelBorder;
import java.awt.event.*;
import javax.swing.Timer;

public class SphereCollision extends JFrame implements ActionListener
{
  //  GUI component declarations not shown …

  //  These fields store sphere data and the coefficient
  //  of restitution.
  private double vx1;
  private double x1;
  private double mass1;
  private double vx2;
  private double x2;
  private double mass2;
  private double e;            //  Coefficient of restitution
  private double sphereRadius; //  Radius of spheres
```

When the Start button is pressed, the `actionPerformed` method declared in the SphereCollision class is called. The values in the text fields are used to update the velocity, mass, and coefficient of restitution values. As with the other programs presented in this book, the SphereCollision class uses a Timer object to control the execution of the simulation. When the start method is called on the Timer, the simulation begins.

```
// The actionPerformed() method is called when
// the Start button is pressed.
public void actionPerformed(ActionEvent event) {

  // Get the initial quantities from the text fields.
  vx1 = Double.parseDouble(vx1TextField.getText());
  mass1 = Double.parseDouble(mass1TextField.getText());
  vx2 = Double.parseDouble(vx2TextField.getText());
  mass2 = Double.parseDouble(mass2TextField.getText());
  e = Double.parseDouble(eTextField.getText());

  // Update the display.
  updateDisplay();

  // Start the box sliding using a Timer object.
  // to slow down the action.
  gameTimer.start();
}
```

The SphereCollision class declares an inner class named GameUpdater that declares its own version of the actionPerformed method. The Timer is set up to call this actionPerformed method every 0.05 seconds. The first thing done in the method is to determine whether the spheres have collided. A collision is defined to occur if the distance between the centers of the spheres is less than or equal to the sum of the radii of the spheres.

```
class GameUpdater implements ActionListener {
  public void actionPerformed(ActionEvent event) {

    // Determine if a collision occurs and if it
    // does, change the velocities of the spheres.
    // A collision occurs if the distance between the
    // centers of the spheres is less than twice their
    // radii.
    double distance = Math.abs(x1 - x2);
    double tmp = 1.0/(mass1 + mass2);
```

If a collision occurs, the velocities of the spheres are updated according to Equation (6.14). Since the spheres only move in the x-direction in this simulation, only the x-direction components of velocity need to be updated.

```
    if ( distance <= 2.0*sphereRadius ) {
      double newVx1 = (mass1 - e*mass2)*vx1*tmp +
                       (1.0 + e)*mass2*vx2*tmp;
      double newVx2 = (1.0 + e)*mass1*vx1*tmp +
                       (mass2 - e*mass1)*vx2*tmp;
      vx1 = newVx1;
      vx2 = newVx2;
    }
```

The new location of the spheres is calculated and the display is updated. The simulation is stopped if either sphere hits the outer edge of the display area.

```
// Compute the new location of the spheres.
double timeIncrement = 0.07;
x1 = x1 + timeIncrement*vx1;
x2 = x2 + timeIncrement*vx2;

// Update the display.
updateDisplay();

// If either of the spheres hits the outer edge
// of the display, stop the simulation.
Graphics g = drawingPanel.getGraphics();
int width = drawingPanel.getWidth() - 1;
int height = drawingPanel.getHeight() - 1;

if ( 10.0*(x1 + sphereRadius) > width ||
     10.0*(x1 - sphereRadius) < 0.0 ||
     10.0*(x2 + sphereRadius) > width ||
     10.0*(x2 - sphereRadius) < 0.0 ) {
  gameTimer.stop();
    }
  }
 }
}
```

Play around with the Linear Collision Simulator. Change the input parameters around and see what the spheres do after they collide. Set the coefficient of restitution to zero and see what happens to the spheres.

General Two-Dimensional Collisions

The equations developed so far in this section have been for a two-body collision in which the line of action is parallel to the x-axis. But what are equations for a general two-body collision where the line of action can have any orientation? The fortunate answer is that the same equations and concepts developed in the previous section can be applied to a general two-body collision. In this section, the equations will be developed to model two-dimensional collisions.

- The collision will affect the velocity components along (that is, parallel to) the line of action of the collision.

- Velocity components perpendicular to the line of action are unchanged by the collision.

The key to general two-dimensional collision analysis is to rotate the frame of reference so that one axis of the rotated coordinate system is parallel to the line of action for the collision. A two-dimensional collision, as the name would suggest, is one where the vector that defines the line of action lies in a two-dimensional plane. For example, consider the collision between object 1 and object 2 shown in Figure 6-6. The collision takes place in the x-y plane, and the line of action of the collision is at an angle θ with respect to the x-axis.

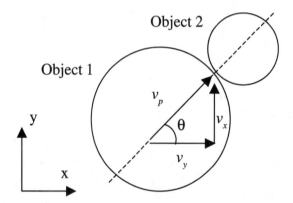

Figure 6-6. *A general two-dimensional collision*

Object 1 has pre-collision velocity components in the x- and y-directions equal to v_x and v_y. In order to analyze the collision, the velocity along the line of action, v_p, must be determined. Once v_p has been calculated, the post collision velocities along the line of action can be calculated according to Equation (6.14a). The velocity along the line of action can be computed from the trigonometric relation shown in Equation (6.16).

$$v_p = v_x \cos\theta + v_y \sin\theta \qquad\qquad (6.16)$$

Let's dig a little deeper into where Equation (6.16) came from. To get the velocity along the line of action, the original Cartesian coordinate system has to be rotated by an angle of θ as shown in Figure 6-7.

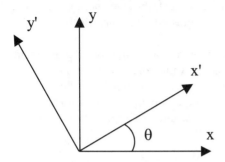

Figure 6-7. *Rotating a coordinate system by an angle*

If you recall from Chapter 1, to determine the velocity components in the rotated (line-of-action-aligned) coordinate system, the original velocity components v_x and v_y are multiplied by the rotation matrix shown in Equation (6.17).

$$\begin{bmatrix} v_p \\ v_n \end{bmatrix} = \begin{bmatrix} \cos\theta & \sin\theta \\ -\sin\theta & \cos\theta \end{bmatrix} \begin{bmatrix} v_x \\ v_y \end{bmatrix} \tag{6.17}$$

The velocity v_n is the velocity component normal to the line of action. The normal velocity component will be unaffected by the collision, and its value is given by Equation (6.18).

$$v_n = -v_x \sin\theta + v_y \cos\theta \tag{6.18}$$

Once the velocity components v_p and v_n have been determined, the post-collision velocity along the line of action, v'_p, can be computed from Equation (6.14). Once the post-collision velocities have been determined, it is usually desirable to convert the rotated velocities back into the original Cartesian velocity components. To do this, the rotated velocity components are multiplied by the inverse rotation matrix shown in Equation (6.19).

$$\begin{bmatrix} v'_x \\ v'_y \end{bmatrix} = \begin{bmatrix} \cos\theta & -\sin\theta \\ \sin\theta & \cos\theta \end{bmatrix} \begin{bmatrix} v'_p \\ v_n \end{bmatrix} \tag{6.19}$$

The equations represented by the matrix in Equation (6.19) are shown in Equation (6.20).

$$v'_x = v'_p \cos\theta - v_n \sin\theta \tag{6.20a}$$

$$v'_y = v'_p \sin\theta + v_n \cos\theta \tag{6.20b}$$

The accent marks, as in v'_x in Equations (6.19) and (6.20), indicate the post-collision velocities. The velocity normal to the line of action, v_n, is not the post-collision value because that velocity component doesn't change due to the collision.

You might be asking yourself why you need to bother with rotating the coordinate system and then later rotating it back again. Why not just use conservation of momentum in the x- and y-directions and be done with it? The problem with that approach is there would be more unknowns than there would be equations. You need to use Equation (6.13) to solve for the post-collision velocities, and Equation (6.13) only applies along the line of action of the collision.

Two-Dimensional Collision Example

Let's go through a sample problem that will demonstrate the process of analyzing a two-dimensional, frictionless collision. In Figure 6-8, two spheres collide. Sphere 1 has a mass of 10 kg and is traveling horizontally with a velocity $v_{1x} = 8$ m/s. Sphere 2 is stationary and has a mass of 5 kg. The line of action for the collision is at an angle of 30 degrees with respect to the x-axis. The coefficient of restitution between the two spheres is 0.9. What will be the post-collision velocities of the two spheres?

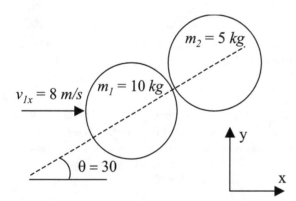

Figure 6-8. *A sample two-dimensional collision*

This problem, like all linear collision problems, can be broken down into four steps:

1. Determine the line-of-action vector for the collision.

2. Use a rotation matrix to determine the velocity components along the line of action and normal to it.

3. Compute the post-collision velocities from Equation (6.14).

4. Rotate the post-collision velocities back to the original Cartesian coordinate system.

The line-of-action vector has already been provided by the problem statement, so we can move on to step 2. The velocity components parallel and normal to the line of action can be computed from Equations (6.16) and (6.18). Sphere 2 is initially not moving, so its velocity components will be zero.

$$v_{1p} = v_{1x} \cos\theta = 8\cos 30 = 6.93 \ m/s \tag{6.21a}$$

$$v_{1n} = -v_{1x} \sin\theta = -8\sin 30 = -4 \ m/s \tag{6.21b}$$

$$v_{2p} = 0 \tag{6.21c}$$

$$v_{2n} = 0 \tag{6.21d}$$

Step 3 in the process is to compute the post-collision velocities for the two spheres according to Equation (6.14).

$$v'_{1p} = \frac{m_1 - em_2}{m_1 + m_2} v_{1p} = \frac{10 - 4.5}{15} 6.93 = 2.54 \ m/s \tag{6.22a}$$

$$v'_{2p} = \frac{(1+e)m_1}{m_1 + m_2} v_{1p} = \frac{19}{15} 6.93 = 8.78 \ m/s \tag{6.22b}$$

The final step in the process is to rotate the post-collision velocities back to the standard Cartesian coordinate system using Equation (6.20) to obtain the post-collision x- and y-components of velocity.

$$v'_{1x} = v'_{1p} \cos\theta - v_{1n} \sin\theta = 2.54\cos 30 + 4\sin 30 = 4.2 \ m/s \tag{6.23a}$$

$$v'_{1y} = v'_{1p} \sin\theta + v_{1n} \cos\theta = 2.54\sin^{v_{1p}} = v_{1x} \cos\theta = 8\cos 30 = 6.93 \tag{6.23b}$$

$$v'_{2x} = v'_{2p} \cos\theta - v_{2n} \sin\theta = 8.78\cos 30 = 7.60 \ m/s \tag{6.23c}$$

$$v'_{2y} = v'_{2p} \sin\theta + v_{2n} \cos\theta = 8.78\sin 30 = 4.39 \ m/s \tag{6.23d}$$

After the collision, both spheres are moving in the positive x-direction, but sphere 1 has slowed down because part of its momentum was transferred to sphere 2 during the collision. Sphere 2 is traveling in the positive y-direction and sphere 1 is traveling in the negative y-direction.

A Paddle Game

Let's use what we know about two-dimensional linear collisions to create a paddle game. A black ball bounces around inside an open-ended box. Your job is to use a paddle to hit the ball and keep it inside the box. If the ball gets past the paddle and reaches the open end of the box (the left-hand side), you lose. If you're old enough to remember, the Paddle Game is essentially a one-person version of the video game Pong.

The only force that will affect the motion of the ball will be the force due to collision with the three walls of the box and with the paddle. All other forces (gravity, drag, wind, etc.) will be ignored. The GUI framework for the Paddle Game is similar to that for the games previously presented in the book, so very little time will be spent describing the GUI aspects of the code. One new feature of the Paddle Game GUI is a slider component that can be moved up or down to change the location of the paddle. A sample screen shot of the Paddle Game is shown in Figure 6-9.

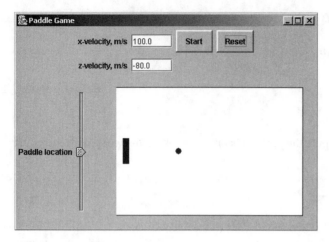

Figure 6-9. *A typical Paddle Game screen shot*

Implementing the collision model for the Paddle Game is quite simple. Because the paddle face and game walls are horizontal or vertical surfaces, the line-of-action vector for the collisions will always be parallel to the horizontal or vertical axis. For the purposes of the collision modeling, the walls and paddle faces are assumed to be immovable objects, so the post-collision velocity of the ball along the line of action can be determined from Equation (6.15). The ball will be modeled as being perfectly elastic, so the coefficient of restitution, *e*, will be equal to 1.

The Paddle Game is implemented inside a class named PaddleGame. The first thing the class does is to declare a number of fields that represent the GUI components for the game and the location and velocity components of the ball and paddle. The ballX and ballZ fields represent the x- and z-locations of the center of the ball.

```
import javax.swing.*;
import java.awt.*;
import javax.swing.border.BevelBorder;
import java.awt.event.*;
import javax.swing.event.*;
import javax.swing.Timer;

public class PaddleGame extends JFrame
        implements ActionListener, ChangeListener
{
  //  GUI component declarations not shown …

  //  These fields store ball data and the coefficient
  //  of restitution.
  private double ballVx;
  private double ballVz;
  private double ballX;
  private double ballZ;
  private double paddleZ;
  private int paddleHeight;
  private double ballRadius; //  Radius of ball
```

As with the games in the earlier chapters of this book, when the Start button is pressed, the actionPerformed method declared in the PaddleGame class is called. The method is quite simple. The horizontal and vertical components of the ball velocity are set according to the values inside the text fields. The GUI display is updated, and then the start method is called on a Timer object to start the ball moving.

```
//  The actionPerformed() method is called when
//  the Start button is pressed.
public void actionPerformed(ActionEvent event) {

  //  Get the initial quantities from the text fields.
  ballVx = Double.parseDouble(vxTextField.getText());
  ballVz = Double.parseDouble(vzTextField.getText());

  //  Update the display.
  updateDisplay();

  //  Start the box sliding using a Timer object
  //  to slow down the action.
  gameTimer.start();
}
```

The PaddleGame class declares an inner class named GameUpdater that declares its own actionPerformed method. The Timer is set up to call this method every 0.05 seconds. The first thing the method does is to determine if a collision has occurred between the ball and either one of the walls or the paddle. The collision determination logic is pretty simple. For example, the ball collides with the right-hand wall if the x-velocity of the ball is positive and the distance from the center of the ball to the wall is less than or equal to the ball radius. The other potential collisions are determined in a similar manner. If a collision occurs, the post-collision velocity along the line of action is determined by Equation (6.15).

```
//  This ActionListener is called by the Timer.
class GameUpdater implements ActionListener {
  public void actionPerformed(ActionEvent event) {
    //  Get dimensions of drawing area.
    Graphics g = drawingPanel.getGraphics();
    int width = drawingPanel.getWidth() - 1;
    int height = drawingPanel.getHeight() - 1;

    //  Determine if ball collides with right wall.
    //  If it does, change the x-velocity of the ball.
    if ( ballVx > 0.0 && ballX + ballRadius >= width ) {
      ballVx = -ballVx;
    }
```

```
// Determine if ball collides with the top wall.
// If it does, change the z-velocity of the ball.
if ( ballVz > 0.0 && ballZ + ballRadius >= height ) {
  ballVz = -ballVz;
}

// Determine if ball collides with the bottom wall.
// If it does, change the z-velocity of the ball.
if ( ballVz < 0.0 && ballZ - ballRadius <= 0.0 ) {
  ballVz = -ballVz;
}

// Determine if ball collides with paddle.
// If it does, change the x-velocity of the ball.
if ( ballVx < 0.0 && ballX - ballRadius <= 20.0 ) {
  if ( ballZ - ballRadius >= paddleZ - paddleHeight/2 &&
       ballZ + ballRadius <= paddleZ + paddleHeight/2 ) {
    ballVx = -ballVx;
  }
}
```

If the paddle misses and the ball reaches the left-hand edge of the game area, the simulation stops and you lose.

```
// If ball travels off the left edge of the game
// area, stop the simulation.
if ( ballX <= 0.0 ) {
  gameTimer.stop();
}
```

After it has been determined whether any collisions have taken place, the location of the ball is updated based on the current x- and z-velocities of the ball, and the GUI display is updated.

```
// Compute the new location of the ball.
double timeIncrement = 0.07;
ballX = ballX + timeIncrement*ballVx;
ballZ = ballZ + timeIncrement*ballVz;

// Update the display.
updateDisplay();

      }
    }
  }
}
```

Play around with the Paddle Game. The ball velocity components can be adjusted to change the speed at which the ball travels inside the GUI. Crank the velocity up real high and see how long you can keep the game going.

The Paddle Game as it is presented here models the collision between the paddle and the ball as if the ball hits the flat face. If you wanted to get more sophisticated, you could account for the possibility that the ball would collide with the corner of the paddle. In this case, the line of action for the collision wouldn't be parallel to the horizontal axis, but would instead be at some angle depending on the point of impact between the ball and corner.

Three-Dimensional Collisions

The most general type of collision is a three-dimensional collision in which the line-of-action vector can point anywhere in three-dimensional space. The same four steps that were used to analyze two-dimensional collisions can be applied to three-dimensional collisions. As you might expect, however, the process is a bit more complicated in three dimensions.

The major increase in complexity between two- and three-dimensional collisions is rotating the coordinate system so one of the coordinate axes is parallel to the line of action of the collision. With two-dimensional collisions, the coordinate rotation is performed through a single rotation angle, and the rotated velocity components can be determined from a simple two-dimensional rotation matrix. A general, three-dimensional collision analysis requires a three-dimensional coordinate system rotation, which requires three separate axis rotations through three separate rotation angles.

The rotation matrix for a three-dimensional coordinate system rotation is a complicated 3×3 matrix. The elements of the matrix depend on the order of the three axis rotations. For example, the matrix shown in Equation (6.24) is a three-dimensional rotation matrix representing a rotation about the z-axis by an angle of ϕ, followed by a rotation about the y-axis by an angle of θ, followed by a rotation about the x-axis by an angle of ψ.

$$R = \begin{bmatrix} \cos\theta\cos\phi & \cos\theta\sin\phi & -\sin\theta \\ -\cos\psi\sin\phi + \sin\psi\sin\theta\cos\phi & \cos\psi\cos\phi + \sin\psi\sin\theta\sin\phi & \cos\theta\sin\psi \\ \sin\psi\sin\phi + \cos\psi\sin\theta\cos\phi & -\sin\psi\cos\phi + \cos\psi\sin\theta\sin\phi & -\cos\theta\cos\psi \end{bmatrix} \quad (6.24)$$

Three-dimensional rotation matrices are messy, and the three rotation angles have to be determined before the rotation can be performed. What's more, the elements of the rotation matrix will be different if the order of the axis rotations is changed. We won't go into any more detail about three-dimensional rotation matrices here, but the topic will come up again when we develop an airplane flight simulator in Chapter 10.

Determining Whether a Collision Occurs

This chapter has spent a considerable amount of time developing the mathematical models to simulate collisions, but another important question is how to tell when a collision occurs. Basically, the question comes down to when the outer surface of one object comes in contact with the outer surface of another object. For complicated, asymmetrical objects, this analysis can be quite difficult, but it simplifies considerably for basic geometrical shapes.

One of the simplest shapes to evaluate collisions with is a sphere, or a circle in two dimensions. As seen in Figure 6-10, two spheres collide with each other if the distance between the centers of the spheres, d, is less than or equal to the sum of the radii, r_1 and r_2, of the spheres.

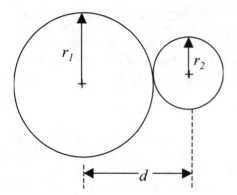

Figure 6-10. *Collision between spheres is a function of the distance between their centers.*

The collision determination is simple if the class that represents the sphere declares fields that store the location of the center of the sphere. In terms of computer code, the conditional statement to evaluate is the following:

```
if ( d <= r1 + r2 ) {
  // Collision has occurred.
}
```

It's also straightforward to determine whether a sphere has collided with a horizontal or vertical surface. If the distance from the center of the circle to the surface is less than or equal to the radius of the sphere, then a collision has occurred.

Another basic geometrical shape that is fairly easy to model is a cylinder. Consider the vertical cylinder shown in Figure 6-11. To determine whether another object collides with the cylinder, the circular criteria apply, but only over the vertical length of the cylinder. If the distance in the x-y plane from the long axis of the cylinder to the surface of another object is less than or equal to the radius of the cylinder, then a collision has occurred if the encounter takes place within the vertical length of the cylinder.

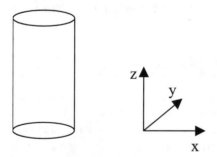

Figure 6-11. *Determining the collision with a cylinder uses the circular criteria.*

The final shape we will consider in this section is a parallelogram. Once again, it is helpful to define whether a collision occurs relative to the center of the parallelogram. If the normal distance from the center of the parallelogram to the surface of another object is less than or equal to the distance from the center of the parallelogram to the corresponding face, then a collision has occurred.

Because determining whether a collision has occurred with a complicated, asymmetric shaped object is difficult, for the purposes of collision modeling you might want to model the objects in your simulations as simple shapes. A person, for example, could be modeled as a sphere on top of a cylinder.

Angular Momentum and Impulse

In the first part of this chapter, you learned about how the linear momentum of an object is equal to its translational velocity multiplied by its mass. We developed the equations that describe linear momentum and explored the concepts of a force impulse and conservation of linear momentum. As we saw in Chapter 3, translational motion is not the only type of motion an object can have. In this section, we will turn our attention to the momentum due to rotation.

Because angular momentum is analogous to linear momentum, the same derivation process is performed to obtain the equations that characterize angular momentum. You learned in Chapter 4 that a net torque, τ, on an object results in an angular acceleration, α, of the object.

$$\hat{\tau} = I\bar{\alpha} \tag{6.25}$$

As was explained in Chapter 4, the moment of inertia, I, is a material and geometrical property that resists a change in angular motion. Equation (6.25) can also be expressed in terms of the derivative of angular velocity. If the moment of inertia is constant, it can be pulled into the derivative as well.

$$\bar{\tau} = \frac{dI\bar{\omega}}{dt} \tag{6.26}$$

The product of the moment of inertia and the angular velocity is known as the **angular momentum**, L.

$$\bar{L} = I\bar{\omega} \tag{6.27}$$

Looking at Equation (6.26), we see that if there is no net torque on an object, then the derivative of angular velocity with respect to time is zero, which means that angular velocity is constant. To determine the changse in angular momentum caused by an applied torque, the left- and right-hand sides of Equation (6.27) can be integrated with respect to time.

$$\int \bar{\tau} dt = \bar{L}_1 - \bar{L}_0 \tag{6.28}$$

In Equation (6.28), L_0 is the initial value of angular momentum, and L_1 is the angular momentum at the end of the time interval being considered. Equation (6.28) indicates that a change in angular momentum of an object is equal to the integral of the net external torque on the object as a function of time. The integration of the torque with respect to time is known as the **angular impulse** of torque.

$$\hat{\tau} = \int \bar{\tau} dt \tag{6.29}$$

Combining Equations (6.5) and (6.6) results in an equation relating an angular impulse to a resulting change in angular momentum.

$$\hat{\tau} = \vec{L}_1 - \vec{L}_0 = I\left(\vec{\omega}_1 - \vec{\omega}_0\right) \tag{6.30}$$

Equation (6.30) states that in the absence of a net applied torque, angular momentum of an object, or of a system of objects, is constant. This concept is known as the **conservation of angular momentum**.

Exercise

3. A figure skater with her arms stretched wide spins at 2 revolutions per second. If she pulls her arms tightly against her body, causing her moment of inertia to decrease from 2.0 *kg-m²* to 1.6 *kg-m²*, how fast will she spin when her arms are next to her body?

Collisions with Friction

Up to this point in the chapter we have dealt with frictionless collisions. In reality, assuming that a collision is frictionless is only strictly valid for **direct impact collisions**. As shown in Figure 6-12, a direct impact collision is one in which the line of action for the collision passes through the center of mass of the two objects, and the velocity vectors of the two objects are parallel to the line of action. After a direct impact collision, the two objects immediately separate, and the collision only affects the velocity along the line of action of the collision.

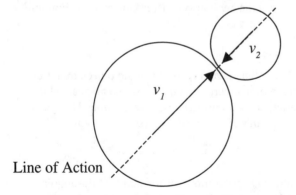

Figure 6-12. *Velocity and line of action are in the same direction for direct impact collisions.*

The other general type of collision is an **oblique** or glancing impact. As shown in Figure 6-13, an oblique collision is one in which the velocity vectors of the two objects aren't aligned with the line of action.

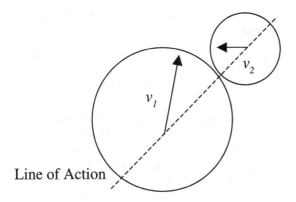

Figure 6-13. *Velocity doesn't line up with line of action for oblique impacts.*

When two objects collide obliquely, they will slide against each other for a brief period of time. In Chapter 3, you learned that when objects slide against each other, a frictional force is generated between the contacting surfaces, which resists the sliding motion. The friction force also generates an applied torque on the two objects. The applied torque generates an angular acceleration. In other words, when the objects slide against each other, they will begin to spin.

The spin acquired due to oblique impact is a very important phenomenon in sports. It is the oblique impact of the golf club head and ball that generates the backspin that golfers use to alter the trajectory of their shots. Soccer players like David Beckham are able to bend their shots because friction between their shoe and the ball generates the required spin.

We will now develop the mathematical equations to predict collision-induced spin. The objective is to find relations that compute the translational and rotational velocity components after an oblique collision. Most of the development will be performed in two dimensions because it is easier to visualize what is going on, but towards the end we will discuss how to apply the techniques to three-dimensional oblique collisions.

Frictional Impulse

In Chapter 3, we learned that friction force, F_F, is related to the normal force acting on an object, F_N, multiplied by the coefficient of friction, μ. The friction force resists motion in the direction perpendicular to the normal force.

$$F_F = \mu F_N \tag{6.31}$$

Earlier in this chapter, we saw that a collision causes a linear impulse of force that acts along the line of action normal to the point of collision of the two objects. The linear impulse of force causes a change in the velocities along the line of action. If the two objects experience an oblique collision and there is friction between them, a frictional impulse, $\hat{F}_F$, will be generated that is equal to the product of the coefficient of friction and the linear impulse of force.

$$\hat{F}_F = \mu \hat{F}_N \tag{6.32}$$

The frictional impulse acts in the direction normal to the line of action and will change the velocity components, v_n, normal to the line of action.

$$\hat{F}_F = m\left(v_{n1} - v_{n0}\right) \tag{6.33}$$

In Equation (6.33), v_{n0} is the pre-collision normal to the line of action, and v_{n1} is the normal velocity after the frictional impulse has been applied.

In the first part of the book, it was emphasized that the velocity components normal to the line of action were unchanged by a collision. This statement is only true for frictionless collisions. If two objects undergo an oblique collision in which friction is involved, the resulting frictional impulse will change the velocity components normal to the line of action. In addition, the frictional impulse will also cause the objects to spin, a subject that will be explored in the next section.

Modeling Two-Dimensional Oblique Collisions

Now that the concept of a frictional impulse has been introduced, we are ready to tackle the problem of modeling a general two-dimensional oblique collision. We will start by looking at a simplified problem, shown in Figure 6-14, of an object striking the face of a ramp that is inclined at an angle of θ. The line of impact of the collision is shown by the dotted line. When the object strikes the ramp, it is traveling at a velocity, v, which can be split into components along the line of action, v_{p0}, and normal to the line of action, v_{n0}.

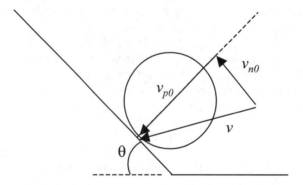

Figure 6-14. *A general, two-dimensional oblique collision*

When the object collides with the ramp, it has a velocity component, v_{n0}, parallel to the face of the ramp, so the object begins to slide up the ramp. The frictional impulse generated by the collision resists the sliding motion and reduces the magnitude of v_{n0} to a new value, v_{n1}, according to Equation (6.33). As shown in Figure 6-15, the frictional impulse causes an angular impulse that causes the object to rotate with an angular velocity, ω. Also shown in Figure 6-15 are the rotated coordinate axes in the p and n directions.

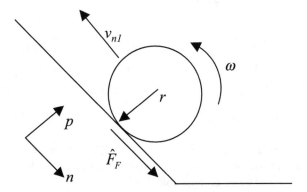

Figure 6-15. *A frictional impulse causes a rotation.*

It is assumed that the object is not rotating when it collides with the ramp, so the initial angular velocity, ω_0, is equal to zero. The angular impulse, frictional impulse, and final angular velocity, ω_1, are related by Equation (6.30).

$$\hat{\tau} = \hat{F}_F r = I\omega_1 \tag{6.34}$$

The quantity, r, is the distance from the center of mass of the object to the point of contact. The negative sign appears on the right-hand side of Equation (6.34) because a positive frictional impulse causes a negative angular velocity. The same frictional force appears in both Equations (6.33) and (6.34), so the two equations can be combined into a single equation that relates the change in velocity normal to the line of action to the change in angular velocity.

$$m\left(v_{n1} - v_{n0}\right) = -\frac{I\omega_1}{r} \tag{6.35}$$

There are two unknowns in Equation (6.35), v_{n1} and ω_1. In order to solve for the two unknowns, one more equation that relates them is needed. This expression can be obtained if we consider the nature of frictional impulses. A frictional impulse only exists as long as there is friction—in other words, as long as the ball is sliding over the ramp. When the translational and angular velocities reach the point where the ball starts rolling without sliding, the frictional impulses no longer act upon the golf ball. The condition for rolling without sliding is when the velocity normal to the line of action, v_{n1}, is equal to the product of the angular velocity, ω_1, and the distance, r.

$$v_{n1} = r\omega_1 \tag{6.36}$$

Using Equations (6.35) and (6.36), expressions can be derived for the velocity normal to the line of action and the angular velocity.

$$v_{n1} = \frac{v_{n0}}{1 + \dfrac{I}{mr^2}} \tag{6.37}$$

$$\omega_1 = \frac{v_{n0}}{r\left(1 + \dfrac{I}{mr^2}\right)} \tag{6.38}$$

Let's apply Equations (6.37) and (6.38) to the specific case of a sphere. The moment of inertia for a sphere is given by Equation (6.39).

$$I = \frac{2}{5}mr^2 \tag{6.39}$$

When the moment of inertia for a sphere is inserted into Equations (6.37) and (6.38), the result is two simple equations that determine the angular velocity and velocity normal to the line of action after the frictional impulse caused by an oblique collision.

$$v_{n1} = \frac{5}{7}v_{n0} \tag{6.40}$$

$$\omega_1 = \frac{5}{7}\frac{v_{n0}}{r} \tag{6.41}$$

The expressions in Equations (6.40) and (6.41) may look familiar to you, because they are the same as the equations developed in the "Bowling Ball Kinematics" section of Chapter 4 to characterize a bowling ball sliding and then rolling down a lane. The equations in Chapter 4 were derived using forces and torques, whereas the equations in this chapter were developed using impulses, but the final results are the same. Notice that the coefficient of friction does not enter into either Equation (6.40) or Equation (6.41). The final velocity and spin rate depend only on the initial velocity and radius.

To summarize the conclusions of this section, when an object is subject to an oblique impact, the frictional impulse caused by the impact will reduce the velocity normal to the line of action of the collision. The frictional impulse will also cause the object to spin. The final value of this velocity component will depend on the moment of inertia of the object. For a sphere, the value of the velocity normal to the line of action after the frictional impulse is equal to 5/7 of the initial velocity. The sphere will also acquire an angular velocity equal to 5/7 of the initial velocity divided by the radius.

Modeling Three-Dimensional Oblique Collisions

As you would probably expect, modeling three-dimensional oblique collisions is more involved than modeling two-dimensional oblique collisions, but the analysis in both cases follows a similar process. For three-dimensional oblique collisions, you must determine the direction in which the objects will slide. The coordinate system is rotated so that one of the rotated axes points along the line of action and another points in the direction that the body will slide. This direction defines the v_{n0} component used for the frictional analysis and will also define the resulting spin axis for the objects. Needless to say, the mathematics for modeling general three-dimensional oblique collisions become pretty daunting because three-dimensional rotation matrices are involved. A detailed discussion of general three-dimensional oblique collisions is beyond the scope of this book.

Summary

In this chapter, you learned the basics of the physics of colliding bodies. Starting with the concepts of linear momentum and impulse of force, equations were developed that compute the post-collision velocities from a linear collision. You learned about how a coefficient of restitution is used to characterize the efficiency of the collision and about inelastic and perfectly elastic collisions. In addition to linear momentum and impulse, the subjects of angular momentum and impulse were discussed. You learned how friction between colliding objects can cause the objects to spin.

Some of the key concepts to take away from this chapter are as follows:

- The change in velocity that results from a collision can be characterized by a linear or angular impulse.

- The post-collision velocities of two objects after a collision can be determined from the principle of conservation of momentum and the coefficient of restitution for the collision.

- For frictionless collisions, only the velocity in the direction of the line of action of a collision is affected by the collision. The other velocity components normal to the line of action are unchanged.

- For collisions that involve friction, the resulting frictional impulse reduces the magnitude of the velocity in the direction normal to the line of action and causes the objects to spin.

- If a sphere rolls without sliding at the end of a frictional impulse, the angular velocity of the sphere will be equal to 5/7 the initial velocity normal to the line of action divided by the radius of the sphere.

We will use our knowledge of collision physics in the next chapter when we explore the physics of sports. The spin caused by frictional collision plays a crucial role in golf, soccer, tennis, baseball, and many other sports as well.

Answers to Exercises

1. The line of action for the collision is along the x-axis so only the x-components of velocities for the two objects will be affected by the collision. The post-collision x-direction velocities can be computed from Equations (6.14a) and (6.14b).

$$v'_{1x} = \frac{1-0.81}{10}20 + \frac{(1+0.9)9}{10}5 = -5.65 \; m/s$$

$$v'_{2x} = \frac{(1+0.9)1}{10}20 + \frac{9-0.9}{10}5 = 7.85 \; m/s$$

2. The time it will take for the object to reach the ground can be found from Equation (5.8c).

$$t = \sqrt{\frac{2d}{g}} = \sqrt{\frac{4}{9.81}} = 0.639 \; s$$

The velocity when the object strikes the ground is equal to the product of the gravitational acceleration and the time.

$$v = at = -9.81 * 0.639 = -6.26 \; m/s$$

Because the object is striking the ground vertically, its rebound velocity is equal to the impact velocity multiplied by the coefficient of restitution.

$$v'_z = ev_z = -0.9 * (-6.26) = 5.63 \; m/s$$

The time it takes the object to reach the apex of its bounce is $5.63/9.81 = 0.574 \; s$. The height that the object will reach at its apex can now be computed.

$$z = -\frac{1}{2}9.81\left(0.574^2\right) + 5.63 * 0.574 = 1.62 \, m$$

3. There is no net torque acting on the skater because gravity is acting along the axis of rotation. Therefore the angular momentum of the skater is conserved as she draws her arms inward.

$$I_\omega = constant = 2.0 * (2.0 * 2\pi) = 1.6(\theta * 2\pi)$$

Here new rotation speed is $= 2.5 \; rev/s$.

CHAPTER 7

■ ■ ■

Sports Simulations

The first six chapters of the book have been pretty generic. You have learned the basics of Newtonian mechanics, kinematics, projectile motion, and collisions. Now it's time to take what you've learned and apply it to specific problems. In this chapter, we will explore the physics of sports simulations. You will learn how to model a golf ball in flight, how to simulate a bank shot in basketball, and many other things besides.

The good news is that you have already learned pretty much everything you need to create realistic sports simulations. When a football, golf ball, or baseball is in flight, it is essentially a projectile. We discussed projectile dynamics in Chapter 5. A basketball hitting the backboard or a tennis racquet making contact with the tennis ball are both examples of collisions. We saw how to model collisions in Chapter 6. The other subjects that we will apply—such as forces, accelerations, friction, and so on—were covered in Chapters 3 and 4.

The sports that we will look at in this chapter include the following:

- Golf

- Baseball

- Basketball

- Soccer

In addition, we'll take a brief look at how to model other sports.

We'll start our exploration of sports simulations with the game of golf.

Golf

Golf is an old game. It originated from a game played in eastern Scotland in the fifteenth century where players would hit a rock around a course of fields and sand dunes with a stick or primitive club. Apparently there wasn't much to do in fifteenth century Scotland for entertainment. Nevertheless, golf became so popular in Scotland that it, along with soccer, was banned in 1457 so the people who played it could prepare to defend the country against an expected invasion from England. The ban lasted until 1502, although it was mostly ignored anyway.

The concept of keeping track of golf strokes was introduced in 1759. The first 18-hole golf course was built at St. Andrews in 1764. Golf has increased in popularity up to this very day when millions of people around the world play the game. Golf technology has become quite sophisticated, with titanium club heads, graphite shafts, and so on, but the basic objective of the game is the same—to hit a ball with a club and have it go straight and far.

The good news is that we have already learned the basic concepts we need to know to create a golf simulation in Chapters 5 and 6. A golf ball in flight is simply a projectile that is subject to the forces of gravity, aerodynamic drag, wind, and spin. In order to create a golf simulation, you simply need to apply what you learned to the specifics of golf.

Equipment Specifications

The first thing to know when developing golf simulations is the size, weight, and other characteristics of the equipment used to play golf. Let's start with the golf ball. Modern two-piece golf balls usually have a hard rubber or synthetic rubber core surrounded by a plastic outer covering. A cross-section view of a typical two-piece ball is shown in Figure 7-1. With a three-piece golf ball, the inner core is surrounded by a tightly wound synthetic rubber string. There are also multilayer balls that consist of three or more solid layers of various materials.

Figure 7-1. *The cross-section of a two-piece golf ball (Photo courtesy of UMX Inc., www.umei.com.)*

■**Tidbit** Early golf balls were made of wood or leather crammed full of wet goose feathers. When the leather ball and the feathers inside it dried, the ball became hard enough to hit 150–175 yards. Early golfers had to stay away from the water hazards, however, because the leather balls became useless when wet.

There are a lot of different golf balls on the market these days, but they all share some standard specifications. According to the United States Golf Association (USGA), the weight of a golf ball should not exceed 1.62 ounces (0.0459 *kg*). The diameter of a golf ball should be 1.68 *in* (0.0427 *m*). You can use these numbers in your golf simulation.

In Chapter 6, the coefficient of restitution was introduced as a measure of how much kinetic energy is lost during a collision. The coefficient of restitution between a golf club face and golf ball depends on the type of golf ball. The value will typically be 0.78 for a standard two-piece ball. Three-piece balls tend to be a bit softer, and the coefficient of restitution for them will be about 0.68. All other things being equal, a higher coefficient of restitution will result in a higher initial velocity for the ball and a longer distance. In response to new-technology drivers that allowed the club faces to exert a spring-like effect on the golf balls they struck, in 1998 the USGA set the maximum allowable coefficient of restitution between a golf ball and club face to be 0.83.

Modern golf balls have dimples on the surface of the ball. The purpose of the dimples is to cause the flow around the ball to become turbulent (a topic discussed in Chapter 5), thereby reducing the aerodynamic drag of the golf ball in flight. There are several commonly used dimple patterns for golf balls, and typically there are 350–500 dimples on the surface of a golf ball.

The coefficient of drag of a golf ball is a function of Reynolds number and how fast the ball is spinning. For a Reynolds number of 150,000 (approximately the value for a golf ball traveling at 60 *m/s*), the drag coefficient will range between 0.21 and 0.25 depending on the spin rate. Lower spin rates will result in lower drag coefficients. The drag coefficient for a smooth sphere at these conditions ranges from 0.4 to 0.47, so the dimpled surface significantly reduces the drag on the golf ball.

The weight and size data of standard golf balls is summarized in Table 7-1.

Table 7-1. *Golf Ball Specifications*

Quantity	Two-Piece Ball	Three-Piece Ball
Mass	0.0459 *kg* (1.62 *oz*)	0.0459 *kg* (1.62 *oz*)
Diameter	0.0427 *m* (1.68 *in*)	0.0427 *m* (1.68 *in*)
Coefficient of restitution	0.78	0.68
Drag coefficient	0.21–0.25	0.22–0.35

A modern golf club consists of a metal or graphite shaft connected to a head. When the golf club is swung, the club head face strikes the ball, causing it to (hopefully) fly through the air. There are different types of clubs—woods, irons, wedges, putters—that are used for different types of golf shots. For the purposes of the golf simulation we will develop in this chapter, we will characterize golf clubs by the mass of the club head and the loft of the club. The loft is the angle, α, the club face makes with the vertical axis as shown in Figure 7-2. The geometry and composition of the club shaft and club head also affects the behavior of the club to a lesser extent, but we will ignore those effects in this chapter.

Loft Angle, α

Figure 7-2. *The loft is the angle the club face makes with the vertical.*

Just as there are a lot of different golf balls on the market today, so are there a lot of different golf clubs. The club head mass and loft angle for a given club can vary from manufacturer to manufacturer, but some typical values of these quantities are shown in Table 7-2.[1] The length of the shaft will vary according to the type of club but also according to the height of the person who will use the club. The length of the club shaft will not be a part of the golf simulation we will develop in this chapter.

Table 7-2. *Typical Loft Angle and Club Head Mass Values*

Club	Loft (Degrees)	Club Head Mass
1 wood	11	0.2 *kg* (7.05 *oz*)
3 wood	15	0.208 *kg* (7.34 *oz*)
5 wood	18	0.218 *kg* (7.69 *oz*)
2 iron	18	0.232 *kg* (8.18 *oz*)
3 iron	21	0.239 *kg* (8.43 *oz*)
4 iron	24	0.246 *kg* (8.67 *oz*)
5 iron	27	0.253 *kg* (8.92 *oz*)
6 iron	31	0.260 *kg* (9.17 *oz*)
7 iron	35	0.267 *kg* (9.42 *oz*)
8 iron	39	0.274 *kg* (9.66 *oz*)
9 iron	43	0.281 *kg* (9.91 *oz*)
Pitching wedge	48	0.285 *kg* (10.05 *oz*)
Sand wedge	55	0.296 *kg* (10.44 *oz*)
Putter	4	0.33 *kg* (11.64 *oz*)

Modeling the Club-Ball Impact

The first thing to decide when developing a golf simulation is what to simulate. The sequence of events in a typical golf shot is as follows: the golfer swings the club, the club impacts the ball, the ball flies through the air (also known as the **carry**), and the ball hits and rolls along the ground (also known as the **roll**).

The golf swing is a complicated process. There are rotations of the wrists, hips, and knees. The golfer's body weight shifts backwards and forwards during the swing. It would be very diffi-cult to develop a general model for a golf swing, but the good news is there really is no need to do so. The flight of the golf ball is determined by the impact between the golf club face and the ball. For the model we will develop in this chapter, we will ignore the swing altogether and start our golf simulation at the time of impact between the club and the ball.

When modeling the impact between the club face and ball, we will make some simplifying assumptions:

- Any effects due to the club shaft or the golfer holding the club will be ignored. The club head will treated as if it is moving through the air by itself.

- At the point of impact, the club head will be traveling at a constant velocity. There will be no net force acting on the club head.

Under these assumptions, the only things that will affect the impact are the mass of the club head, the mass of the ball, the velocity of the club head at impact, and the angle of the impact. Figure 7-3 shows a high-speed photography picture of the initial point of impact between a club head and golf ball. The side of the ball in contact with the club face is being compressed by the impact.

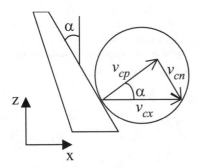

Figure 7-3. *A golf ball at the point of impact (Photo courtesy of Acushnet Company)*

The impact of a golf ball and club head face is really just a simple collision, similar to those we studied in Chapter 6. The ball is initially at rest either on the ground or on a tee. A simple impact model, shown in Figure 7-4, assumes that the club head is traveling in the x-direction with a velocity equal to v_{cx}. The swing is taken to be "ideal," meaning that the club face strikes the ball such that the line of action is perpendicular to the club face in the x-z plane.

Figure 7-4. *Schematic of a club head—golf ball collision*

For the "ideal" impact shown in Figure 7-4, the line of action of the collision is along a vector whose angle is equal to the loft of the club, α. The club head velocity along the line of action, v_{cp}, is normal to the club head face and is therefore equal to the velocity in the x-direction multiplied by the cosine of the loft angle.

$$v_{cp} = v_{cx}\cos\alpha \tag{7.1}$$

The component of initial club head velocity normal to the line of action, v_{cn}, which will be important in determining the spin of the golf ball, can be found using the sine of the loft angle.

$$v_{cn} = v_{cx}\sin\alpha \tag{7.2}$$

The post-impact velocity of the golf ball can be determined from Equation (6.14a) developed in Chapter 6. It is a function of the mass of the ball, m_b, the mass of the club head, m_c, the coefficient of restitution, e, and the velocity component in the direction of the line of action of the collision, v_{cp}.

$$v'_{bp} = \frac{(1+e)m_c}{m_b + m_c}v_{cp} = \frac{(1+e)m_c}{m_b + m_c}v_{cx}\cos\alpha \tag{7.3}$$

Equation (7.3) represents the post-impact velocity of a golf ball after an "ideal" hit, but as we all know in the real world, the "ideal" hit rarely ever occurs. The club face may not strike the ball at the bottom of the swing, thereby changing the effective loft of the club. The club face might also strike the ball at an angle, changing the line-of-action vector of the collision from the x-z plane. We'll discuss how to deal with nonideal impacts in the "Impact Modeling Decisions" section a little later in this chapter.

Friction Effects

When the club face strikes the ball, there will be friction between the two surfaces, and this friction effect is very important in golf simulations. It not only affects the initial velocity of the ball, but is also responsible for the ball acquiring spin. For the purposes of developing some basic relations in this section, we will assume an "idealized" impact where the line of action of the collision is in the x-z plane and the spin axis of the golf ball is parallel to the y-axis.

As we saw in Figure 7-4, because the club is lofted when it impacts the ball, it will have velocity components both normal to and parallel to the club face. At the moment of impact, the ball starts to slide up the face of the club. The relative velocity between the ball club as the sliding begins is equal to the velocity of the club normal to the line of action, v_{cn}. Because the ball is sliding over the club face, a friction force is generated that resists this motion. The friction force does two things: it reduces the relative velocity between the club and ball, and it generates a torque on the ball that causes it to spin. The general situation is illustrated in Figure 7-5.

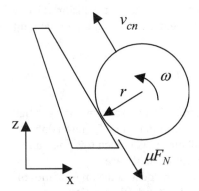

Figure 7-5. *Friction between the ball and club face causes the ball to spin.*

When analyzing the friction effects on a golf ball, there are two questions to answer: what is the resulting velocity of the golf ball parallel to the club face, and what is the spin rate that is imparted to the golf ball? Both questions can be answered by analyzing the frictional impulse that is generated between the golf ball and club face, a concept that was introduced in Chapter 6. If the ball is assumed to roll without slipping at the end of the frictional impulse, the post-collision velocity normal to the line of action, v'_{bc}, and the post-collision angular velocity of the ball, ω, can be computed from Equations (6.40) and (6.41).

$$\omega_b = \frac{5}{7}\frac{v_{cn}}{r_b} = -\frac{5}{7}\frac{v_{cx}\sin\alpha}{r_b} \tag{7.4}$$

$$v'_{bc} = \frac{5}{7}v_{cn} = -\frac{5}{7}v_{cx}\sin\alpha \tag{7.5}$$

As we saw in Chapter 6, the post-collision normal velocity component and angular velocity are independent of the coefficient of friction between the ball and club face. The spin rate only depends on the initial club velocity, v_{cx}, and ball radius, r_b.

The collision between the ball and club face will change the velocity of both the ball and club head. The post-velocity component in Equation (7.5) is designated as v'_{bc} because it represents the post-collision velocity of the ball relative to the club face. It is equal to the difference between the post-collision velocities of the ball, v'_{bn}, and club head, v'_{cn}.

$$v'_{bc} = v'_{cn} - v'_{bn} = -\frac{5}{7}v_{cx}\sin\alpha \tag{7.6}$$

What we really want is the post-collision velocity of the ball in the direction normal to the line of action. To obtain this quantity, we can assume that there is conservation of momentum in the normal direction.

$$m_b v'_{bn} + m_c v'_{cn} = m_c v_{cn} \tag{7.7}$$

Combining Equations (7.6) and (7.7) results in an expression for the post-collision velocity of the golf ball normal to the line of action of the collision. As before, the result is independent of the coefficient of friction between the ball and club face.

$$v'_{bn} = \frac{2}{7} \frac{m_c v_{cn}}{(m_c + m_b)} = -\frac{2}{7} \frac{m_c v_{cx} \sin\alpha}{(m_c + m_b)} \tag{7.8}$$

One thing to keep in mind about the preceding development is that it assumes the golf ball eventually rolls without sliding along the club face. This assumption is good for lower-loft angle clubs. At higher loft angles, 45 degrees and up, the ball may never reach this point and will be in a combined state of sliding and rolling when it leaves the club face.

The last step in the golf ball collision analysis is to convert the post-collision velocities of the golf ball parallel and normal to the line of action back to the standard Cartesian x- and z-components, v_{bx} and v_{bz}. This operation can be performed using the inverse rotation matrix shown in Equation (6.19).

$$v'_{bx} = v'_{bp} \cos\alpha - v'_{bn} \sin\alpha \tag{7.9}$$

$$v'_{bz} = v'_{bp} \sin\alpha + v'_{bn} \cos\alpha \tag{7.10}$$

If you want to get fancy, Equations (7.3), (7.8), (7.9), and (7.10) can be combined into expressions that relate the post-collision x- and z-velocity components of the golf ball to the initial velocity, ball mass, club head mass, coefficient of restitution, and loft angle.

$$v'_{bx} = v_{cx} \frac{m_c}{(m_c + m_b)} \left((1+e)\cos^2\alpha + \frac{2}{7}\sin^2\alpha \right) \tag{7.11}$$

$$v'_{bz} = v_{cx} \frac{m_c}{(m_c + m_b)} \sin\alpha \cos\alpha \left(\frac{5}{7} + e \right) \tag{7.12}$$

A Sample Collision Analysis

The equations developed in the previous section may seem rather complicated, but the process for computing the post-collision velocities of a golf ball is really pretty straightforward. Let's go through an example to see how it all fits together so far. A driver with a club head mass of 0.2 *kg* and a loft angle of 10 degrees strikes a two-piece ball with an impact velocity of 50 *m/s*. Assume the coefficient of restitution between the ball and the club is 0.78. We want to compute the post-collision velocities and spin rate of the ball.

The first step in the process is to compute the velocity components normal and parallel to the line of action for the collision. The parallel and normal velocities of the club head, v_{cp} and v_{cn}, can be obtained from Equations (7.1) and (7.2).

$$v_{cp} = 50\cos\left(\frac{10\pi}{180} \right) = 49.24 \ \frac{m}{s} \tag{7.13}$$

$$v_{cn} = -50\sin\left(\frac{10\pi}{180} \right) = -8.68 \ \frac{m}{s} \tag{7.14}$$

The angles in Equations (7.13) and (7.14) have been converted from degrees to radians. The post-collision velocity of the golf ball along the line of action can be obtained from Equation (7.3).

$$v'_{bp} = \frac{(1+0.78)0.2}{(0.2+0.0459)}49.24 = 71.3 \ \frac{m}{s} \tag{7.15}$$

The post-collision velocity normal to the line of action and the spin rate can be found using Equations (7.4) and (7.8).

$$v'_{bn} = \frac{-2*8.68*0.2}{7*(0.2+0.0459)} = -2.02 \ \frac{m}{s} \tag{7.16}$$

$$\omega_b = -\frac{5*8.68}{7*0.02135} = -290.4 \ \frac{rad}{s} = -46.2 \ \frac{rev}{s} \tag{7.17}$$

The final step in the process is to rotate the post-collision velocity components of the golf ball back into the standard Cartesian reference frame using Equations (7.9) and (7.10).

$$v'_{bx} = 71.3\cos\left(\frac{10\pi}{180}\right) + 2.02\sin\left(\frac{10\pi}{180}\right) = 70.6 \ \frac{m}{s} \tag{7.18}$$

$$v'_{bz} = 71.3\sin\left(\frac{10\pi}{180}\right) - 2.02\cos\left(\frac{10\pi}{180}\right) = 10.4 \ \frac{m}{s} \tag{7.19}$$

The initial flight angle of the ball, θ, is defined by the arctangent of the z-component of velocity divide by the x-component of velocity.

$$\theta = \tan^{-1}\left(\frac{10.4}{70.6}\right) = 8.4 \ degrees \tag{7.20}$$

Since the impact occurred in the x-z plane, the pre- and post-collision velocity of the golf ball in the y-direction is zero. Because of friction, the initial flight angle of the golf ball is not equal to the loft angle of the club (10 degrees) but instead has a slightly lower value of 8.4 degrees. The final results could also have been obtained directly from Equations (7.11) and (7.12).

Impact Modeling Decisions

So far in this section, we have discussed how to model an idealized collision between a golf ball and club face where the line of action for the impact is in the x-z plane and the spin axis is aligned with the y-axis. Now as we all know, the idealized golf swing rarely ever happens. The club face can strike the ball at an angle, causing the ball to slice or hook. Depending on the mechanics of the swing, the loft of the club face when it strikes the ball can be greater or smaller than its nominal value. The club face can "top" the ball, striking it above the centerline, or it can dig into the ground before impact, causing the impact velocity to decrease.

Because there are so many variables with a golf swing, for game programming purposes it may be best to start with the idealized swing and then add variations to the loft, club speed, and axis of rotation to account for "mistakes" in the swing. You could also give the option of intentionally adding a slice or hook as professional golfers sometimes do to curve a shot around a "dogleg" in the golf course.

Modeling the Golf Ball in Flight

The impact with the golf club determines the initial velocity (both angular and translational) of the golf ball. Once the ball is in flight, it behaves like a projectile. The force diagram for the golf ball is shown in Figure 7-6. It will experience acceleration in the vertical direction due to Earth's gravity. Aerodynamic drag and wind will affect the flight of a golf ball, as will the Magnus force due to spin, so these effects will have to be incorporated into the physical model. In Figure 7-6, the golf ball is spinning in the counterclockwise direction (i.e., backspin), so the Magnus force will be directed upward.

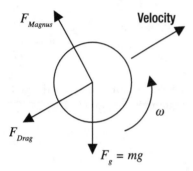

Figure 7-6. *Force diagram for a golf ball in flight*

The basic governing equations and modeling ideas for all of the forces experienced by a golf ball were covered in Chapter 5, but we will spend a little time discussing how to model the Magnus force on a golf ball.

Computing the Magnus Force for a Spinning Golf Ball

In Chapter 5, you learned how a spinning object generates a lifting force known as Magnus force. Golf balls can have very high spin rates, so the effects of the resulting Magnus force must be included in a golf simulation. In Chapter 5, an equation was developed that represented the Magnus force generated by a spinning object as a function of the density of air, ρ, the frontal area of the object, A, the square of the velocity magnitude, v, and a quantity known as the lift coefficient, C_L.

$$F_M = \frac{1}{2} C_L \rho v^2 A \qquad (7.21)$$

The density, velocity, and frontal area of the golf ball are readily obtainable, but what value should be given to the lift coefficient? The simplest approximation, and the one predicted by the Bernoulli equation, is to set the lift coefficient for a sphere equal to the ratio of the radius multiplied by the angular velocity divided by the translational velocity.

$$C_L = \frac{r\omega}{v} \qquad (7.22)$$

The ratio in Equation (7.22) is also known as the **rotational spin ratio**. According to Bernoulli's equation, the Magnus force lift coefficient is equal to the rotational spin ratio. But how good is this approximation? The results from Equation (7.22) can be compared against experimental measurements of the lifting force exerted on a spinning golf ball. Figure 7-7 displays the experimental measurements of lift coefficient on a standard dimpled golf ball as a function of the rotational spin ratio.[2] Also shown in Figure 7-7 is the lift coefficient predicted by Equation (7.22), which is a straight line.

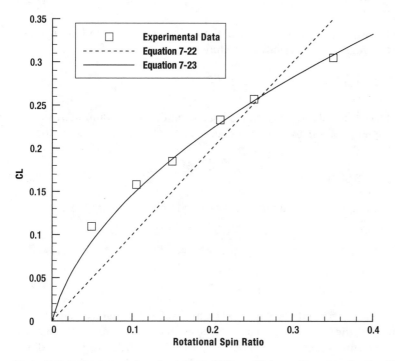

Figure 7-7. *Experimental and computed lift coefficients for a standard golf ball*

In looking at Figure 7-7, we can see that the Bernoulli equation approximation for the lift coefficient, shown in Equation (7.22), underpredicts the lift coefficient for rotational spin ratios below 0.3 and overpredicts the lift coefficient for rotational spin ratios above 0.3. A more accurate estimation of C_L can be obtained by using the expression shown in Equation (7.23), which models the relationship between rotational spin ratio and C_L as a curve.

$$C_L = -0.05 + \sqrt{0.0025 + 0.36\left(\frac{r\omega}{v}\right)} \tag{7.23}$$

The values from Equation (7.23) are also shown in Figure 7-7 and are closer to the experimental values. One thing to keep in mind when using Equation (7.23) is that it is based on the absolute magnitude of the angular and translational velocities. When you plug the value of the rotational spin ratio into Equation (7.23), make sure the value is positive.

Let's use Equations (7.21) and (7.23) to compute the Magnus force and acceleration on the golf ball analyzed in the "A Sample Collision Analysis" section. The golf ball had post-collision x- and z-components of velocity equal to 70.6 and 10.4 *m/s*. The post-collision angular velocity of the ball was –290.4 *rad/s*. We'll assume the air density is equal to the sea-level value of 1.225 *kg/m³*. The Magnus force equation is based on the translational velocity magnitude, v, which can be found from Equation (5.15).

$$v = \sqrt{70.6^2 + 10.4^2} = 71.4 \ \frac{m}{s} \tag{7.24}$$

The rotational spin ratio is equal to the product of the golf ball radius, r_b, and the angular velocity, ω, divided by the translational velocity magnitude.

$$\frac{r_b \omega}{v} = -\frac{0.02135 * 290.4}{71.4} = -0.087 \tag{7.25}$$

The Magnus force lift coefficient is found by plugging the rotational spin ratio value shown in Equation (7.25) into Equation (7.23), making sure to use the absolute value of the rotational spin ratio.

$$C_L = -0.05 + \sqrt{0.0025 + 0.36(0.087)} = 0.134 \tag{7.26}$$

The magnitude of the Magnus force can now be computed from Equation (7.21).

$$F_M = \frac{1}{2} C_L \rho v^2 A = 0.6 \ N \tag{7.27}$$

A Golf Game

Let's take what we've covered so far and develop a golf game. Similar to the golf games that were developed in Chapter 5, the object of this game will be to hit the ball onto the green from a certain distance away. The user selects a club and an impact velocity. Other text fields allow the user to specify the wind velocity, air density, distance to hole, and spin axis. If your shot lands within 8 *m* of the hole, you are "on the green" and you win. A sample screen shot of the GUI is shown in Figure 7-8.

The nice thing about the Golf Game from a code developer point of view is that most of the work has already been done. A class named GolfBall will be written to represent the golf ball. The GolfBall class will be written as a subclass of the SpinProjectile class that was developed in Chapter 5. The Golf Game GUI is very similar to the GUIs for the Golf Games developed in Chapter 5 except that here the user chooses a club rather than specifying the initial velocity components of the ball.

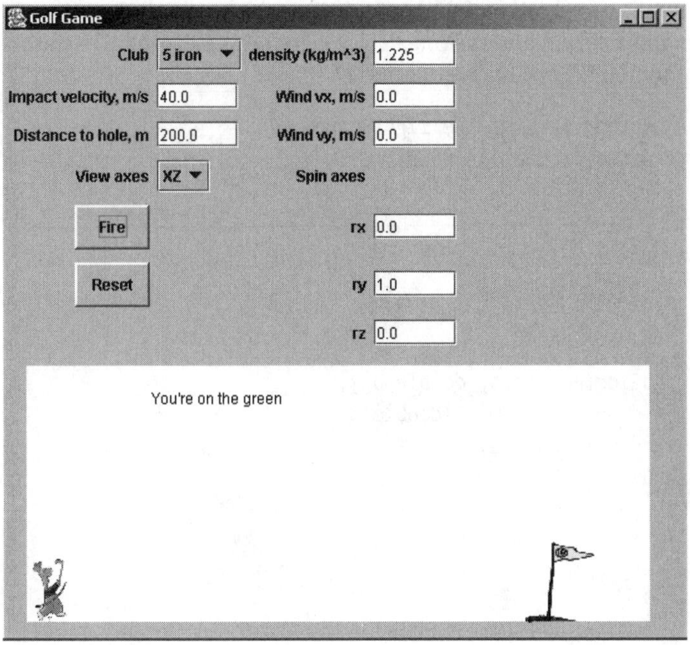

Figure 7-8. *Golf simulator screen shot*

Let's start the discussion with the GolfBall class. The only reason to even write a GolfBall class is to use Equation (7.23) to compute the lift coefficient for the Magnus force term. Everything else about the class will be the same as in the SpinProjectile class. The GolfBall class doesn't declare any new fields, and its constructor simply calls the SpinProjectile constructor.

```
public class GolfBall extends SpinProjectile
{
  public GolfBall(double x0, double y0, double z0,
            double vx0, double vy0, double vz0, double time,
            double mass, double area, double density, double Cd,
            double windVx, double windVy, double rx, double ry,
            double rz, double omega, double radius) {
    // Call the SpinProjectile class constructor.
    super(x0, y0, z0, vx0, vy0, vz0, time, mass, area,
        density, Cd, windVx, windVy, rx, ry, rz, omega, radius);
  }
```

The GolfBall class declares its own version of the getRightHandSide method. The only significant difference between this method and the one declared in the SpinProjectile class is that the lift coefficient is computed according to Equation (7.23).

```
//  The getRightHandSide() method returns the right-hand
//  sides of the six first-order projectile ODEs.
//  q[0] = vx = dxdt
//  q[1] = x
//  q[2] = vy = dydt
//  q[3] = y
//  q[4] = vz = dzdt
//  q[5] = z
public double[] getRightHandSide(double s, double q[],
                            double deltaQ[], double ds,
                            double qScale) {
  double dQ[] = new double[6];
  double newQ[] = new double[6];

  //  Compute the intermediate values of the
  //  dependent variables.
  for(int i=0; i<6; ++i) {
    newQ[i] = q[i] + qScale*deltaQ[i];
  }

  //  Declare some convenience variables representing
  //  the intermediate values of velocity.
  double vx = newQ[0];
  double vy = newQ[2];
  double vz = newQ[4];

  //  Compute the apparent velocities by subtracting
  //  the wind velocity components from the projectile
  //  velocity components.
  double vax = vx - getWindVx();
  double vay = vy - getWindVy();
  double vaz = vz;

  //  Compute the apparent velocity magnitude. The 1.0e-8 term
  //  ensures there won't be a divide by zero later on
  //  if all of the velocity components are zero.
  double va = Math.sqrt(vax*vax + vay*vay + vaz*vaz) + 1.0e-8;
```

```
//  Compute the total drag force and the dirctional
//  drag components.
double Fd = 0.5*getDensity()*getArea()*getCd()*va*va;
double Fdx = -Fd*vax/va;
double Fdy = -Fd*vay/va;
double Fdz = -Fd*vaz/va;

//  Compute the velocity magnitude.
double v = Math.sqrt(vx*vx + vy*vy + vz*vz) + 1.0e-8;

//  Evaluate the Magnus force terms.
double Cl = -0.05 + Math.sqrt(0.0025 +
                0.36*Math.abs(getRadius()*getOmega()/v));
double Fm = 0.5*getDensity()*getArea()*Cl*v*v;
double Fmx =  (vy*getRz() - getRy()*vz)*Fm/v;
double Fmy = -(vx*getRz() - getRx()*vz)*Fm/v;
double Fmz =  (vx*getRy() - getRx()*vy)*Fm/v;

//  Compute the right-hand sides of the six ODEs.
dQ[0] = ds*(Fdx + Fmx)/getMass();
dQ[1] = ds*vx;
dQ[2] = ds*(Fdy + Fmy)/getMass();
dQ[3] = ds*vy;
dQ[4] = ds*(G + (Fdz + Fmz)/getMass());
dQ[5] = ds*vz;

    return dQ;
  }
}
```

The GUI for this version of the Golf Game is implemented in a class named GolfGame.
The GolfGame class is so similar to the GUI classes developed in Chapter 5 that only the
actionPerformed method that is called when the Fire button is pressed will be discussed here.
The first thing the method does is to define some parameters for the golf ball and extract the
input values for velocities, density, spin axis, and distance-to-hole from the text fields. The drag
coefficient for the golf ball is assumed to be a constant 0.22.

```
//  The actionPerformed() method is called when
//  the Fire button is pressed.
public void actionPerformed(ActionEvent event) {

  //  Define golf ball parameters.
  double ballMass = 0.0459;
  double radius = 0.02135;
  double area = Math.PI*radius*radius;
  double cd = 0.22;   //  Drag coefficient
  double e = 0.78;    //  Coefficient of restitution
```

```
//  Get some initial quantities from the text fields.
double velocity = Double.parseDouble(velocityTextField.getText());
double density = Double.parseDouble(densityTextField.getText());
distanceToHole = Double.parseDouble(distanceTextField.getText());
double windVx = Double.parseDouble(windVxTextField.getText());
double windVy = Double.parseDouble(windVyTextField.getText());
double rx = Double.parseDouble(rxTextField.getText());
double ry = Double.parseDouble(ryTextField.getText());
double rz = Double.parseDouble(rzTextField.getText());
```

The club head mass and loft angle are set according to the club the user has selected. The mass and angle values are those shown in Table 7-2.

```
//  Set the club mass and loft based on the combo box
//  selection.
double clubMass;
double loft;
String club = (String)clubComboBox.getSelectedItem();
if ( club.equals("Driver") ) {
  clubMass = 0.2;
  loft = 11.0;
}
else if ( club.equals("3 wood") ) {
  clubMass = 0.208;
  loft = 15.0;
}
else if ( club.equals("3 iron") ) {
  clubMass = 0.239;
  loft = 21.0;
}
else if ( club.equals("5 iron") ) {
  clubMass = 0.253;
  loft = 27.0;
}
else if ( club.equals("7 iron") ) {
  clubMass = 0.267;
  loft = 35.0;
}
else {
  clubMass = 0.281;
  loft = 43.0;
}
```

The method then computes the post-collision velocities in the x- and z-directions for the golf ball according to the process outlined in the "A Sample Collision Analysis" presented earlier in the chapter.

```
// Convert the loft angle from degrees to radians and
// assign values to some convenience variables.
loft = loft*Math.PI/180.0;
double cosL = Math.cos(loft);
double sinL = Math.sin(loft);

// Calculate the pre-collision velocities normal
// and parallel to the line of action.
double vcp = cosL*velocity;
double vcn = -sinL*velocity;

// Compute the post-collision velocity of the ball
// along the line of action.
double vbp = (1.0+e)*clubMass*vcp/(clubMass+ballMass);

// Compute the post-collision velocity of the ball
// perpendicular to the line of action.
double vbn = (2.0/7.0)*clubMass*vcn/(clubMass+ballMass);

// Compute the initial spin rate assuming ball is
// rolling without sliding.
double omega = (5.0/7.0)*vcn/radius;

// Rotate post-collision ball velocities back into
// standard Cartesian frame of reference. Because the
// line of action was in the xy plane, the z-velocity
// is zero.
double vx0 = cosL*vbp - sinL*vbn;
double vy0 = 0.0;
double vz0 = sinL*vbp + cosL*vbn;
```

Once the initial translational and angular velocities have been determined, a GolfBall object is created. The start method is called on a Timer object to start the simulation.

```
// Create a GolfBall object representing the golf ball.
golfball = new GolfBall(0.0, 0.0, 0.0, vx0, vy0, vz0,
    0.0, ballMass, area, density, cd, windVx, windVy,
    rx, ry, rz, omega, radius);

// Update the display.
updateDisplay();

// Start the box sliding using a Timer object
// to slow down the action.
gameTimer.start();
}
```

When you play the Golf Game, select different clubs and impact velocities and see what happens. Keep in mind that because the clubs are different lengths that a realistic impact velocity will be different for different clubs. A professional golfer might be able to swing a driver such that the impact velocity is 50 *m/s*, but he or she (or you) would be unable to swing a 7 iron with the same impact velocity.

An interesting effect occurs if the impact velocity is set too high for a given loft angle. The spin rate will be high enough such that the resulting Magnus force will significantly exceed the force of gravity over part of the flight of the ball, causing a sharper peak in the ball trajectory. This type of shot is known as a "blow-up" shot, and a typical example is shown in Figure 7-9.

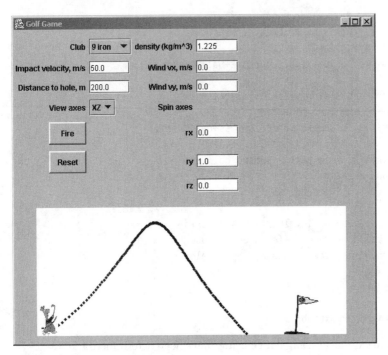

Figure 7-9. *A blow-up shot results from too much spin on the ball.*

Putting

At the end of every golf hole is an area of tightly mowed grass known as the **green**. The objective of golf is to hit the ball into a hole located on the green. Once the ball is on the green (or sometimes even if it is off the green), a shot called a putt is performed to roll the ball towards the hole. Putters are clubs with low loft angles—3 degrees is a typical number. The putter club head mass can vary quite a bit, but a typical value is 0.33 *kg*. The green upon which the ball rolls is an area of closely mowed grass that can slope in any direction. The movement of the golf ball after it is putted can be broken up into three segments—the impact phase, the skid phase, and the roll phase.

The Impact Phase

The impact of the putter and golf ball can be modeled in exactly the same way as the impact of the ball and any other club. For the time being, we will assume that the green is horizontal and at the point of impact the head of the putter is in the x-direction. The line of action for the collision will be equal to the loft angle of the putter. The post-impact velocity normal and parallel to the line of action can be determined from Equations (7.3) and (7.8). As before, the velocities are a function of the mass of the putter head and ball, the impact velocity, the coefficient of restitution, and the loft of the putter.

$$v'_{bp} = \frac{(1+e)m_c}{m_b + m_c} v_{cx} \cos\alpha \tag{7.28}$$

$$v'_{bn} = -\frac{2}{7} \frac{m_c v_{cx} \sin\alpha}{(m_c + m_b)} \tag{7.29}$$

If the putter has a nonzero loft angle, the ball will be given a small spin rate due to the collision. The spin rate is a function of the impact velocity, loft angle, and ball radius, and can be calculated from Equation (7.4).

$$\omega_{b0} = -\frac{5}{7} \frac{v_{cx} \sin\alpha}{r_b} \tag{7.30}$$

The normal component of velocity, v'_{bn}, is usually small enough compared to the parallel component that it can be ignored. The post-collision velocity of the ball in the x-direction can be assumed to be equal to the post-collision velocity along the line of action.

$$v'_{bx} = v'_{bp} \tag{7.31}$$

If the putter is lofted, the ball will initially take a small hop. The distance of the hop could be determined from Equations (7.28) and (7.29), and the basic projectile relations presented in Chapter 5, but the final equations become pretty complicated, with lots of sine and cosine terms. The bottom line is this: depending on the putter loft angle and the speed of impact, a golf ball will usually hop between 0.04 and 0.08 m. For game programming purposes, you can assume a middle range value for the hop, say 0.06 m, and proceed to the skid phase calculations.

The Skid Phase

After the collision with the putter face and the initial hop, the ball skids along the green for a certain distance. As computed during the collision phase, the translational velocity at the start of the skid is equal to v'_{bx} and an angular velocity equal to ω_{b0}. When the ball skids along the putting green, a friction force develops between the ball and the ground in the direction opposite to the motion of the ball. The magnitude of the friction force is equal to the normal force exerted by the ball multiplied by the coefficient of friction. A schematic of the forces and velocities of the ball at the start of the skid is shown in Figure 7-10.

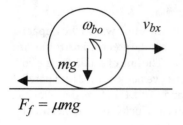

Figure 7-10. *The forces and velocities at the beginning of the skid phase*

We want to determine the time it takes until the golf ball is rolling without skidding and the distance it travels during that time. To determine these results, a process similar to the one discussed in the "Collisions with Friction" section of Chapter 6 can be used. The angular velocity of the ball at a given time is equal to the initial angular velocity plus the torque exerted on the golf ball divided by the moment of inertia of the ball.

$$\omega = \omega_{b0} + \frac{\mu m g r}{I} t \tag{7.32}$$

The translational velocity of the golf ball at any point during the skid phase is equal to the initial velocity plus the acceleration due to friction multiplied by the elapsed time. Friction works to slow the ball down, so the acceleration is negative.

$$v = v'_{bx} - \mu g t \tag{7.33}$$

Since we know that the point the ball begins to roll without skidding is when $v = r\omega$, we can use this fact along with Equations (7.32) and (7.33) to obtain an expression for the time that this occurs.

$$t = \frac{2\left(v'_{bx} - r\omega_{b0}\right)}{7\mu g} \tag{7.34}$$

Plugging this time value into Equations (7.32) and (7.33) results in the translational and angular velocity at the point where the ball begins rolling without skidding.

$$v_{br} = \frac{5}{7} v'_{bx} + \frac{2}{7} r\omega_{b0} \tag{7.35}$$

$$\omega_{br} = \frac{v_{br}}{r} = \frac{5}{7} \frac{v'_{bx}}{r} + \frac{2}{7} \omega_{b0} \tag{7.36}$$

Once again, we get the interesting result that the velocities of the ball when it begins to roll without sliding are independent of the coefficient of friction between the ball and green. The distance traveled during the skid phase can be computed from the standard expression relating distance, velocity, and acceleration.

$$x = v'_{bx} t - \frac{1}{2} \mu g t^2 \tag{7.37}$$

In looking at Equation (7.37), we see that the distance traveled during the skid phase does depend on the coefficient of friction between the ball and putting green. The coefficient of sliding friction between the ball and green will typically range from 0.4 to 0.5.[3]

The Rolling Phase

After the skid is complete, we can assume the golf ball to be in a pure rolling motion across the green. Even though the ball is no longer sliding, and therefore there is no force due to sliding friction, the ball will eventually slow down and come to rest. According to Newton's second law, if a body slows down, a force is acting upon it. In this case, the golf ball slows down due to the force of **rolling friction**.

Rolling friction is somewhat misnamed because it really is a force due to the contact of the golf ball and the green. When a golf ball, or any other object, rolls on a surface, both the golf ball and the surface it is rolling on are slightly deformed by the force each object exerts on the other. This deformation moves the effective point of contact between the ball and green slightly forward on the golf ball as shown in Figure 7-11.

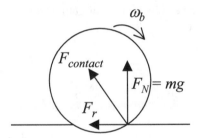

Figure 7-11. *The contact force on a rolling object acts slightly forward of the center of gravity.*

The normal component of the contact force, F_N, is equal to mg (or $mg\cos\theta$ if the ball is rolling on an inclined surface). The parallel component of the contact force, F_r, is known as the force of rolling friction. While it is essentially a contact force, rolling friction is modeled similar to the force of static or sliding friction. The magnitude of the rolling friction force is equal to the normal force exerted on the ball multiplied by the coefficient of rolling friction, μ_r.

$$F_r = \mu_r mg \qquad (7.38)$$

Rolling friction acts to slow a rolling object down. For a ball rolling on a flat surface, the velocity of the golf ball at any time during the roll will be equal to the initial velocity minus the acceleration due to rolling friction.

$$v_b = v_{br} - \mu_r gt \qquad (7.39)$$

The total distance traveled by the golf ball until it stops can be computed from the standard Newtonian mechanics relation.

$$x = v_{br}t + \frac{1}{2}at^2 = \frac{1}{2}\frac{v_{br}^2}{\mu_r g} \qquad (7.40)$$

The coefficient of rolling friction, μ_r, depends on the height of the grass, the type of grass, and the relative dampness of the green. Typically, the value of μ_r might range from 0.05 to 0.075.[4] A dry, tightly mowed green is considered "hard" and would have a lower coefficient of rolling friction, whereas a damp green with longer grass would be considered "soft" and would have a higher coefficient.

Sample Problem: Compute the distance of a putt

Let's take what we have learned about putting and compute how far a typical putted ball will travel. We'll assume that the putting surface is flat. We'll also assume that the putter has a loft of 3 degrees, the mass of the putter head is 0.33 kg, and the coefficient of restitution is 0.78. The impact velocity will be taken to be 1.65 m/s.

We'll start by modeling the collision between the putter and the ball. The post-collision velocity of the ball can be found from Equation (7.3).

$$v'_{bp} = \frac{(1+0.78)0.33}{0.0459+0.33}1.65\cos\left(\frac{3\pi}{180}\right)=2.57\ \frac{m}{s} \tag{7.41}$$

Because the putter loft angle is small, the post-collision velocity in the x-direction will be assumed to be the same as the post-collision normal velocity.

$$v'_{bx} = v'_{bp} = 2.57\ \frac{m}{s} \tag{7.42}$$

The initial spin rate of the ball is determined from Equation (7.4).

$$\omega_{b0} = -\frac{5}{7}*\frac{1.65\sin\left(\frac{3\pi}{180}\right)}{0.02135}=-2.89\ \frac{rad}{s} \tag{7.43}$$

We won't go to the trouble to compute the distance that the ball will hop but will assume it is 0.06 m.

$$x_h = 0.06 \tag{7.44}$$

Now, we'll move on to the skid phase. The angular and x-direction velocities at the end of the skid phase when the ball is in a pure-rolling motion can be computed from Equations (7.35) and (7.36).

$$v_{br} = \frac{5}{7}*2.57-\frac{2}{7}*0.02135*2.89=1.82\ \frac{m}{s} \tag{7.45}$$

$$\omega_{br} = \frac{v_{br}}{r} = \frac{1.82}{0.02135}=85.2\ \frac{rad}{s} \tag{7.46}$$

The elapsed time during which the ball will be skidding can be found from Equation (7.34). We'll assume that the coefficient of sliding friction between the ball and green is 0.5.

$$t = \frac{2(2.57+0.02135*2.89)}{7*0.5*9.8}=0.15\ s \tag{7.47}$$

The distance the ball will travel during its skid can be determined from Equation (7.37).

$$x_s = 2.57 * 0.15 - \frac{1}{2} * 0.5 * 9.8 * 0.15^2 = 0.33 \ m \tag{7.48}$$

The ball is now rolling, and the distance the ball will travel when it is rolling can be computed from Equation (7.40). We'll assume a medium-hard green with a coefficient of rolling friction of 0.065.

$$x_r = \frac{1}{2} * \frac{1.82^2}{0.065 * 9.8} = 2.6 \ m \tag{7.49}$$

The final distance the putt will travel is the sum of the distances during the collision, skid, and roll phases.

$$x_{putt} = 0.06 + 0.33 + 2.6 = 2.99 \ m \tag{7.50}$$

Slope Effects

Up to now we have been considering the physics of putting on a flat surface. Most greens are not flat, however, but have slopes, ridges, undulations, and other physical features. Accounting for slope does add complexity to a putting simulation, but we have already covered all the necessary elements. The line-of-action vector of the collision is measured relative to the vector parallel to the slope in the direction the ball is struck. For example, if the ball is struck with a 3-degree lofted putter on a 5-degree upslope, the angle of the line of action will be 8 degrees.

If the golf is rolling on a slope, a moment is generated that causes an angular acceleration of the ball. If the ball is hit on a downslope, the moment will cause the ball to roll farther than it would on a flat green, and the opposite is true if the ball is hit on an upslope. If the geometry of the green is complicated, the motion of the putted ball can be quite complicated as well, since the axis of the moment due to slope may be different from the initial roll axis of the ball.

Soccer

Soccer, or football as it is known in most of the world, is probably the most widely played, widely watched sport in the world. When the World Cup Championships are held every four years, well over one billion people watch the competition on television. In this book, the sport will be referred to as soccer to differentiate it from American football, which will be discussed later in this chapter.

People have been playing games involving kicking a ball around for over 2000 years. During the Han Dynasty of China in 2nd–3rd century BC, men kicked a leather ball stuffed with feathers and hair into a net attached to a bamboo cane as part of their military training. An early brand of soccer (called football) was played in the British Isles during medieval times.

Modern soccer dates its origin to 1863 in England when a set of rules was set down to standardize the various incarnations of football that were being played at that time. The rules forbid tripping, shin-kicking, and other acts of violence that had often been a part of early versions of soccer. With some dissension, it was also agreed that players could not carry the ball. Those who were unhappy with this rule split off to form the sport of rugby. The now mostly standardized sport of soccer quickly spread outside Great Britain to Europe, South America, and eventually all over world.

While there are a lot of other aspects to the game of soccer, such as headers, throw ins, and the like, in this chapter we will focus on the physics of a kicked soccer ball and how to model the trajectory of a soccer ball in flight. As was the case with modeling the flight of a golf ball, we already know everything we need to model a soccer ball in flight. To start our soccer simulation, let's go over some information about the size, weight, and other specifications of the equipment used to play soccer.

Equipment Specifications

The equipment used in soccer is pretty simple. All you need are a ball, a field, some chalk or paint to draw lines, and some goal posts. As shown in Figure 7-12, a soccer ball is not a smooth sphere but rather a shape known as a truncated icosahedron (yikes!). It has 12 pentagon- and 20 hexagon-shaped patches built into the surface of the ball. The specifications of an official soccer ball are controlled by the Federation Internationale de Football Association (FIFA), which is the governing body for international soccer. According to FIFA, the ball will have a circumference of between 0.68 and 0.70 m and a mass between 0.41 and 0.45 kg. The corresponding radius of an official soccer ball ranges from 0.108 to 0.111 m.

Figure 7-12. *A typical soccer ball with hexagon- and pentagon-shaped patches*

Soccer is played on a field also known as the pitch. Just as with the soccer ball, FIFA allows a range of field dimensions for an "official" soccer field. For standard play, the length of the field must be between 90 and 120 m, and the width of the field must be between 45 and 90 m. For international match play, the field specifications are a bit tighter. The length of the field must be between 100 and 110 m and the width can range from 64 to 75 m. A soccer field also has various lines, circles, and boxes drawn on it. We won't go into detail on all of them here, but you can find out exactly what lines should be drawn on a soccer field from the FIFA website at www.fifa.com.

The objective in soccer is to kick the ball into the opponent's goal. According to FIFA, the distance between the goal posts should be 7.32 m. The distance from the lower edge of the crossbar between the goal posts to the ground should be 2.44 m (8 ft). The goal posts and crossbars themselves must be less than 0.12 m wide.

Modeling the Impact of Ball and Foot

The initial phase of the flight of a soccer ball is conceptually similar to the flight of a golf ball. In soccer, there is an initial impact of the player's foot with the ball, creating a force impulse along the line of action of the collision. The ball will also be given a spin due to friction between the foot and ball. However, modeling the collision between the foot and ball is complicated because the shoe worn over the foot is not a simple shape. To properly determine the line of action of the collision, it is necessary to know where on the foot and where on the ball the collision occurs.

Fortunately, for game programming purposes, there really is no reason to try to model the impact between the foot and soccer ball. It is enough to simply specify the initial velocity components, spin rate, and spin axis of the ball. A top-rate professional soccer player can kick a soccer ball such that it has an initial velocity of 25–35 *m/s* with an initial spin rate of 8–10 *rev/s*. You can use these values as upper limits in your game simulations.

Modeling the Soccer Ball in Flight

Just like a golf ball or a cannonball, once a soccer ball leaves the ground, it's a projectile and is subject to the forces caused by gravity, aerodynamic drag, wind, and spin. The gravity force is constant and acts in the vertical direction, as always. The force due to wind and spin can be treated the same as we have done previously in this book. The force due to aerodynamic drag, however, is a bit more complicated for soccer balls, because the differences between laminar and turbulent drag must be taken into account.

Laminar and Turbulent Drag

We learned in Chapter 5 that there are basically two ways that air can flow over an object. Laminar flow is when the air flows smoothly over the object and generally speaking occurs at low Reynolds number conditions. As the Reynolds number increases, a point is reached where the flow no longer smoothly travels over the object but instead becomes chaotic. This condition is known as turbulent flow. The laminar/turbulent distinction has significance for computing aerodynamic drag because the drag over an object is higher for laminar flow than it is for turbulent flow.

As with all of the other projectiles we have studied, the force on soccer ball due to aerodynamic drag is typically expressed as a function of the density of the air, the square of the velocity of the ball, the frontal area of the ball, and a quantity known as the drag coefficient.

$$F_D = \frac{1}{2}\rho v^2 A C_D \tag{7.51}$$

Researchers at the University of Sheffield[5] performed wind tunnel tests to determine the drag coefficient of a nonspinning soccer ball as a function of Reynolds number. The results are shown in Figure 7-13. At lower Reynolds numbers, the flow is laminar and the drag coefficient value is about 0.47. When the Reynolds number reaches a value of approximately 100,000, the flow begins to transition from laminar to turbulent flow and the drag coefficient decreases. At a Reynolds number of 130,000–140,000 the flow around the soccer ball is fully turbulent, and the drag coefficient levels off at a value of about 0.22.

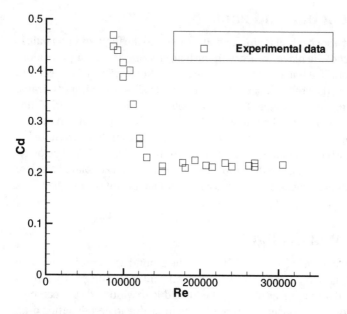

Figure 7-13. *Drag coefficient of a nonspinning soccer ball*

The question now becomes which drag coefficient should be used—the laminar one or the turbulent one? The answer is maybe one, maybe the other depending on the velocity of the soccer ball. As we saw in Chapter 5, the Reynolds number is the ratio of the air density, object velocity, and characteristic length divided by the air viscosity.

$$\text{Re} = \frac{\rho v L}{\mu} \qquad (7.52)$$

For soccer balls the characteristic length, L, is taken to be the diameter of the ball. The viscosity of a fluid can be thought of as a measure of how easily an object can move through a fluid. The viscosity of maple syrup, for instance, would be quite high. The viscosity of air at low-to-moderate temperatures can be approximated using the relation shown in Equation (7.53).

$$\mu = 1.458e - 6 \frac{T^{1.5}}{T + 110.4} \quad \frac{kg}{m - s} \qquad (7.53)$$

Let's use Equations (7.52) and (7.53) to compute the Reynolds number of a soccer ball flying through the air at various velocities at sea level where the temperature is 294 K (70°F). The density of the air at is 1.2 kg/m^3 and the viscosity is 1.82e − 5 kg/m-s. The Reynolds number at these conditions for various velocities using the diameter of the ball as the characteristic length is shown in Table 7-3.

Table 7-3. *Reynolds Number for a Typical Soccer Ball*

Velocity (*m/s*)	Reynolds Number
3.0	45300
5.0	75500
7.0	105700
9.0	136000
10.0	151000
15.0	226500
20.0	302000

In comparing the values shown in Table 7-3 with the drag coefficient data shown in Figure 7-11, it is clear that at ball velocities of greater than 9.0 *m/s* the flow around the ball will be fully turbulent, and the lower drag coefficient value of approximately 0.22 can be applied. At velocities between 9.0 and 7.0 *m/s*, the flow is transitioning from turbulent to laminar flow, and the drag coefficient will be between 0.22 and 0.47. At velocities below 7.0 *m/s*, the flow around the ball is fully laminar, and the drag coefficient will be about 0.47.

Now it is perfectly conceivable for a soccer ball to start its flight at a velocity faster than 9 *m/s* and slow down during its flight to a velocity of less than 7 *m/s*. When this happens, the ball experiences all three flight regimes during its flight—turbulent, transitional, and laminar—and the drag characteristics of the ball will change dramatically as well. Some of the most dramatic shots in soccer history where the ball seemed to change course in midair were made possible by the transition from turbulent to laminar flow.

Building this type of drag coefficient behavior into a soccer simulation is quite easy. The Reynolds number is computed and a simple "if" test is used to determine the drag coefficient value. When the flow is transitioning between laminar and turbulent flow, the drag coefficient can be assumed to vary linearly between 0.47 and 0.22.

$$C_D = 0.47 \qquad\qquad\qquad \text{for } Re < 100000 \tag{7.54a}$$

$$C_D = 0.47 - 0.25 * \frac{Re - 100000}{35000} \qquad \text{for } 100000 < Re < 135000 \tag{7.54b}$$

$$C_D = 0.22 \qquad\qquad\qquad \text{for } Re > 135000 \tag{7.54c}$$

Figure 7-14 shows the linear approximation curves on top of the experimental data. As you can see, the three straight lines do a pretty good job of modeling the soccer ball drag coefficient data.

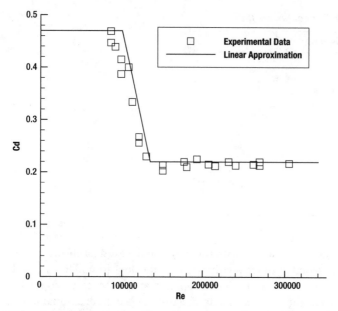

Figure 7-14. *A linear approximation to soccer drag coefficient data*

Magnus Force

Just as it is with golf balls, the force due to spinning, or Magnus force, is very important in modeling the flight of a soccer ball. Players use spin to bend the ball around defenders on penalty or corner kicks. For soccer balls, we'll use the same expression for Magnus force that we used for golf balls in which the magnitude of the force is a function of the density, velocity, frontal area, and a lift coefficient.

$$F_M = \frac{1}{2} C_L \rho v^2 A \tag{7.55}$$

In order to evaluate the Magnus force experienced by a soccer ball, we need to calculate the lift coefficient, C_L. Fortunately, there is some experimental data on which we can base our estimation. Tests were conducted at the University of Sheffield in which a soccer ball was fired at a constant velocity of 18 *m/s* with varying spin rates.[5] The lift and drag coefficients experienced by the ball were measured, and the results are shown in Figure 7-15.

To use this information in a soccer simulation, a function is defined, shown in Equation (7.56), that approximates the lift coefficient experimental data. The results from Equation (7.56) are included in Figure 7-15.

$$C_L = 0.385 \left(\frac{r\omega}{v} \right)^{0.25} \tag{7.56}$$

Just as was the case with modeling golf balls, the expression for computing the lift coefficient of a soccer ball shown in Equation (7.56) is still a function of the rotational spin ratio, but it is more accurate than the Bernoulli approximation of assuming that the lift coefficient is equal to the rotational spin ratio.

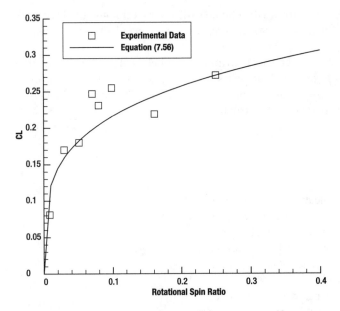

Figure 7-15. *Experimental and computed soccer ball lift coefficients*

Free-Kick Game

Let's use what we know about the flight of a soccer ball to create a "free kick" game. You have been given a free kick at a spot 20 *m* for your opponent's goal. Five defenders (represented by black dots) will attempt to block your shot with their bodies. It is your job to select the initial velocity and spin values of your kick so you can score a goal. The user can also select the spin axis, which will affect the direction of the Magnus force. A sample screen shot of the Free-Kick Game is shown in Figure 7-16.

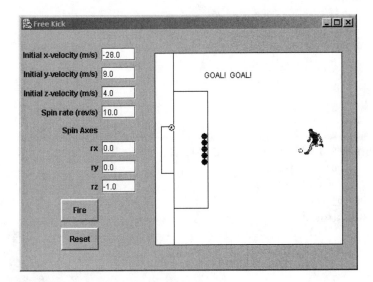

Figure 7-16. *The Free-Kick Game screen shot*

As was the case with the golf simulator we developed earlier in this chapter, the Free-Kick Game requires two classes—the SoccerBall class that represents a soccer ball and a FreeKick class that defines the GUI. We'll start by looking at the SoccerBall class.

Like the GolfBall class, the SoccerBall class is written as a subclass of the SpinProjectile class. The SoccerBall class declares one field that will store the value of the air temperature, which will be used to compute the Reynolds number later in the class. The SoccerBall constructor simply calls the SpinProjectile constructor.

```
public class SoccerBall extends SpinProjectile
{
  private double temperature;

  public SoccerBall(double x0, double y0, double z0,
          double vx0, double vy0, double vz0, double time,
          double mass, double area, double density, double Cd,
          double windVx, double windVy, double rx, double ry,
          double rz, double omega, double radius,
          double temperature) {
    // Call the SpinProjectile class constructor.
    super(x0, y0, z0, vx0, vy0, vz0, time, mass, area,
        density, Cd, windVx, windVy, rx, ry, rz, omega, radius);

    this.temperature = temperature;
  }
```

The getRightHandSide method declared in the SoccerBall class is similar to the SpinProjectile class version with two exceptions: the drag coefficient for the soccer ball is computed according to Equation (7.54), and the lift coefficient for the Magnus force term is determined from Equation (7.56). The first part of the method, which is identical to that of the SpinProjectile class, is not shown.

```
// The getRightHandSide() method returns the right-hand
// sides of the six first-order projectile ODEs.
// q[0] = vx = dxdt
// q[1] = x
// q[2] = vy = dydt
// q[3] = y
// q[4] = vz = dzdt
// q[5] = z
public double[] getRightHandSide(double s, double q[],
                      double deltaQ[], double ds,
                      double qScale) {
  double dQ[] = new double[6];
  double newQ[] = new double[6];
```

```
//  First part of the method code listing not shown …

//  Compute the drag coefficient, which depends on
//  the Reynolds number.
double viscosity = 1.458e-6*Math.pow(temperature,1.5)/
                   (temperature + 110.4);
double Re = getDensity()*v*2.0*getRadius()/viscosity;
double cd;
if ( Re < 1.0e+5 ) {
  cd = 0.47;
}
else if ( Re > 1.35e+5 ) {
  cd = 0.22;
}
else {
  cd = 0.47 - 0.25*(Re - 1.0e+5)/35000.0;
}

//  Compute the total drag force and the directional
//  drag components.
double Fd = 0.5*getDensity()*getArea()*cd*va*va;
double Fdx = -Fd*vax/va;
double Fdy = -Fd*vay/va;
double Fdz = -Fd*vaz/va;

//  Evaluate the Magnus force terms.
double rotSpinRatio = Math.abs(getRadius()*getOmega()/v);
double Cl = 0.385*Math.pow(rotSpinRatio, 0.25);
double Fm = 0.5*getDensity()*getArea()*Cl*v*v;
double Fmx =  (vy*getRz() - getRy()*vz)*Fm/v;
double Fmy = -(vx*getRz() - getRx()*vz)*Fm/v;
double Fmz =  (vx*getRy() - getRx()*vy)*Fm/v;

//  Compute the right-hand sides of the six ODEs.
dQ[0] = ds*(Fdx + Fmx)/getMass();
dQ[1] = ds*vx;
dQ[2] = ds*(Fdy + Fmy)/getMass();
dQ[3] = ds*vy;
dQ[4] = ds*(G + (Fdz + Fmz)/getMass());
dQ[5] = ds*vz;

  return dQ;
 }
}
```

The GUI class for the Free-Kick Game is named FreeKick and is very similar to the GUI for the Golf Game presented earlier in the chapter. When the Fire button is pressed, the actionPerformed method declared in the FreeKick class is called. The first thing the method does is to extract input values from the text fields and compute the angular velocity of the ball.

```
public void actionPerformed(ActionEvent event) {

    //  Extract input values from text fields.
    double vx0 = Double.parseDouble(vxTextField.getText());
    double vy0 = Double.parseDouble(vyTextField.getText());
    double vz0 = Double.parseDouble(vzTextField.getText());
    double spinRate = Double.parseDouble(spinRateTextField.getText());
    double rx = Double.parseDouble(rxTextField.getText());
    double ry = Double.parseDouble(ryTextField.getText());
    double rz = Double.parseDouble(rzTextField.getText());

    //  Calculate the angular velocity from the spin rate.
    double omega = spinRate*2.0*Math.PI;
```

The method sets the initial location of the ball and the values of the density and temperature. Wind was not included as a user input in the GUI (although the SoccerBall class itself does model wind effects), so the wind velocity is set to zero.

```
    //  The ball starts at a spot 18 meters from and directly
    //  in front of the goal.
    double x0 = 23.2;
    double y0 = 15.0;
    double z0 = 0.0;

    //  Set the density to be sea level, the wind
    //  velocity to zero, and temperature to be 294 K.
    double density = 1.2;
    double temperature = 294.0;
    double windVx = 0.0;
    double windVy = 0.0;
```

Values are given to the fields that represent the mass, radius, and area of the soccer ball. The drag coefficient is given a dummy value that is overwritten in the getRightHandSide method of the SoccerBall class.

```
    //  Define some soccer ball variables. The cd value will be
    //  overridden in the getFunction method of the SoccerBall class.
    double ballMass = 0.43;
    double radius = 0.11;
    double area = Math.PI*radius*radius;
    double cd = 0.25;
```

When all of the initial values are specified, a SoccerBall object is created. The start method is called on a Timer object to start the simulation.

```
    // Create a SoccerBall object representing the soccer ball.
    soccerBall = new SoccerBall(x0, y0, z0, vx0, vy0, vz0,
        0.0, ballMass, area, density, cd, windVx, windVy,
        rx, ry, rz, omega, radius, temperature);

    // Update the display.
    updateDisplay();

    // Start the box sliding using a Timer object
    // to slow down the action.
    gameTimer.start();
}
```

Play around with the Free-Kick Game. If the ball crosses the goal line, hits the ground, or hits one of the defenders, the simulation stops. A message written across the GUI informs the user the result of the shot—"Wide left," "Wide right," "GOAL!," and so on. Try scoring goals to both the left and right of the defenders. Because of the way the lift coefficient is computed, the Magnus force term will always be positive. To change the direction that the ball will curve, change the direction of the spin axis. For example, you could change the value of r_z from -1.0 to 1.0.

Basketball

The sport of basketball was invented by Dr. James Naismith. In 1891 at the YMCA Training School in Springfield, Massachusetts, Dr. Naismith was looking for a game that students could play indoors when it was too cold outside for them to play. He was interested in creating a game in which success would be based on skill rather than on brute strength. The first basketball game was played using a soccer ball and two peach baskets as goals.

From these rather humble beginnings, basketball has grown into an international sport played and watched by millions of people. In thinking about the sport in terms of game programming, basketball is similar to the other sports we have studied in this chapter in that it involves throwing and bouncing a ball. We'll start our investigation in building a basketball simulation by looking at the equipment that is used to play the game.

Equipment Specifications

Basketball, like soccer, is a relatively simple game to play in that it doesn't require much equipment. All you need is a ball, a flat area called the **court**, and two (or even just one) baskets. There are at least three standards for determining the specifications of the ball, court, and basket for men's basketball. Additional standards exist for women's play. In this section, details will be provided according to the National Basketball Association (NBA), Federation Internationale de Basketball (FIBA), and NCAA college specifications.

The Ball

The circumference, radius, and mass of a regulation men's basketball, as shown in Figure 7-17, depends on whether the NBA, FIBA, or NCAA standards are used. There are slight differences between them, and these are highlighted in Table 7-4. The values shown in Table 7-4 are for men's basketballs. The regulation ball for women is slightly smaller and lighter. The exact specifications for women's balls can be found at the WNBA, FIBA, and NCAA websites.

Figure 7-17. *An NBA regulation basketball*

Table 7-4. *The Radius, Diameter, and Mass of Regulation Men's Basketballs*

	FIBA	NBA	NCAA
Circumference (m)	0.78	0.749–0.762	0.76
Radius (m)	0.124	0.119–0.121	0.121
Mass (kg)	0.567–0.650	0.567–0.624	0.624

The Court

Basketball is played on a rectangular area known as the court. In a full-court game, the court would be divided into halves with a basket at either end. A half-court game, as the name implies, is played on only half of the court. The lines at either end of the court are known as the end lines. Surrounding the basket is a smaller rectangle known as the lane. The back end of the lane is known as the free-throw line where players can take a free shot in certain situations if they are fouled. A general schematic of the area of the court around the basket is shown in Figure 7-18.

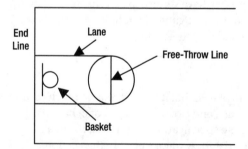

Figure 7-18. *A schematic of the location of the basket, lane, and free-throw line*

The size and location of the various elements of a basketball court depend on whether the FIBA, NBA, or NCAA standards are used. Some of the more important court dimensions are listed in Table 7-5. The free-throw line is along the back edge of the lane, so it would be 5.79–5.8 meters from the end line. Another feature of a basketball court is a 3-point line that is drawn a certain distance around the location of the hoop. If a player makes a basket from beyond the 3-point line, it is worth 3 points instead of 2.

Table 7-5. *Court Dimensions*

	FIBA	NBA	NCAA
Court length (*m*)	28	28.65	28.65
Court width (*m*)	15	15.24	15.24
Lane length (*m*)	5.8	5.79	5.79
Lane width (*m*)	6.0	4.88	3.66
3-point line distance (*m*)	6.25	6.71–7.24	6.02

The Basket and Backboard

The objective in basketball is to shoot or dunk the ball through a basket that consists of a metal ring, also known as the hoop, and a net that is suspended below the hoop. The basic schematic of the basket and backboard is shown in Figure 7-19. The basket is attached to a backboard that is either at the top of a metal post or suspended from the ceiling. The basket hoop is 5.79 *m* (10 *ft*) above the court, and the center of it is located at a distance of 1.6 *m* from the end line. The backboard is a flat surface placed behind the basket to allow for bank shots and to help keep the ball in the field of play.

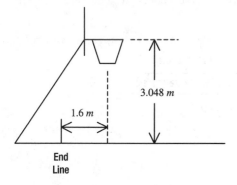

Figure 7-19. *Basket and backboard schematics*

The basic dimensions and locations of the basket and backboard are shown in Table 7-6. The term "hoop diameter" refers to the diameter of the metal circle that forms the basket hoop.

Table 7-6. *Basket and Backboard Dimensions*

	FIBA	NBA/NCAA
Basket inside diameter (*m*)	0.45–0.475	0.4572
Hoop diameter (*m*)	0.016–0.02	0.016–0.02
Backboard height (*m*)	1.05	1.07
Backboard width (*m*)	1.8	1.83

Modeling the Jump Shot

The jump shot is the most common shot in basketball. The shooter jumps in the air and the ball is released above the shooter's head towards the basket. In this section, we develop a model to simulate the flight of a jump shot. Creating a basketball simulation is similar in some ways to creating a golf or soccer simulation. When a basketball leaves the shooter's hand, it becomes a projectile and may be subject to the forces due to gravity, aerodynamic drag, wind, and spin. However, the velocities and spin rates of a basketball are significantly lower than those experienced by golf or soccer balls. Before we can create a jump shot model, we need to evaluate which forces need to be considered.

Evaluating the Forces on a Basketball in Flight

Let's compute the forces experienced by a basketball traveling through the air at 7.5 m/s, approximately the velocity one would use when trying to make a jump shot from a distance of 5 m. The mass and radius of the ball are 0.62 kg and 0.12 m respectively, and the density of the air is 1.2 kg/m^3. We'll assume that the coefficient of drag for the basketball is 0.5 and that the ball is spinning at 1.5 rev/s when it leaves the shooter's hand. The lift coefficient for the Magnus force due to spin is set equal to the rotational spin ratio, which is equal to 0.15.

The forces and accelerations due to gravity, drag, and spin can be computed using the equations presented in this chapter. We'll ignore the effects of wind by assuming that the basketball game is being played indoors. The results for the theoretical jump shot are shown in Table 7-7.

Table 7-7. *Force and Acceleration Components Acting on a Basketball*

Force Type	Force Value (N)	Acceleration Value (m/s^2)
Gravity	$F_g = mg = -6.08$	$a_g = g = -9.81$
Drag	$F_D = \dfrac{1}{2}C_D\rho v^2 A = 0.76$	$a_D = 1.23$
Spin	$F_M = \dfrac{1}{2}C_L\rho v^2 A = 0.23$	$a_M = 0.37$

Under these conditions, the acceleration on the basketball due to aerodynamic drag is equal to 12.5% of the gravitational acceleration value. Some basketball simulations ignore the effects of drag on the ball. Since we already have the DragProjectile class written, we will include drag in our basketball simulation.

The acceleration due to spin, on the other hand, is less than 4% of the gravitational acceleration, so it can safely be ignored. Even though spin doesn't really affect the flight of the basketball, there are two reasons spin is put on a basketball during a jump shot. The first reason is that the spin is a natural consequence of the one-handed jump shot where the ball rolls off the fingers. The second reason is that spin can help "soften" the bounce off of the top of the hoop and background. The spin reduces the rebound angle and makes it more likely that the ball will bounce into the basket.

Determining If a Shot Is Good

One element that is important to a basketball simulation is a way to determine whether a shot is good. One way to accomplish this objective is by the knowledge that if a shot is good, the center of the basketball must travel through the hoop. Consider the schematic shown in Figure 7-20. The radius of the hoop is approximately 0.23 *m*, and the radius of the ball is about 0.12 *m*. Therefore, the center of the basketball doesn't have to travel right through the center of the hoop, but can be 0.11 *m* away in any direction. Actually, the margin of error is larger than 0.11 *m* because glancing impacts with the hoop will cause the ball to fall through the hoop.

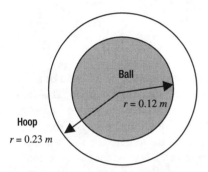

Figure 7-20. *For a shot to be good, it must travel through the hoop.*

Modeling Backboard Impacts

Another important element of basketball simulations is to model impacts that might occur between the ball and backboard. The simplest way to model this situation is to assume a friction-less collision between the ball and backboard. If the x-coordinate direction is down the length of the court (perpendicular to the backboard), then the y- and x-components of the ball velocity would be unchanged by the collision. The post-collision velocity in the x-direction would be equal to the opposite of the pre-collision velocity multiplied by a coefficient of restitution.

$$v_x' = -ev_x \qquad (7.57)$$

The coefficient of restitution for a basketball is about 0.75. Equation (7.57) does not take into account the effects of spin, which might change the post-collision velocities in all three directions.

A Free-Throw Game

Let's use what we know about the flight of a basketball to develop a game that simulates a player taking a free throw. A screen shot from the Free-Throw Game is shown in Figure 7-21. The player is assumed to be facing directly at the basket, so the motion of the basketball is restricted to the x-z plane. The user selects the initial velocity and angle of the ball. When the Fire button is pressed, the shot is taken and the result printed on the screen.

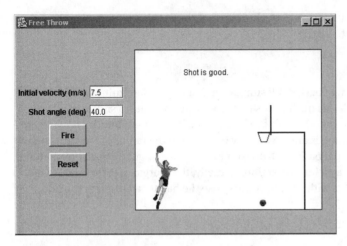

Figure 7-21. *A screen shot of the Free-Throw Game*

The hoop is assumed to have a radius of 0.23 *m* and the ball a radius of 0.12 *m*. For a shot to be good, the center of the ball must travel to within 0.14 *m* of the center of hoop. This value represents the difference in radius between the hoop and ball plus a 0.03 *m* "fudge factor" to account for glancing collisions where the ball would still fall through the hoop. Backboard collisions are assumed to be frictionless. The coefficient of restitution between the ball and backboard is assumed to be 0.75. A constant drag coefficient of 0.5 is used for the basketball.

One nice thing about the Free-Throw Game is that we do not have to write a class that models a basketball. We can simply use the DragProjectile class we developed in Chapter 5, which has all of the elements required to model the flight of a basketball. The FreeThrow class that defines the GUI for the application is very similar to the other GUI classes in this chapter. The FreeThrow class code listing can be downloaded from the Apress website.

Baseball

Most cultures invent a game that involves hitting a ball with a stick. In the middle part of the nineteenth century, Americans began to modify an English game called rounders into what would become baseball. In 1845 Alexander Cartwright (not Abner Doubleday as is commonly believed) wrote down a series of rules to govern team baseball. Many of these rules are still in use today.

The first recorded baseball game took place in 1846 between the New York Knickerbockers and the New York Baseball Club. The first organized baseball league formed in 1857, but the first completely professional team, the Cincinnati Red Stockings, did not appear until 1869. Baseball has a rich and storied history over the past 160 years and is played in countries all over the world today.

Equipment Specifications

A baseball, as shown in Figure 7-22, is made from yarn tightly wound around an inner core of cork. The outer cover of the ball is two dumbbell-shaped pieces of horsehide or leather that are stitched together to form a spherical shape. The seams are used to help grip the ball and are also employed by pitchers to put different types of spin on their pitches.

Figure 7-22. *An official MLB baseball*

The mass and dimensions of an official baseball, as defined by Major League Baseball (MLB), are shown in Table 7-8. As was the case with soccer, there is some range of possible mass and dimension values. The coefficient of restitution for a baseball is somewhat dependent on the velocity of the ball and ranges from 0.525 to 0.55.

Table 7-8. *Specifications of an MLB Baseball*

Quantity	Value
Mass	0.142–0.149 kg
Circumference	0.229–0.235 m
Radius	0.0364–0.0374 m
Coefficient of restitution	0.525–0.55

The other piece of baseball equipment we will discuss is the bat. According to MLB regulations, the bat is a "smooth, round stick" made from "one piece of solid wood." Aluminum bats are allowed in college and youth baseball. Bats are tapered. The end of the bat the player grabs onto, known as the **handle**, has a smaller diameter than the other end of the bat, which is known as the **barrel**. Two typical baseball bats are shown in Figure 7-23.

Figure 7-23. *Typical baseball bats*

The mass and dimension specifications for a baseball bat are shown in Table 7-9. The MLB regulations specify a maximum diameter and length of the bat. The mass of a bat can vary, but typical values are 0.79–0.96 kg (28–34 oz).

Table 7-9. *Baseball Bat Specifications*

Quantity	Value
Maximum diameter	0.07 m
Maximum length	1.067 m
Mass	0.79–0.96 kg

Modeling the Pitch

In the movie *Bull Durham*, Kevin Costner summed up the game of baseball: "You throw the ball, you hit the ball, you catch the ball." One of the key elements of the game is that the pitcher, who stands 18.44 *m* (60 *ft* 6 *in*) from home plate, has to throw the baseball in such a way that either the batter can't hit the ball or he hits it to one of the defenders, who can either catch the ball or throw him out. The pitcher aims for an imaginary "strike" zone whose boundaries are the width of the plate (0.43 *m*) and the distance between the batter's knees and the lettering across his jersey.

The two key elements of a baseball pitch are velocity and spin. The pitcher gives the ball an initial velocity when he releases it towards home plate. The velocity components of the ball are then affected by the accelerations caused by gravity and aerodynamic drag. The pitcher also puts a spin on the ball when he throws. Let's discuss in a little more detail how spin affects the flight of a baseball.

The Effects of Spin on the Flight of a Baseball

From what you have learned about Magnus force, you know that a spinning baseball generates lift in the direction perpendicular to the velocity vector and spin axis. Spin is critically important in baseball because it is what defines the various pitches and allows the ball to move and curve as it travels to home plate. It doesn't matter how hard you can throw a baseball; if you throw it straight, batters can hit it.

The spin axis and direction of spin defines the type of a given pitch. The velocity of the ball and the spin rate will determine the amount of movement experienced by a given pitch. The spin axis and spin directions for three commonly used baseball pitches are shown in Figure 7-24. The point of view of Figure 7-24 is that of the pitcher looking towards home plate. The arrows show the direction of the spin.

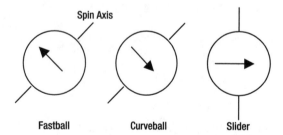

Figure 7-24. *Spin dynamics for three types of baseball pitches*

In looking at Figure 7-24, we can determine how the pitches will move due to their spin. A slider is a pitch that spins about the vertical axis. The Magnus force will therefore be in the horizontal direction. The slider shown in Figure 7-24 will break from left to right. The curveball spins in the downward direction. The Magnus force for the curveball will be downward as well.

The curveball shown in Figure 7-24 will break downwards and to the right. The spin on the fast-ball will tend to loft the flight of the pitch. It will show less break than any of the other types of pitches.

To evaluate the Magnus force on a fastball according to Equation (7.55), we must determine the lift coefficient for the baseball. Researchers at the University of California, Davis, came up with two equations that estimate C_L as a function of the rotational spin ratio of the ball.[6] The equations, shown in Equation (7.58), were created as a best fit to the available experimental data.

$$C_L = 1.5 \frac{r\omega}{v} \qquad \text{for } \frac{r\omega}{v} < 0.1 \qquad (7.58a)$$

$$C_L = 0.09 + 0.6 \frac{r\omega}{v} \qquad \text{for } \frac{r\omega}{v} > 0.1 \qquad (7.58b)$$

The Drag Coefficient of a Baseball

An estimation of the drag coefficient is necessary to compute the aerodynamic drag experienced by a baseball. Experimental data[6] suggests that C_D is approximately 0.5 until a Reynolds number of between 130,000 and 150,000, when the drag coefficient drops sharply due to the transition of the flow over the baseball from laminar to turbulent. The drag coefficient reaches a minimum value of about 0.15 at a Reynolds number of about 160,000 and then rises again as the Reynolds number continues to increase, leveling off at a value of about 0.35 at Reynolds numbers above 200,000–250,000. The Reynolds number of 160,000 corresponds roughly to a ball velocity of 32 *m/s* (72 *mph*).

For game programming purposes, the drag coefficient could be modeled by finding equations that fit the experimental C_D data, including the downward spike that occurs at Re = 160,000. A simpler, although somewhat less accurate, approach is to assume that $C_D = 0.5$ for $\text{Re} < 140,000$, $C_D = 0.35$ for $\text{Re} > 225,000$, and decrease C_D linearly from 0.5 to 0.35 for $140,000 < \text{Re} < 225,000$.

Modeling the Hit

The objective of the batter is to hit the ball either over the outfield wall or into the field of play such that the batter can reach base before he is thrown out. Modeling the collision of the baseball bat, shown schematically in Figure 7-25, is a complicated problem. At the point of collision, both the bat and ball will have three-dimensional velocity components. The ball will certainly be spinning at the point of impact, and the bat may be rotating as well. The point of impact can be almost anywhere on the ball depending on the relative positions of the ball and bat at the time of impact.

Rather than trying to model all of the variables that go into an impact between a baseball and bat, for game programming purposes it's probably a better idea to simply specify the post-collision velocity, spin rate, and spin axis of the ball. It's relatively easy to specify velocity and spin components that would reproduce a single to left field, a pop-up, or any other type of hit that you would want to model.

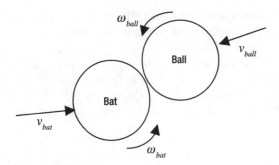

Figure 7-25. *A schematic of the collision of a baseball and bat*

Simulating Other Sports

The list of sports is endless, and there is not room in this chapter to cover the modeling aspects of all of them. The good news is that many of the concepts covered in this chapter are applicable to many different sports. For example, when balls (or people for that matter) are thrown, kicked, or pushed into the air, they become projectiles, and the same basic concepts can be used to model their flight.

No matter what other sport you are trying to model, the same force considerations will apply. The force of gravity will always be present. Depending on the sport that you are modeling, you may also have to account for the forces of aerodynamic drag, wind, and spin. In some sports, such as hockey, friction will be an important force. In other sports, such as football, the ball may tumble in strange ways. In any case, the general modeling process is the same:

1. Define the force diagram for the required objects.

2. Determine the equations of motion that need to be solved.

3. Solve the equations of motion either directly or with an ODE solver.

Football

American football is one of the relatively few sports in which the ball isn't round, but rather is an oblong spheroid. When a quarterback throws the football, he imparts a spin to it known as a spiral. The spin acts to stabilize the football in flight in a similar way that spin is given to a bullet to stabilize its flight.

A football in flight will be subject to the forces of gravity, aerodynamic drag, and wind. The Magnus force experienced by a football is probably not great enough to significantly affect its trajectory. The drag coefficient for a football depends on whether the ball is in a spiral or is tumbling. A football that is tumbling will experience a higher drag coefficient.

Hockey

One of the unique aspects about hockey is that it is played on ice. The puck used in hockey is not round, but instead is a hard rubber cylindrical disk. Most of the time the puck will either be sliding over the ice or flying through the air. To model the sliding puck requires accounting for the friction between the ice and puck. The flight of a puck in the air will be affected by the forces due to gravity, aerodynamic drag, and possibly spin. Unless the game simulation is set outdoors, wind effects can be ignored.

Tennis

The final sport we will briefly discuss is tennis, where players must hit the ball over a net and keep it inside the opponent's side of the court. Spin is very important in tennis. Putting topspin on the ball allows players to hit the ball harder without hitting the ball out of bounds. In developing a tennis simulation, collisions between the ball and ground would have to be modeled as well as possibly collision of the ball and top of the net.

Summary

In this chapter, you learned how to apply some basic Newtonian mechanics and kinematics to the problem of developing sports simulations. Specific details were presented on how to model golf, soccer, basketball, and baseball—sports that involve hitting, kicking, or throwing balls. The basic physics is really very similar for many sports simulations. It's just a matter of knowing which forces to consider.

Here are some specific points to remember about creating sports simulations:

- When a ball (or person for that matter) is in the air, it can be treated as projectile and will be subject to the forces due to gravity, aerodynamic drag, wind, and spin.

- The Magnus force due to spin is very important for the sports of golf, soccer, and baseball. The magnitude of the force due to spin can be obtained by determining the lift coefficient for the object in question.

- At times the effects of wind and spin can be ignored, for example, when simulating the flight of a basketball.

- There are also instances, for example soccer and baseball, when it is probably better for game programming purposes not to try to model the initial collision, but rather to begin the simulation by specifying the post-collision velocity, spin rate, and spin axis of the ball.

References

1. S. Atkinson, Brown, J., and McElheny, J., The Physics of Golf, www.homewood.k12.al.us/compsci/projects98/eteam.

2. P.W. Bearman and Harvey, J.K., "Golfball Aerodynamics," *Aeronautical Quarterly*, May 1976, pp. 112–122.

3. A. Weber, "Green Speed Physics," *USGA Green Section Record*, March/April 1997, http://turf.lib.msu.edu/1990s/1997/970312.pdf.

4. K. Tanner, Probable Golf Instruction, www.probablegolfinstruction.com.

5. University of Sheffield Sports Engineering Research Group, www.shef.ac.uk/mecheng/sports.

6. G. Sawicki, Hubbard, M., and Stronge, W., "How to Hit Home Runs: Optimum Baseball Bat Swing Parameters for Maximum Range Trajectories," *American Journal of Physics*, Vol. 71, No. 11, November 2003, pp. 1152–1162.

CHAPTER 8

■ ■ ■

Cars and Motorcycles

Car racing games are a lot of fun. You can drive high-powered vehicles that you couldn't possibly afford in real life, and you can drive them into trees. Between the speed, the power, and the spectacular fiery crashes, you can create a lot of exciting game scenarios using cars, motorcycles, and other motorized vehicles. But it's important to get the physics right in a car or motorcycle simulation. Your game should properly model, for example, whether a Nissan 350Z can outrun a police cruiser.

In this chapter, we will explore the physics of cars and motorcycles, but the basic principles we will explore are equally applicable to other types of motorized vehicles. The focus will be on the external physics of the vehicles—how they accelerate, how they brake, how they travel around curves. We won't go into the physics of the internal workings of motor vehicles. As a game programmer, you don't really need to know the physics of the internal combustion engine or how disk brakes work.

Some of the topics we will cover in this chapter include the following:

- A brief history of the automobile

- The basic force diagram of a car

- Engine torque and power: how to compute them from the engine turnover rate

- Gears and gear shifting: how gears are used to increase the torque applied to the wheels

- Rolling friction of car tires: what it is and how to calculate it

- Computing the acceleration and velocity of a car

- Braking: how brakes work and how to model braking in game programs

- Wheel traction and how it can limit the acceleration of a car

- Turning: how to compute turn radius and turn rate and how to model the effects of high-speed turns

- Motorcycles and how they turn

We'll also develop a car simulator that will model the performance and operation of a sports car.

Cars

You can create a lot of exciting game simulations involving cars, whether it's car races, car chases, or just simulating the life of a taxi driver. Putting realistic physics into a car simulation really just involves applying some basic concepts from Newtonian mechanics and kinematics with a little knowledge about how power is transferred from the engine to the wheels.

In this section, we'll start with the basics of straight-line driving and explore topics such as the forces that act upon a moving car, engine torque, and how gears and a transmission transfers the engine power to the wheels. We'll revisit the subjects of aerodynamics and rolling friction as they apply to the motion of a car. With these topics in hand, we'll explore how to model the acceleration and velocity of a car. Later, we'll investigate such topics as what happens when a car drives around a curve and wheel traction, and we'll also develop a simple car simulator.

Keep in mind when reading this section that it provides the basic theory of car physics. It will give you the information you need to create a fairly realistic car simulation. Advanced topics such as weight transfer during braking and cornering are not included in the model we will develop, but if you want to get "fancy" with your car simulation, it would be pretty straightforward to add advanced effects to the basic model. We'll discuss briefly how to go about adding advanced effects at the end of the chapter.

A Brief History of the Automobile

People have been thinking about, designing, and building motorized vehicles for a very long time. The first working motorized vehicle was a steam-powered tractor built by a French engineer named Nicolas Cugnot in 1769. It was intended to pull cannons and had a top speed of 4 *km/hr*. Mr. Cugnot was also the first person to have a car accident when he drove his vehicle into a stone wall in 1771.

The development of automobiles took a big leap forward towards the end of the nineteenth century when a German engineer named Karl Benz designed and built the first vehicle powered by an internal combustion gasoline-powered engine. While cars gained in popularity over the next 20 years, they were quite expensive and considered mostly toys for the rich. In 1913, the American Henry Ford perfected the assembly line, which could assemble a Model T car in only 93 minutes. Such improved productivity greatly reduced the cost of buying a car. By 1927, over 15 million Model T's had been built and sold.

Obviously, cars have never looked back, and they are a crucial element of the transportation systems of almost every country on Earth. Cars have also become a form of entertainment for people who like to drive fast, look good, or just generally have a good time.

Basic Force Diagram

A schematic of the forces acting on a car driving in a straight line on an inclined surface is shown in Figure 8-1. The angle of the slope is equal to θ. The car is influenced by the forces of gravity, static friction, rolling friction, and aerodynamic drag—all subjects you have learned about earlier in the book. The engine applies a torque, T_e, to the car wheels that generates the force that moves the car forward. In Figure 8-1, the torque is applied to the front wheels of the car.

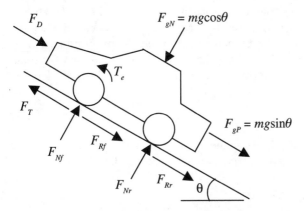

Figure 8-1. *Force balance on a car driving in a straight line on a horizontal surface*

As you can see from Figure 8-1, there are quite a few forces acting on the car, so let's go over them one by one. The force of gravity pulls the car towards the earth. It acts both normal to the slope with a force, $F_{gN} = mg\cos\theta$, as well as parallel to the slope with a force, $F_{gP} = mg\sin\theta$. Depending on whether the car is pointing uphill or downhill, the parallel component of gravitational force can pull the car either forwards or backwards.

This force of gravity in the normal direction, F_{gN}, is balanced by normal forces, F_{Nf} and F_{Nr}, that act along the surfaces of the front and rear tires that are in contact with the ground. The total normal force, F_N, is the sum of the forces on the front and rear tires and is equal to the mass of the car multiplied by the acceleration due to gravity and the cosine of the slope angle, θ.

$$F_N = F_{Nf} + F_{Nr} = mg\cos\theta \tag{8.1}$$

The engine generates torque, which when applied to the wheels causes them to rotate. Friction between the tires and the ground resists this motion, resulting in a force applied to the tires in the direction opposite to the rotation of the tires. The force applied to the tires, F_T, is equal to the torque applied to the wheels, T_w, divided by the wheel radius, r_w.

$$F_T = \frac{T_w}{r_w} \tag{8.2}$$

As we shall see in the "Gears and Wheel Torque" section a little later in this chapter, the torque applied to the wheels is generally not equal to the torque generated by the engine.

When the car is in motion, an aerodynamic drag force will develop that will resist the motion of the car. As we saw in Chapter 5, drag force can be modeled as a function of the air density, ρ, frontal area, A, the square of the velocity magnitude, v, and a drag coefficient, C_D.

$$F_D = \frac{1}{2}C_D\rho v^2 A \tag{8.3}$$

As was the case with projectiles, aerodynamic drag acts in the opposite direction to the velocity of the vehicle. We'll discuss aerodynamic drag in more detail a little later in this chapter. The final force in the basic force diagram is due to rolling friction, which was introduced in Chapter 7. This force acts on all four wheels and resists the rolling motion of the car. The total rolling friction force, F_R, is equal to the total normal force, F_N, multiplied by the coefficient of rolling friction for the vehicle, μ_r.

$$F_R = \mu_r F_N = \mu_r mg \cos\theta \qquad (8.4)$$

The net force on the car parallel to the direction the car is driving, F_{Total}, is equal to the sum of the forces due to engine torque, gravity, aerodynamic drag, and rolling friction.

$$F_{Total} = \frac{T_w}{r_w} - \mu_r mg \cos\theta - mg \sin\theta - \frac{1}{2} C_D \rho v^2 A \qquad (8.5)$$

For the car shown in Figure 8-1, the sign on the parallel gravity force term, $mg\sin\theta$, in Equation (8.5) is negative to indicate that it is pulling the car backwards. The acceleration of the car at any given time is equal to the net force on the vehicle divided by the mass of the vehicle, m.

$$a = \frac{T_w}{r_w m} - \mu_r g \cos\theta - g \sin\theta - \frac{1}{2} \frac{C_D \rho v^2 A}{m} \qquad (8.6)$$

The velocity of the vehicle at any given time can be found by integrating Equation (8.6). Before we can integrate Equation (8.6), however, we need to evaluate the torque that is applied to the wheels.

Engine Torque and Power

When the engine runs, it generates a torque that is used to drive the car forwards or backwards. As we shall see later in this chapter, the torque generated by the engine is typically not the same as the torque applied to the wheels. The engine torque is a function of the rate at which the engine is turning over.

$$T_e = T_e(\Omega_e) \qquad (8.7)$$

The engine turnover rate, Ω_e, in Equation (8.7) is usually expressed in terms of revolutions per minute, or *rpm*. If the engine torque is plotted as a function of engine turnover rate, the result is what is known as a **torque curve**. These curves are usually available for a given car from the manufacturer or from other sources. A typical torque curve is shown in Figure 8-2. One characteristic of engine torque is that it does not always increase with increasing engine turnover rate. The torque in the curve shown in Figure 8-2 increases with increasing *rpm* until it reaches a peak value of 309 *N-m* at about 4600 *rpm*. As the engine turnover rate increases beyond 4600 *rpm*, the torque delivered by the engine decreases.

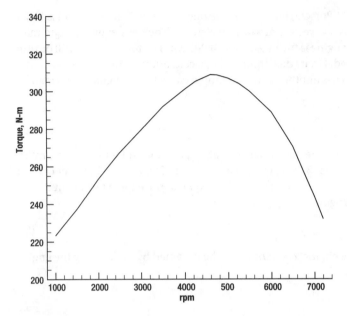

Figure 8-2. *A typical torque curve*

The 2004 Porsche Boxster S

To help you understand how to apply the equations presented in this chapter, we will use as a test case the 2004 Porsche Boxster S sports car, a picture of which is shown in Figure 8-3. The Boxster S was chosen because it is a fast, sporty-looking car and because the author has always wanted to own one.

Figure 8-3. *The Porsche Boxster S (Photo courtesy of Tony Straughn, www.pictures-of-cars.com)*

The torque curve for a 2004 Porsche Boxster S is the one shown in Figure 8-2 and is based on data obtained from the Porsche website at www.porsche.com. The peak engine torque value of 309.2 *N-m* occurs when the engine is turning over at 4600 *rpm*. The torque curve will be used a little later on to develop a model that will compute the acceleration of the Boxster S at any point in time. But first let's discuss another important topic concerning engine performance, namely engine power.

Power and Torque

Generally, when people talk about the performance of an engine, they refer to its power rather than its torque. Recall from Chapter 3 that power is an amount of work done in a unit of time. When applied to the output of a car engine, power, P_e, is equal to the engine torque multiplied by the angular velocity of the engine.

$$P_e = T_e \omega_e \tag{8.8}$$

The angular velocity of the engine, ω_e, in *rad/s* can be obtained by multiplying the engine turnover rate by 2π and dividing by 60.

$$\omega_e = \frac{2\pi\Omega_e}{60} \tag{8.9}$$

A plot of the power generated by the Boxster S as a function of engine turnover rate, known as a **power curve**, is shown in Figure 8-4. Similar to the torque curve, the peak power occurs at a certain *rpm* level and decreases after that. The peak power output of the Boxster engine is 1.92e + 5 *W* and occurs at about 6200 *rpm*. Comparing the power and torque curves in Figure 8-2 and 8-4, the peak power for the engine occurs at a higher *rpm* level than does the peak torque.

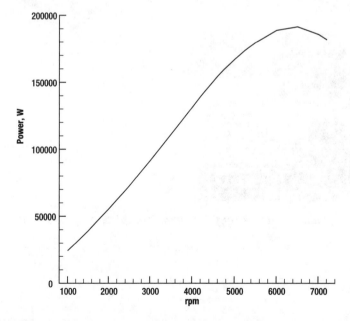

Figure 8-4. *The power curve for the 2004 Boxster S*

Gears and Wheel Torque

The torque applied to the wheels of a car determines its acceleration. In general, the torque applied to the wheels is not the same as the engine torque because before the engine torque is applied to the wheels it passes through a **transmission**. A typical transmission cross-section is shown in Figure 8-5. You can see that a modern transmission is quite complicated, with a lot of gears, shafts, and other strange-looking things.

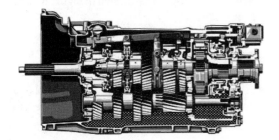

Figure 8-5. *A cross-section of a transmission (Photo courtesy of Daimler-Chrysler)*

You might ask yourself, "Why bother with a transmission? Why not connect the torque from the engine directly to the wheels?" A big reason for the existence of transmissions is performance. In looking at Figure 8-2, when the engine turnover rate is low, the torque and therefore acceleration is relatively low as well. In fact, if the engine was connected directly to the wheels, it would take the Boxster S over 16 seconds to accelerate to 100 *km/hr*. That would be pretty boring performance for a sports car.

Fortunately, the acceleration of a car can be greatly increased by using a transmission. What the gears inside the transmission do is to change the angular velocity and torque transferred from the engine. To see how this is done, consider the two gears shown in Figure 8-6. The second gear has twice the diameter of the first gear, so for every revolution the second gear makes, the first gear will make two. The second gear has half the angular velocity of the first gear. However, the torque that the second gear can exert is twice that of the first gear.

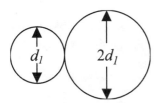

Figure 8-6. *Gears are used to change angular velocity and torque.*

The **gear ratio** between two gears is the ratio of the gear diameters. In Figure 8-6, the gear ratio between the second and first gears would be 2:1. Car transmissions will typically have between three and six forward gears and one reverse gear. There is also an additional set of gears between the transmission and the wheels. In many cars, this gearset is known as the **differential**. The gear ratio of this final gearset is known as the **final drive ratio**.

So what the transmission does is to (generally) increase the torque that comes out of the engine at the cost of reducing the gear turnover rate. To determine the acceleration of the car, we need the torque applied to the wheels. The wheel torque, T_w, is equal to the engine torque, T_e, multiplied by the gear ratio, g_k, of whatever gear the car is in and the final drive ratio, G, of the car.

$$T_w = T_e g_k G \tag{8.10}$$

Using Equation (8.10), the equation for the acceleration for the car shown in Figure 8-1 can be modified in terms of the engine torque and gear ratios.

$$a = \frac{T_e g_k G}{r_w m} - \mu_r g \cos\theta - g \sin\theta - \frac{1}{2} \frac{C_D \rho v^2 A}{m} \tag{8.11}$$

Another effect of the transmission gears is to change the angular velocity of the wheel relative to the turnover rate of the engine. The relationship between the engine turnover rate, Ω_e, and wheel angular velocity, ω_w, becomes the following:

$$\omega_w = \frac{2\pi\Omega_e}{60 g_k G} \tag{8.12}$$

The "60" term in Equation (8.12) is to convert the minutes in *rpm* to seconds. If the tires roll on the ground without slipping, the translational velocity of the car, v, can be related to the angular velocity of the wheel, and therefore to the engine turnover rate.

$$v = r_w \omega_w = \frac{r_w 2\pi\Omega_e}{60 g_k G} \tag{8.13}$$

In looking at Equations (8.11) and (8.13), we can make the following observations about gear and final drive ratios:

- The higher the gear ratio, the higher the acceleration and the lower the car velocity for a given *rpm*.

- Increasing the final drive ratio increases the acceleration for all gears but likewise decreases the car velocity for a given *rpm* for all gears.

As an example of the gear ratios for a typical sports car, Table 8-1 shows the gear ratios for the six forward gears of the 2004 Porsche Boxster S. The final drive ratio for the car is 3.44.

Table 8-1. *Porsche Boxster S Gear Ratios*

Gear	Gear Ratio
First	3.82
Second	2.20
Third	1.52
Fourth	1.22
Fifth	1.02
Sixth	0.84

Determining Wheel Radius

The acceleration and velocity expressions shown in Equations (8.11) and (8.13) are functions of the wheel radius, but how can this quantity be determined? Fortunately, the wheel radius can be calculated from information on the tire itself. Every tire will have a series of letters and numbers that identify the tire. For example, the front tires of the Porsche Boxster S have the identification 225/40ZR-18. The first number, 225 for the Boxster, indicates the width of the tire in millimeters. The number after the slash symbol, /, is the ratio of the tire thickness to the tire width expressed as a percentage. The letters indicate the conditions for which the tire is designed. The last two numbers represent the diameter of the wheel that fits the tire in inches. The tire radius is equal to the wheel radius added to the tire thickness. Based on the tire designation, 225/40ZR-18, the radius of the Boxster S front tire is 0.3186 *m*.

Gear Shifting

We learned in the last section that a lower gear (with a higher gear ratio) results in a greater acceleration. So why not just stay in first gear all the time? Wouldn't that optimize the acceleration of the car? This is the flip side to the question, "Why not connect the engine directly to the wheels?" The answer is, "No, you shouldn't stay in first gear all the time." The reason is that the velocity of the car is a function of engine turnover rate and gear ratios, and there is a limit to how fast the engine can turn over.

Every car engine has a characteristic known as a **redline** *rpm* value. The engine cannot exceed this turnover rate for more than a brief period of time without causing damage to the engine. On the Porsche Boxster S, the redline value is 7200 *rpm*. Using Equation (8.13) and the data in Table 8-1, the theoretical maximum velocity for each gear at 7200 *rpm* can be computed, and the results are shown in Table 8-2.

Table 8-2. *Theoretical Maximum Velocity for Each Gear for the Boxster S*

Gear	Maximum Velocity (*m/s*)	Maximum Velocity, (*km/hr*)
First	18.3	65.8
Second	31.7	114.3
Third	45.9	165.4
Fourth	57.2	206.0
Fifth	68.5	246.4
Sixth	83.1	299.3

We can see from Table 8-2 that although the maximum acceleration occurs in first gear, the maximum velocity the car can attain in first gear is 65.8 *km/hr*. At this point, you would reach the redline *rpm* value and have to shift into second gear, which would provide the optimum acceleration between 65.8 and 114.3 *km/hr*. At this point, the *rpm* level would reach the redline value again, and the car would have to be shifted into third gear. Most transmissions are designed so the shift point for optimum acceleration is at the redline value of the car.

Keep in mind that the values in Table 8-2 are theoretical maximum velocities. The Boxster S can't really reach 299.3 *km/hr* in sixth gear. According to the manufacturer's specifications, the top speed of the car is "only" 266 *km/hr*. The reason the car can't reach the theoretical maximum velocity in sixth gear is because the car is also subject to the decelerating forces of aerodynamic drag and rolling friction.

Equation (8.13) can also be used to calculate what the engine *rpm* value will be after a gear shift. If the car is shifted into a higher gear, the gear ratio is reduced. If the velocity of the car is assumed to be constant before and after the gear shift, the engine *rpm* level will decline because of the lower gear ratio. The new engine turnover rate, $\Omega_e(new)$, will be equal to the engine turnover rate before the gear shift, $\Omega_e(old)$, multiplied by the ratio of the new gear ratio to the previous gear ratio.

$$\Omega_e(new) = \Omega_e(old)\frac{g_k(new)}{g_k(old)} \tag{8.14}$$

For example, if the Boxster S shifts from first gear to second gear at 7200 *rpm*, the new *rpm* level of the engine after the gear shift will be the following:

$$\Omega_e = 7200\frac{2.2}{3.82} = 4147 \; rpm \tag{8.15}$$

This is an effect you've probably seen quite a bit. If you are driving a car and shift from a lower gear to a higher gear, the *rpm* level of the engine falls. The opposite is also true; if you shift from a higher gear into a lower gear, the *rpm* level of the engine will surge.

Manual and Automatic Transmissions

There are two general types of transmissions. With a **manual transmission** the driver must make all of the gear shifts manually. An **automatic transmission** is one where the transmission shifts automatically. When the automatic transmission will shift varies from transmission to transmission but usually is dependent on the car velocity, the engine turnover rate, and the load being put on the engine. If you wanted to use an automatic transmission in your game programs, you could just specify when the transmission would shift. The automatic transmission in the author's 1997 Toyota Camry shifts when the engine turnover rate is between 3000 and 4000 *rpm*.

Aerodynamic Drag

A car in motion is subject to the force of aerodynamic drag. As we know, drag acts in the opposite direction to the velocity vector of an object, so drag force will cause the car to slow down. As shown in Equation (8.3), the drag force on a car is expressed as a function of the air density, velocity of the car squared, the frontal area of the car, and a drag coefficient.

To evaluate Equation (8.3), we need to determine the drag coefficient and frontal area of the car.

Drag Coefficients for Motor Vehicles

The drag coefficient for a car or other motor vehicle will depend on the shape of the vehicle. A sports car will have a lower drag coefficient than will a garbage truck. Typical drag coefficient ranges for several vehicle types[1] are shown in Table 8-3.

Table 8-3. *Drag Coefficients for Some Typical Vehicle Types*

Vehicle Type	Drag Coefficient
Sports car	0.27–0.38
'60s muscle car	0.38–0.5
Sedan	0.34–0.5
Truck	0.6–1.0
Tractor-Trailer	0.6–1.2
Motorcycle	0.5–1.0

While there may be some variation in vehicle drag coefficient due to its Reynolds number and other effects, for game programming purposes, you can assume a constant drag coefficient for the vehicles you are simulating. The drag coefficient for the 2004 Porsche Boxster S that we have been using as an example in this chapter is 0.31.

Frontal Area

The drag force, as expressed by Equation (8.3), is a function of the frontal area of the car. The simplest estimate of the frontal area of a vehicle is the product of the width and height of the vehicle. This method assumes that the frontal cross-section of the vehicle is rectangular. In reality, sides of most cars are sloped so the true frontal area is less than the product of the width and height. One way to account for frontal area slope is to multiply the width and height of the vehicle by a factor between 0 and 1. For the car simulator we will develop later in this chapter, a factor of 0.85 is used to compute the frontal area of the Boxster S.

$$A = 0.85 * width * height \tag{8.16}$$

The Boxster S has a width of 1.78 m and a height of 1.28 m. Using Equation (8.16), the frontal area of the vehicle, for purposes of computing the drag force, would be 1.94 m^2.

Rolling Friction

As you learned in Chapter 7, rolling friction is a force that resists the rolling motion of an object. While it is referred to as friction, it really is a contact force caused by the deformation of the object and the surface it is rolling over. As shown in Equation (8.4), the force due to rolling friction, F_r, between the tires and the ground is equal to the normal force exerted on the object, F_N, multiplied by a coefficient of rolling friction, μ_r. If the car is traveling over flat ground, the normal force will be equal to mg.

The value of the coefficient of rolling friction tends to be significantly lower than the coefficients of static or kinetic friction for the same object. For car tires, the coefficient of rolling friction ranges from 0.01 to 0.02.[2]

Computing Acceleration and Velocity

In order to create a car simulation, it is necessary to determine the acceleration and velocity of the car at any point in time. The starting point for this analysis is Equation (8.11). In the preceding sections, values were presented for the coefficient of rolling friction and drag coefficient of a car. If the slope angle, frontal area, and air density are known, the only unknown quantity in Equation (8.11) is the wheel torque, T_w.

According to Equation (8.10), the wheel torque is the product of the engine torque, T_e, the current gear ratio, g_k, and the final drive ratio, G. The engine torque, T_e, can be obtained from the torque curve of the engine. Torque curve data is usually presented either as a plot or as a table of numbers. For game programming purposes, the torque curve needs to be expressed as a mathematical expression. The easiest way to mathematically model a torque curve is with a series of straight lines.

For example, the torque curve for the Boxster S as shown in Figure 8-2 can be approximated by three straight lines. The first line extends from a torque value of 220 *N-m* at 1000 *rpm* up to 4600 *rpm* where the torque peaks at 309.2 *N-m*. A second line is drawn from 4600 *rpm* to the redline value of 7200 *rpm* where the torque is approximately 227 *N-m*. Below 1000 *rpm*, the idle speed of the engine, the torque will be assumed to be 220 *N-m*. The simplified torque curve is shown in Figure 8-7.

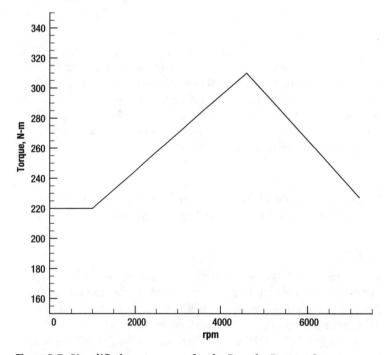

Figure 8-7. *Simplified torque curve for the Porsche Boxster S*

CHAPTER 8 ■ CARS AND MOTORCYCLES   **223**

Using the simplified torque curve, the torque for the Boxster S can be modeled by three equations. The units for engine torque in all three equations are in *N-m*.

$$T_e = 220 \qquad \Omega_e \leq 1000 \tag{8.17a}$$

$$T_e = 0.025\Omega_e + 195 \quad 1000 < \Omega_e < 4600 \tag{8.17b}$$

$$T_e = -0.032\Omega_e + 457.2 \qquad \Omega_e \geq 4600 \tag{8.17c}$$

All three of the lines described by Equations (8.17a) through (8.17c) are specific cases of the general equation for a straight line.

$$T_e = b\Omega_e + d \tag{8.18}$$

The b parameter in Equation (8.18) is the slope of the line. Of course, straight lines aren't the only way to mathematically model a torque curve. Depending on the shape of the curve, a parabolic or exponential function could also be used to approximate a torque curve.

Having a mathematical expression for the torque curve is all well and good, but to solve for the acceleration of the car what we really need is an equation for the wheel torque as a function of the current velocity of the car. An equation that relates wheel torque to car velocity can be derived if the assumption is made that the tires roll without slipping. Under this condition, the velocity of the car, v, is equal to the wheel radius, r_w, multiplied by the angular velocity of the wheel, ω_w. As seen in Equation (8.12), the angular velocity is a function of the engine turnover rate and the gear and final drive ratios.

$$v = r_w\omega_w = \frac{2\pi r_w\Omega_e}{60 g_k G} \tag{8.19}$$

As a reminder, the "60" term in Equation (8.19) converts the engine turnover rate from *rpm* to *rev/s*. Plugging Equations (8.18) and (8.19) into Equation (8.11) results in an expression for the acceleration of the car as a function of the current velocity of the car.

$$a = \frac{60 g_k^2 G^2 b v}{2\pi m r_w^2} + \frac{g_k G d}{m r_w} - \frac{1}{2}\frac{C_D \rho v^2 A}{m} - \mu_r g \cos\theta - g \sin\theta \tag{8.20}$$

Equation (8.20) looks really messy, but it's really just an algebraic equation. The constants can be grouped together to form a simpler equation in which the acceleration of the car is a function of the current velocity of the car.

$$a = \frac{dv}{dt} = c_1 v^2 + c_2 v + c_3 \tag{8.21}$$

The constants, c_1, c_2, and c_3, in Equation (8.21) are the following:

$$c_1 = -\frac{1}{2}\frac{C_D \rho A}{m} \tag{8.22a}$$

$$c_2 = \frac{60 g_k^2 G^2 b}{2\pi m r_w^2} \tag{8.22b}$$

$$c_3 = \frac{g_k G d}{m r_w} - \mu_r g \cos\theta - g \sin\theta \tag{8.22c}$$

In looking at Equation (8.20), we can observe what parameters influence the acceleration value of the car. Some conclusions are pretty obvious—the heavier the car, the lower the acceleration. If the gear and final drive ratios are increased, the acceleration is increased. Reducing the rolling friction of the wheels increases the acceleration.

Keep in mind that Equation (8.20) represents the maximum acceleration available at a given velocity. It's based on the wheel torque that would result if you pushed the gas pedal all the way to the floor. In real life, using the maximum acceleration all the time would be a pretty extreme way of driving. If the gas pedal was pushed only part way down, the actual torque applied to the wheels would be some fraction of the maximum possible torque. For game programming purposes, you might apply the maximum possible wheel torque if the gas pedal were pushed all the way down, half the torque if the pedal were pushed halfway down, and so on.

The acceleration shown in Equation (8.20) assumes that the tires roll without slipping on the ground. In many cases, the maximum available torque will generate a force that is greater than the maximum frictional force between the tires and the ground. When this happens, the wheels won't roll without slipping; instead, the wheels will spin across the road surface in the classic "burning rubber" effect. We'll discuss tire slippage in the "Wheel Traction" section a little later in this chapter.

Another thing to remember is that the acceleration equation shown in Equation (8.20) is really an idealized case. It assumes there is no loss in engine torque as it goes through the transmission and differential. In reality, there is some loss due to friction between the mechanical parts. On the other hand, using straight lines to model the torque curve tends to underpredict the engine torque. The two assumptions would somewhat cancel each other out, and for game programming purposes, Equation (8.20) is probably sufficient.

Equation (8.20) or the alternative form shown in Equation (8.21) can be used to solve for the velocity of the car over time. It turns out that there is a closed-form solution to Equation (8.21), but it is quite messy and has different forms depending on the relative values of the c_1, c_2, and c_3 constants. It's easier if slightly slower to solve Equation (8.21) using our ODE solver, and that's exactly what we'll do when we develop a car simulator later in this section.

Maximum Velocity

Equation (8.21) can be used to compute the theoretical maximum velocity that a car can achieve. The maximum velocity will be the point where the net acceleration on the car is zero. But there is a catch, because at lower gears the redline *rpm* will be reached before the net acceleration on the car reaches zero. In this case, the maximum velocity, v_{max}, of a car is limited by the redline *rpm* value of the engine.

$$v_{max} = \frac{2\pi r_w \Omega_{redline}}{60 g_k G} \tag{8.23}$$

At higher gears (with lower gear ratios) the maximum velocity of a car is drag-limited. Drag will stop the car from accelerating any further before the redline *rpm* value is reached. If you recall, the drag force is proportional to the square of the velocity of the car. As velocity increases, the aerodynamic drag increases until a velocity is reached where the torque applied to the wheels is exactly balanced by the aerodynamic drag and rolling friction experienced by the vehicle. At this point the acceleration of the car, a, is zero.

$$a = c_1 v^2 + c_2 v + c_3 = 0 \tag{8.24}$$

The maximum velocity can be found using the standard equation for finding the roots of a quadratic equation.

$$v_{max} = \frac{-c_2 \pm \sqrt{c_2^2 - 4c_1c_3}}{2c_1} \tag{8.25}$$

Let's use Equation (8.25) to compute the maximum velocity of the Porsche Boxster S when the car is in sixth gear. The drag coefficient of the car is 0.31, the empty mass is 1323 kg, and the radius of the front wheels is 0.3186 m. We'll assume that the coefficient of rolling friction is 0.015, the frontal area of the car is 1.94 m^2, and the weight of the driver is 70 kg. The air density value will be taken to be 1.2 kg/m^3. The car is assumed to be driving over flat, level ground, so the slope angle, θ, is equal to zero.

The maximum velocity will occur in the higher rpm range, so the engine torque will be approximated by Equation (8.17c). This means that the b coefficient is equal to –0.032 and the d coefficient has a value of 457.2. In sixth gear, the maximum velocity of the car is likely to be drag-limited, so we'll use Equation (8.25) to compute the maximum velocity.

$$c_1 = -\frac{1}{2}\frac{C_D\rho A}{m} = -\frac{1}{2}\frac{0.31*1.2*1.94}{1393} = -2.59e-4 \tag{8.26a}$$

$$c_2 = \frac{60g_k^2G^2b}{2\pi mr_w^2} = -\frac{60*0.84^2*3.44^2*0.032}{2\pi*1393*0.3186^2} = -0.018 \tag{8.26b}$$

$$c_3 = \frac{g_k Gd}{mr_w} - \mu_r g = \frac{0.84*3.44*457.2}{1393*0.3186} - 0.015*9.8 = 2.83 \tag{8.26c}$$

$$v_{max} = \frac{0.018 \pm \sqrt{0.018^2 + 4*2.59e-4*2.83}}{-2*2.59e-4} = 75.4 \ \frac{m}{s} = 271.5 \ \frac{km}{hr} \tag{8.26d}$$

The other solution to the v_{max} equation gives a negative value and can be ignored. The manufacturer's published value for the top speed of the Boxster S is 266 km/hr. Considering the assumptions and simplifications that went into our model, it did a pretty good job of computing the top speed of the vehicle.

The value of 271.5 km/hr is the drag-limited maximum velocity of the Boxster S. Let's compare it to the redline-limited value calculated using Equation (8.23).

$$v = \frac{2\pi r_w\Omega_{redline}}{60g_k G} = \frac{2\pi*0.3186*7200}{60*0.84*3.44} = 83.1 \ \frac{m}{s} = 299.3 \ \frac{km}{hr} \tag{8.27}$$

So the Boxster S could go 299 km/hr in sixth gear if there were no aerodynamic drag and no rolling friction. To get a feeling for the relative magnitudes for some of the force terms, let's compare the magnitude of aerodynamic drag and rolling friction on the Boxster S when it has reached a speed of 271.5 km/hr. The drag force can be calculated from Equation (8.3).

$$F_D = \frac{1}{2}0.31*1.2*75.4^2*1.94 = 2051 \ N \tag{8.28}$$

The force of rolling friction can be computed from Equation (8.4).

$$F_R = 0.015*1393*9.81 = 205 \ N \tag{8.29}$$

In comparing the results from Equations (8.28) and (8.29), the aerodynamic drag force is 10 times as large as the rolling friction force when the car is traveling at 271.5 km/hr. The rolling friction force is not a function of velocity. If the car were going 10 km/hr, the rolling friction force would still be 205 N, whereas the drag force would only be 2.8 N.

Braking

Driving a car is not all acceleration; sometimes you need to slow down, too. In this section, we will discuss two general ways a car can slow down (and no, one of them is not running into a tree). It turns out that an engine will slow itself down just by the nature of how the cylinders move up and down inside the engine. This effect is known as **engine braking**. The torque due to engine braking, T_{eb}, is modeled mathematically by a constant known as the **engine braking coefficient**, μ_{eb}, multiplied by the turnover rate of the engine in *rev/s*.

$$T_{eb} = \mu_{eb} \frac{\Omega_e}{60} \tag{8.30}$$

It can be difficult to obtain the value of the engine braking coefficient for a given car. For an F1 race car, the coefficient has a value of 0.74.[3] If this value is applied to the Boxster S, the torque due to engine braking at 6000 *rpm* is equal to 74 N-m corresponding to an acceleration of –0.17 m/s^2. If you want to include the effects of engine braking in your car simulation and don't have the precise value of engine braking coefficient for the car you are modeling, assuming a value of 0.74 is probably a reasonable estimate.

Another way a car can be slowed down is if its brakes are applied. When the driver steps on the brake pedal, a brake pad is pressed up against a flat metal disk attached to the wheel. Friction between the brake pad and disk generates a torque that slows the wheels down. The torque caused by the brake pad acts in the opposite direction that the wheel is rotating.

It can be difficult to find information about brake torque for a given car. Information on braking is usually presented as the distance it takes to brake a car from an initial velocity to a full stop. For example, the Boxster S requires 34 m to brake from a velocity of 26.8 m/s (60 mi/hr) to a full stop. If braking distance data is available, the braking acceleration, a_b, can be obtained from the Newtonian mechanics as a function of the initial velocity, v_0, and braking distance, x.

$$a_b = -\frac{v_0^2}{2x} = -10.4 \ \frac{m}{s^2} \tag{8.31}$$

Keep in mind when looking at the results in Equation (8.31), the driver who performed this test was trying to get the shortest braking distance possible, so he or she probably slammed on the brakes. The –10.4 value therefore can be considered the maximum braking deceleration for the Boxster S.

For game programming purposes, if the value for the brake torque for a given car isn't available, you can calculate the braking acceleration from braking distance data and apply that in your code. Keep in mind that the braking distance is based on the maximum braking force—if you slammed on the brakes. To simulate a more gentle braking action, you could simply take some fraction of the maximum braking acceleration.

A Car Simulator

Let's take what we've learned about modeling the physics of cars and develop a car simulator. The GUI display for the car simulator is shown in Figure 8-8. At the top of the simulator is a display area that shows a picture of the car. Above the car are two rectangular markers. When the simulator runs, the car location remains fixed on the screen, and the markers move from left to right to simulate the forward motion of the car. The speed at which the markers move is proportional to the speed of the car.

On the left-hand side of the GUI are three radio buttons that determine whether the car is accelerating, cruising at a constant velocity, or slowing down by braking. The radio buttons are mutually exclusive, so only one may be selected. Below the radio buttons are five buttons. The Start button starts or resumes the simulation. The Shift Up and Shift Down buttons cause the car to shift gears up or down. The Stop button stops the car, shifts the car into first gear, and lowers the engine turnover rate to 1000 *rpm*. The Reset button does the same things as the Stop button, but it also resets the distance and time values to zero.

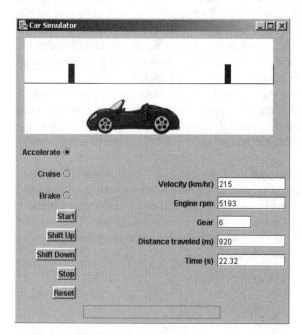

Figure 8-8. *Car Simulator screen shot*

On the right-hand side of the display are text fields that show the current velocity and engine turnover rate of the car as well as what gear the car is currently in. Also included are text fields that display the distance the car has traveled and the total elapsed time of the simulation. At the bottom of the display is a text field used to present warning messages. If the engine turnover rate exceeds the redline *rpm* value, a message to that effect is shown in the text field. If the engine turnover rate exceeds 8000 *rpm*, you've "blown" the engine and the simulation will stop, as shown in Figure 8-9.

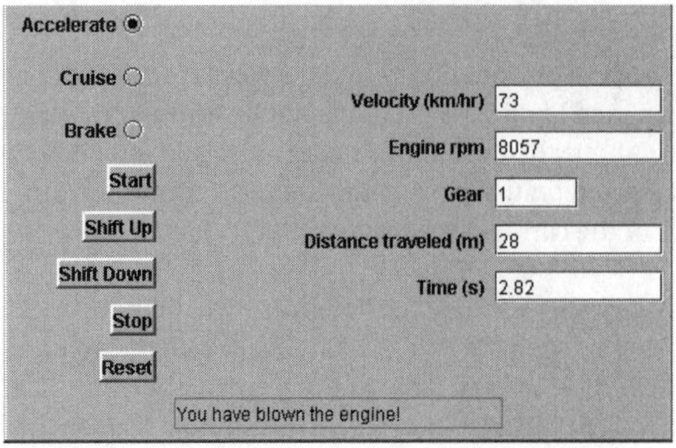

Figure 8-9. *If the* rpm *exceeds 8000, you've blown the engine.*

The GUI for this car simulation is pretty primitive, but the physics inside it are real and are based on the equations developed in this chapter. The effects of aerodynamic drag and rolling friction are included in the model. Some simplifications were made, however. The car is assumed to be driving in a straight line on flat ground. When the car is braking, the acceleration due to braking is assumed to be a constant $-5.0 \; m/s^2$ at all times. We are also not modeling the reverse gear in this simulation, so the car is either stopped or is moving forward.

The tires of the car in the Car Simulator are assumed to roll without slipping at all times. In real life, if too much torque is applied to the wheels, the maximum frictional force between the tires and the ground will be exceeded, and the tires will slip along the ground—the "burning rubber" effect. We'll explore how to model tire slippage in more detail in the "Wheel Traction" section a little later in this chapter.

Creating the car simulation requires two general types of classes—one representing the car and the other defining the GUI. We'll start by discussing the classes that represent the cars. Two car classes will be written. The first class is called the Car class and represents a generic car. The Car class will declare the fields and methods that are common to all cars. The Car class will be written as a subclass of the DragProjectile class so it can reuse the code declared in the DragProjectile, SimpleProjectile, and ODE classes.

```
public class Car extends DragProjectile
{
  private double muR;
  private double omegaE;
  private double redline;
  private double finalDriveRatio;
  private double wheelRadius;
  private int gearNumber;     //  Gear the car is in
  private int numberOfGears;  //  Total number of gears
  private String mode;
  private double[] gearRatio;  //  Gear ratios
```

The muR field represents the coefficient of rolling friction. The gearNumber field is the gear the car is currently in. The numberOfGears field contains the total number of forward gears in the transmission. The mode field defines whether the car is accelerating, cruising at constant velocity, or braking. The omegaE field is the engine turnover rate in *rpm*. The names of the other Car class fields are self-explanatory.

The Car constructor is used to initialize the fields in the Car, DragProjectile, SimpleProjectile, and ODE classes. The first thing the constructor does is to call the DragProjectile class constructor.

```
// The Car constructor calls DragProjectile constructor and
// then initializes the car-specific variables.
public Car(double x, double y, double z,
          double vx, double vy, double vz,
          double time, double mass, double area,
          double density, double Cd, double redline,
          double finalDriveRatio, double wheelRadius,
          int numberOfGears) {

   super(x, y, z, vx, vy, vz, time, mass, area,
        density, Cd);
```

The Car constructor then initializes the fields declared in the Car class with values passed to the constructor. The size of the gearRatio array is set according to the value of the numberOfGears field. The gear ratios are initially given dummy values of 1.

```
// Initialize some fields based on values passed
// to the constructor.
this.redline = redline;          // Redline rpm
this.finalDriveRatio = finalDriveRatio;  // Final drive ratio
this.wheelRadius = wheelRadius;   // Wheel radius
this.numberOfGears = numberOfGears;   // Number of gears

// Initialize the array that stores the gear ratios.
// The array is shifted so the first index in the
// array correpsonds to first gear and so on.
// Give all gear ratios the dummy value of 1.0
gearRatio = new double[numberOfGears + 1];
gearRatio[0] = 0.0;
for(int i=1; i<numberOfGears+1; ++i) {
  gearRatio[i] = 1.0;
}
```

Some of the Car field values will be set to the same value for all car classes including the fields that represent the coefficient of rolling friction, initial engine *rpm*, starting gear number, and mode.

```
// Set some fields the same for all cars.
muR = 0.015;              // Coefficient of rolling friction
omegaE = 1000.0;          // Engine rpm
gearNumber = 1;           // Gear the car is in
mode = "accelerating";    // Accelerating, cruising, or
                          // braking
}
```

After the constructor, the Car class declares a series of get/set methods to access or change the value of the fields declared in the class. Only some of the get/set methods are shown here. Download the complete code listing from the Apress website to see all of the get/set methods.

```
// These methods return the value of the fields
//   declared in this class.
public double getMuR() {
  return muR;
}

public double getFinalDriveRatio() {
  return finalDriveRatio;
}

// Other get methods not shown ...

public void setOmegaE(double value) {
  omegaE = value;
}

// Other set methods not shown ...
```

One of the features of this car simulation is that you can shift gears. This functionality is implemented in the shiftGear method. The first thing the method does is to determine whether the desired shift is outside the possible range of gear numbers, in which case the method returns. If the shift is possible, the value of the gearNumber field is changed, and the new engine turnover rate is computed by multiplying the old turnover rate by the ratio of the new gear ratio to the old gear ratio.

```
// This method simulates a gear shift.
public void shiftGear(int shift) {
  // If the car will shift beyond highest gear, return.
  if ( shift + getGearNumber() > getNumberOfGears() ) {
    return;
  }
  // If the car will shift below 1st gear, return.
  else if ( shift + getGearNumber() < 1 ) {
    return;
  }
  // Otherwise, change the gear and recompute
  //   the engine rpm value.
  else {
    double oldGearRatio = getGearRatio();
    setGearNumber(getGearNumber() + shift);
    double newGearRatio = getGearRatio();
    setOmegaE(getOmegaE()*newGearRatio/oldGearRatio);
  }

  return;
}
```

Since the ODE solver will be used to update the position and velocity of the car, the `Car` class has to declare a `getRightHandSide` method to define the right-hand sides of the equations to be solved. The first part of the `getRightHandSide` method is similar to that found in many of the classes we've written previously. The intermediate values of location and velocity for the car are computed. In this simulation, we only are concerned with the x-components of location and velocity, but the y- and z-components are included in the method to make the class easily extendable to a car traveling in all three directions.

```
public double[] getRightHandSide(double s, double q[],
                                 double deltaQ[], double ds,
                                 double qScale) {
  double dQ[] = new double[6];
  double newQ[] = new double[6];

  //  Compute the intermediate values of the
  //  dependent variables.
  for(int i=0; i<6; ++i) {
    newQ[i] = q[i] + qScale*deltaQ[i];
  } getRightHandSide
```

The next thing the method does is to define the torque curve. We're going to use the simplified torque curve shown in Figure 8-7 where three straight lines approximate the torque curve. The three lines are defined in Equations (8.17a) through (8.17c). Which line to use depends on the engine turnover rate.

```
//  Compute the constants that define the
//   torque curve line.
double b, d;
if ( getOmegaE() <= 1000.0 ) {
  b = 0.0;
  d = 220.0;
}
else if ( getOmegaE() < 4600.0 ) {
  b = 0.025;
  d = 195.0;
}
else {
  b = -0.032;
  d = 457.2;
}
```

The `getRightHandSide` method computes the total drag and rolling friction forces from Equations (8.3) and (8.4). Because the field that represents the gravitational acceleration, G, was given a value of –9.81 in the `SimpleProjectile` class, the value of the rolling friction force will be negative.

```
// Compute velocity magnitude.
double vx = newQ[0];
double vy = newQ[2];
double vz = newQ[4];
double v = Math.sqrt(vx*vx + vy*vy + vz*vz) + 1.0e-8;

// Compute the total drag force.
double Fd = 0.5*getDensity()*getArea()*getCd()*v*v;

// Compute the force of rolling friction. Because
// the G constant defined in the SimpleProjectile
// class has a negative sign, the value computed here
// will be negative.
double Fr = getMuR()*getMass()*G;
```

The final part of the getRightHandSide method defines the right-hand side of the ODEs that describe the motion of the car. If the car is accelerating, the acceleration of the car is computed from Equation (8.20). If the car is braking and the velocity is positive, the acceleration of the car is set to –5.0 m/s^2. If the car is cruising at constant velocity, the acceleration is set to zero. The equations for the y- and z-components of velocity are all set to zero.

```
// Compute the right-hand sides of the six ODEs
// newQ[0] is the intermediate value of velocity.
// The acceleration of the car is determined by
// whether the car is accelerating, cruising, or
// braking. The braking acceleration is assumed to
// be a constant -5.0 m/s^2.
if ( mode.equals("accelerating") ) {
  double c1 = -Fd/getMass();
  double tmp = getGearRatio()*getFinalDriveRatio()/
               getWheelRadius();
  double c2 = 60.0*tmp*tmp*b*v/(2.0*Math.PI*getMass());
  double c3 = (tmp*d + Fr)/getMass();
  dQ[0] = ds*(c1 + c2 + c3);
}
else if ( mode.equals("braking") ) {
  // Only brake if the velocity is positive.
  if ( newQ[0] > 0.1 ) {
    dQ[0] = ds*(-5.0);
  }
  else {
    dQ[0] = 0.0;
  }
}
else {
  dQ[0] = 0.0;
}
```

```
      dQ[1] = ds*newQ[0];
      dQ[2] = 0.0;
      dQ[3] = 0.0;
      dQ[4] = 0.0;
      dQ[5] = 0.0;

      return dQ;
  }
}
```

The Car class represents a generic car and declares the fields and methods common to all cars. Classes for specific car types can be written as subclasses of the Car class and can define the field values for a specific car. For example, the Car Simulator will simulate the Boxster S, so we will write a BoxsterS class to represent that specific type of car.

Because Java is an object-oriented programming language, writing the BoxsterS class is really easy because almost all of the functionality the BoxsterS class needs has already been defined in earlier classes. All the BoxsterS class needs to do is to define fields that contain the specs for the Boxster S. The BoxsterS constructor simply calls the Car constructor with the appropriate Boxster S values and then sets the gear ratio value by calling the setGearRatio method.

```
public class BoxsterS extends Car
{
  //  The BoxsterS constructor calls the Car constructor
  //  and then sets the gear ratios for the BoxsterS.
  //  Here are some specs for the BoxsterS
  //  mass = 1393.0 kg (with 70 kg driver)
  //  area = 1.94 m^2
  //  Cd = 0.31
  //  redline = 7200 rpm
  //  finalDriveRatio = 3.44
  //  wheelRadius = 0.3186
  //  numberOfGears = 6;

  public BoxsterS(double x, double y, double z, double vx,
              double vy, double vz, double time, double density) {

    super(x, y, z, vx, vy, vz, time, 1393.0, 1.94,
          density, 0.31, 7200.0, 3.44, 0.3186, 6);

    //  Set the gear ratios.
    setGearRatio(1, 3.82);
    setGearRatio(2, 2.20);
    setGearRatio(3, 1.52);
    setGearRatio(4, 1.22);
    setGearRatio(5, 1.02);
    setGearRatio(6, 0.84);
  }
}
```

Now that the Car and BoxsterS classes are defined, they can be incorporated into the Car Simulator GUI. The class that implements the GUI is named CarSimulator. As with the other GUIs in this book, we will not go over every detail of the CarSimulator class, but you are encouraged to download the source code from the Apress website. As with most of the other sample games in this book, the CarSimulator class makes use of a Timer object to control the execution speed of the game. Among the fields declared in the CarSimulator class is a BoxsterS object that represents the car being modeled in the simulation.

```
import javax.swing.*;
import java.awt.*;
import javax.swing.border.BevelBorder;
import java.awt.event.*;
import javax.swing.Timer;

public class CarSimulator extends JFrame implements ActionListener
{
  // Other field declarations not shown ...

  private BoxsterS car;
```

When the Start button is pressed, the start method is called on the Timer object to start the simulation. The Timer object is set up to call the actionPerformed method every 0.05 seconds. The first thing the actionPerformed method does is to determine whether the car is accelerating, cruising at a constant speed, or braking, and sets the value of the mode field accordingly.

```
// This ActionListener is called by the Timer
class GameUpdater implements ActionListener {
  public void actionPerformed(ActionEvent event) {
    // Figure out if the car is accelerating,
    // cruising, or braking, and set the mode of
    // the car accordingly.
    if ( accelButton.isSelected() == true ) {
      car.setMode("accelerating");
    }
    else if ( cruiseButton.isSelected() == true ) {
      car.setMode("cruising");
    }
    else {
      car.setMode("braking");
    }
```

The updateLocationAndVelocity method is called to update the location and velocity of the car. This method is implemented in the DragProjectile class, but since the BoxsterS class is a subclass of DragProjectile, the method can be accessed inside the BoxsterS class.

```
// Update the car velocity and position at the next
// time increment.
double timeIncrement = 0.06;
car.updateLocationAndVelocity(timeIncrement);
```

The new *rpm* value of the engine is computed using Equation (8.13). If the value exceeds the redline value for the car, a warning message is displayed. If the *rpm* value exceeds 8000, the engine is blown and the simulation stops.

```
// Compute the new engine rpm value.
double rpm = car.getVx()*60.0*car.getGearRatio()*
    car.getFinalDriveRatio()/(2.0*Math.PI*car.getWheelRadius());
car.setOmegaE(rpm);

// If the rpm exceeds the redline value, put a
// warning message on the screen. First, clear the
// message text field of any existing messages.
messageTextField.setText("");
if ( car.getOmegaE() > car.getRedline() ) {
  messageTextField.setText("Warning: Exceeding redline rpm");
}
if ( car.getOmegaE() > 8000.0 ) {
  messageTextField.setText("You have blown the engine!");
  gameTimer.stop();
}
```

Two rectangular markers are used to simulate the motion of the car. The car stays in a set location in the GUI display, and the rectangular markers move from right to left. The location of the markers is updated based on the velocity of the car. The factor of 10 is a scaling factor that relates the size of the car image to the actual length of the car. After the new marker locations have been determined, the GUI display is updated.

```
// Update the location of the rectangular markers.
rectangleOneX = rectangleOneX + 10.0*car.getVx()*timeIncrement;
rectangleTwoX = rectangleTwoX + 10.0*car.getVx()*timeIncrement;

// If the markers have gone off the display, move them
// back to zero.
if ( rectangleOneX > 401.0 ) {
  rectangleOneX = 0.0;
}
if ( rectangleTwoX > 401.0 ) {
  rectangleTwoX = 0.0;
}

// Update the display.
resetDisplay();
    }
  }
}
```

Play around with the Car Simulator. Switch the mode to "accelerate" and push the Start button to start the simulation. Be sure to watch the *rpm* value and shift up before it hits the redline value. When you get to sixth gear, let the car run and see what the maximum velocity of the car is. Then select the "brake" mode and watch the car slow down. If you want to play with shifting gears up and down, you can set the mode to "cruise", which will hold the velocity constant. If for some reason the entire GUI is not rendered, press the Reset button to redraw the GUI.

Keep in mind that the Car Simulator uses the maximum possible acceleration of the car according to Equation (8.20). In the Car Simulator, you're driving "pedal to the metal."

Wheel Traction

Up to this point, we have been modeling the car tires under the assumption they roll without sliding along the ground. In certain situations, however, this may not be the case. If a car is stopped and the accelerator is pushed to the floor, the tires may spin in place for a moment before the car starts to move forward. If a car tries to drive around a corner at too high a speed, it may slide outward.

If you recall from the beginning of this section, the tires move the car forward because of the friction that exists between the tire and the surface of the ground. This force, known as the **traction force**, is equal to the normal force exerted on the tire multiplied by the coefficient of friction between the tire and road.

$$F_T = \mu_k F_N = \mu_k mg \cos\theta \tag{8.32}$$

The traction force, shown in Equation (8.32), is the maximum force that can be applied to the tire for it to roll without sliding on the ground. The traction force for a given car is typically determined by putting the car through what is known as a **skidpad** test. The car is driven around a level, circular track. The velocity of the car is increased until centripetal acceleration of the car is equal to the traction force of the tires.

$$\mu_k mg = m\frac{v^2}{r} \tag{8.33}$$

The r parameter in Equation (8.33) is the radius of the track. If the velocity of the car increases beyond this point, the centripetal force is greater than the traction force, and the car begins to slide outward on the track. The results of the skidpad test are usually expressed in terms of the maximum acceleration the tires can be subject to without sliding. On dry pavement, the 2004 Porsche Boxster S has a maximum tire frictional force of $0.91g$, where g is the gravitational acceleration.

This limiting acceleration applies to straight-line motion as well. If the torque applied to the wheels results in a force that is greater than the maximum frictional force, the tires will spin against the ground. The maximum frictional force is therefore a limiting value on the acceleration of the car. No matter how much torque the engine is applying to the wheels, the acceleration of the car won't be greater than that defined by the maximum frictional force.

For game programming purposes, the implementation of wheel traction effects is fairly straightforward. The first thing to do is to compute the force applied to the wheels from the engine, which is a function of the engine torque, gear ratios, and wheel radius.

$$F_T = \frac{T_w}{r_w} = \frac{T_e g_k G}{r_w} \tag{8.34}$$

Next we compute the maximum frictional force from Equation (8.32). If the engine torque force is less than the maximum frictional force, the engine torque force is used in the equations of motion. If the engine torque force is greater than the maximum frictional force, then the wheels are sliding, and the maximum frictional force should be used in the equations of motion.

The value of the coefficient of friction in Equation (8.32) depends on the condition of the tires and the surface on which the car is driving. A bald tire will have a lower coefficient of friction than will a tire with a normal tread. A tire will have a lower coefficient of friction on ice than it will on dry pavement.

One final note about maximum tire frictional force is that it applies to the total acceleration of the car. A car going around a curve will experience a centripetal acceleration. The total acceleration of the car is equal to the square root of the sum of the squares of the centripetal and straight-line acceleration of the car.

$$a_{total} = \sqrt{a_{straightline}^2 + \left(\frac{v^2}{r}\right)^2} \tag{8.35}$$

One conclusion from Equation (8.35) is that a car that is accelerating into a curve is more likely to skid than a car traveling at a constant velocity around the same curve.

Driving Around Curves

Up to this point the discussion on the physics of cars has focused on the straight-line motion of a car. Of course, cars can't drive in a straight line forever. At some point they need to turn or drive around a curve. Modeling a car driving around a curve can be separated into two areas depending on whether the car is performing a high-speed or low-speed turn.

We'll start with the subject of a car driving around a curve at low speeds. As you would expect, modeling low-speed curves is easier than modeling high-speed curves because some factors, such as centripetal acceleration, can be ignored. The wheels can be assumed to be rolling without slipping. Consider the car shown in Figure 8-10. The front wheels of the car are turned at an angle, δ, such that the car is making a right turn. If the car is traveling at a constant speed, it will drive in a circle of radius, r_c.

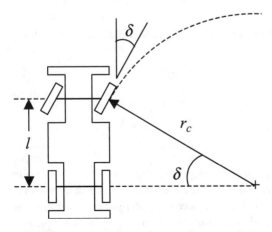

Figure 8-10. *A car making a turn at low speeds*

The center of the circle that the car is traveling on is located at the intersection of lines drawn perpendicular to the front and rear right wheels. The radius of the circle can be found from trigonometric relations. The distance from the centers of the front and back wheels, l, is known as the **wheelbase**. The ratio of the wheelbase to the circle radius is equal to the sine of the wheel angle, δ. Rearranging this relation results in an equation for the circle radius.

$$r_c = \frac{l}{\sin \delta} \tag{8.36}$$

Another important quantity to determine is the rate that a car will make the turn—that is, the angular velocity of the car during its turn. If the wheels are rolling without friction, the angular turn velocity, ω_t, is equal to the translational velocity magnitude, v, of the car divided by the turn radius.

$$\omega_t = \frac{v}{r_c} \tag{8.37}$$

Using Equation (8.36), the angular turn velocity can be expressed in terms of the wheelbase and wheel angle.

$$\omega_t = \frac{v \sin \delta}{l} \tag{8.38}$$

Equations (8.36) and (8.38) provide all the information needed to model a low-speed turn. The turn radius can be determined from the wheelbase and wheel angle. The car then travels along this circle at an angular velocity determined from Equation (8.38). Let's look at an example to see how it all fits together. Let's say the driver of a Boxster S car wants to perform a low-speed 90-degree turn at a translational velocity of 10 *m/s* (36 *km/hr*). To make this turn, the wheels are turned at an angle of 10 degrees. The wheelbase of the Boxster S is 2.41 *m*. What is the radius of the turn, and how long will it take the car to make the turn?

The turn radius can be computed from Equation (8.36).

$$r_c = \frac{2.41}{\sin\left(\dfrac{10\pi}{180}\right)} = 13.9 \ m \tag{8.39}$$

The time required to make a 90-degree turn is equal to the number of radians in the turn, $\pi/2$, divided by the angular turn velocity.

$$t = \frac{\pi}{2\omega_t} = \frac{\pi l}{2v \sin \delta} = \frac{\pi * 2.41}{2 * 10 * \sin\left(\dfrac{10\pi}{180}\right)} = 2.2 \ s \tag{8.40}$$

High-Speed Turns

A general model for describing high-speed car turns is complicated by several factors. For one thing, as the car goes around the curve, the centripetal force experienced by the car may cause the tires to slide outward. In other words, the tires will have a velocity component normal to the direction in which they are rotating. The normal force component can also generate a torque about the center of mass of the car, causing the entire vehicle to rotate. You have probably seen this effect in watching a car take a high-speed turn where the back end of the car slides outward or "fishtails."

The simplest way to model high-speed turns is to compute the lateral force, $F_{lateral}$, on the car as being equal to the difference between the centripetal force on the car and the frictional force acting on the tires.

$$F_{lateral} = \frac{mv^2}{r_c} - \mu_k mg \cos \theta \tag{8.41}$$

The angle θ is the angle of any slope that the car might be driving on. In Equation (8.41), a positive lateral force is one acting outwards. Because the frictional force will never exceed the centripetal force (the car won't be sucked into the center of the turn circle), the lateral force term will always be greater than or equal to zero.

Equation (8.41) provides a rough approximation to lateral force, but it doesn't model effects such as fishtailing or spinouts when a car tries to take a curve too fast. To get the more sophisticated high-speed turning effects requires that the lateral force be evaluated for each tire as it goes around the curve. This analysis is pretty complicated, involving concepts such as wheel slip angles, and is beyond the scope of this book.

Modeling Car Crashes

As we all know, cars sometimes run into things. In real life, hitting something with your car is generally a bad thing to have happen to you. In car simulations, sometimes it seems like half the fun is running into or bouncing off of other objects. We learned about the basics of collision modeling in Chapter 6, and many of the same concepts can be applied to cars. Cars are not solid blocks of metal. When they hit something, unless it is at very low speeds, the body of the car will crumple as a result of the collision. The collision is inelastic because some of the kinetic energy of the car and whatever it hits will be converted into work that is performed in damaging the car.

In Chapter 6, equations were presented to compute the post-collision velocities of two objects in the direction of the line of action of the collision. Those expressions are repeated here in Equations (8.42a) and (8.42b). The post-collision velocities, v'_1 and v'_2, are functions of the masses of the two objects, m_1 and m_2, the pre-collision velocities, v_1 and v_2, and the coefficient of restitution, e. One of the objects will be the car. The other object could be almost anything—another car, a tree, a fast food restaurant, and so on.

$$v'_1 = \frac{m_1 - em_2}{m_1 + m_2} v_1 + \frac{(1+e) m_2}{m_1 + m_2} v_2 \tag{8.42a}$$

$$v'_2 = \frac{(1+e) m_1}{m_1 + m_2} v_1 + \frac{m_2 - em_1}{m_1 + m_2} v_2 \tag{8.42b}$$

If any part of the car is deformed during the collision, then the collision is inelastic, and the coefficient of restitution will be less than one. As a reminder, a more extensive discussion of elastic and inelastic collision can be found in Chapter 6. An extreme case for the car collision would be if the collision were completely inelastic, meaning that the coefficient of restitution is equal to zero. In this case, the car and the object it collided with would stick together, and they would have the same post-collision velocity shown in Equation (8.43).

$$v_1' = v_2' = \frac{m_1 v_1 + m_2 v_2}{m_1 + m_2}$$

(8.43)

In most cases, the collision won't be completely inelastic, and the coefficient of restitution will have some nonzero value. The car will suffer a certain amount of damage, and it will bounce off the object it hits. The F1-Spirit Formula One racing game uses a value of 0.25 for the coefficient of restitution.

Motorcycles

Motorcycles are another type of motor vehicle that can be used to create exciting game scenarios. Generally speaking, motorcycles are lighter, more agile, and have greater acceleration potential than cars, but much of the general physics to describe the acceleration and braking is the same between motorcycles and cars. Motorcycle engines generate torque that is applied to the back wheel, and friction between the wheel and the ground propels the motorcycle forward. Motorcycles are subject to the forces of aerodynamic drag, rolling friction, and traction, just as cars are.

Table 8-4 compares some physical and performance characteristics between a sports car and a performance motorcycle. The sports car is the 2004 Porsche Boxster S we used in the "Cars" section of this chapter. The motorcycle is the 2004 Honda CBR1000RR. As you would expect, the mass of the motorcycle is considerably less than that of the car. The Boxster S has a higher top speed, but the motorcycle has greater acceleration. It can reach 100 km/hr in a little over half the time it takes the car. The car engine is more powerful in terms of peak torque, but the motorcycle engine has a much higher redline rpm value (which is one reason why the acceleration potential is higher).

Table 8-4. *A Comparison of Motorcycle and Car Characteristics*

Quantity	Honda CBR1000RR	Porsche Boxster S
Vehicle mass (kg)	180	1323
0–100 km/hr (sec)	2.95	5.5
Top speed (km/hr)	225	266
Redline rpm	11650	7200
Peak engine torque (N-m)	106 @ 8500 rpm	310 @ 4600 rpm
Peak engine horsepower	153.5 @ 11000 rpm	258 @ 6400 rpm

As we said before, many similarities exist in the physics that describe the motion of a motorcycle and car. There is one important area of difference that we will explore in a little more detail—how a motorcycle turns.

Turning a Motorcycle

Turning a car is pretty straightforward. The wheels are turned in the direction of the turn. If you try to turn in this manner on a motorcycle, except at very low speeds, you will crash the bike. The reason is an effect called **gyroscopic precession**. When the wheel of the bike is turned in one direction, a torque is applied to the wheel in the opposite direction, causing the bike to lean. In other words, if you turn the front wheel of a bike to the left, the bike will lean to the right and vice versa. Because of this effect, if you try to turn the front wheel of a motorcycle in the direction of the turn, you will fall forward off the bike.

■**Tidbit** It's easy to demonstrate gyroscopic precession, and the bike doesn't have to be moving to do it. Stand your motorcycle or bicycle straight up and turn the front wheel 90 degrees in either direction. The bike will lean in the opposite direction.

The secret to successfully turning a motorcycle at higher speeds is to lean *into* the turn as shown in Figure 8-11. This type of leaning stabilizes the motion of the motorcycle during the turn. There are several ways to get a bike to lean into a turn. The first technique makes use of gyroscopic precession and is known as **countersteering**. To initiate a turn, the driver must turn the front wheel in the *opposite* direction of the turn. This maneuver may seem strange, but remember that turning the front wheel in the opposite direction of the turn causes the bike to lean into the turn. The proper lean can also be created or augmented by having the driver lean his shoulders into the direction of the turn.

Figure 8-11. *To successfully turn, a motorcycle must lean into the turn. (Photo courtesy of Brett McLeod)*

The mathematical equations that describe the forces and moments that exist during a countersteered motorcycle turn are quite complicated, with various moments of inertia terms and angular velocities. Unless you are building a very detailed motorcycle simulation, there is probably no reason to try to include that level of complexity in your game. The way to include countersteering is probably more as a visual effect than anything else. When the motorcycle riders in your games make a turn, have the motorcycle lean into the turn.

Adding Sophisticated Effects to the Car or Motorcycle Models

This chapter has covered the basics of modeling the motion of cars and motorcycles. As you might imagine, certain sophisticated physical effects that govern the motion of cars and motorcycles were not covered in detail. This chapter already mentioned that a true representation of the lateral force experienced by a car during a turn involves analyzing the lateral force experienced by each of the four wheels. Another effect that happens during a turn is that weight is shifted to the outside wheels.

To add more sophisticated effects to your car or motorcycle model, use the same sequence of steps that have been used to come up with the basic model. First, create a force diagram to determine what forces and torques act on the vehicle and the direction in which they act. Second, come up with equations that describe the motion of the vehicle based on the force diagram. Finally, code up and solve the equations of motion using an ODE solver.

Summary

In this chapter, once again armed with a basic knowledge of Newtonian mechanics and kinematics, you learned the basic physics behind the forces and accelerations that act upon cars and motorcycles. Many of the concepts covered in this chapter are equally applicable to other types of motor vehicles such as snowmobiles or tanks. You should now be able to create fun and realistic motor vehicle simulations.

Some of the specific things you learned in this chapter include the following:

- How transmission gears are used to increase engine torque

- How to model aerodynamic drag and rolling friction for a car

- What the redline *rpm* value is and its effect on car performance

- How the wheel torque is a function of the engine torque, the gear ratio, and the final drive ratio

- How wheel traction limits the maximum acceleration of a car

- How to calculate the turn radius and turn rate for a car driving around a curve

- How motorcycles turn by leaning into the turn

References

1. B. Bowling, "Air Drag Coefficients and Frontal Area Calculation," www.bgsoflex.com/airdragchart.html.

2. C.E. Mungan, "Rolling Friction of a Free Wheel," http://usna.edu/Users/physics/mungan/Scholarship/RollingFriction.pdf.

3. R. van Gaal, "Car Physics Basics," www.racer.nl/reference/carphys.htm#enginebraking.

■ ■ ■

CHAPTER 9

Boats and Things That Float

So far in this book we've focused on land-based activities. It's time to hit the water. In this chapter, we will explore the basic physics behind boats and things that float. As with the chapters on sports and car simulations, we'll start armed with an understanding of Newtonian mechanics and kinematics. The concepts of force, acceleration, torque, and velocity apply just as well to boats as they do to projectiles or cars. The big difference with boats, of course, is that they float, so we will learn about a new force that allows this to happen.

The emphasis of this chapter will be on powerboats, but an introduction will be provided on the more complicated physics of sailboats. At the end of the chapter, the physics of surfing will be explored. Some of the specific topics this chapter will cover include the following:

- A review of some basic nautical terminology

- Different boat hull types and what they are used for

- The basic forces that act on a boat

- The force of buoyancy, what it is and how it is modeled

- How the power from a boat engine is converted into thrust to propel the boat

- The different drag forces that act on a boat

- How to obtain an acceleration profile for a boat or other watercraft from performance test data

- An introduction to jet skis

Some Nautical Terminology

People have been sailing and floating on boats for thousands of years, and over time seafarers have developed a rather unique terminology for describing the various components of a boat and many other things besides. Before we get into details on how a boat moves through the water, let's spend a little time going over some basic terminology.

The first things to discuss are the words "boat" and "ship." They are both generic terms for a vessel that travels on the water. The word "boat" is generally used for smaller vessels, whereas "ship" is generally used to describe larger, seagoing vessels. One commonly used distinction is that a boat is a vessel that can be carried aboard a ship. The focus of this chapter will be on powerboats and speedboats, so the term "boat" will be used throughout.

There are specialized terms for just about every piece of the boat geometry. Some of the more commonly used terms are shown in Figure 9-1. The arrow in Figure 9-1 indicates the direction of forward travel for the boat.

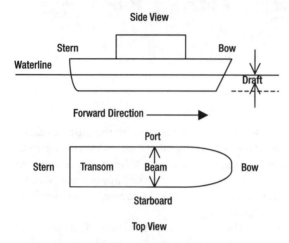

Figure 9-1. *Boat geometry terminology*

Here are definitions for the terms shown in Figure 9-1 and for some other commonly used nautical terminology:

- **Beam**: The width of the boat. Also called the breadth.

- **Bow**: The front or forward part of the boat.

- **Displacement**: The weight of the water displaced by the boat. We'll discuss what "water displacement" means in the "Buoyancy" section later in the chapter.

- **Draft**: The depth of the boat below the waterline. Also used to describe the depth of water necessary to float a boat.

- **Hull**: The outer shell of the boat.

- **Knot**: A unit of velocity commonly used for boats. 1 *knot* = 0.514 *m/s* = 1.852 *km/hr*.

- **Port**: The left-hand side of the boat when facing the front of the boat.

- **Starboard**: The right-hand side of the boat when facing the front of the boat.

- **Stern**: The back or aft part of the boat.

- **Transom**: The flat, vertical (or nearly vertical) aft end of the hull.

Boat Hull Types

As you learned in the last section, the hull is the outer shell of a boat. There are several general types of hulls. A **displacement hull** is one that stays relatively low in the water when the boat is traveling and plows its way through the water. The cross-section of a displacement hull has a relatively constant U shape from bow to stern. Displacement hulls are used in long-distance powerboats such as cruise liners and trawlers. They are the most fuel-efficient type of hull, but they also experience the highest drag forces in the water, which limits their speed to relatively low values.

With a **semi-displacement** hull, the forward section of the hull is V shaped, which allows the front end of the boat to lift up when the boat is traveling forward. The lifting motion reduces the water drag (also called **hydrodynamic drag**) experienced by the boat. The top speed of a semi-displacement hull is higher than that of a comparable displacement hull. Lobster boats and coastal trawlers will typically have semi-displacement hulls.

High-speed powerboats and jet skis have what is known as a **planing hull**. This type of hull has a V shape over much of the hull, allowing the hull to rise up out of the water when the boat is traveling forward. The angle that the hull rises out of the water is known as the **planing angle** (see Figure 9-2).

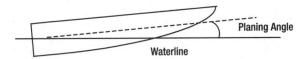

Figure 9-2. *A planing hull can rise up out of the water.*

Since the portion of the hull still in the water is reduced during planing, the hydrodynamic drag experienced by the boat is reduced as well. Planing boats can achieve speeds of 160 *km/hr* or more. The downside is that planing boats have the highest fuel consumption rates and are the least stable in heavy seas, but that is rarely an issue in game programming situations. Since most boat game simulations involve speed, you will probably most often be dealing with planing hulls.

Basic Force Diagram

Just like the projectiles, sports balls, and motor vehicles that we have studied in the previous chapters of this book, a boat traveling across the water is subject to various forces that determine the acceleration, velocity, and position of the boat. The basic force diagram for a boat is shown in Figure 9-3.

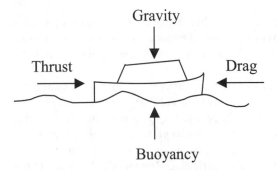

Figure 9-3. *Basic force diagram on a boat*

There are four forces that we will consider to act upon the boat. You are already well acquainted with the force due to gravity. It pulls the boat downward. In order for the boat to float on the water, another force must be there to counteract the force of gravity. This force is referred to as the **buoyancy** of the boat. We will look at buoyancy in more detail in the next section, but for now it suffices to say that if the buoyancy force is large enough to counteract the gravitational force, the boat will float.

The two forces that act in the horizontal direction are thrust and drag. In a powerboat, propellers that are connected to the boat's engine provide the thrust. This chapter will cover the different types of boat engines and how to determine the power and thrust that they provide later in this chapter. Drag forces resist the forward motion of the boat. You will learn more about boat drag a bit later in this chapter as well.

There are additional forces that might be included but won't be discussed in detail in this chapter. For example, there may be a current in the water that would affect the boat in a way similar to the way wind affects the trajectory of a projectile. Some types of boats, in particular sailboats, are greatly affected by the direction and magnitude of the wind.

Buoyancy

You know from your own experience that some things float and some things don't. You also know that the force of gravity will pull any object on a body of water downwards to the bottom of the body of water. For an object to float, there must be another force that balances the gravitational pull. This force is referred to as the buoyancy force.

Buoyancy has been studied for a very long time. Archimedes discovered the principles of buoyancy over 2200 years ago. Archimedes, who lived in Syracuse, Sicily, is considered the greatest mathematician and scientist of the ancient world. Along with the field of hydrostatics (of which buoyancy is a part), Archimedes also discovered how pulleys and levers could be used to lift heavy objects.

■**Tidbit** Archimedes allegedly discovered the principles of buoyancy while he was taking a bath. When the idea came to him, he jumped out of the bath and ran through the streets yelling "Eureka!," which means "I have found it!" Hopefully, he wrapped a towel around himself first.

To understand buoyancy, consider what happens when a rock is dropped into a pail of water and sinks to the bottom. The water that used to be in the space now occupied by the rock has been pushed away, or displaced, by the rock. The volume of water displaced is equal to the volume of the rock.

Archimedes discovered that the weight of an object submerged in water is less than the weight of the object in air. In other words, the net force on the submerged object is lower, which means a force must be acting on the body that opposes the force of gravity. This force is due to the buoyancy of an object. Archimedes also discovered that the reduction in weight of a submerged or floating object is equal to the weight of the water displaced by the object. The buoyancy force, F_B, is therefore equal to the weight of the displaced water, which is equal to the density of the water, ρ_w, multiplied by the volume of the displaced water, V_w, and the gravitational constant, g.

$$F_B = \rho_w V_w g \tag{9.1}$$

The buoyancy force acts through the geometrical center of an object, which is not always the same as the center of mass of an object. If the geometrical center and center of mass are in different locations, the buoyancy force and gravitational force will create a torque that will cause the object to rotate. This fact has potentially serious consequences for boats. For example, if all of the people on a crowded boat move to one side of a boat, the center of mass of the boat may shift enough to create a torque large enough to capsize the boat.

If you recall from Chapter 3, the density of an object is equal to the mass of the object divided by its volume. Equation (9.1) isn't just for objects floating in water. It is applicable to any fluid, including air. The densities of fresh water, salt water, and air at sea-level conditions are shown in Table 9-1. It probably comes as no surprise that water is significantly more dense than air, which means that objects will have a much easier time floating in water than they would floating in air.

Table 9-1. *Density of Water and Air*

Substance	Density (kg/m^3)
Fresh water	1000
Seawater	1025–1030
Air (sea level)	1.2

When a boat floats, the buoyancy force due to the water displaced by the boat balances the gravitational force acting on the boat. If the weight of the boat increases, if more people get on the boat, for example, the boat will sink a little lower in the water as shown in Figure 9-4. By doing so, more water is displaced, which increases the buoyancy forces acting on the boat, which balances out the additional weight of the boat.

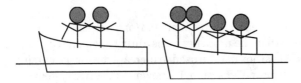

Figure 9-4. *If weight is added to a boat, it will float lower in the water.*

Equation (9.1) can be used to compute the maximum loading that can be placed on a boat (or any other object) and have it still float. The maximum buoyancy force the boat can generate is equal to the volume of the boat hull multiplied by the density of the fluid in which the boat is floating and the gravitational constant. The weight of the boat and whatever is inside the boat must be less than this value.

$$m_b g < \rho_w V_w g \tag{9.2}$$

The gravitational constant appears on both sides of Equation (9.2) and can be cancelled out.

Exercise

1. A canoe has a volume of 0.5 m^3 and has a mass of 30 kg. What is the total mass of passengers and cargo that can be loaded into the canoe before it will sink?

Buoyancy and Density

Another way to think of buoyancy and whether a boat or other object will float is in terms of density. Equation (9.2) can be rewritten if the mass of the boat is expressed in terms of the density of the boat multiplied by the volume of the boat.

$$\rho_b V_b < \rho_w V_w \tag{9.3}$$

When the boat or other object just begins to sink below the surface of the water, its volume will be equal to the volume of the displaced water, so the two volume terms in Equation (9.3) cancel each other out. When this is done, we see that for an object to float, its density must be less than the density of water.

$$\rho_b < \rho_w \tag{9.4}$$

But wait a minute, boats are sometimes made out of steel or concrete. Steel has a density of 7850 kg/m^3, which is more than the density of water. So a boat made out of steel should sink, right? The problem with this line of thought is that you can't think of a boat as a solid object. If the boat consisted of a solid block of steel, it would sink. In applying Equation (9.4) to boats, the density of the boat is equal to the mass of the boat divided by the total volume of the boat, including the volume of any empty space inside the boat. Steel boats float because there is a lot of empty space inside the hull of the boat that gets added to the total volume.

Thrust

A boat engine generates torque that is transferred to a drive shaft and/or a propeller shaft, which in turn is connected to a propeller. When the propeller turns, thrust is generated that propels the boat forwards or backwards. A gearbox may be used to increase the torque coming from the engine. The engine-gearbox-shaft-propeller system is known as the drive system of the boat. Before we begin to mathematically model the thrust imparted to a boat from its engine, let's go over some drive system basics.

Drive System Types

There are several different ways to configure the drive system of a boat. They have different advantages and disadvantages and are used for different types of boats. The simplest and least expensive drive system, shown in Figure 9-5, is **direct drive**. The engine is placed in the middle of the boat and is connected to the propeller by a single, straight shaft that enters the water at an angle. This type of drive system is known as an **inboard drive system** since the engine, gearbox, and most of the shaft is contained inside the hull.

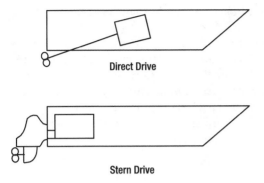

Figure 9-5. *Drive system types*

Because the weight of the engine is moved forward and because the propeller thrust is directed upward with the direct drive system, a direct drive boat will have a lower planing angle at high speed and will experience more hull drag.

The most commonly used type of drive system with modern, planing powerboats is the **stern drive** and is also shown in Figure 9-5. The engine is located inside the hull and is placed very close to the transom (the aft end of the hull). The drive shaft goes through the transom into a gearbox located outside the hull aft of the transom. The engine torque is transmitted downward to the propeller shaft located below the gearbox. The stern drive is also known as an **Inboard/Outboard** (I/O) drive system because some of the drive components are inside the hull and some are outside.

The angle of the propeller shaft in a stern drive can be rotated somewhat up or down to make it easier for the boat to plane and to reduce hull drag at high speeds. Stern drives are also more maneuverable than direct drives because the boat can be turned by rotating the propeller shafts from side to side. Because the engine torque must pass through two 90-degree gearboxes to reach the propeller shaft, a stern drive is somewhat less efficient than a direct drive. A stern drive is also more complicated mechanically than a direct drive and is therefore more prone to failure.

In addition to direct drive and stern drive systems, there are other drive system configurations that have been developed over the years including **Vee drives** and **surface drives**. These are inboard drive systems that involve different configurations of the engine, gearbox, and shafts. There are also **outboard drive** systems where the engine and propeller are located at the stern of the boat outside of the hull.

Another completely different type of drive system is a **jet drive** system. Rather than a mechanical drive system based on turning drive and propeller shafts, a jet drive works as a powerful, engine-driven water pump. Water is sucked in through an opening in the bottom of the boat and shot out at high velocities through a nozzle at the stern. The nozzle discharge provides the propulsion for the boat. Jet drives are used for some types of powerboats and are widely used with jet skis, a topic that will be explored in more detail later in this chapter.

Propeller Basics

The purpose of the drive system of a boat is to transfer the torque from the boat's engine to the propeller. When the propeller (also known as the screw) turns, thrust is generated that propels the boat forwards or backwards. Let's take a little time now to understand how a boat propeller works.

When the propeller rotates, as shown in Figure 9-6, the underside of each propeller blade pushes the water next to it down and back, similar to the hand motion of a swimmer doing the backstroke. Because the propeller blades are pushing on the water, the pressure on the rearward-facing side of the propeller blade is greater than the pressure on the forward-facing side of the blade. This pressure difference generates a thrust that pushes the propeller, and therefore the boat, forward. This effect is similar to that seen with airplane wings where the pressure difference between the top and bottom surfaces of the wing generates lift.

Figure 9-6. *Side view of a typical boat propeller pushing water away from it. (Photo courtesy of Piranha Propellers, www.piranha.com)*

There are two important numbers that are used to characterize boat propellers. These numbers are usually listed after the propeller name. For example, you might see the numbers "20×24." The first number is the diameter of the propeller, usually in inches. The second number is called the **pitch** of the propeller and represents the theoretical distance, again usually in inches, that the propeller will move relative to the water around it for every revolution of the propeller.

The theoretical forward velocity of the propeller, v_T, is equal to the pitch of the propeller, $\bar{P}$, multiplied by the propeller turnover rate, n (in revolutions per second).

$$v_T = \bar{P}n \tag{9.5}$$

Unfortunately, the theoretical velocity is never achieved because some losses will occur due to propeller blade bending, air bubbles in the water, and other causes. The actual distance traveled per propeller revolution to be less than the pitch of the propeller. The actual forward velocity of the propeller relative to the water around it, also known as the **speed of advance**, is less than the theoretical maximum velocity by a quantity, s_r, known as the **real slip ratio**.

$$v_a = (1 - s_r)v_T = (1 - s_r)\bar{P}n \tag{9.6}$$

The real slip ratio is a dimensionless quantity with a value between 0 and 1. We've been careful to note that the speed of advance is the forward velocity of the propeller relative to the water around it. In general, this will not be the same as the velocity of the boat. When a boat moves forward in the water, the water just behind the boat will acquire a forward motion in the same direction as the ship. The forward moving water is known as the **wake** of the boat. The **wake velocity**, v_w, is equal to the difference between the velocity of the boat, v_b, and the speed of advance, v_a.

$$v_w = v_b - v_a \tag{9.7}$$

The ratio of the wake velocity to the boat velocity is called the **wake fraction,** w_f.

$$w_f = \frac{v_w}{v_b} = \frac{v_b - v_a}{v_b} \tag{9.8}$$

The boat velocity and speed of advance of the propeller can be related using the wake fraction.

$$v_a = (1 - w_f)v_b \tag{9.9}$$

In looking at Equation (9.6), we see it doesn't really provide the velocity of the boat because the wake velocity at a given point in time is also required. A variation of Equation (9.6) exists that relates the boat velocity to the turnover rate of the propeller. The quantity, s_a, in Equation (9.10) is called the **apparent slip ratio.**

$$v_b = (1 - s_a)\bar{P}n \tag{9.10}$$

A final note about propeller geometry is that propellers generally have two, three, four, or five blades. Having fewer blades increases the forces experienced by each blade, known as the **blade loading.** If the blade loading is too high, the performance and even structural integrity of the propeller can be compromised. Increasing the number of blades shifts the loading from the blades to the engine, possibly preventing the engine from producing its theoretical maximum power.

Thrust

The thrust of a boat due to the propellers can be analyzed in terms of power. The engine generates a certain power level, P_e, which will typically not be constant, but will be a function of the turnover rate of the engine. This power is transferred through shafts, gearboxes, and other mechanical devices to the propeller. There are losses along the way, so the power that is available to the propeller, P_p, is some fraction of the engine power.

$$P_p = \eta_s P_e \tag{9.11}$$

The **shaft transmission efficiency,** η_s, in Equation (9.11) will generally have a value fairly close to 1.

When the boat moves through the water a certain velocity, v_b, a certain power level called the **effective power,** P_{eff} is necessary to overcome the resistance, R, experienced by the boat at that velocity. The effective power is equal to the resistance acting on the boat multiplied by the boat velocity.

$$P_{eff} = Rv_b \tag{9.12}$$

The effective power can be related to the engine power using the **coefficient of propulsive efficiency,** η_p.

$$P_{eff} = \eta_p P_e \tag{9.13}$$

Typical values for the coefficient of propulsive efficiency range from 0.5 to 0.7.[1]
Equations (9.12) and (9.13) can be used to estimate the maximum velocity for a boat. If the overall

resistance is known at a certain velocity, the effective power required can be computed. If the coefficient of propulsive efficiency is known, it can be compared against the maximum power output of the engine to determine whether the engine can provide this level of power.

When the propeller rotates through the water, it generates a thrust. The thrust power, P_T, is equal to the thrust force, F_T, multiplied by the speed of advance of the propeller.

$$P_T = F_T v_a = F_T v_b (1 - w_f) \tag{9.14}$$

The effective power and thrust power are related by the coefficient of **hull efficiency**, η_H.

$$P_{eff} = \eta_H P_T \tag{9.15}$$

Combining Equations (9.13), (9.14), and (9.15) results in an equation for the thrust produced by the boat engine as a function of the engine power, boat velocity, wake fraction, and the coefficients of propulsive and hull efficiency.

$$F_T = \frac{\eta_p P_e}{\eta_H v_b (1 - w_f)} \tag{9.16}$$

The key to using Equation (9.16), however, is that you need values for the two efficiency coefficients, η_p and η_H, and for the wake fraction, w_f.

Drag

A boat traveling through the water will experience drag forces that will resist the motion of the boat. Boats are a bit different from the projectiles and cars we have previously explored because part of the boat is below water and part of the boat is above water. A boat will therefore experience both hydrodynamic drag due to interactions with the water and aerodynamic drag on the boat structures that are exposed to the air.

The good news is that the same equation that was used for aerodynamic drag can also be applied to hydrodynamic drag, namely that the hydrodynamic drag force, F_{HD}, is equal to the product of the square of the boat velocity, v_b, the fluid density, ρ, a characteristic area, A, and a coefficient, C_R, known as the **coefficient of resistance**.

$$F_{HD} = \frac{1}{2} C_R \rho v_b^2 A \tag{9.17}$$

The area, A, in Equation (9.17) is the wetted area of the boat, meaning the surface of the hull that is in contact with the water. Many different phenomena contribute to the total hydrodynamic drag experienced by a boat. The three major components are skin friction drag, wave drag, and form drag. The overall coefficient of resistance can be written as the sum of these three components.

$$C_R = C_f + C_w + C_{Form} \tag{9.18}$$

Let's look at the three main components of hydrodynamic drag in a bit more detail starting with skin friction drag.

Skin Friction Drag

Skin friction drag is caused by the contact between the water and the hull as the hull slides through the water. The water clings to the hull and resists the hull motion. Skin friction drag is the dominant hydrodynamic drag component at lower boat velocities and is still significant at higher velocities. The skin friction coefficient, C_f, is a function of the Reynolds number of the boat. Recall from Chapter 5 that the Reynolds number is a nondimensional ratio of fluid density, velocity, and a characteristic length, L, divided by the viscosity of the fluid, μ.

$$\text{Re} = \frac{\rho v_b L}{\mu} \tag{9.19}$$

The length term, L, in Equation (9.19) is generally taken to be either the length of the boat or the length of the waterline (the line where the hull meets the water). The viscosity of fresh and salt water is a function of temperature, and values for some typical water temperatures are shown in Table 9-2. For game programming purposes, assuming the viscosity is a constant 0.001 *kg/(m-s)* is probably a reasonable approximation.

Table 9-2. *Viscosity of Fresh Water and Seawater,* kg/(m-s)

Temperature (*K*)	Temperature (*°C*)	Temperature (*°F*)	Viscosity, Fresh Water	Viscosity, Seawater
283	10	50	1.304e – 3	1.400e – 3
288	15	60	1.122e – 3	1.210e – 3
294	21	70	0.974e – 3	1.060e – 3
300	27	80	0.858e – 3	0.920e – 3

Several equations and techniques have been developed over the years to estimate the skin friction coefficient. In 1957, the International Towing Tank Conference (ITTC) came up with an equation that is still commonly used today.[1]

$$C_f = \frac{0.075}{\left(\log_{10} \text{Re} - 2\right)^2} \tag{9.20}$$

As an example of computing the skin friction coefficient, consider a boat traveling through salt water at 10 *m/s*. The temperature of the water is 283 *K*, and the length of the waterline of the boat is 8 *m*. The Reynolds number based on waterline length can be computed from Equation (9.19).

$$\text{Re} = \frac{1025 * 10 * 8}{0.0014} = 5.86e + 7 \tag{9.21}$$

The skin friction coefficient based on this Reynolds number can be computed from Equation (9.20).

$$C_f = \frac{0.075}{\left(\log_{10}\left(5.86e+7\right)-2\right)^2} = 2.25e-3 \qquad (9.22)$$

Form Drag

Form drag on boat hulls is similar to form drag on projectiles. As the hull pushes its way through the water, the pressure on the front of the hull is greater than the pressure on the back of the hull. The pressure difference sets up a drag force that acts in the opposite direction to the boat motion. The magnitude of form drag for a given hull depends on the geometry of the hull and is a weak function of the boat velocity, the water density, and the water velocity. The value of form drag for a given boat is usually obtained experimentally. As we shall see in the next section, the evaluation of form drag and wave drag are sometimes combined.

Wave Drag

When the hull of a boat travels through water, waves are created by the action of the hull pushing water away from its surface. The waves radiate away from the body and carry with them a certain amount of energy that is dissipated in the ocean, lake, or river. The wave drag experienced by the boat is a consequence of the work performed by the hull in maintaining the wave structure.

When a boat with a displacement hull travels slowly, there will be a wave created at the bow of the boat and many other smaller waves behind it. As the velocity of the boat increases, the bow wave increases in height and the spacing between the waves increases. If the boat velocity continues to increase, there will be a point where there will be a wave crest at the bow, a crest at the stern, and a trough at in the middle as shown in Figure 9-7. The distance between the wave crests is equal to the waterline length of the hull, L_w.

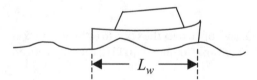

Figure 9-7. *Wave structure caused by a displacement hull*

■**Tidbit** The waves created by large ships can be quite substantial. Off the coast of the Gulf of Mexico, surfers ride the waves caused by large container ships.

William Froude, a nineteenth century English engineer and naval architect, determined that the velocity of the waves, v_{wv}, produced by a displacement hull relative to a fixed coordinate system was proportional to the square root of the length of the wave, L_{wv}.

$$v_{wv} = 1.34\sqrt{L_{wv}} \qquad (9.23)$$

The highest wave velocity will occur when the length of the wave is equal to the waterline length of the boat. It turns out that wave drag is a limiting factor in the maximum speed of a boat with a displacement hull. The reason is that for the boat to travel faster than the wave it is generating, it essentially has to pull the wave along with it, causing the wave drag to increase dramatically. The velocity described by Equation (9.23) is also known as the **hull speed**. The hull speed limitation on maximum boat velocity only applies to boats with displacement hulls. A boat with a planing hull can overcome the hull speed limit by lifting itself on top of the bow wave. The lifting action greatly reduces the wave (and friction) drag experienced by the boat.

To compute wave drag for a boat analytically requires knowledge of the size and frequency of the wave pattern. Many attempts have been made to develop an analytical wave drag model. The models involve horrible-sounding things like "weight integrals" and "thin ship theory." For game programming applications, you probably won't want to tackle anything so involved.

A commonly used approach to estimating wave drag is through experimental measurements. The total drag resistance of a boat is measured, the contribution due to skin friction is subtracted out, and what's left is the resistance due to wave drag, form drag, and any other drag that might be present. The remainder is also called the **residual drag**. Under this system, the total drag coefficient, C_R, is expressed as the sum of the skin friction drag coefficient, C_f, and the residual drag coefficient, C_r.

$$C_R = C_f + C_r \qquad\qquad\qquad (9.24)$$

For large displacement hulls, the residual drag coefficient can range from 0.001 to 0.003.[1]

Other Hydrodynamic Drag Components

The main components of hydrodynamic drag are skin friction, form, and wave drag, but there are other things going on in the water that can contribute to hydrodynamic drag. If wind-generated waves are present, they will increase the drag. If there are any boat appendages in the water such as keels, rudders, struts, and so on, they will add to the hydrodynamic drag. If the boat is traveling in shallow water, it will affect the drag experienced by the boat by changing the wave pattern generated by the hull of the boat.

Unless you are developing a highly accurate boat simulation, you can probably ignore the "other" hydrodynamic drag components. If you want to include the effects of some or all of them, one way to do so would be to add a factor onto the residual drag coefficient to account for them.

Determining the Wetted Area

The drag force equations presented in the previous sections are a function of the wetted area of the boat, the surface area of the hull that is in contact with the water. For displacement hulls, the wetted area can be determined from the hull geometry and from the draft of the boat (the depth of the hull that is underwater) at a given time.

For planing hulls, estimating the wetted area is a bit more complicated. When the boat reaches a certain speed, part of the hull will lift out of the water. This action reduces the wetted area (which is the whole point of a planing hull). Determining the wetted area for a planing hull requires information on when the boat begins to plane and how much of the hull lifts out of the water at a given boat velocity.

Aerodynamic Drag

So far we have been discussing how to model the hydrodynamic drag forces experienced by a boat. Part of a boat will be above water and will be subject to the forces of aerodynamic drag. Generally speaking, aerodynamic forces for boats traveling at low to moderate speeds don't contribute significantly to the overall drag resistance experienced by the boat. Aerodynamic drag is significant, however, for high-speed planing powerboats.

To model the aerodynamic drag on a boat, the familiar drag equation can be applied once again.

$$F = \frac{1}{2} C_D \rho v^2 A \tag{9.25}$$

The area, A, in Equation (9.25) is the frontal area of the boat that is above water. Aerodynamic drag coefficients for displacement hull boats tend to range from 0.6 to 1.1 depending on the type of boat. Supertankers, obviously, have higher aerodynamic drag coefficients than do powerboats.

Computing the aerodynamic drag of a high-speed boat with a planing hull is complicated by the fact that when the boat lifts up, its frontal area and drag coefficient will change and will be a function of how much of the hull is out of the water and the angle of the boat relative to the water.

Modeling the Acceleration and Velocity of a Boat

In the previous sections, we have discussed some of the theoretical aspects of boat thrust and drag. To create a boat simulator, a model must be developed to predict the acceleration profile for the boat, ideally an expression that relates the potential acceleration of the boat as a function of the current velocity of the boat.

One way to come up with an acceleration profile is to try to model the various thrust and drag components. The problem with this approach is that so many unknowns are involved. For example, to compute the drag, we need to calculate not only the wetted area, but also the time history of the wetted area, because the value will change as the speedboat begins to plane. The aerodynamic drag coefficient and frontal area of the boat will similarly change as the boat begins to plane.

A similar situation exists with trying to evaluate the thrust produced by the boat engines. Using Equation (9.16) requires knowledge of the engine power level, wake fraction, and the coefficients of propulsive and hull efficiency. The engine power level will likely be a function of the engine turnover rate. The wake fraction will be a function of boat velocity. As you can see, it takes a lot of research and a lot of information to realistically model the forces and accelerations of a boat.

Fortunately, there is a much simpler approach for game programmers, one that will generally give pretty accurate results as well. Most speedboats are performance tested either by the manufacturer or by publications such as *Powerboat* magazine. The performance data typically includes things such as velocity vs. time and engine *rpm* vs. velocity data. The performance data represents experimental measurements on the performance of the boat. From this data, an acceleration profile can be determined for the boat that includes all of the various thrust and drag components experienced by the boat.

The drawback to this approach is that it really only replicates the performance of the boat for the conditions on the day it was tested. But given the complexities and uncertainties in trying to develop a general analytical model for the performance of a boat, using the performance data to develop an acceleration profile is a reasonable approach for game programming applications.

As an example of how to develop an acceleration profile from performance test data, let's use as a test case the performance test of a Fountain 35' Lightning speedboat that was presented in the January 2004 issue of *Powerboat* magazine (www.powerboatmag.com/2004tests/01_04_fountain.php). The Fountain Lightning is 10.7 *m* (35 *ft*) long and has a beam of 2.5 *m*. The boat weighs 3909 *kg* and is powered by twin 550 *hp* engines. The performance test took place in the ocean near Ft. Myers, Florida, under relatively calm conditions. Acceleration results from the performance test are shown in Table 9-3.

Table 9-3. *Acceleration Data for the Fountain Lightning*

Time (*s*)	Velocity (*m/s*)
5.0	11.2
6.4	13.4
8.2	17.9
10.0	22.4
12.1	26.8
15.0	31.3
20.0	35.8

From the time and velocity data, the acceleration at each time in Table 9-3 can be estimated by the equation $a = \Delta v / \Delta t$. In addition, according to the performance test, the top speed of the boat is 46.1 *m/s* (103 *mph*) at which point the net acceleration of the boat is zero.

The next step in the process is to come up with an equation for the acceleration of the boat as a function of the velocity of the boat that will match the performance test measurements. This technique is called **curve fitting** and is widely used in science and engineering. There are several ways to find an equation that approximates a set of data. One way to accomplish this task is by a method called **least squares approximation**. This technique determines a curve through a set of data points that minimizes the distance (that is, error) between the data points and the curve. For more information on the least squares approximation method, read *Technical Java: Applications for Science and Engineering* by Grant Palmer (Prentice Hall PTR, 2003).

The least squares approximation technique was used to come up with a fourth-order algebraic equation for the acceleration of the Fountain Lightning as a function of the boat velocity. The equation consists of four velocity terms and five coefficients:

$$a = c_1 v^4 + c_2 v^3 + c_3 v^2 + c_4 v + c_5 \tag{9.26}$$

where

$$c_1 = -4.44e - 7 \tag{9.27a}$$

$$c_2 = 2.56e - 4 \tag{9.27b}$$

$$c_3 = -0.0216 \tag{9.27c}$$

$$c_4 = 0.527 \tag{9.27d}$$

$$c_5 = -1.51 \tag{9.27e}$$

A plot of the acceleration as a function of velocity curve predicted by Equation (9.26) is shown in Figure 9-8. Also shown on the plot are the performance test measurement data points that were used to determine the curve fit equation. Above the maximum velocity of 46.1 m/s, the acceleration can be set to zero. For velocities below 11.2 m/s (the first point from the performance test data), the acceleration can be assumed to be the same as when the velocity is 11.2 m/s.

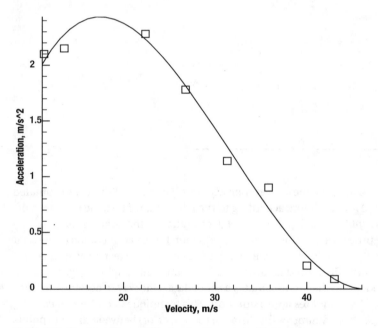

Figure 9-8. *Acceleration profile for the Fountain Lightning*

The estimated acceleration profile shown in Figure 9-8 is not ideal. The curve is a bit steep at the high end, so the transition to zero acceleration at $v = 46.1$ m/s will be somewhat abrupt. If the coefficients of Equation (9.27) were tweaked around a bit, it might be possible to flatten the curve out a bit at the higher velocities.

The acceleration curve also doesn't account for the effects of wind or additional wave drag (if the sea was choppy, for instance). If there were a headwind, the acceleration would be lower, whereas a tailwind would increase the acceleration. Also keep in mind that the performance data and the approximation shown in Figure 9-8 represents the maximum, full-throttle acceleration of the boat. If the engines weren't at full throttle, the acceleration experienced at a given boat velocity would be less.

Speedboat Simulator

Let's use the estimated acceleration profile for the Fountain Lightning to develop a boat simulator program. The GUI for the simulator, shown in Figure 9-9, looks very similar to the Car Simulator GUI we developed in Chapter 8. The Boat Simulator computes and displays values of velocity and distance of a powerboat as a function of elapsed time. On the left-hand side of the GUI are three radio button components that allow the user to specify whether the boat is accelerating, cruising at constant speed, or decelerating. Below the radio buttons are three buttons that start, stop, or reset the simulation. A Timer object is used to slow the action down, so the velocity and distance values are updated in approximately real-time.

A drawing panel at the top of the GUI shows the powerboat. As with the Car Simulator from Chapter 8, a rectangular marker is used to simulate the forward motion of the boat. The powerboat cartoon stays in a fixed location on the screen, and the marker moves from right-to-left with a velocity proportional to the velocity of the boat. The Boat Simulator also models the planing action of the powerboat. When the boat reaches the velocity at which planing begins, the boat cartoon will tilt upwards.

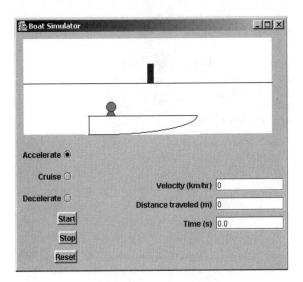

Figure 9-9. *Boat Simulator GUI*

Two classes will be written that will represent boats. The first, named Powerboat, will model a generic powerboat and will define the fields and methods common to all powerboats. The second class, FountainLightning, will define the data specific to the Fountain 35' Lightning speedboat.

We'll start by discussing the Powerboat class. Since the curve fit expression shown in Equation (9.26) is used to compute the acceleration as a function of the current velocity of the boat, there is no need to calculate the aerodynamic or hydrodynamic drag terms. The Powerboat class can therefore be written as a subclass of the SimpleProjectile class. The Powerboat class declares two fields: one named mode that determines whether the boat is accelerating, cruising at constant speed, or slowing down; and the other named planingSpeed that stores the speed at which the powerboat begins to plane.

```java
public class Powerboat extends SimpleProjectile
{
  private String mode;
  private double planingSpeed;
```

The Powerboat constructor only consists of three lines of code. The first thing done is to call the SimpleProjectile constructor to initialize the location and velocity components of the boat. The mode and planingSpeed fields are initialized according to the value passed to the constructor.

```java
// The Powerboat constructor calls the
// SimpleProjectile constructor and initializes
// the value of the mode variable.
public Powerboat(double x, double y, double z, double vx,
                double vy, double vz, double time) {
  super(x, y, z, vx, vy, vz, time);

  mode = "accelerating";   // Accelerating, cruising, or
                           // decelerating
  this.planingSpeed = planingSpeed;
}
```

The Powerboat class declares methods to return or change the value of the mode and planingSpeed fields and implements the getLocationAndVelocity method to update the location and velocity of the boat.

```java
// These methods access or change the value of the
// mode and planingSpeed fields.

public String getMode() {
  return mode;
}

public void setMode(String value) {
  mode = value;
}

public double getPlaningSpeed() {
  return planingSpeed;
}

public void setPlaningSpeed(double value) {
  planingSpeed = value;
}
```

```
//  This method updates the velocity and location
//  of the boat using a 4th order Runge-Kutta
//  solver to integrate the equations of motion.
public void updateLocationAndVelocity(double dt) {
  ODESolver.rungeKutta4(this, dt);
}
```

Because the Powerboat class is a subclass of the SimpleProjectile class, which itself
is a subclass of the ODE class, the Powerboat class must provide an implementation of the
getRightHandSide method. The Powerboat class version of this method sets all of the location
and velocity updates to zero. The intention is that Powerboat subclasses will override this
method with the acceleration and velocity functions, like Equation (9.26) for instance, that
correspond to the specific boat being modeled.

```
//  The getRightHandSide() method returns the right-hand
//  sides of the two first-order ODEs. The Powerboat
//  implementation of this method does nothing. It is
//  meant to be overridden by subclasses of Powerboat.
//  q[0] = vx = dxdt
//  q[1] = x
//  q[2] = vy = dydt
//  q[3] = y
//  q[4] = vz = dzdt
//  q[5] = z
public double[] getRightHandSide(double s, double q[],
                        double deltaQ[], double ds,
                        double qScale) {
  double dQ[] = new double[6];

  dQ[0] = 0.0;
  dQ[1] = 0.0;
  dQ[2] = 0.0;
  dQ[3] = 0.0;
  dQ[4] = 0.0;
  dQ[5] = 0.0;

  return dQ;
  }
}
```

Similar to the approach taken with the Car Simulator in Chapter 8, classes that represent
specific powerboats are written as subclasses of the Powerboat class. We want to include the
Fountain Lightning in the Boat Simulator, so a FountainLightning class is written. The main
thing the FountainLightning class does is to provide a real implementation of the getRightHandSide
method according to the acceleration expression shown in Equation (9.26). The FountainLightning
class doesn't declare any new fields, and its constructor simply calls the Powerboat constructor.

```
public class FountainLightning extends Powerboat
{
  //  The FountainLightning constructor calls the
  //  SimpleProjectile constructor and initializes
  //  the value of the mode variable.
  public FountainLightning(double x, double y, double z,
                           double vx, double vy, double vz,
                           double time, double planingSpeed) {
    super(x, y, z, vx, vy, vz, time, planingSpeed);
  }
```

The FountainLightning class implements the getRightHandSide method to compute the right-hand sides of the equations of motion. The first part of the method is the same as always in that it computes intermediate values of the location and velocity of the boat.

```
public double[] getRightHandSide(double s, double q[],
                         double deltaQ[], double ds,
                         double qScale) {
    double dQ[] = new double[6];
    double newQ[] = new double[6];

    //  Compute the intermediate values of the
    //  dependent variables.
    for(int i=0; i<6; ++i) {
      newQ[i] = q[i] + qScale*deltaQ[i];
    }
```

The powerboat in this simulation moves in the x-direction only. If the mode is set to "accelerate" and if the velocity is equal to the maximum velocity of 46.1 *m/s*, the acceleration is set to zero. If the velocity is less than 11.2 *m/s*, the acceleration is set to a constant value of 2.1 *m/s*^{2}. Otherwise, the acceleration is determined from the curve fit relation shown in Equation (9.26).

```
    double v = newQ[0];
    double ax;    //  x-direction acceleration

    if ( getMode().equals("accelerating") ) {
      //  If the velocity is at or above the maximum
      //  value, set the acceleration to zero.
      if ( v >= 46.1 ) {
        ax = 0.0;
      }
      //  If the velocity is less than 11.2 m/s, set the
      //  acceleration equal to the value at 11.2 m/s.
      else if ( v < 11.2 ) {
        ax = 2.1;
      }
```

```
  //  Otherwise, evaluate the acceleration according
  //  to the curve fit equation.
  else {
    ax = -4.44e-7*Math.pow(v,4.0) + 2.56e-4*Math.pow(v,3.0) -
        0.0216*v*v + 0.527*v - 1.51;
  }
}
```

If the mode is "decelerate," the x-direction acceleration is set to –2.0 m/s^2. If the mode is "cruising," the acceleration is set to zero.

```
else if ( getMode().equals("decelerating") ) {
  //  Only decelerate if the velocity is positive.
  if ( newQ[0] > 0.1 ) {
    ax = -2.0;
  }
  else {
    ax = 0.0;
  }
}
//  If the mode is "cruising," set the acceleration
//  to zero.
else {
  ax = 0.0;
}
```

Once the x-direction acceleration is computed, the right-hand sides of the equation of motion ODEs can be filled.

```
  //  Fill the right-hand sides of the equation of
  //  motion ODEs.
  dQ[0] = ds*ax;
  dQ[1] = ds*newQ[0];
  dQ[2] = 0.0;
  dQ[3] = 0.0;
  dQ[4] = 0.0;
  dQ[5] = 0.0;

  return dQ;
  }
}
```

The GUI for the Boat Simulator is implemented in a class named BoatSimulator. As with the other GUIs in this book, the BoatSimulator class will not be discussed in detail. You can download the complete code listing from the Apress website for this book.

We will highlight one feature of the BoatSimulator class. The planing speed for the Fountain 35' Lightning speedboat is 8.44 *m/s* (30.4 *km/hr*). When the boat reaches this speed, the planing action of the hull begins and the hull tilts upward. While the physical details of the planing process are not modeled in the Boat Simulator, the appearance of planing is modeled. The resetDisplay method is used to update the GUI display. The BoatSimulator class uses three pictures to display the boat. If the x-component of boat velocity is less than the planing speed, the "no planing" picture of the boat is used. If the boat has reached planing speed, the "half-plane" picture is used, which shows the boat beginning to tilt upward. If the boat velocity is greater than the planing speed plus 2.0 *m/s*, the "full-plane" picture is used to show the boat at the full-plane tilt angle.

```
// Get the graphics object on the JPanel.
Graphics g = drawingPanel.getGraphics();
int width = drawingPanel.getWidth() - 1;
int height = drawingPanel.getHeight() - 1;

g.clearRect(0, 0, width, height);
g.setColor(Color.WHITE);
g.fillRect(0, 0, width, height);

g.setColor(Color.BLACK);
g.drawLine(0, 70, width, 70);

// Draw the boat depending on whether the boat
// is planing or not.
if ( boat.getVx() < boat.getPlaningSpeed() ) {
  g.drawImage(noPlaneIcon.getImage(), 100, 95,
          noPlaneWidth, noPlaneHeight, drawingPanel);
}
else if ( boat.getVx() < boat.getPlaningSpeed() + 2.0 ) {
  g.drawImage(halfPlaneIcon.getImage(), 100, 95,
          halfPlaneWidth, halfPlaneHeight, drawingPanel);
}
else {
  g.drawImage(fullPlaneIcon.getImage(), 100, 95,
          fullPlaneWidth, fullPlaneHeight, drawingPanel);
}
```

The effect (although somewhat primitive) of the three pictures is to show the boat tilting upward when it passes through its planing speed. If the boat slows down below its planing speed, the boat in the GUI tilts back down. Play around with the Boat Simulator. The boat doesn't do much more than speed up or slow down, but the simulation does a good job of reproducing the performance test data for the Fountain Lightning speedboat.

There are a couple of things to keep in mind about the Boat Simulator. The acceleration as modeled by the Boat Simulator is the maximum, full-throttle acceleration. No attempt was made to simulate variable-throttle acceleration. One of the problems with the performance test data was that it only included acceleration data. There was no information on how fast the boat will slow down if the engines are throttled back. The deceleration of the boat could be simulated by modeling the drag resistance forces on the boat as a function of velocity. For this simple boat simulation, when the Decelerate radio button is selected, the boat decelerates at a constant -2.0 m/s^2.

Powerboat Turns

The way that a powerboat turns depends on the type of drive system that it has. Boats with direct drives turn by way of underwater rudders. Boats with outboard or inboard/outboard drives turn by rotating the engine or the propeller shafts to the desired turn angle. As shown in Figure 9-10, rotating the engine or propeller shafts rotates the direction of the thrust force of the engine, F_T.

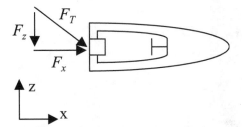

Figure 9-10. *Rotating the thrust force vector creates a torque that turns the boat.*

When the thrust force vector is rotated, there will be force components normal and perpendicular to the direction that the boat is traveling. The normal force component, F_z in Figure 9-10, will create a torque about the center of mass of the boat. As we saw in Chapter 4, the torque will result in an angular acceleration of the boat.

$$\tau = F_z r = I\alpha \tag{9.28}$$

The quantity, r, in Equation (9.28) is the distance from the center of mass to the propeller. The angular acceleration, α, represents the rate at which the orientation (that is, angle) of the boat will change during the turn. One thing that must be determined is the moment of inertia, I, of the boat. The moment of inertia will depend on the shape and weight distribution of the boat. For game programming purposes, a rough approximation for the moment of inertia of the boat would be to assume it was the same as a cylinder.

$$I = \frac{1}{12}m_b l^2 + \frac{1}{4}m_b \left(\frac{b}{2}\right)^2 \tag{9.29}$$

In Equation (9.29), m_b is the mass of the boat, l is the boat length, and b is the beam, or width, of the boat. Equation (9.29) is based on a vertical spin axis that goes through the center of the boat.

Jet Skis

Jet skis, or more generally personal watercraft (PWC), are small, highly maneuverable water-craft that offer a lot of possibilities for game simulations. Although different manufacturers refer to them by different names, in this section we will use the term "jet ski." As shown in Figure 9-11, jet skis are powerful, highly maneuverable watercraft. They are usually designed to carry from 1 to 3 people and are ridden like a motorcycle. Jet skis have V-shaped planing hulls, and as such they rise out of the water when they reach a certain speed.

Figure 9-11. *Masao Fujisama goes airborne in his jet ski. (Photo courtesy of JetSkiNews, www.jetskinews.com)*

Jet Drives

Jet skis and other personal watercraft are powered by jet drives. A low-pressure water pump sucks in water from an opening in the bottom of the hull and accelerates the water backwards through a nozzle out the back of the hull. The acceleration of the water generates a thrust that propels the jet ski forward. Typically, the exit velocity of the water coming out of the nozzle will be about twice the top speed of the jet ski.

The water is accelerated inside the pump by means of an **impeller**, which can be thought of as an internal propeller. The function of an impeller is exactly the same as an external propeller. The impeller blades push the water back and down, which sets up a pressure difference between the forward and rearward faces of the blades. Impellers are safer than external propellers for the obvious reason that they operate inside the jet ski so riders or swimmers aren't exposed to the blades.

Optimum performance of a jet drive depends on getting a clean, steady supply of water into the pump. The flow can be disrupted, for example, if the jet ski makes sharp, high-speed turns. Another risk to performance is if seaweed or other water-borne debris gets sucked up into the pump.

Thrust and Drag

The basic relations between thrust and drag are the same for a jet ski as they are for a planing speedboat. The engine generates thrust that propels the jet ski forward. Various aerodynamic and hydrodynamic drag forces including skin friction, wave drag, form drag, and aerodynamic drag resist the forward motion. To develop a general model for the motion of a jet ski, as was the case with planing speedboats, requires a lot of detailed information including drag coefficients, wetted area time histories, propulsive and hull efficiencies, and so on.

Unless you have access to all of this technical information, you may be better off modeling the jet ski motion by generating an acceleration profile from existing performance test data. Table 9-4 contains acceleration data taken from a performance test of a Kawasaki 800 SX-R (superstock model) jet ski that was performed by *Personal Watercraft Illustrated* magazine.

Table 9-4. *Acceleration Data for the Kawasaki 800 SX-R*

Time (*s*)	Velocity (*m/s*)
0.0	0.0
0.78	8.9
1.9	15.6
12.4	64.5

Comparing the jet ski acceleration data in Table 9-4 with the Fountain Lightning speedboat data from Table 9-3, we can see that the jet ski initially has significantly greater acceleration than the speedboat. It takes the jet ski less than 2 seconds to reach 15.6 *m/s*, a velocity that takes the speedboat almost 8 seconds to achieve. However, the speedboat eventually catches up to the jet ski in that the two watercraft are at about the same velocity after 12 seconds.

To model the performance of a jet ski, we can use the same process as that for modeling the powerboat. An acceleration curve can be developed based on the measured velocity as a function of time. The more data points that are available, the more accurately the curve fit relation will approximate the acceleration performance of the jet ski.

The Physics of Sailing

Up to this point in the chapter, the discussion has been on modeling powerboats. As you have learned, with a powerboat, a propeller or jet drive provides the thrust. With a sailboat, the thrust for the boat is provided by the wind blowing into or over the sails. Figure 9-12 shows a schematic of a typical sailboat. Some of the terms that apply to a sailboat (bow, stern, beam, and so on) are the same as for a powerboat and are not shown in the figure. The **mast** is a vertical pole on which the sails are raised. Most mid- to large-sized sailboats have more than one sail. The boat in Figure 9-12 has two sails, a **mainsail** behind the mast and a smaller **jib** in front of the mast. Sailboats also have an extension of the hull known as the **keel**, which is used to help stabilize the boat.

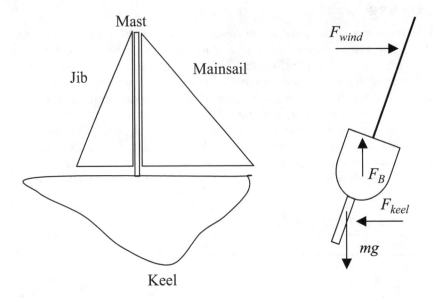

Figure 9-12. *A schematic of a typical sailboat*

The right-hand side of Figure 9-12 shows a sideways force diagram on the sailboat where the wind is coming from the left. The force due to the wind on the sail pushes the boat to the right. The keel resists this movement, and a force is exerted on the keel, acting to the left. The wind and keel forces create a torque that causes the boat to rotate, or heel, over to the right.

The reason the sailboat doesn't just topple over is because a counterbalancing torque is generated from the buoyancy and gravitational forces. The keel of the sailboat is weighted such that the center of mass for the sailboat will be somewhere in the keel. The buoyancy force acts through the geometric center of the sailboat. The separation between the buoyancy and gravitational force vectors is what causes the counterbalancing torque.

The real trick to modeling a sailboat is to compute the thrust force generated by the sail. This force will depend on the direction of the wind, the magnitude of the wind, the size of the sail, the shape of the sail, and many other factors besides. The development of a detailed model of sail thrust force is beyond the scope of this book. To learn more about the physics of sailing, try *The Physics of Sailing Explained* by Bryon Anderson (Sheridan House, 2003).

The Physics of Surfing

Surfing is a sport that combines athletic ability, speed, and balance, with a little danger thrown into the mix. In this section, we'll see a brief overview of the physics of surfing. Figure 9-13 shows a surfer riding a wave off the coast of Southern California. It turns out that you've already learned pretty much all you need to know to create a realistic surfing simulation, because in essence a surfboard is a boat with a solid, planing hull.

Figure 9-13. *A surfboard is really just a boat. (Photo courtesy of Kevin Schmidtchen)*

Buoyancy and Balance

Consider a surfer standing on a surfboard as shown in Figure 9-14. The surfer's weight acts through the center of mass of the surfer and presses down on the board. The buoyancy force resists the downward force, and it acts through the geometrical center of the surfboard. This point is also known as the center of buoyancy. If the center of mass of the surfer is over or near the center of buoyancy, as shown in left-hand side of Figure 9-14, the surfer and board are balanced.

If the surfer moves back on the board, as shown in the right-hand side of Figure 9-14, the center of mass of the surfer no longer lines up with the center of buoyancy. A moment is created that pushes the nose of the board up and the aft end of the board down. The rotation continues until the buoyancy force is once again lined up with the center of mass of the surfer. If the surfer shifts her weight to one side of the board, a similar moment is generated that will cause the board to roll.

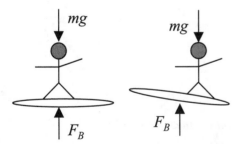

Figure 9-14. *Moving the center of mass away from the center of buoyancy causes the board to rotate.*

Surfers can control the speed they are traveling by moving their center of mass forward or backward on the board. If the surfer moves back, causing the nose of the board to lift up, the speed of the board is reduced. If the surfer moves forward, the nose of the board tips down, and the speed increases. If the center of mass is moved too far forward, the tip of the board will dip underneath the surface of the water. This effect is known as **pearling** and usually causes the surfer to fall off the board.

The Physics of a Wave

Most ocean waves are caused by wind, although a ship traveling through the water can also cause waves. A wave caused by a storm in the middle of the Pacific or Atlantic oceans can travel hundreds or even thousands of miles before hitting the shore. The velocity of a wave when it hits the shore is a function of the size of the wave. A typical wave velocity is 6 *knots* or about 3.1 *m/s*.

When the wave reaches shallow water, the water that is carried along with the wave begins to interact with the bottom of the ocean. Friction between the water and the ocean floor causes the water at the bottom of the wave to slow down while the water at the top of the wave maintains its velocity. The result is that the wave begins to steepen. The velocity mismatch between the water at the top of the wave eventually reaches a point where the wave **breaks** and falls over on top of itself.

Some waves seem to break everywhere at once. This type of wave is called a **close-out** and is not ideal for surfing. The best waves for surfing are those where the break begins at one point and then the break continues sequentially in one direction or sometimes both. This type of wave can be ridden sideways, and the surfer typically tries to stay just ahead of the break point.

Catching a Wave

The critical element in catching a wave is to gather speed by paddling so the velocity of the surfboard is fairly close to the velocity of the wave. If this is done, the wave will "pick up" the surfboard and carry it along at the velocity of the wave. The force diagram of a surfer at the point of catching a wave is shown in Figure 9-15. When the surfer catches the wave, the nose of the surfboard is tipped downwards. Since the buoyancy force now acts at an angle from the vertical, a net forward force is generated that accelerates the surfer to the velocity of the wave.

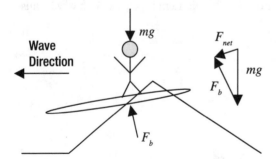

Figure 9-15. *When a surfer catches a wave, a net force pushes the surfboard forward.*

When the surfer catches a wave, she is essentially standing on top of a hill of water. If the surfer moves forward on the board, the board will speed up and slide down the slope of the wave. If the surfer slows down the board by moving her weight back or by turning, the wave will catch up to the surfer, and the board will climb back up the wave slope.

Turning

A surfboard is turned very much like a skateboard or snowboard is turned. To turn a surfboard to the right, a surfer shifts his weight back and to the right. This causes the board to rotate onto its right side (known as the right rail), and the board will curve to the right. As a general rule, the longer and heavier the surfboard, the slower and harder it is to turn.

Coming up with an analytical model for the turn of a surfboard requires an estimation of the drag acting on the board. Modeling the drag of a surfboard is a difficult problem because the wetted area of the board and the drag coefficient will change as the surfer changes his position on the board and the board rotates up or down. One way to approximate drag in a game simulation is to assume that the drag when the surfer is in a neutral position on the board balances the forward force on the board so the velocity of the surfer matches the velocity of the wave.

Summary

In this chapter, we went nautical and saw some basic physics about boats and things that float. Starting with basic Newtonian mechanics and kinematics, we explored how to model the forces that result in the acceleration and velocity of boats, jet skis, and surfboards. We discussed buoyancy, the force that keeps things afloat. Some of the specific things covered in the chapter include the following:

- The different types of ship hulls including displacement, semi-displacement, and planing hulls

- The basic forces that act on a boat—gravity, buoyancy, thrust, and drag

- How an boat engine works and how power is transferred from the engine to the propeller to generate thrust

- The different drag forces experienced by a boat including skin friction, wave, form, and aerodynamic drag

- How an acceleration profile for a boat or other watercraft can be obtained from performance test data

- An introduction to the physics of surfing including the forces and moments that act upon a surfboard

Answers to Exercises

1. The maximum buoyancy force that can be exerted on the canoe is equal to the volume of the canoe multiplied by the density of water.

   $$F_B = \rho_w V_c g = 1000 * 0.5 * g = 500g$$

   Since the canoe itself weighs 30 kg, an additional 470 kg can be loaded into it before it will sink. In real life, however, you would never want to load a boat to its theoretical buoyancy limit.

References

1. F. Papoulias, "Ship Resistance and Propulsion," http://web.nps.navy.mil/~me/tsse/TS4001/support/1-4-1.pdf.

CHAPTER 10

■ ■ ■

Airplanes

People have always had a fascination with flying. It would be so convenient and so fun to soar with the birds. For thousands of years, people dreamed of ways that man could fly. In a Greek legend, Icarus and his dad built wings out of wax to escape King Minos. Unfortunately, Icarus flew too close to the sun and his wings melted. Leonardo Da Vinci came up with elaborate contraptions to allow people to fly. Most of the early attempts at creating flying machines involved trying to imitate the way birds fly.

It wasn't until the late nineteenth century that researchers began making breakthroughs in the concepts of lift and aerodynamic drag that would make heavier-than-air flight possible. In this chapter, we will explore the basic physics of how an airplane takes off from the ground, flies, and then lands. We will discuss how an airfoil maintains lift and stability. Some other specific topics this chapter will cover include the following:

- A brief history of the early days of flight

- Some airplane terminology

- The basic forces acting on an airplane in flight—lift, drag, thrust, and gravity

- What an airfoil is and how it generates lift

- How airplanes generate thrust using propeller or jet engines

- The various components of aerodynamic drag

- Moments and stability

- Full-body aerodynamics

The physical models developed in this chapter will be an extension of the Newtonian mechanics, kinematics, and projectile physics material that was covered in Chapters 3, 4, and 5. After we discuss the physics of how airplanes fly, we'll take what was covered and create a basic flight simulator. The airplane in the simulator can take off, fly around, and come back in for a landing. Let's get started with a brief history of the beginnings of powered flight.

Historical Stuff

One of the biggest obstacles to the development of heavier-than-air flight was that it was widely considered to be physically impossible. Famous scientists came up with elaborate "proofs" of why it couldn't be done. In the 1890s, a German mechanical engineer named Otto Lilienthal dispelled this motion by building and flying a series of gliders, one of which flew a distance of 244 meters (800 feet). Being an aviation pioneer was a dangerous pastime, however. Otto died in 1896 from injuries he sustained from a crash in one of his gliders.

The glider development performed by Lilienthal inspired two American bicycle repair shop owners, Wilbur and Orville Wright. The Wright brothers wanted to take the glider concept a step further and construct a powered aircraft. The Wright brothers were remarkably systematic in their approach. They conducted research in propeller shapes. They developed valuable tables of wind pressure and drift. They designed, built, and tested numerous airplane prototypes until they finally achieved sustained powered flight on December 17, 1903 near Kitty Hawk, North Carolina. The airplane, shown in Figure 10-1, only flew a distance of 120 feet on its first flight, but the era of powered flight had begun.

Figure 10-1. *The 1903 Wright Flyer (Photo courtesy of U.S. Library of Congress)*

Once the "genie was out of the bottle" and people saw that powered flight was possible, airplane development proceeded at a rapid pace. Less than 15 years after the first powered flight, airplane technology and performance had progressed to the point where airplanes were used in combat in World War I. Aeronautical advancement continues even today with the development of new supersonic jet fighters and fuel-efficient passenger planes.

Airplane Terminology

Before we get into detail about the physics of airplanes, let's spend a little time defining some airplane terminology. A typical propeller-driven airplane is shown in Figure 10-2. The **fuselage** is the body of the airplane. It houses the cargo and/or passenger compartments as well as the engine. The **wing** is the generally flat structure that generates most of the lift that allows the airplane to fly. The airplane in Figure 10-2 has its wing on top of the fuselage, but wings can be located in the middle or bottom of the fuselage as well. The **tail** is located at the back of the plane and is used to stabilize the plane and to help it turn. The tail consists of two parts—a horizontal, wing-like structure called the **horizontal stabilizer** and a vertical structure called the **vertical stabilizer** or **vertical fin.**

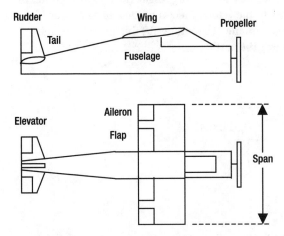

Figure 10-2. *Airplane schematic*

Here is a short glossary defining the terms shown in Figure 10-2 and some other airplane geometry terms as well:

- **Aileron**: Movable areas on the trailing (back) edge of the wing that when deflected cause the airplane to roll.

- **Aspect ratio**: The ratio of the span of the wing to its chord. A high-aspect ratio wing is long and slender, with a wide span and narrow chord.

- **Chord**: The distance from the front (or leading) edge of the wing to the back (or trailing) edge.

- **Elevator**: A movable part of the horizontal part of the tail that controls the pitch of the aircraft.

- **Flap**: A movable, usually hinged part of the wing used to increase the lift or drag of the wing.

- **Landing gear**: The wheels or other structures used during takeoff or landing.

- **Pitch**: The nose-up/nose-down rotation of the airplane.

- **Rudder**: The movable part of the vertical stabilizer used to control the yaw of the aircraft.

- **Span**: The width of the wing from wing tip to wing tip.

- **Yaw**: The side-to-side rotation of the nose of the airplane.

Basic Force Diagram

As shown in Figure 10-3, four basic forces act upon an airplane. **Thrust** generated by the airplane engine propels the aircraft forward. **Aerodynamic drag** resists the forward motion of the aircraft and acts in the opposite direction to the velocity vector of the aircraft. When air flows over the wing and other surfaces of the airplane, it generates **lift** that overcomes the gravitational force pulling the airplane towards the earth.

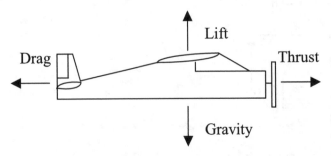

Figure 10-3. *Basic force diagram for an airplane*

A comparison of Figure 10-3 to the boat force schematic in Chapter 9, Figure 9-3, shows that the two figures are very similar. In fact, the buoyancy force that causes a boat to float is a type of lifting force. Let's explore the forces on an airplane in more detail starting with a discussion of aerodynamic lift.

Lift

Airplanes fly because the wing and other surfaces of the airplane generate a force called **lift**. Most of the lift is generated by the wing surface, so we will focus on wing lift in this section, but the general concepts apply to other surfaces (the tail and fuselage primarily) that can also generate lift. Lift is generated when air flows over the wing, so the shape of the wing plays a critical part in lift generation. To start the discussion of lift, let's talk about the shape of a wing.

Airfoils

An **airfoil** is the cross-section of a surface, such as a wing, that is shaped to generate lift. A typical airfoil is shown in Figure 10-4. The front edge of the airfoil is called the **leading edge**. The back edge is called the **trailing edge**. In Figure 10-4, the airfoil is traveling from right to left. The **chord line** is a straight line drawn from the leading edge to the trailing edge. Airfoils don't have to be symmetric. The curvature of the top surface of the airfoil can be different from the curvature on the bottom surface. The **camber line** is defined such that there is an equal airfoil thickness above and below the camber line. For a symmetric airfoil, the camber would be the same as the chord line.

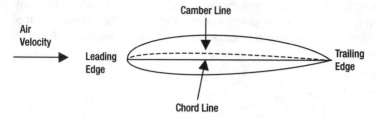

Figure 10-4. *An airfoil schematic*

The **angle of attack** for an airfoil, typically represented by the Greek letter α as shown in Figure 10-5, is the angle the chord line makes with the velocity vector of the airfoil. As we shall see later in this section, the lift and drag characteristics of an airfoil are often evaluated as a function of angle of attack.

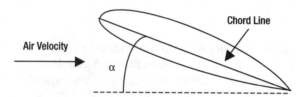

Figure 10-5. *Angle of attack*

The **incidence angle** of a wing is the angle the chord line makes with the longitudinal axis of the airplane. Incidence angles tend to be small, usually 1 to 3 degrees. For an airplane in straight-and-level flight, the angle of attack of the wing will be equal to its incidence angle.

How Lift Is Created

To understand how an airfoil generates lift, consider the airfoil shown in Figure 10-6. To simplify the discussion, let's assume that the airfoil is two-dimensional, is at a fixed location, and that air is being blown over it. Initially, the air is traveling in the x-direction only, but when the air strikes the airfoil, it can no longer travel exclusively in the x-direction. Instead the air flow turns and moves around the shape of the airfoil.

Chapter 3 introduced Newton's second law, which relates a force, F, to an acceleration a.

$$\bar{F} = m\bar{a} = m\frac{d\bar{v}}{dt} \tag{10.1}$$

Newton's second law tells us that a force is required to change a velocity. Force and velocity are vector quantities, so a change in velocity in any direction requires a force in that direction. Applying Newton's second law to the airfoil in Figure 10-6, the velocity direction is clearly changing over both the top and bottom surfaces of the wing, which means that the airfoil is exerting a force on the air. By Newton's third law of equal and opposite forces, if the airfoil is exerting a force on the air, then the air is applying an equal and opposite force on the airfoil. The net force on the airfoil due to air turning, that is, the difference in force between the top and bottom surfaces, is the lift generated by the airfoil.

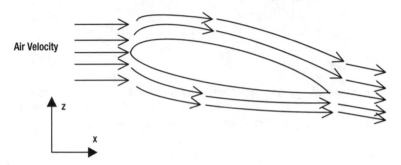

Figure 10-6. *Air is turned as it flows over an airfoil.*

Another way to describe the lift generated by an airfoil is by using Bernoulli's equation, first introduced in Chapter 5. If you recall, Bernoulli's equation states that for frictionless, incompressible (that is, constant density) flow, the sum of the pressure, kinetic energy, and potential energy is constant.

$$p + \frac{1}{2}\rho v^2 + \rho gh = const \tag{10.2}$$

In Equation (10.2), p is the air pressure, ρ is the air density, and h is the altitude. If the airfoil is asymmetric or if it is flying at an angle of attack, the amount of flow turning, and therefore the flow velocity, will be different over the top and bottom surfaces of the airfoil. According to Bernoulli's equation, if the velocity is different along the top and bottom surfaces, the pressure will be different as well. The pressure difference between the top and bottom surfaces is what generates lift.

The lift generated by an airplane will come primarily from the wings, but some additional lift is created by the fuselage and by the horizontal stabilizer of the tail. The lift generated by the horizontal stabilizer is important in maintaining aerodynamic stability, as we will see a little later in this chapter.

Evaluating Airfoil Lift

To compute the magnitude of the lifting force, the pressure distribution along the top and bottom surfaces of the airfoil must be calculated. There are two ways to obtain the lift generated by a given airfoil—the lift can be computed analytically or it can be measured experimentally. Decades of research have been devoted to coming up with analytical models to predict airfoil lift. Before the age of computers, analytical methods focused on coming up with mathematical equations to simulate lift that could be solved directly. An example of such a methodology is the **thin airfoil theory** in which a three-dimensional airfoil was modeled as a curved, flat plate.

As high-speed computers became available in the 1970s and 1980s, a new methodology called **computational fluid dynamics** was developed that divided the airfoil into small subsections.

The surface pressure on each subsection could be computed using the principles of conservation of mass, momentum, and energy. The overall surface pressure, and therefore lift, of the airfoil is determined by summing up the contributions from each subsection. Computational fluid dynamics is a powerful tool, but it is too complicated and requires too much computer power for game programming purposes.

In addition to analytical methods, the lift of an airfoil can also be determined by experimental measurements. Typically, a scale model of the airfoil is put inside a facility called a **wind tunnel**, and large fans are used to blow air over the airfoil. The airfoil is attached to springs or other force measuring devices, and the lift generated by the airfoil is obtained. Until the availability of high-speed computers, experimental measurement was the primary means to obtain airfoil lift data and is still widely used today.

For game programming purposes, you aren't going to want to perform computational fluid dynamic calculations, and you won't want to perform your own experiments. The best way to obtain lift data for your game simulations is to use existing lift data, which is widely available from government, academic, or industrial sources. The data is usually presented in terms of a lift coefficient, C_L, a concept we have seen in modeling Magnus force in Chapter 5. As in Chapter 5, the lift force for an airfoil, F_L, is a function of the lift coefficient; the air density, ρ; the square of the air velocity, v; and the wetted surface area of the airfoil, A. In this case, "wetted surface area" refers to the airfoil surface that is exposed to the air.

$$F_L = \frac{1}{2} C_L \rho v^2 A \tag{10.3}$$

Lift coefficient data, whether it is obtained experimentally or analytically, is typically presented as a function of angle of attack. Let's take a look at the lift coefficient curves for two airfoils. The airfoil shapes are shown in Figure 10-7. The NACA 0012 airfoil is a symmetric airfoil with a maximum thickness 12% of its chord length. The NACA 2412 airfoil is also a 12% thick airfoil, but it is asymmetrical with a 2% camber line.

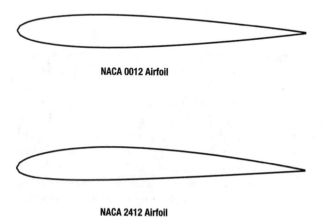

NACA 0012 Airfoil

NACA 2412 Airfoil

Figure 10-7. *The shapes of the NACA 0012 and 2412 airfoils*

Lift coefficient data as a function of angle of attack for the NACA 0012 and 2412 airfoils is shown in Figure 10-8. The data is from experimental measurements taken in a wind tunnel at the NASA Langley Research Center.[1]

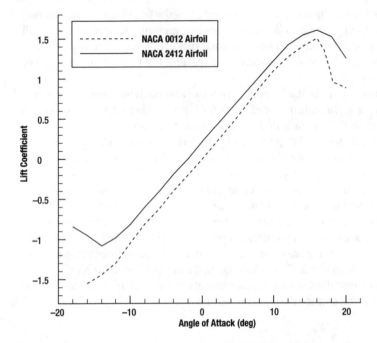

Figure 10-8. *Lift coefficient data for the NACA 0012 and 2412 airfoils*

One thing that is obvious from looking at Figure 10-8 is that changing the angle of attack of an airfoil changes its lift. This phenomenon makes sense because tilting the airfoil up or down changes the way that air flows around it, which changes the surface pressure distribution over the wing. If the airfoils are tilted downward (given a negative angle of attack), they generate a negative, or downward, lift force.

Stall

If you look at Figure 10-8, the lift coefficient of the NACA 0012 and 2412 airfoils increases with increasing angle of attack until about $\alpha = 16$ degrees, at which point the lift coefficient begins to decrease. This effect is known as a **stall** condition. What has happened is that when the angle of attack reaches a certain value, the air is no longer able to follow the shape of the airfoil on the upper surface. Instead, as shown in Figure 10-9, the air flow **separates** from the airfoil. Inside the separation region, the flow is turbulent and chaotic and the surface pressure increases. The pressure increase on the upper surface reduces (or eliminates) the pressure differential between the top and bottom wing surfaces, reducing the lift generated by the airfoil.

Gaining speed and reducing the angle of attack so the air flow can **reattach** itself to the top surface of the airfoil can correct a stall condition. Stall is most dangerous at low velocities where it can be difficult to make the necessary corrections.

The **stall speed** of an airplane is the minimum speed at which the wings can generate enough lift to sustain level flight. It is the point where $F_L = mg$, with m being the mass of the airplane. Knowing that the lift force must equal the weight of the airplane, the stall speed can be computed from Equation (10.3).

$$v_{stall} = \sqrt{\frac{mg}{\frac{1}{2}C_{L,max}\rho A}}$$

(10.4)

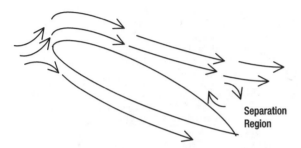

Separation
Region

Figure 10-9. *Flow separation reduces the lift generated by an airfoil.*

You will most likely want to include the possibility of stall in your flight simulation, particularly when you are modeling takeoffs and landings.

■**Tidbit** Many modern airplane wings have a row of tiny vanes called vortex generators along the top surface of the wing. The vortex generators make it less likely that the airflow will separate over the top surface of the wing and lower the stall speed of the airplane.

Flaps

As seen in Figure 10-10, flaps are movable sections on the aft end of the wing. They are deflected up or down to change the lift characteristics of the wing. Specifically, flap deflection shifts the lift coefficient curve up or down and may change the **stall angle**, the angle of attack where the maximum lift coefficient occurs. Flaps are commonly used during takeoff and landing. In Figure 10-10, the flap is deflected downwards, which will increase the lift coefficient of the airfoil.

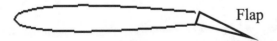

Flap

Figure 10-10. *Flaps are used to alter the lift coefficient.*

As an example of the effect of flaps, Figure 10-11 shows the lift coefficient profiles for the NACA 2412 airfoil with no flap deflection and with a 20-degree downward flap deflection.[1] The peak lift coefficient is higher and the stall angle is somewhat less when the flaps are deflected.

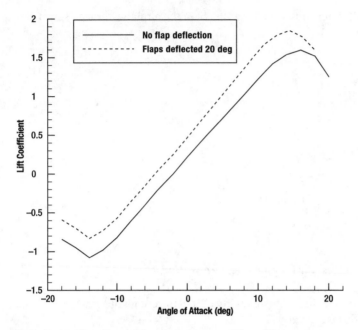

Figure 10-11. *The effect of flap deflection on lift coefficient*

Center of Pressure

In the "How Lift Is Created" section of this chapter, you learned that according to Bernoulli's equation the pressure on the surface of the wing is related to the air velocity as it flows over the wing. Because the air velocity will vary over the surface of the wing, so will the surface pressure. Figure 10-12 shows what a typical pressure distribution curve over the top and bottom surfaces of an airfoil might look like.

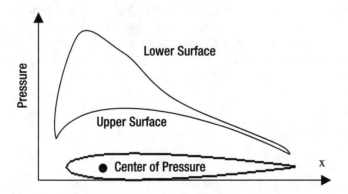

Figure 10-12. *A typical surface pressure distribution*

In the "Rigid Body Motion" section of Chapter 4, you learned that when modeling translational motion, the mass of an object can be considered to be concentrated at a point known as the center of mass. A similar concept is applied to the pressure distribution of airfoils.

The lift force of an airfoil can be determined by integrating (that is, summing up) the pressure distribution over the top and bottom surfaces of the wing. The resulting lift force can be modeled by assuming that it is concentrated at a single point known as the **center of pressure** of the airfoil. This point is important in the analysis of airfoils and other lifting bodies, so let's state it again. *The lift force on an airfoil will act through the center of pressure of the airfoil.*

The location of the center of pressure of an airfoil is determined by the geometry and orientation of the airfoil. The mass distribution inside the airfoil has no bearing on the center of pressure. The center of gravity, on the other hand, depends both on the geometry and weight distribution of the airfoil. More commonly than not, the center of pressure and center of gravity will be in different locations. Another feature of the center pressure is that it won't necessarily remain in a fixed location but will move as the angle of attack changes because the pressure distribution over the airfoil will change with angle of attack.

Up to this point the discussion in this section has been on the centers of pressure and gravity of an airfoil, but the airplane as a whole will have a center of pressure and a center of gravity as well. The relative locations of the centers of pressure and gravity for an airplane have important ramifications for the stability of the airplane in flight—a topic that will be discussed in the "Trim and Stability" section later in the chapter.

Thrust

The thrust created by an airplane engine serves two purposes. It propels the airplane forward, and it also creates the airflow over the wing that generates the lifting force that keeps the plane in the air. Of the four forces that act on an airplane, thrust is the most difficult to model and predict. For one thing, thrust is a function of altitude. At higher altitudes, an engine will generate less thrust than it will at sea level. Different types of engines generate thrust in different ways.

There are four basic types of airplane engines—propeller, jet, turbojet, and rocket. Of these four, propeller and jet engines are the most commonly used, and are the ones that will be covered in this section. A discussion of rocket engines will be deferred until the next chapter.

Propeller Engines

Starting with the Wright brothers and for about 40 years after, airplanes primarily used internal combustion engines connected to a propeller to generate thrust. Even today, most smaller general aviation or private planes still use propellers and internal combustion engines, because it is an efficient engine type for low-speed flight. The engine itself is similar to the internal combustion engines found in cars. The engine burns a mixture of fuel and air to drive pistons up and down, which turn a shaft connected to the propeller. When the propeller turns, it pushes air backwards and downwards, which pushes the airplane forward.

Instead of being characterized in terms of thrust, propeller engines are normally described in terms of the power they can deliver. An aircraft engine generates a certain engine power, P_E. Due to inefficiencies and losses, not all of the engine power can be converted into thrust by the propeller. The thrust power of the propeller, P_T, is equal to the engine power multiplied by a **propeller efficiency coefficient**, η_p.

$$P_T = \eta_p P_E \tag{10.5}$$

The engine power is sometimes referred to as the **engine brake power** because engine power is tested by applying a brake to the engine shaft. The thrust power is equal to the thrust produced by the propeller multiplied by the airplane velocity, v.

$$P_T = F_T v \tag{10.6}$$

The propeller efficiency, which has a value between 0 and 1, is not constant but instead is a function of propeller forward velocity and turnover rate. Propeller efficiency is usually plotted as a function of a quantity called the **propeller advance ratio**, J, which is the ratio of the velocity divided by the propeller turnover rate, n, and the propeller diameter, d.

$$J = \frac{v}{nd} \tag{10.7}$$

In Equation (10.7), the engine turnover rate is in units of revolutions per second. The propeller efficiency curve for a typical propeller,[2] the McCauley 7557, is shown in Figure 10-13. It is clear from the figure that the propeller efficiency coefficient is not constant. The efficiency reaches a peak value of about 0.83 at an advance ratio value of 0.65 and then decreases quite sharply after that.

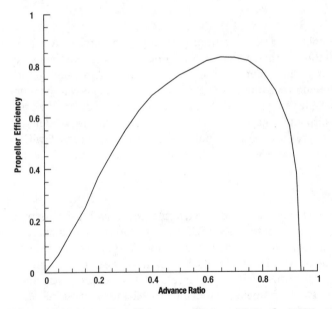

Figure 10-13. *Propeller efficiency coefficient, McCauley 7557 propeller*

In order to use the propeller efficiency data shown in Figure 10-13, a mathematical equation must be found that simulates the propeller efficiency curve. One way to model the curve is with a simple cubic equation that is a function of the advance ratio, J.

$$\eta_p = aJ + bJ^3 \tag{10.8}$$

The expression shown in Equation (10.8) satisfies the requirement that the propeller efficiency must be zero when the advance ratio is zero. The constants a and b can be chosen to match significant features of the curve. For example, in Figure 10-13 the maximum propeller efficiency value of approximately 0.83 occurs at an advance ratio value of about 0.65. The slope of the curve at this point will be zero. Using this information, the values of the constants to match Figure 10-13 can be obtained.

$$\eta_p = 1.83J - 1.32J^3 \tag{10.9}$$

The results of the curve fit are shown in Figure 10-14. Equation (10.9) does a good job of matching the original data up to and a little beyond the peak efficiency coefficient value at $J = 0.65$. The curve fit loses accuracy at high advance ratio values, but propellers are generally not intended to reach such high advance ratio values anyway, so for simulation purposes, Equation (10.9) is sufficient.

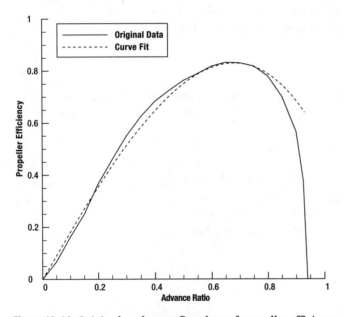

Figure 10-14. *Original and curve fit values of propeller efficiency*

Now that a curve fit expression for the propeller efficiency coefficient is available, a general expression for the propeller thrust as a function of the advance ratio or velocity can be obtained. The starting point is the equation relating thrust, propeller power, and engine power.

$$F_T = \frac{P_T}{v} = \frac{\eta_p P_e}{v} = \frac{\eta_p P_e}{Jnd} \tag{10.10}$$

Using the general form of the curve fit relation shown in Equation (10.8), the propeller efficiency in Equation (10.10) can be written in terms of the advance ratio, J.

$$F_T = \frac{P_e}{Jnd}\left(aJ + bJ^3\right) = \frac{P_e}{nd}\left(a + bJ^2\right) \tag{10.11}$$

Equation (10.11) can also be expressed in terms of the airplane velocity.

$$F_T = \frac{P_e}{nd}\left(a + b\frac{v^2}{n^2 d^2}\right) \tag{10.12}$$

Equation (10.12) is what we will use when we create a flight simulator a little later in the chapter. It states that the thrust generated by the propeller at any time is a function of the engine power, airplane velocity, propeller turnover rate, and propeller diameter.

Altitude Effects

One of the complications in computing the thrust of a propeller engine is that the engine thrust is a function of altitude. The power generated by the engine, and therefore the thrust generated by the propeller, decreases as the altitude increases. The power decrease is largely a function of atmospheric density and is represented by a **power drop-off factor, Φ**.

$$\Phi = \frac{\sigma - C}{1 - C} \tag{10.13}$$

The C parameter in Equation (10.13) is an altitude-independent mechanical power loss factor. It is normally assigned a constant value of 0.12.[2] The σ parameter is the ratio of the current atmospheric density to sea-level density.

$$\sigma = \frac{\rho}{\rho_o} \tag{10.14}$$

Atmospheric density is a function of altitude and is also a function of the air pressure and temperature. For altitudes below 11 km, the pressure and temperature can be found by equations that are a function of the altitude, h, and the sea-level values of pressure and temperature.[3]

$$T = 288.15 - 0.0065h \tag{10.15}$$

$$p = 101325\left(1 - 0.0065\frac{h}{288.15}\right)^{5.25} \tag{10.16}$$

The temperature in Equation (10.15) is in K, and the pressure in Equation (10.16) is in N/m^2. The altitude in both equations is in m. Once the pressure and temperature are known for a given altitude, the density can be computed.

$$\rho = 0.00348\frac{p}{T} \tag{10.17}$$

To incorporate altitude effects into the airplane thrust model, the power drop-off factor is simply added to the thrust equation.

$$F_T = \frac{\Phi P_e}{nd}\left(a + b\frac{v^2}{n^2 d^2}\right) \tag{10.18}$$

Example: Computing the Thrust of the Cessna 172 Skyhawk

Let's apply what we've learned about propeller engine thrust to compute the thrust profiles of the Cessna 172 Skyhawk airplane. The Skyhawk, shown in Figure 10-15, is a small, single-engine airplane that has been flying for many years and is still quite popular in the world of private aviation.

Figure 10-15. *The Cessna 172 Skyhawk (Photo courtesy of Steve Ashley)*

According to the manufacturer specifications,[4] the Skyhawk engine delivers 160 *hp* at 2400 *rpm*. The propeller diameter is 75 *in*. We'll assume the Skyhawk is using a McCauley 7557 propeller, so we can use the curve-fit relation shown in Equation (10.9) for the propeller efficiency. In order to compute the thrust profiles, the engine and propeller specifications will be converted to SI units.

$P_e = 160 \ hp = 119310 \ Watts$

$n = 2400 \ rpm = 40 \ \frac{rev}{s}$

$d = 75 \ in = 1.905m$

$a = 1.83$

$b = -1.32$

The thrust profiles will be computed at several altitudes so the power drop-off factor will be computed for each altitude. Table 10-1 shows the atmospheric density and power drop-off factor for four altitudes.

Table 10-1. *Atmospheric Density and Power Drop-Off Factors*

Altitude (*m*)	Density (*kg/m³*)	Power Drop-Off Factor (*Φ*)
0.0 (sea level)	1.225	1.0
1500	1.058	0.845
3000	0.909	0.707
4500	0.819	0.623

The input parameters are inserted into Equation (10.18), and thrust values are computed as a function of velocity up to the maximum rated velocity of the plane of 63 *m/s*. The results are shown in Figure 10-16. Because the *b* coefficient in the curve fit equation is negative, the calculated thrust generated by the engine is highest when the airplane velocity is zero and decreases in a parabolic fashion with increasing velocity. As predicted by the power drop-off factor, the thrust generated at an altitude of 4500 meters (close to the maximum altitude for the plane) is only 62% of the thrust generated at sea level.

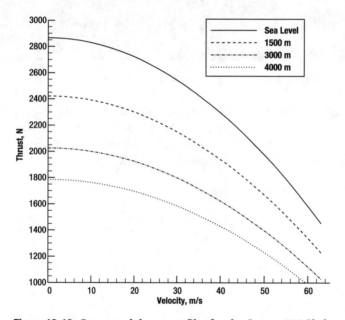

Figure 10-16. *Computed thrust profiles for the Cessna 172 Skyhawk*

The most recent Cessna 172 Skyhawk models feature an engine with better performance than earlier versions of the airplane. Previous Skyhawks featured an engine that delivered 160 *hp* at 2700 *rpm*. Because the current Skyhawk engine delivers the same power with a lower propeller turnover rate, it delivers about 10% more thrust than the earlier models.

Jet Engines

The second main type of airplane engine we will see in this chapter is the jet engine. This type of engine uses a series of spinning blades known as a turbine to generate thrust. A turbine can be thought of as a propeller with many blades. People have been playing around with turbines and turbine engines for a long time. The ancient Egyptians made toys that rotated on top of boiling pots of water. Leonardo Da Vinci invented a type of automated barbecue that was based on hot gases from a fire passing through a turbine that turned a roasting spit.

Research on the development of a gas turbine for airplane propulsion was carried on independently in England and Germany in the 1930s. The first successful jet engine, built in England in 1937, generated 445 N of thrust. The first jet-powered plane, the Heinkel HE-178, flew in 1939. After World War II, military and commercial airplanes increasingly used jet engines because of the superior power and performance that they offered.

The cross section of a typical jet engine is shown in Figure 10-17. Air enters the engine at the inlet. A compressor compresses the air and forces it into the combustor. Fuel is mixed with the compressed air and ignited, resulting in a high-temperature, high-pressure gas mixture. The gas passes through a turbine, causing the turbine blades to rotate. The turbine rotation is used to drive the compressor. The gas mixture then expands through a nozzle at the rear of the engine, generating thrust that moves the engine (and the airplane attached to it) forward.

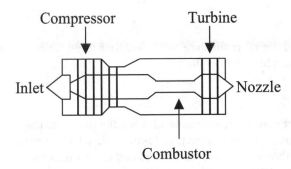

Figure 10-17. *A jet engine schematic*

There are different types of jet engines. The one described in the previous paragraph is called a **turbojet** engine. A **turboprop** engine is a jet engine that drives an external propeller. Turboprop engines are somewhat of a bridge between propeller and turbojet engines. They allow higher speeds than a propeller engine and offer greater efficiency than a turbojet engine at speeds below 225 *m/s* (500 *mph*). A **turboshaft** engine is similar to a turboprop and is used to turn the shaft of a helicopter rotor. A **turbofan** engine includes a fan at the front of the engine that is used to increase engine thrust. Most airliners today use turbofan engines.

The thrust generated by a jet engine is equal to the change of momentum of the gas traveling through the engine plus the pressure difference between the inlet and nozzle.

$$F_T = \dot{m}_e v_e - \dot{m}_0 v_0 + \left(p_e - p_0 \right) A_e \qquad (10.19)$$

The subscript 0 in Equation (10.19) represents the inlet conditions and the subscript e corresponds to exit conditions. The variable $\dot{m}$ is the inlet or exit mass flow rate in *kg/s*. Jet engines are usually characterized by thrust, and this number can be used in your simulations if the mass flow rate and pressure data is not available. For example, the General Electric F110 turbofan engine used in F-16 fighter planes generates between 120,000 to 142,000 N of force at sea level.[5]

It turns out that jet engines are easier to model in game simulations than are propeller engines, because the thrust produced by a jet engine at a given altitude will be constant. There is no need to use an equation like Equation (10.18) to model jet engine thrust. The thrust produced by a jet engine is affected by changing altitude and will decrease with increasing altitude.

Drag

Like baseballs, bullets, or anything else that travels through the air, an airplane is subject to aerodynamic drag forces that will resist the motion of the airplane. While the wing generates most of the lift of the airplane, the same is not true with drag. The drag caused by the fuselage and tail structures must be considered. If the landing gear is exposed, it will contribute to the overall drag as well. The overall drag on an airplane, F_D, can be computed from the familiar drag equation.

$$F_D = \frac{1}{2}C_D \rho v^2 A \qquad (10.20)$$

The overall drag on the airplane, and therefore the drag coefficient, has three main components. Let's discuss each of them in a bit more detail.

Skin Friction and Form Drag

Skin friction drag results from the contact between the air molecules and the surface of the airplane. As the air slides over the airplane, it tries to pull the plane along with it. **Form drag** is caused by the difference in pressure distribution between the forward and rearward facing surfaces of the airplane. Form drag is also referred to as **pressure drag**.

Skin friction drag and form drag are sometimes combined into what is called **parasitic drag**. Like all other drag forces we have studied, parasitic drag, F_{Dp}, can be expressed in terms of a parasitic drag coefficient, C_{Dp}.

$$F_{Dp} = \frac{1}{2}C_{Dp} \rho v^2 A \qquad (10.21)$$

An interesting characteristic about the parasitic drag coefficient is that it is not a function of angle of attack but is only a function of the airplane geometry. For example, the parasitic drag coefficient won't change if the airplane changes its pitch angle, but the coefficient will change if the wing flaps are deflected.

Induced Drag

A third type of drag experienced by airplanes, known as **induced drag**, is caused by the generation of lift. Recall from earlier in this chapter that lift occurs because the pressure is higher on the bottom of the wing than it is on the top of the wing. In the region of the wing tip, the higher-pressure air on the bottom of the wing flows in a swirling vortex structure towards the upper surface of the wing. This effect is shown schematically in Figure 10-18. The vortices are "shed" from the aft end of the wing tip and continue for some distance behind the plane. The generation of the wing tip vortex structure creates drag.

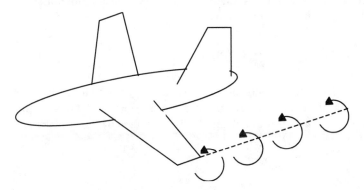

Figure 10-18. *Wing tip vortices are due to air circulation from the bottom side of the wing to the top.*

Induced drag is characterized by a coefficient of induced drag, C_{Di}. The coefficient is a function of the square of the lift coefficient, C_L; the wing aspect ratio, A_R; and a constant, e, known as the **airplane efficiency factor**.

$$C_{Di} = \frac{C_L^2}{\pi A_R e}$$

(10.22)

The airplane efficiency factor has a value between 0 and 1. Its value depends on the shape of the pressure distribution over the wing. If the shape of the pressure distribution is elliptic, as it was for the RAF Spitfire, then the efficiency factor is equal to 1. Nonelliptic pressure distributions have an efficiency factor less than 1. The Cessna 172 Skyhawk, for example, has an airplane efficiency factor of 0.77.

The **wing aspect ratio** is defined as the ratio of the square of the wing span, s, divided by the wing reference area, A.

$$A_R = \frac{s^2}{A} \tag{10.23}$$

The wing reference area in Equation (10.23) is the wetted area of the wing, the same value that is used in the lift and drag equations. In looking at Equation (10.22), the induced drag coefficient is inversely proportional to aspect ratio. A long, slender wing will have a greater aspect ratio, and therefore less induced drag, than will a short, stubby wing.

Total Drag Equation Revisited

The total drag experienced by an airplane can be divided into parasitic and induced drag components that are a function of the parasitic and induced drag coefficients. As you learned in the previous section, the induced drag coefficient is a function of the lift coefficient. An updated version of the total drag equation is shown in Equation (10.24).

$$F_D = F_{Dp} + F_{Di} = \frac{1}{2}\left(C_{Dp} + C_{Di}\right)\rho v^2 A = \frac{1}{2}\left(C_{Dp} + \frac{C_L^2}{\pi A_R e}\right)\rho v^2 A \tag{10.24}$$

To use Equation (10.24) requires the parasitic drag coefficient, C_{Dp}, as well as the lift coefficient, C_L. In some situations, the lift coefficient can be related to other quantities. For example, when an airplane is traveling in straight-and-level flight, the lift generated by the airplane is equal to the weight of the airplane.

$$L = W = \frac{1}{2}C_L\rho v^2 A \tag{10.25}$$

In Equation (10.25), the weight of the airplane, W, is simply equal to the mass of the airplane multiplied by the gravitational acceleration. When Equation (10.25) is incorporated into Equation (10.24), the total drag equation for straight-and-level flight becomes the following:

$$F_D = F_{D,p} + F_{D,i} = \frac{1}{2}C_{D,p}\rho v^2 A + \frac{2W^2}{\pi e \rho v^2 s^2} \tag{10.26}$$

Let's use Equation (10.26) to compute the straight-and-level flight drag profiles for the Cessna 172 Skyhawk. The airplane has a wingspan of 11.0 m, an airplane efficiency factor of 0.77, and a reference wing area of 16.2 m^2. The weight of the airplane will be assumed to be 10675 N (2400 lb). The coefficient of parasite drag will be assumed to be 0.035. The density will be taken to be 1.2 kg/m^3. The calculations will be performed from the stall speed of 25.5 m/s up to the maximum velocity the airplane can achieve, which is 62.6 m/s.

The total drag profile for the Skyhawk is shown in Figure 10-19. Also shown on the curve are the parasitic and induced drag profiles. It is apparent from Equation (10.26) that parasitic drag is a function of velocity squared, whereas induced drag is an inverse function of velocity squared. The maximum induced drag will therefore occur at the lowest velocity, and the maximum parasitic drag occurs at the highest velocity. The minimum total drag occurs somewhere in the middle, at a velocity of 37.5 m/s.

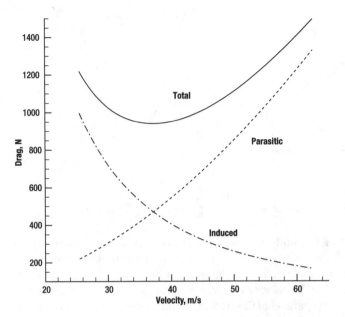

Figure 10-19. *Straight-and-level drag profiles for the Cessna 172 Skyhawk*

Keep in mind that the drag profiles shown in Figure 10-19 are for straight-and-level flight. If the airplane was climbing or sinking, the lift would not be equal to the weight of the airplane, and the induced drag profile would be somewhat different.

Lift over Drag Ratio

A commonly used method for characterizing the performance of airfoils and airplanes is by the **lift over drag ratio**, or L/D ratio. The L/D ratio is simply the ratio of the lift coefficient (or lift force) at a given condition to the drag ratio (or drag force).

Full-Body Aerodynamics

We've covered quite a bit of ground so far in this chapter. As you have learned, the physics of airplanes is quite complicated. There is one more step to go until we're ready to build a flight simulator game. The equations that model lift, drag, thrust, and gravity have to be pulled into a single, integrated model that will be referred to as **full-body aerodynamics**. We'll start by examining a force diagram for an airplane that is in a climb.

The net aerodynamic force on an airplane consists of all the lift, drag, thrust, and gravitational forces acting on the plane. The basic force diagram shown in Figure 10-3 was for an airplane traveling in straight-and-level flight. Let's examine the more general case of an airplane that is climbing and therefore has a vertical velocity component. The force diagram for such a flight situation is shown in Figure 10-20. For simplicity, we'll look at a two-dimensional case where the motion of the airplane is restricted to the x-z plane.

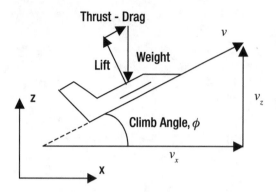

Figure 10-20. *Force diagram for an airplane that is climbing*

For the purposes of analyzing full-body aerodynamics, the lift force, F_L, as shown in Figure 10-20 will be defined as the aerodynamic force component that acts perpendicular to the velocity vector of the airplane. Similarly, the drag force, F_D, is defined as the aerodynamic force component that acts parallel to the velocity vector. For the purposes of this analysis, the thrust force from the engine, F_T, acts parallel to the velocity vector as well. The net force in the direction parallel to the velocity vector is equal to the thrust force minus the drag force, $F_T - F_D$.

Because the airplane is climbing, it will have both vertical and horizontal velocity components. The **climb angle** is the angle between the flight path of the airplane and the ground. The **pitch angle** of the airplane is the angle between the longitudinal axis of the airplane and the ground. In Figure 10-20 the pitch and climb angles are the same, but this will not always be the case. The angle of attack of the wing is equal to the sum of the pitch and incidence angles minus the climb angle. A wing on an airplane in straight-and-level flight with a pitch angle of 5 degrees will have the same angle of attack as when the airplane is at a pitch angle of 15 degrees while climbing at an angle of 10 degrees.

As was previously mentioned, the thrust and drag forces act along the flight path of the airplane. Thrust acts in the forward direction and drag acts in the backward direction. The net thrust on the airplane is equal to the difference between the thrust and drag forces. The lift generated by the airplane acts in a direction perpendicular to the flight path. Using the climb angle and the schematic shown in Figure 10-20, the net force acting on the airplane can be expressed in terms of vertical, F_z, and horizontal, F_x, components. The angle, ϕ, in Equations (10.27) and (10.28) is the climb angle.

$$F_z = ma_z = \left(F_T - F_D \right) \sin\phi + F_L \cos\phi - W \tag{10.27}$$

$$F_x = ma_x = \left(F_T - F_D \right) \cos\phi - F_L \sin\phi \tag{10.28}$$

Turning

A standard way to change the direction an airplane is traveling is to perform a banking turn. The ailerons on the wing are deflected, causing the airplane to roll or bank to one side. As shown in Figure 10-21, when this happens, the lift force vector is rotated by the bank angle, ψ.

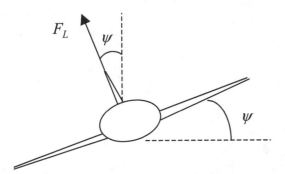

Figure 10-21. *Banking the airplane creates a sideways force component.*

When the airplane banks, a sideways component to the lift force causes the airplane to turn in a circular arc. When the bank angle is brought back to zero, the sideways lift force component disappears, and the airplane once again flies in a straight line. The rudder is not used to turn the airplane but is used during the turn to keep the nose of the airplane pointed in the direction of the flight path.

If the airplane is performing a level turn (that is, the pitch angle is zero), the radius of the turn is equal to the square of the velocity divided by the gravitational acceleration multiplied by the tangent of the bank angle.

$$r = \frac{v^2}{g \tan \psi} \tag{10.29}$$

One consequence of a plane performing a banking turn is that the stall speed of the airplane will decrease. For an airplane performing a level turn, the stall speed during the turn, v_{sb}, is equal to the straight-and-level stall speed, v_s, divided by the square root of the cosine of the bank angle.

$$v_{sb} = \frac{v_s}{\sqrt{\cos \psi}} \tag{10.30}$$

Aircraft Orientation

The lift, thrust, and drag forces that act on an airplane are evaluated relative to the velocity vector of the airplane. This velocity vector can be pointing in any direction. To determine the location and velocity of the airplane relative to a fixed point on the ground, the forces normal and parallel to the velocity vector need to be rotated to the standard Cartesian coordinate system. We've managed to avoid a detailed discussion of 3-D rotation matrices up to this point in the book, but now it's time to bite the bullet and talk about them.

The orientation of an airplane relative to its center of gravity is defined by three angles, called **pitch**, **roll**, and **yaw**. The three angles represent three coordinate system rotations about the center of gravity. The three angles are shown schematically in Figure 10-22. We've already spoken about pitch angle quite a bit in this chapter. Pitch represents a nose-up or nose-down rotation of the airplane. Yaw is a side-to-side rotation of the nose of the airplane. The roll angle, also called the bank angle, is an up-or-down rotation of the wing tips.

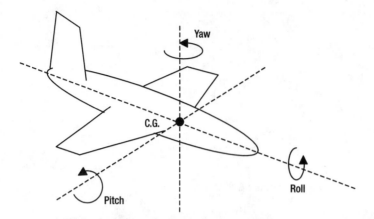

Figure 10-22. *The pitch, roll, and yaw rotations relative to the center of gravity.*

Pitch, roll, and yaw are relative to the center of gravity of the airplane. For game simulation purposes, it is usually valuable to define the airplane orientation relative to a fixed point on the ground in terms of climb, heading, and roll angles. The climb angle was previously introduced in Figure 10-20. The tangent of the climb angle is equal to the vertical velocity component, v_z, divided by the horizontal velocity component, v_h.

$$\tan\phi = \frac{v_z}{v_h} \tag{10.31}$$

The horizontal velocity component is equal to the sum of the squares of the x- and y-velocity components.

$$v_h = \sqrt{v_x^2 + v_y^2} \tag{10.32}$$

As shown in Figure 10-23, the heading angle, θ, of the airplane is defined as the orientation of the velocity vector of the airplane in the x-y plane. The x-axis is assumed to point north and is at a heading angle of zero.

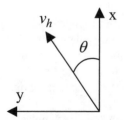

Figure 10-23. *The heading angle is the orientation of the velocity vector in the x-y plane.*

The cosine and sine of the heading angle is equal to the ratio of the x- and y-velocity components to the horizontal velocity component.

$$\cos\theta = \frac{v_x}{v_h} \qquad \sin\theta = \frac{v_y}{v_h} \tag{10.33}$$

The bank angle relative to a fixed point on the ground is the same as the bank angle relative to the center of gravity. Its definition remains the same as was defined in Figure 10-21.

The lift, thrust, and drag forces acting on an airplane are evaluated parallel and normal to the velocity vector of the airplane. The directions parallel and normal to the velocity vector are defined by the climb, heading, and bank angles. In Chapter 2, the concept of a two-dimensional rotation matrix was introduced as a way to perform a coordinate system rotation about a coordinate axis. With airplanes there are three angles (climb, heading, bank) representing three coordinate system rotations. Therefore, to transform the lift, thrust, and drag forces into x-, y-, and z-direction components requires multiplying three two-dimensional rotation matrices together.

$$\begin{bmatrix} F_x \\ F_y \\ F_z \end{bmatrix} = \begin{bmatrix} 1 & 0 & 0 \\ 0 & \cos\psi & -\sin\psi \\ 0 & \sin\psi & \cos\psi \end{bmatrix} \begin{bmatrix} \cos\phi & 0 & -\sin\phi \\ 0 & 1 & 0 \\ \sin\phi & 0 & \cos\phi \end{bmatrix} \begin{bmatrix} \cos\theta & -\sin\theta & 0 \\ \sin\theta & \cos\theta & 0 \\ 0 & 0 & 1 \end{bmatrix} \begin{bmatrix} F_T - F_D \\ 0 \\ F_L \end{bmatrix} \tag{10.34}$$

In Equation (10.34), the climb angle is ϕ, the heading angle is θ, and the bank angle is ψ. When the three rotation matrix multiplications are performed, the result is three equations for the x-, y, and z-components of force on the airplane.

$$F_x = \cos\theta\cos\phi\left(F_T - F_D\right) + \left(\sin\theta\sin\psi - \cos\theta\sin\phi\cos\psi\right)F_L \tag{10.35a}$$

$$F_y = \sin\theta\cos\phi\left(F_T - F_D\right) + \left(-\cos\theta\sin\psi - \sin\theta\sin\phi\cos\psi\right)F_L \tag{10.35b}$$

$$F_z = \sin\phi\left(F_T - F_D\right) + \cos\phi\cos\psi F_L \tag{10.35c}$$

The expressions shown in Equation (10.35) are the force equations that will be used when we create the Flight Simulator.

Takeoff

For an airplane to fly, it must first gain enough lift to take off from the ground. While the airplane is traveling down a flat runway, the climb angle is zero, and the lift and gravity forces are vertical. The velocity required for takeoff is a function of the weight of the airplane, the lift coefficient, the air density, and the reference area of the wing.

$$v = \sqrt{\frac{2W}{C_L \rho A}} \tag{10.36}$$

The key to minimizing takeoff velocity for a given airplane at a given atmospheric density condition is to maximize the lift coefficient. Lift increases with angle of attack, but the airplane is rolling along the ground so the angle of attack is equal to the incidence angle of the wing, which is usually quite small. Deflecting the flaps downward during takeoff can increase the lift coefficient, and therefore the flaps are usually deflected during takeoff.

Another way to make it easier for an airplane to lift off the ground is to take off into wind. The velocity in Equation (10.36) is relative velocity between the airplane and the air traveling over it. The relative velocity is a combination of the velocity the airplane is traveling relative to the ground, known as the **ground speed**, and the direction and magnitude of any wind that is present. Whenever possible, pilots try to take off into the wind to add the wind velocity to the relative velocity of the airplane.

Ground Effect

The lift coefficient of an airfoil depends on its geometry, angle of attack, and whether its flaps are deflected. When an airplane is close to the ground, there is also an effect known as **ground effect** that can increase the apparent lift coefficient of the airplane. Ground effect is very fortuitous when it comes to airplane flight because some airplanes would have a difficult time taking off without it. Ground effects also influence an airplane that is landing, reducing the rate of descent of the airplane near the ground.

Tidbit Some critics have claimed that Howard Hughes's enormous "Spruce Goose" airplane only flew because of ground effect and would have been incapable of achieving an altitude of more than a few feet.

If you remember from the "Induced Drag" section earlier in this chapter, when a wing travels through the air, vortices are shed off from the wing tips, and the swirling air vortices continue for some distance behind the airplane. When the airplane is flying at an altitude far away from the ground, the shape of the vortex structure is cylindrical.

When the wing is close to the ground, less than a wingspan distance or so, the presence of the ground disturbs the structure of the vortices. The shape of the vortices is no longer cylindrical, it becomes flattened, and the induced drag on the wings is reduced. Ground effect also increases the apparent lift coefficient of the wing.

The easiest way to incorporate ground effects into your flight simulator is to simply add a ground effect factor to the normally computed lift coefficient when the wing is within a wingspan distance of the ground. You could either multiply the "normal" lift coefficient by a number greater than 1 or you could add a value, say 0.5, to the "normal" lift coefficient value. Once the wing is higher than a wingspan's distance above the ground, the ground effect factors would no longer be applied. Keep in mind that this is a very simplified treatment of ground effects. A full discussion of the complicated physics of ground effects is beyond the scope of this book.

Exercise

1. Compute the liftoff velocity for the Cessna 172 Skyhawk that uses a NACA 2412 airfoil for its wing. Assume for this problem that the incidence of the wing is zero. The weight of the plane is 10245 N (2300 lb), the reference wing area is 16.2 m^2, and the plane is taking off at sea level where the air density is 1.22 kg/m^3. Assume that the flaps are deflected at 20^0 during takeoff, resulting in an increase in lift coefficient of 0.25 over the nominal value, and that the lift coefficient is increased by 0.25 due to ground effects.

Landing

If the lift generated by an airplane is less than its weight, the airplane will descend. The maximum rate of descent for landing is limited by the ability of the landing gear to absorb the impact. The pitch angle of the airplane at landing has maximum and minimum values as well. If the pitch angle is negative, the nose of the airplane might strike the ground before the wheels do. If the pitch angle is positive but at too high a value, the tail might scrape the ground.

The simplest way to evaluate a landing in an airplane simulator is to define a maximum vertical velocity and pitch angle for a given airplane. If the plane hits the ground and is exceeding these maximum values, the simulation can assume that the plane has crashed.

A Basic Flight Simulator

At long last all of the physical model development is complete, and we are ready to create a basic flight simulator. If we know the geometrical and performance characteristics of an airplane, the lift, drag, and thrust forces acting on the airplane can be evaluated using the equations presented in this chapter. As with the other games developed in this book, the flight simulator will be displayed using a very simple Java GUI. The graphics aren't very sophisticated, but the physics inside the Flight Simulator are real.

A lot of elements go into modeling an airplane in flight, but to make the Flight Simulator a bit simpler to program, we will ignore some of them. Here is a list of some of the features, assumptions, and simplifications in the Flight Simulator:

- The engine thrust, lift, and drag are modeled according to the equations presented in this chapter.

- The lift coefficient will be modeled by straight-line curve fits to the experimental data for the NACA 2412 airfoil shown in Figure 10-8.

- The pilot will have control over the angle of attack, throttle, and bank angle of the airplane. The plane will have the ability to pitch, yaw, and roll.

- There is no wind in this simulation.

- Flap, elevator, and aileron deflections are assumed to happen instantaneously. No attempt will be made to model the dynamic behavior of these flight control surfaces.

- When the plane is traveling down the runway, the rolling friction between the wheels and ground will be ignored. If you wanted to include that effect in your flight simulator, a reasonable value for the coefficient of rolling friction for an airplane is $\mu_r = 0.015$.

- The display window in the Flight Simulator will only show the vertical motion of the airplane. While pitch, yaw, and roll are modeled in the flight simulator, the airplane cartoon in the display window will not show the airplane pitching or turning.

The GUI display for the flight simulator is shown in Figure 10-24. On the left-hand side of the display are the user controls. The pilot can change the throttle percentage, angle of attack, bank angle, and flap deflection of the airplane. Angle of attack was chosen as a user control rather than pitch angle because it made it easier to control the airplane in flight. Rather than trying to model a continuously varying flap deflection angle, three flap deflection angles are available—0, 20, and 40 degrees. The airplane is assumed to take off from sea level where the altitude (z-location) of the plane is zero. On the right-hand side of the GUI window are text fields that display the current state of the airplane including the heading angle, climb angle, airspeed, climb rate, and altitude. At the bottom of the GUI is a status text field that displays useful information such as "You landed safely" or "The throttle is set to zero."

When the Reset button is hit, the controls reset to default values and the plane appears on the ground. To fly the plane, move the throttle control to 100% and press the Start button. The plane will start to move forward. Actually, the plane will remain in a fixed location in the GUI and the marker will begin to move. The airspeed as indicated in the text field on the right-hand side of the GUI will start to increase. If you press the Start button and nothing happens, make sure that the throttle setting is not set to zero.

When the takeoff speed is reached, the lift generated by the wing is sufficient to overcome the weight of the airplane. The climb rate, climb angle, and altitude values will start to increase. When this happens, increase the angle of attack to a positive value to increase lift. Once the plane is airborne, you can play around with the throttle and angle of attack settings. The plane can turn by setting the bank angle to a nonzero number. When the plane starts to turn, the heading angle will change. Setting the bank angle back to zero stops the turn.

Landing is also a part of the Flight Simulator. To decrease altitude, lower the throttle setting and/or decrease the angle of attack. The quality of your landing is determined by the z-velocity component when the plane hits the ground. Any value in excess of –5.0 *m/s* is considered a crash. A smaller negative z-velocity indicates a safe landing.

The flaps aren't necessary for takeoff in the Flight Simulator, but they can be used to shorten the distance required for takeoff. The flaps can also be used when landing to increase the lift and therefore reduce the rate of descent when the airplane is traveling at low speeds.

The Flight Simulator is implemented by three classes, one that defines the GUI and two that represent propeller airplanes. This version of the Flight Simulator features a Cessna Skyhawk as the airplane being flown. We'll start by discussing the airplane classes. The PropPlane class is written to represent a generic propeller airplane. Because the ODE solver will be used to update the location and velocity of the airplane, the PropPlane class is written as a subclass of the SimpleProjectile class, which itself is a subclass of the ODE class.

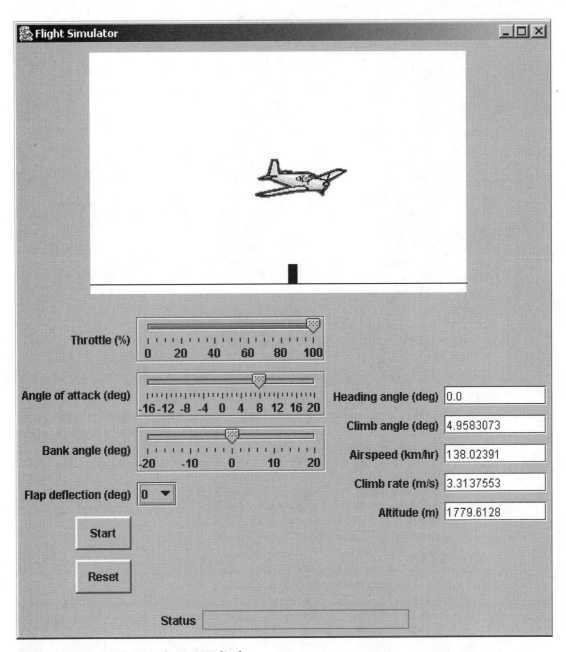

Figure 10-24. *The Flight Simulator GUI display*

The first thing the PropPlane class does is to declare a number of fields that define various aspects of the airplane. Many of the field names are self-explanatory. The lift coefficient curve for the airplane wing is approximated by two straight lines to model the pre- and post-stall lift coefficient.

```
public class PropPlane extends SimpleProjectile
{
  // Declare fields.
  private double bank;
  private double alpha;    // Angle of attack
  private double throttle;
  private double wingArea;
  private double wingSpan;
  private double tailArea;
  private double clSlope0;     // Slope of Cl-alpha curve
  private double cl0;          // Intercept of Cl-alpha curve
  private double clSlope1;     // Post-stall slope of Cl-alpha curve
  private double cl1;          // Post-stall intercept of Cl-alpha curve
  private double alphaClMax;   // Alpha when Cl=Clmax
  private double cdp;          // Parasite drag coefficient
  private double eff;          // Induced drag efficiency coefficient
  private double mass;
  private double enginePower;
  private double engineRps;    // Revolutions per second
  private double propDiameter;
  private double a;            // Propeller efficiency coefficient
  private double b;            // Propeller efficiency coefficient
  private String flap;         // Flap deflection amount
```

The PropPlane constructor calls the SimpleProjectile constructor to initialize the initial location and velocity of the airplane. It then assigns values to the fields declared in the class based on arguments passed to the constructor. Initially, the bank angle, angle of attack, throttle setting, and flap deflection are all set to zero.

```
public PropPlane(double x, double y, double z,
        double vx, double vy, double vz, double time,
        double wingArea, double wingSpan, double tailArea,
        double clSlope0, double cl0, double clSlope1,
        double cl1, double alphaClMax,
        double cdp, double eff, double mass,
        double enginePower, double engineRps,
        double propDiameter, double a, double b) {
    super(x, y, z, vx, vy, vz, time);

    this.wingArea = wingArea;
    this.wingSpan = wingSpan;
    this.tailArea = tailArea;
    this.clSlope0 = clSlope0;
    this.cl0 = cl0;
    this.clSlope1 = clSlope1;
    this.cl1 = cl1;
    this.alphaClMax = alphaClMax;
```

```
    this.cdp = cdp;
    this.eff = eff;
    this.mass = mass;
    this.enginePower = enginePower;
    this.engineRps = engineRps;
    this.propDiameter = propDiameter;
    this.a = a;
    this.b = b;

    //  Initially, set bank, angle of attack,
    //  and throttle to zero.
    bank = 0.0;
    alpha = 0.0;
    throttle = 0.0;
    flap = "0";
  }
```

The PropPlane class declares a collection of get/set methods to access or change the value of the fields declared in the class. Not all of the get/set methods are shown here.

```
//  These methods access or change the value of the
//  fields declared in the PropPlane class.
public double getBank() {
  return bank;
}

public double getAlpha() {
  return alpha;
}

//  Other get/set methods not shown …
```

The heart of the PropPlane class is the getRightHandSide method that defines the right-hand sides of the equations of motion that will be solved using the ODE solver. The method begins by computing intermediate values of the location and velocity of the plane and declaring a series of convenience variables.

```
public double[] getRightHandSide(double s, double q[],
                        double deltaQ[], double ds,
                        double qScale) {
  double dQ[] = new double[6];
  double newQ[] = new double[6];

  //  Compute the intermediate values of the
  //  location and velocity components.
  for(int i=0; i<6; ++i) {
    newQ[i] = q[i] + qScale*deltaQ[i];
  }
```

```
//  Compute the intermediate values of the various
//  velocities.
double vx = newQ[0];
double vy = newQ[2];
double vz = newQ[4];
double x = newQ[1];
double y = newQ[3];
double z = newQ[5];
double vh = Math.sqrt(vx*vx + vy*vy);
double vtotal = Math.sqrt(vx*vx + vy*vy + vz*vz);
```

The method then computes the forces that act on the airplane starting with the thrust. The air density at the current altitude is computed using Equation (10.17). The power drop-off factor and thrust force are calculated from Equations (10.13) and (10.18).

```
//  Compute the air density.
double temperature = 288.15 - 0.0065*z;
double grp = (1.0 - 0.0065*z/288.15);
double pressure = 101325.0*Math.pow(grp, 5.25);
double density = 0.00348*pressure/temperature;

//  Compute power drop-off factor.
double omega = density/1.225;
double factor = (omega - 0.12)/0.88;

//  Compute thrust.
double advanceRatio = vtotal/(engineRps*propDiameter);
double thrust = throttle*factor*enginePower*
        (a + b*advanceRatio*advanceRatio)/(engineRps*propDiameter);
```

The next force that is evaluated is the lift. The Skyhawk uses a NACA 2412 airfoil for its wing cross-section. The lift coefficient profile for the NACA 2412 is shown in Figure 10-8. For the purposes of the flight simulator, the lift coefficient profile is approximated by two straight lines.

$$C_L = 0.889\alpha + 0.178 \quad for\ \alpha \le 16 \tag{10.37a}$$

$$C_L = -0.1\alpha + 3.2 \quad for\ \alpha > 16 \tag{10.37b}$$

The slopes and intercepts of these two lines are contained in the clSlope0, cl0, clSlope1, and cl1 fields.

```
//  Compute lift coefficient. The Cl curve is
//  modeled using two straight lines.
double cl;
if ( alpha < alphaClMax ) {
  cl = clSlope0*alpha + cl0;
}
else {
  cl = clSlope1*alpha + cl1;
}
```

The nominal value of lift coefficient is modified according to whether the flaps are deflected or if ground effects are present. A simplified approach is taken to account for flap deflection. If the flaps are deflected 20 degrees, the C_L is increased by 0.25. If the flaps are deflected 40 degrees, C_L is increased by 0.5. In looking at Figure 10-11, the difference in C_L for the NACA 2412 airfoil for no-flap and 20-degree flap deflection is approximately 0.25.

If the plane is within 5 m of the ground, ground effects are assumed to be present and the lift coefficient is increased by 0.5. Once C_L has been determined, the lift force is computed using Equation (10.3).

```
//  Include effects of flaps and ground effects.
//  Ground effects are present if the plane is
//  within 5 meters of the ground.
if ( flap.equals("20") ) {
  cl += 0.25;
}
if ( flap.equals("40") ) {
  cl += 0.5;
}
if ( z < 5.0 ) {
  cl += 0.25;
}

//  Compute lift.
double lift = 0.5*cl*density*vtotal*vtotal*wingArea;
```

The next force to be computed is the drag force experienced by the airplane. The drag coefficient and drag force are calculated using Equation (10.24). The cdp field represents the parasitic drag coefficient.

```
//  Compute drag coefficient.
double aspectRatio = wingSpan*wingSpan/wingArea;
double cd = cdp + cl*cl/(Math.PI*aspectRatio*eff);

//  Compute drag force.
double drag = 0.5*cd*density*vtotal*vtotal*wingArea;
```

The thrust, lift, and drag forces that were computed in the preceding sections of code are the forces parallel and normal to the velocity vector of the airplane. The x-, y-, and z-components of the parallel and normal forces are determined based on the bank, heading, and climb angles using a 3-D rotation matrix and Equation (10.35). The force of gravity, which always acts in the vertical direction, is added to the z-direction force component.

```
//  Define some shorthand convenience variables
//  for use with the rotation matrix.
//  Compute the sine and cosines of the climb angle,
//  bank angle, and heading angle;

double cosW = Math.cos(bank); //  Bank angle
double sinW = Math.sin(bank); //  Bank angle
```

```
      double cosP;      // Climb angle
      double sinP;      // Climb angle
      double cosT;      // Heading angle
      double sinT;      // Heading angle

   if ( vtotal == 0.0 ) {
      cosP = 1.0;
      sinP = 0.0;
   }
   else {
      cosP = vh/vtotal;
      sinP = vz/vtotal;
   }

   if ( vh == 0.0 ) {
      cosT = 1.0;
      sinT = 0.0;
   }
   else {
      cosT = vx/vh;
      sinT = vy/vh;
   }


   //  Convert the thrust, drag, and lift forces into
   //   x-, y-, and z-components using the rotation matrix.
   double Fx = cosT*cosP*(thrust - drag) +
               (sinT*sinW - cosT*sinP*cosW)*lift;
   double Fy = sinT*cosP*(thrust - drag) +
               (-cosT*sinW - sinT*sinP*cosW)*lift;
   double Fz = sinP*(thrust - drag) + cosP*cosW*lift;

   //  Add the gravity force to the z-direction force.
   Fz = Fz + mass*G;
```

Once the x-, y-, and z-components of force are determined, the right-hand sides of the ODEs that describe the motion of the airplane can be filled.

```
   //  Load the right-hand sides of the ODEs
   dQ[0] = ds*(Fx/mass);
   dQ[1] = ds*vx;
   dQ[2] = ds*(Fy/mass);
   dQ[3] = ds*vy;
   dQ[4] = ds*(Fz/mass);
   dQ[5] = ds*vz;

   return dQ;
  }
}
```

Now that a generic PropPlane class has been created, it is a simple matter to declare subclasses of it that represent specific types of airplanes. All that the airplane-specific subclasses have to do is to pass the proper input parameters to the PropPlane constructor. All of the methods and fields needed to describe the state and behavior of the airplane have already been implemented in the PropPlane class.

The Flight Simulator will model the flight of a Cessna Skyhawk, so we will write a class named CessnaSkyhawk that will represent the airplane. The only thing the CessnaSkyhawk class does is to declare a constructor that calls the PropPlane constructor passing it the proper input values for a Cessna Skyhawk.

```
public class CessnaSkyhawk extends PropPlane
{
  //  Cessna Skyhawk data
  //  wingArea = 16.2    = wing wetted area, m^2
  //  wingSpan = 10.9    = wing span, m
  //  tailArea = 2.0     = tail wetted area, m^2
  //  clSlope0 = 0.0889  = slope of Cl-alpha curve
  //  cl0 = 0.178        = Cl value when alpha = 0
  //  clSlope1 = -0.1    = slope of post-stall Cl-alpha curve
  //  cl1 = 3.2          = intercept of post-stall Cl-alpha curve
  //  alphaClMax = 16.0  = alpha at Cl(max)
  //  cdp = 0.034        = parasitic drag coefficient
  //  eff = 0.77         = induced drag efficiency coefficient
  //  mass = 1114.0      = airplane mass, kg
  //  enginePower = 119310.0 = peak engine power, W
  //  engineRps = 40.0       = engine turnover rate, rev/s
  //  propDiameter = 1.905   = propeller diameter, m
  //  a = 1.83               = propeller efficiency curve fit coefficient
  //  b = -1.32              = propeller efficiency curve fit coefficient

  //  The CessnaSkyhawk constructor calls the
  //  PropPlane constructor.
  public CessnaSkyhawk(double x, double y, double z,
        double vx, double vy, double vz, double time) {
    super(x, y, z, vx, vy, vz, time, 16.2, 10.9, 2.0,
        0.0889, 0.178, -0.1, 3.2, 16.0, 0.034, 0.77,
        1114.0, 119310.0, 40.0, 1.905, 1.83, -1.32);
  }
}
```

The GUI aspects of the Flight Simulator are implemented in a class named FlightSimulator. The code listing for the FlightSimulator class is quite long, and it is similar to all of the other GUIs previously created in this book. Details of the FlightSimulator class will not be discussed here, but you can download the complete code listing from the Apress website.

When your airplane takes off and reaches a reasonable altitude, try turning the plane by setting a nonzero bank angle. To stop the simulation, you can press the Reset button or you can cut throttle, set the angle of attack to be negative, and auger your Skyhawk into the ground.

If you want to try for a more gentle landing experience, decrease the angle of attack and/or throttle and try to set the plane down with a vertical velocity smaller than –5.0 *m/s.*

Trim and Stability

The final topics that will be discussed in this chapter are the trim and stability of an airplane. As you have learned in the previous sections, airplanes are subject to various forces that act through different locations on the airplane. These forces create moments that can cause undesirable rotational motion of the airplane. If left unchecked, the moments can cause the airplane to spin out of control. The study of trim and stability is an effort to predict, minimize, and control the moments experienced by an airplane in flight

Moments

Earlier in the chapter, you learned that lift acts through the center of pressure of the airfoil. The force of gravity acts through the center of gravity (or c.g.). As shown in Figure 10-25, if the center of gravity and center of pressure are in different locations, then the opposing forces of lift and gravity will create a moment that will pitch the airfoil up or down. The "+" symbol in Figure 10-25 indicates the center of rotation for the moment.

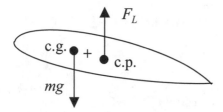

Figure 10-25. *Gravitational and lift forces can generate a moment.*

The moment generated by an airfoil is characterized by an equation very similar to the standard lift and drag expressions. The moment, *M*, is a function of a moment coefficient, C_M; the air density, ρ; the square of the air velocity, v; the wing wetted area, *A*; and the chord length, $\bar{c}$. If you recall, the chord is the distance from the leading edge of the wing to the trailing edge.

$$M = \frac{1}{2} C_M \rho v^2 A \bar{c} \qquad (10.38)$$

Moments are always defined with respect to a center of rotation, the point at which the moment is applied. A given force will result in a different moment, for example, if the moment is evaluated at the leading edge than it will be if it is evaluated at the center of gravity. It was found both experimentally and analytically that if the moment is evaluated at a point approximately ¼ of the distance from the leading edge to the trailing edge (called the **quarter chord point**) that the moment value is relatively independent of the angle of attack. The point at which moment is independent of the angle of attack is also known as the **aerodynamic center** (or a.c.) of the airfoil.

Figure 10-26 shows moment coefficient data for the NACA 2412 airfoil.[1] The moment coefficient shown in the figure is relative to the quarter chord point. It is fairly constant for angle of attack values ranging from −10 to 10.

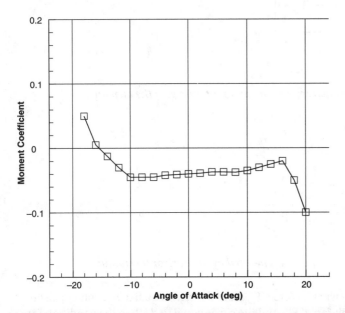

Figure 10-26. *Moment coefficient data for the NACA 2412 airfoil*

While the moment about the aerodynamic center of an airfoil is relatively independent of the angle of attack, this is not the case if the center of rotation of the moment is evaluated somewhere else on the airfoil. The moment taken about the center of gravity, for example, will change if the angle of attack is changed.

Trim

Figure 10-26 showed the moment that can be generated in an airfoil, but the same considerations can be applied to an airplane as a whole. Consider the tailless airplane shown in Figure 10-27. The lift from the wing acts through the center of pressure of the wing. If the center of gravity is aft of the center of pressure, a positive (counterclockwise) moment is created about the center of gravity that will pitch the nose of the plane upwards. Obviously, if this moment isn't counterbalanced, the plane will flip over backwards.

To counteract the moment generated by wing is the reason planes have a horizontal stabilizer as part of the tail. The horizontal stabilizer is a lifting surface; in effect it is a small wing. When a tail with a horizontal stabilizer is added to the airplane, as shown in Figure 10-28, the lift generated by the horizontal stabilizer creates a negative (clockwise) moment that pushes the nose of the plane down and counteracts the moment generated by the wing.

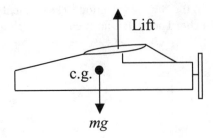

Figure 10-27. *Lift from the wing generates a moment about the c.g. of the airplane.*

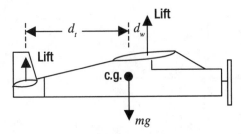

Figure 10-28. *A counterbalancing moment is generated by the horizontal stabilizer.*

If the distance between the wing lift force, F_{Lw}, and the c.g. is equal to d_w, and the distance from the horizontal stabilizer lift force, F_{Lt}, and the c.g. is equal to d_t, then the condition for zero moment about the center of gravity is when the magnitudes of the two moments are equal.

$$M_{cg} = 0 = F_{Lt}d_t - F_{Lw}d_w \tag{10.39}$$

An airplane is said to be **trimmed** if there is no moment about its center of gravity. The angle of attack at which trim occurs is called the **trim angle of attack.**

In Figures 10-27 and 10-28, the center of gravity of the airplane is behind the center of pressure of the wing. For many airplanes, large jetliners for instance, the center of gravity will be in front of the center of pressure of the wing. In this case, as shown in Figure 10-29, the moment caused by the wing lift will pitch the nose of the airplane downwards. To counteract this moment, the tail must produce negative lift. This can be accomplished by either orienting the horizontal stabilizer at a negative angle of attack or by using an upside-down cambered airfoil for the horizontal stabilizer.

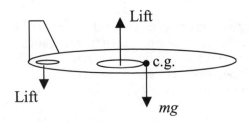

Figure 10-29. *To create the proper counterbalancing moment, sometimes the horizontal stabilizer lift must be negative.*

Stability

The previous section introduced the concept of trim, which is a condition where the moment through the center of gravity of an airplane is equal to zero. What happens when the angle of attack deviates from the trim angle defines the **stability** of the airplane. In this section we will discuss pitch stability, in which moments applied to the airplane cause the nose of the airplane to rotate up or down. Moments applied to an airplane can also cause the nose of the airplane to rotate side-to-side (yaw) or cause the airplane to roll.

The pitch stability of an airplane can be assessed by determining how the pitching moment about the center of gravity changes with changing angle of attack. Consider the plot of moment coefficient about the center of gravity, $C_{M,CG}$, versus angle of attack, α, shown in Figure 10-30. A negative moment coefficient indicates a moment that will push the nose of the airplane down. A zero moment coefficient signifies the trim condition.

Let's say there are two airplanes flying at their trim angle of attack, α_{trim}. The solid line indicates the moment coefficient curve for the first airplane. If the angle of attack of the first airplane increases beyond its trim angle, that is, the nose of the airplane pitches upwards, the resulting moment coefficient is negative. The negative moment acts to pitch the nose of the airplane back downwards. If the nose of the airplane pitches down, decreasing the angle of attack, the resulting moment is positive, which acts to pitch the nose of the airplane back up. Therefore, any moments that are generated for the first airplane are restoring moments in that they work to return the airplane to its trim angle of attack. This situation is known as **pitch stability**.

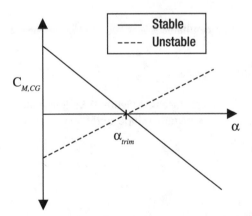

Figure 10-30. *Stability depends on the slope of the moment-angle of attack curve.*

On the other hand, let's say the dashed line signifies the moment coefficient curve for the second airplane. The slope of the moment coefficient curve is now positive. If the angle of attack of the second airplane increases beyond the trim value, a positive moment is generated. This moment acts to pitch the nose of the airplane even higher, increasing the angle of attack even more. This action generates an increased positive moment, which pitches the nose up, and so on, and so on. The airplane will continue to pitch upwards until it tumbles out of control. A moment coefficient curve with a positive slope therefore represents an unstable situation.

The condition for pitch stability can be expressed mathematically. For pitch stability, the derivative of pitching moment coefficient with respect to angle of attack for an airplane must be negative. This situation corresponds to the moment curve having a negative slope.

$$\frac{dC_{M,CG}}{d\alpha} < 0 \tag{10.40}$$

Stability and Trim

Ideally, an airplane should be stable, and it should be able to be trimmed. The condition for pitch stability is given by equation (10.40). Whether an airplane can be trimmed can also be determined by looking at the moment coefficient versus angle of attack curve. For trim to occur, there must be an angle of attack at which the moment coefficient about the center of gravity is zero. The moment coefficient when angle of attack is zero is designated as C_{MO}. Depending on the value of C_{MO} and the slope of the moment coefficient curve, there are four different stability trim outcomes, and they are summarized in Equation (10.41).

If $\dfrac{dC_{M,CG}}{d\alpha} < 0$ and $C_{M0} > 0$ airplane is stable and trimmable. $\hspace{1cm}$ (10.41a)

If $\dfrac{dC_{M,CG}}{d\alpha} > 0$ and $C_{M0} > 0$ airplane is unstable and untrimmable. $\hspace{1cm}$ (10.41b)

If $\dfrac{dC_{M,CG}}{d\alpha} < 0$ and $C_{M0} < 0$ airplane is stable but untrimmable. $\hspace{1cm}$ (10.41c)

If $\dfrac{dC_{M,CG}}{d\alpha} > 0$ and $C_{M0} < 0$ airplane is trimmable but unstable. $\hspace{1cm}$ (10.41d)

The four expressions from Equation (10.41) are shown graphically in Figure 10-31. Remember that for stability, the moment coefficient line has to have a negative slope, and for an airplane to trim, there must be an angle of attack where $C_{M.CG} = 0$.

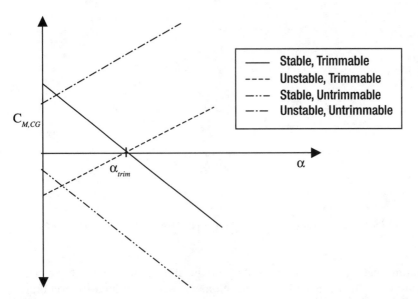

Figure 10-31. *The four stability trim possibilities*

Dynamic Stability

The preceding discussion on stability has actually been on the **static stability** of the airplane. The term "static" means that there is no time component to the analysis. Static stability deals only with the initial tendency of the airplane to return to an equilibrium orientation or not. Another important aspect of airplane stability is the **dynamic stability**, which is concerned with the time history of the airplane motion when it deviates from its equilibrium orientation.

An airplane is defined to be dynamically stable if it naturally returns to its equilibrium orientation over time. For example, assume that Figure 10-32 shows the moment about the center of gravity of an airplane as a function of time. Initially, there is a positive moment about the c.g. The moment oscillates both positively and negatively, but the magnitude of the moment decreases over time so the plane is dynamically stable.

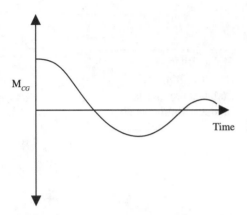

Figure 10-32. *A plane is dynamically stable if deviations from the equilibrium orientation die out over time.*

The moment time history shown in Figure 10-33, on the other hand, represents a dynamically unstable airplane in that the magnitude of the moment oscillations increase over time.

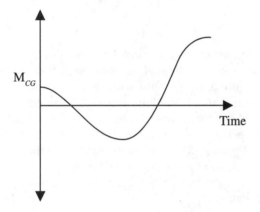

Figure 10-33. *A plane is dynamically unstable if oscillations get larger and larger.*

Summary

In this chapter, we took our knowledge of Newtonian mechanics, kinematics, and projectiles into the wild blue yonder and learned about the physics of flight. We studied the four basic forces that act on an airplane—lift, drag, thrust, and gravity—and learned how to evaluate these forces. Some of the other things we saw include the following:

- What an airfoil is and how its shape generates the lift that keeps an airplane in the air

- What aerodynamic stall is and how it can be corrected

- The moments that are generated due to lift and how they affect the stability and trim of an airplane

- The three types of drag experienced by an airplane, skin friction, form, and induced drag, and how induced drag is related to the lift generated by a wing

- How to compute the thrust of propeller and jet engines and how to account for altitude effects on thrust

- The physics of takeoffs and landings

- How a plane turns and the effect turns have on lift and stall

Answer to Exercise

1. When the plane is rolling down the runway, the angle of attack is zero (assuming that the incidence of the wing is zero). Looking at Figure 10-11, the lift coefficient for the NACA 2412 airfoil at zero degrees angle of attack is about 0.25. Adding 0.25 for the flap deflection and 0.25 for ground effects gives an effective lift coefficient of 0.75. The takeoff velocity can be determined from Equation (10.36).

$$v = \sqrt{\frac{2W}{C_L \rho A}} = \sqrt{\frac{2*10245}{0.75*1.22*16.2}} = 37.2 \ m/s$$

References

1. University of Tennessee Aerodynamic Database, www.engr.utk.edu/~rbond/airfoil.html

2. J. Lowery, "Propeller Aircraft Performance and the Bootstrap Approach," www.allstar.fiu.edu/aero/BA-Background.htm

3. U.S. Standard Atmosphere 1976, http://nssdc.gsfc.nasa.gov/space/model/atmos/us_standard.html

4. http://skyhawk.cessna.com

5. www.geae.com/engines/military/f110/index.html

CHAPTER 11

■ ■ ■

Rockets and Missiles

In previous chapters in this book, we explored how to model the motion of cars, boats, and airplanes. Now it's time to leave the confines of the lower atmosphere and learn about the physics of rockets. Rockets have been around for 800 years or so. At first they were used mostly for military purposes, but starting in the twentieth century, people have used rockets to explore the solar system or to put satellites into orbit.

In analyzing the physics of rockets, we will once again turn to the "four forces"—thrust, drag, lift, and gravity. You will learn about the different types of rockets and rocket engines and how they generate thrust. Because rockets can travel into the upper atmosphere and beyond, we will explore how altitude affects gravity, thrust, and drag. We will use what we discuss about rockets to create a rocket simulator that will model the flight of a rocket as it rises into the atmosphere. Some of the other topics this chapter will cover include the following:

- A brief history of rockets

- A general force diagram of a rocket in flight

- The rocket equation and how it can be used to compute the velocity of a rocket

- An introduction to planetary orbits

- How multistage rockets can be used to improve rocket performance

- An introduction to modeling rocket-powered missiles

Let's start the rocket rolling with a brief history of rocketry.

A Brief History of Rockets

Some people think of rockets as being part of the Space Age, but they have actually been around for a long time. The Chinese are generally credited with discovering the rocket. The Chinese used rockets they called "arrows of fire" against the attacking Mongols in 1232. The English monk Roger Bacon developed an improved form of gunpowder in the mid-thirteenth century that increased the range of rockets and improved their military potential.

For the next 700 years, rockets were used primarily for warfare with varying degrees of success. The term "rocket" itself was first used in a book written in 1577 by a German armorer named Leonhart Fronsperger. Rockets were used in the Napoleonic Wars, the American Revolutionary War, and in the American Civil War. There were some nonmilitary applications of rockets in the early days. In the early 1800s, an Italian named Claude Ruggieri entertained people by rocketing small animals into the air and recovering the animal-carrying payloads by parachute.

Up until the early twentieth century, rockets were typically powered by gunpowder. In 1903, a Russian schoolteacher named Konstantin Tsiolkovskii published a manuscript titled "Exploration of Cosmic Space by Rocket Devices" in which he suggested the possibility of using liquid propellants for rocket propulsion. Tsiolkovskii's manuscript also introduced the idea of using rockets for space travel. Robert Goddard, an American, flew the first liquid-fueled rocket in 1926. The rocket, shown in Figure 11-1, was powered by gasoline and liquid oxygen and reached an altitude of 41 feet.

Figure 11-1. *Robert Goddard with his liquid-fueled rocket (Photo courtesy of Clark University Archives)*

After Goddard's pioneering work, the development of liquid-fueled rockets proceeded at a rapid pace. German scientists designed and built sophisticated V2 rockets and used them against England in World War II. After the war, the Russian and American governments "borrowed" the Germans' expertise (by moving the German scientists to their countries) and began developing large rockets to move satellites and men into Earth's orbit. Yuri Gagarin, a Soviet, became the first man in space in 1961. The Americans Neil Armstrong and Edwin Aldrin flew a rocket to Earth's moon in 1969.

Today rockets are routinely used to transport satellites, experiments, and people into space. They still have widespread military uses as well, as every branch of the military includes missiles as part of their weaponry. In addition to liquid and solid propulsion, some modern rockets make use of nuclear propulsion and other exotic types of propulsion.

Before we dive into the physics of how rockets work, let's spend a little time and learn some terminology that will be used in the rest of the chapter.

Some Rocket Terminology

A schematic of a **liquid-propellant rocket** is shown in Figure 11-2. The rocket engine requires two liquids. The first is an oxidizer that is stored in an **oxidizer tank**. Typically, liquid oxygen is used for the oxidizer. The **fuel tank** holds a liquid that contains hydrogen. Liquid hydrogen and a highly refined form of kerosene known as RP-1 are two commonly used rocket fuels. The fuel and oxidizer are sent to a **combustion chamber** where they are mixed and burned, creating a high-pressure gas mixture. The combustion gas travels through a **nozzle** where it accelerates. The velocity of the gas when it leaves the nozzle is called the **exhaust velocity**. The acceleration of the combustion gases through the nozzle generates thrust that propels the rocket forward.

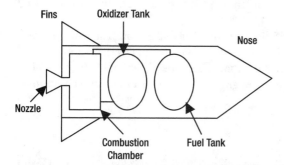

Figure 11-2. *A cross section of a liquid-propellant rocket*

The propellant tanks, combustion chamber, and other internal structures of the rocket are stored inside the rocket body, which generally is a cylindrical metal tube. The front part of the body is called the **nose**. Rockets have fins that stabilize the rocket in flight. Most rockets carry a **payload** that is stored inside the rocket body as well.

Another general type of rocket is a **solid-propellant rocket**. The propellant for a solid-propellant rocket is called the **grain** and contains both the fuel and the oxidizer needed for ignition. Solid-propellant rockets are mechanically simpler, but less powerful than liquid-propellant rockets. You'll learn more about both liquid- and solid-propellant rockets a bit later in the chapter.

Rocket Engine Types

Many different types of rocket engines have been developed over the years. Some of the engine types use liquid propellants and some use solids. Most engines burn the propellants in a combustion chamber, but some use other methods to eject mass out of the rocket nozzle. Let's take a brief look at some of the engine types in use today and some that may someday be developed.

Liquid-Cryogenic Engines

Cryogenic means "low temperature," and cryogenic rocket engines use propellants that exist in liquid form only at very low temperatures. The most commonly used oxidizer in cryogenic rocket engines is liquid oxygen, commonly abbreviated as LOX. Liquid oxygen is only a liquid at temperatures below 90 K (-297°F). Commonly used fuels in liquid-cryogenic rocket engines include liquid hydrogen and kerosene, although kerosene does not have to be kept at very low temperatures. Cryogenic propellants provide better performance than solid propellants, but the internal structure of a liquid-cryogenic rocket must be designed to deal with the very low temperature requirements. One advantage of liquid-cryogenic rocket engines and liquid rocket engines in general is that they can be throttled up or down to provide variable thrust.

Solid-Propellant Engines

Modern solid rocket engines are descendants of the very first rockets that used gunpowder as the propellant. Solid rocket engines are simpler than liquid engines in that there are no fuel pumps or propellant feed systems to worry about. The oxidizer and fuel are mixed together and generally held in a casing made out of steel.

Solid rocket propellants can be quite exotic in their chemical makeup and can look nothing like the gunpowder used of old. The Space Shuttle solid rocket boosters use a mixture of ammonium perchlorate and powdered aluminum that has a consistency similar to a pencil eraser. Unlike liquid rocket engines, solid rocket engines are generally not throttleable and can't be shut down once they are ignited.

Liquid-Hypergolic Engines

Liquid-hypergolic engines use volatile propellants that ignite when they come in contact with each other. There is no need to provide an ignition source. Because of their easy start and restart capability, liquid-hypergolic engines are typically used to make small changes to the attitude or position of a rocket or spacecraft once it is in outer space. Despite their volatile nature, hypergolic propellants have a storage advantage over cryogenics in that they do not need to be kept at ultra-low temperatures.

Hybrid Engines

A hybrid rocket engine is one that uses both liquid and solid fuels. Burt Rutan's privately built SpaceShipOne rocket uses liquid nitrous oxide and a special type of rubber as the propellants for the rocket engine.

Nuclear Engines

Nuclear rocket engines use a fission reaction to heat a reactor core to a very high temperature. The propellant gas hydrogen is commonly used; it flows through the core and becomes super-heated. The propellant gas exits the rocket nozzle at very high velocity. Nuclear engines can achieve greater thrust for a given rate of propellant flow than liquid or solid rocket engines.

Exotic Engines

The great thing about being a game developer is that you can let your imagination run wild a bit when you are creating a rocket simulation. Most of us are familiar with *Star Trek* and the Warp Drive engines used to power the starships. You might also conceive of a rocket engine driven by antimatter or by other exotic means. The key to using an exotic rocket engine in a game simulation is coming up with an estimate of the thrust produced by the engine.

General Force Diagram

The forces that act upon a rocket during ascent are shown in Figure 11-3. By this time in the book, it probably comes as no shock to you that a rocket is acted upon by the forces of thrust, drag, lift, and gravity. The thrust force is generated by the rocket engines. Drag, as always, acts in the opposite direction of the velocity vector of the rocket. If the longitudinal axis of the rocket is at an angle of attack relative to the flight path, a lift force will be generated. Gravity acts in the vertical direction.

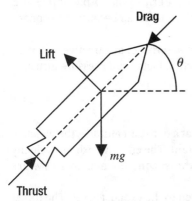

Figure 11-3. *A rocket during ascent experiences thrust, drag, lift, and gravity forces.*

The angle θ is called the pitch angle of the rocket. Most rockets lift off vertically, so the pitch angle at liftoff will be 90°. The rocket force diagram shown in Figure 11-3 is very similar to the airplane force diagram, Figure 10-20, that was presented towards the end of Chapter 10. The net vertical force, F_v, and horizontal force, F_h, are functions of the thrust force, F_T, drag force, F_D, lift force, F_L, and the pitch angle, θ.

$$F_h = \left(F_T - F_D\right)\cos\theta - F_L \sin\theta \tag{11.1}$$

$$F_v = \left(F_T - F_D\right)\sin\theta + F_L \cos\theta - mg \tag{11.2}$$

In this book, we are using the convention that the vertical axis is in the z-direction. The horizontal force component could be divided into x- and y-direction components depending on the heading angle of the rocket.

Now that we have seen what the basic forces that act upon a rocket are, let's look at the four forces in a bit more detail starting with the engine thrust.

Thrust

When the fuel and oxidizer are burned in the combustion chamber, the resulting high-temperature, high-pressure gases are used to generate thrust. The thrust generated by a rocket engine comes from two sources—the change in momentum imparted to the exhaust gases and from the pressure difference at the exit plane of the nozzle.

$$F_T = \lambda v_{ex} \frac{dm}{dt} + \left(p_e - p_a\right) A_e \tag{11.3}$$

The first term in Equation (11.3) is called the **momentum thrust** and is caused by the rocket engine ejecting exhaust gases from the rocket nozzle. The momentum thrust is equal to the **exhaust velocity** of the combustion gases, v_{ex}, multiplied by the mass flow rate. The λ term in the momentum thrust expression is a correction factor that accounts for losses due to the shape of the nozzle. It generally has a value less than but close to 1.

The second term in Equation (11.3) is called the **pressure thrust** and is due to the pressure difference at the exit plane of the nozzle. The quantities p_e and p_a are the exit and ambient air pressures respectively, and A_e is the area of the exit plane of the nozzle. The pressure thrust can be positive, negative, or zero depending on the relative values of the exit and atmospheric pressure. The value of pressure thrust will also change as the rocket climbs into the air because atmospheric pressure decreases with increasing altitude.

The thrust generated by a rocket engine is often written in terms of an **effective exhaust velocity**, v_e, which incorporates the effects due to the correction factor and pressure thrust.

$$F_T = v_e \frac{dm}{dt} \tag{11.4}$$

For most rockets running at a constant throttle setting at a constant altitude, the effective exhaust velocity and mass flow rate are assumed to be constant. The effective exhaust velocity will increase with increasing altitude because the pressure thrust component increases with increasing altitude.

The thrust shown in Equation (11.4) is the force imparted to the exhaust gases. The thrust force applied to the rocket is equal and opposite to the force applied to the exhaust gases.

$$F_T = -v_e \frac{dm}{dt} \tag{11.5}$$

The Rocket Equation

The force applied to the rocket from the engines causes the rocket to accelerate according to Newton's second law. The thrust force on the rocket, F_T, is equal to the mass of the rocket, m, times the acceleration of the rocket, and is also equal to the effective exhaust velocity times the change in mass with respect to time.

$$F_T = m \frac{dv}{dt} = -v_e \frac{dm}{dt} \tag{11.6}$$

Multiplying the two sides of Equation (11.6) by the time increment, dt, and dividing by mass results in a differential equation that is a function of mass and velocity only.

$$dv = -v_e \frac{dm}{m} \tag{11.7}$$

The two sides of Equation (11.7) can be integrated, yielding an expression for the velocity at any point in time as a function of the mass at that point in time.

$$v(t) = v_0 + v_e \ln\left(\frac{m_0}{m(t)}\right) \tag{11.8}$$

Equation (11.8) is called the **rocket equation** and was first presented by Tsiolkovskii in 1903. It states that in the absence of any external forces, the velocity of a rocket at any point in time is a function of the original mass and velocity of the rocket, m_0 and v_0, the effective exhaust velocity of the combustion gases, v_e, and the current mass of the rocket, $m(t)$. Since propellant is being burned and expelled during the flight of the rocket, the mass at time t will be less than the original mass.

The rocket equation as shown in Equation (11.8) is not applicable to all rocket problems because it does not include the effects of drag or gravity. If a rocket was flying through the atmosphere, Equation (11.8) would overpredict the velocity. The rocket equation as shown in Equation (11.8) would be able to predict the velocity of a rocket that was traveling in outer space.

Specific Impulse

Rocket engines are often characterized by a quantity known as the **specific impulse**, I_{sp}, defined as the thrust produced by the engine divided by the mass flow rate and the gravitational acceleration.

$$I_{sp} = \frac{F_T}{g\,\frac{dm}{dt}} \tag{11.9}$$

Specific impulse has units of seconds and can also be expressed in terms of the effective exhaust velocity.

$$I_{sp} = \frac{v_e}{g} \tag{11.10}$$

In looking at Equation (11.9), we can see that a rocket engine with a higher specific impulse will deliver more thrust for a given mass flow rate than will an engine with a lower specific impulse. Table 11-1 shows typical specific impulse values for some general types of rocket engines.[1, 2]

Table 11-1. *Specific Impulse for Some Rocket Engine Types*

Rocket Engine Type	Specific Impulse (*s*)
Liquid oxygen—liquid hydrogen	425–460
Liquid oxygen—kerosene	260–330
Hypergolic	260–290
Nuclear	825–925
Antimatter	10^7

The specific impulse for the antimatter is a rough estimate, of course. Specific impulse is sometimes defined as being equal to the effective exhaust velocity of the engine.

$$I_{sp} = v_e \tag{11.11}$$

This definition is equal to the previous one without the gravitational acceleration scaling. The units for the specific impulse as defined in Equation (11.11) are typically expressed in terms of *(N-s)/kg*, which is equivalent to *m/s*. You can use either definition for I_{sp} in your game programming; just make sure that the units of the I_{sp} value that you are using match the definition of I_{sp}.

Altitude Effects

Looking at Equation (11.3), one of the contributions to engine thrust is the pressure thrust caused by the difference between the nozzle exit pressure and the surrounding atmospheric pressure. As altitude increases, the atmospheric pressure decreases, so the thrust generated by the engine will increase. For example, the F-1 rocket engine used with the Saturn 5 rocket generates a specific impulse of 260 *s* at sea level and 304 *s* in a vacuum. The corresponding sea-level thrust for the F-1 engine is $6.67e + 6$ *N*, and the vacuum thrust is $7.86e + 6$ *N*.

One way to model altitude effects on thrust is to simply vary the thrust from the sea-level to vacuum values using the pressure ratio as the scale factor.

$$F_T = F_{T,vacuum} - \left(F_{T,vacuum} - F_{T,SL}\right)\frac{p}{p_0} \qquad (11.12)$$

In Equation (11.12), the quantity p is the atmospheric pressure at the current altitude and p_0 is the pressure at sea level. The quantity $F_{T,SL}$ is the sea-level thrust and $F_{T,vacuum}$ is the vacuum thrust.

It turns out that pressure decreases quite rapidly with altitude, so that the pressure ratio gets small when the rocket is still at a relatively low altitude. Table 11-2 lists the pressure and pressure ratio over a range of altitudes. Also shown in Table 11-2 is the thrust produced by an F-1 engine according to Equation (11.12). At 10 *km*, the pressure ratio is down to 0.262 and the engine thrust is 96% of the vacuum thrust value of $7.86e + 6$ *N*. At 30 *km*, the pressure ratio has dropped to about 0.011.

Table 11-2. *Pressure and Pressure Ratio As a Function of Altitude*

Altitude (*km*)	Pressure (*N/m²*)	Pressure Ratio	F-1 Engine Thrust (*N*)
0	101,325	1.0	$6.672e + 6$
5	54,054	0.533	$7.276e + 6$
10	26,506	0.262	$7.549e + 6$
20	5531	0.055	$7.795e + 6$
30	1198	0.011	$7.847e + 6$
40	287	0.003	$7.856e + 6$

For game programming purposes, one way to incorporate altitude effects on thrust would be to compute the thrust according to Equation (11.12) up to an altitude of 40–50 *km* and just use the vacuum thrust value at higher altitudes.

Computing Atmospheric Pressure, Density, and Temperature

The atmospheric pressure as a function of altitude is necessary to properly evaluate the thrust of a rocket engine. When we study drag a little later in this chapter, we will find that we need the density as a function of altitude as well. The pressure, temperature, and density relations that were presented in Chapter 10 are valid only up to an altitude of 11 *km*. A more extensive atmosphere model is required for modeling rockets, which can travel significantly higher than 11 *km*.

The U.S. Committee on Extension to the Standard Atmosphere (COESA) is a government organization that developed an earth atmosphere model known as the U.S. Standard Atmosphere 1976 model, which is an industry standard for computing the pressure, density, temperature, and other atmosphere quantities as a function of altitude.

We won't go into details about the equations that make up the U.S. Standard Atmosphere 1976 model. They are fairly complicated, involving things like geopotential altitudes. As a brief overview, Earth's atmosphere is divided into a series of altitude ranges. Temperature is modeled using a series of straight lines between control points. Pressure and density are modeled using exponential or power equations. If you want, you can find out more about the nitty-gritty details of the U.S. Standard Atmosphere 1976 model at http://nssdc.gsfc.nasa.gov/space/model/atmos/us_standard.html.

For use in the rocket simulator we will develop a bit later in this chapter, a class named USatm76 was written that encapsulates the U.S. Standard Atmosphere 1976 model. Actually, the USatm76 class represents a simplified version of the model in that only the pressure, density, and temperature quantities are computed. The code listing for the USatm76 class is shown next. To make use of the atmosphere model, a program would create a USatm76 object and call the updateConditions method on that object.

```
public class USatm76
{
  private static final double R = 287.1;      //  Gas constant for air
  private static final double G = 9.80665;    //  Gravity acceleration
  private static final double RE = 6356766.0; // Earth radius in meters

  private double pressure;
  private double density;
  private double temperature;

  public USatm76(double altitude) {
    //  Set the field values according to an
    //  initial altitude.
    updateConditions(altitude);
  }

  //  Declare methods to return field values.
  public double getPressure() {
    return pressure;
  }
```

```java
public double getDensity() {
  return density;
}

public double getTemperature() {
  return temperature;
}

// This method computes atmospheric density,
// pressure, and temperature based on the U.S.
// Standard Atmosphere 1976 model.
public void updateConditions(double altitude) {
  double slope;   // Slope of the temperature line
  double T0;      // Reference temperature value
  double p0;      // Reference pressure value
  double h0;      // Reference altitude
  double geoAltitude; // Geopotential altitude
  double grp;     // Temporary variable
  double grp2;    // Temporary variable

  // The 1976 U.S. Standard Atmosphere model equations
  // are functions of geopotential altitude, so we
  // need to compute it. Geopotential altitude is an
  // equivalent altitude assuming gravity is constant
  // with altitude.
  geoAltitude = altitude*RE/(altitude + RE);

  // Assign values to the reference temperature,
  // pressure, and altitude based on the current
  // altitude.
  if (geoAltitude <= 11000.0) {
    slope = -0.0065;
    T0 = 288.15;
    p0 = 101325.0;
    h0 = 0.0;
  }
  else if (geoAltitude < 20000.0) {
    slope = 0.0;
    T0 = 216.65;
    p0 = 22631.9;
    h0 = 11000.0;
  }
```

```
    else if (geoAltitude < 32000.0) {
      slope = 0.001;
      T0 = 216.65;
      p0 = 5474.8;
      h0 = 20000.0;
    }
    else if (geoAltitude < 47000.0) {
      slope = 0.0028;
      T0 = 228.65;
      p0 = 868.0;
      h0 = 32000.0;
    }
    else if (geoAltitude < 51000.0) {
      slope = 0.0;
      T0 = 270.65;
      p0 = 110.9;
      h0 = 47000.0;
    }
    else if (geoAltitude < 71000.0) {
      slope = -0.0028;
      T0 = 270.65;
      p0 = 66.9;
      h0 = 51000.0;
    }
    else if (geoAltitude < 84000.0) {
      slope = -0.002;
      T0 = 214.65;
      p0 = 3.96;
      h0 = 71000.0;
    }
    else {
      slope = 0.0;
      T0 = 186.9;
      p0 = 0.373;
      h0 = 84000.0;
    }

    //  Compute temperature and pressure. The equations
    //  used depend on whether the temperature is constant
    //  in the current altitude range.
    if ( slope == 0.0 ) {
      temperature = T0;
      grp = -G*(geoAltitude - h0)/(R*temperature);
      pressure = p0*Math.exp(grp);
    }
```

```
    else {
      temperature = T0 + slope*(geoAltitude - h0);
      grp = T0/temperature;
      grp2 = G/(slope*R);
      pressure = p0*Math.pow(grp,grp2);
    }

    density = pressure/(R*temperature);

    return;
  }
}
```

The USatm76 class computes the pressure, density, and temperature for a given altitude by curve fit relations between seven known data points. An exponential equation is used to compute the pressure. Temperature is calculated by drawing straight lines between the known data point temperature values. The code contained in the USatm76 class can be useful for other game programming situations as well. You could, for example, make use of the USatm76 class in a high-altitude airplane flight simulator.

Gravity

For the other physical models we have created in earlier chapters of this book, gravitational acceleration has been a nice, dependable constant. It could be assumed to be constant because the altitude changes of the projectiles, balls, cars, boats, and planes were small relative to the radius of the earth. This situation is not necessarily the case when dealing with rockets, as they can travel hundreds, thousands, or even millions of kilometers away from the earth.

The gravitational acceleration due to the earth is proportional to the square of the distance from the center of the earth. The acceleration at a given altitude above the surface of the earth is equal to the acceleration at the surface multiplied by the ratio of the square of the distances.

$$g = 9.81 \frac{r_e^2}{(r_e + h)^2} \tag{11.13}$$

The quantity h is the altitude above the surface of the earth. The radius of the earth, r_e, is equal to 6356.8 km. Figure 11-4 shows the change in gravitational acceleration with increasing altitude from the surface of the earth. For the range of altitudes shown in Figure 11-4, the gravitational acceleration curve as a function of altitude is nearly a straight line. At an altitude of 100 km, the acceleration is 9.51 m/s^2. At an altitude of 400 km, the gravitational acceleration has decreased to 8.68 m/s^2.

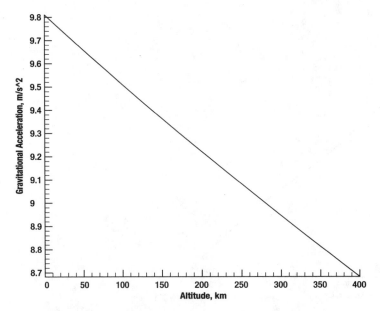

Figure 11-4. *Gravitational acceleration as a function of altitude*

Drag

By this point in the book, you should be very familiar with the concept of aerodynamic drag and with the equation that is used to evaluate drag. Just to refresh your memory, the drag experienced by a rocket as it travels through the atmosphere is proportional to the atmospheric density, the square of the velocity, the frontal area of the rocket, and the coefficient of drag for the rocket.

$$F_D = \frac{1}{2}C_D\rho v^2 A \qquad (11.14)$$

Unlike most of the vehicles, balls, and projectiles we have been exploring in this book, altitude effects must be included when evaluating the drag of a rocket. If a rocket ascends into the upper atmosphere or into outer space, the density value will change by several orders of magnitude during the ascent. The density at any altitude can be computed using the USatm76 class that was discussed earlier in this chapter. Figure 11-5 shows the variation of density with altitude up to an altitude of 84 *km*.

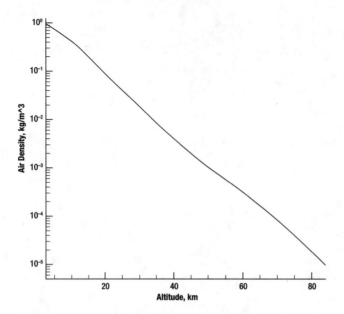

Figure 11-5. *Variation of atmospheric density with altitude*

It's apparent from Figure 11-5 that density changes quite significantly with increasing altitude. The density at 80 *km* is almost 100,000 times less than the density at sea level.

Another quantity needed to compute aerodynamic drag is the drag coefficient for the rocket. The drag coefficient will be a function of Reynolds number, and there will be a spike in drag coefficient if and when the rocket exceeds the speed of sound. Typically, values of rocket drag coefficients range from 0.2 to 1.0. If you don't want to go through the trouble of modeling drag coefficient more precisely for your game simulation, you can assume a constant drag coefficient somewhere in the typical range.

It turns out that drag isn't such a big deal with large rockets, because the thrust generated by the rocket engines tends to be much greater than the drag force. Furthermore, because the density decreases by orders of magnitude as the altitude increases, the peak drag force level occurs at relatively low altitudes and declines significantly after that point. Figure 11-6 presents the computed velocity profiles with and without drag effects for the Saturn 1B rocket during a vertical ascent. A constant drag coefficient of 0.5 was used in the calculations.

The inclusion of drag effects has a small but noticeable effect on the velocity profile of the Saturn 1B rocket. If drag is included in the calculation, the velocity of the rocket at 150 seconds is equal to 1500 *m/s*. If drag is not included, the velocity of the rocket at 150 seconds is equal to 1560 *m/s* for a difference of about 4%.

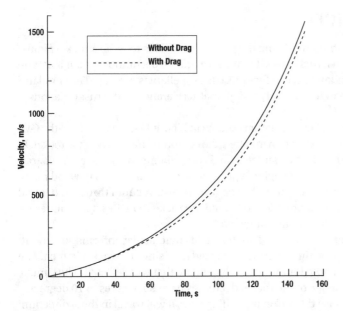

Figure 11-6. *Saturn 1B velocity profiles with and without drag*

Lift

When a rocket is in flight, its longitudinal axis may be at a nonzero angle to the flight path of the rocket. If this is the case, the rocket will experience a lift force. Usually, the lift force on a rocket is quite small, but it does have ramifications for the stability of the rocket in flight.

Stability

Many large rockets, such as the Saturn 5 rocket that took men to the moon, are statically unstable during ascent. Small deviations in the pitch and yaw angles of the rocket would promote larger deviations that would eventually cause the rocket to tumble out of control. Stability of large rockets in flight is maintained by continually adjusting the angle (called **gimbaling**) of the rocket nozzles. If you wanted to build a really sophisticated rocket simulation, you would need to include a stability and control model in your rocket simulation; however, the development of such a model is beyond the scope of this book. Less sophisticated rocket simulations can simply assume that the rocket maintains stability during its flight.

Wind

For obvious reasons, rockets are always launched outdoors and as such may be subject to the forces caused by any wind that may be present during launch. The effect of wind is to change the magnitude and direction of the air velocity vector relative to the rocket. If you want to include wind in your rocket simulation, you could incorporate wind into the drag calculations similar to what was used when we discussed projectile wind effects in Chapter 5.

A Rocket Simulator

Let's use what we have learned about modeling the physics of rockets to write a rocket simulator. The user gets to build her own rocket by selecting an engine type, number of engines, and payload mass. When the rocket is launched, it flies until its propellant is used up. The simulator will include the effects of aerodynamic drag and gravitational acceleration and thrust variations due to altitude.

A typical screen shot for the Rocket Simulator is shown in Figure 11-7. At the top of the GUI is a display area that shows a rocket cartoon moving along the computed trajectory of the rocket. In the bottom left-hand corner are combo box and text field components that display the characteristics of the rocket. The user selects the engine type, number of engines, and payload mass. Based on these inputs, the simulator computes the sea-level thrust, vacuum thrust, and initial mass of the rocket. A Launch button is provided to launch the rocket. The Reset button resets the display and brings the rocket back to the launch pad.

In the bottom right-hand corner of the GUI are text fields that display information about the rocket trajectory. The rocket burn time shows the elapsed time since the rocket launch. The simulation runs up until the burn time for the particular engine that was selected. The simulation is set up such that the pitch angle of the rocket decreases from 90 degrees to 10 degrees over the course of the flight. Because the rocket is pitching over, it will travel in the x-direction. The distance traveled in the x-direction is shown in the Cross range text field. The Rocket mass text field shows the current mass of the rocket. As propellant is expended, the mass of the rocket will decrease.

The Rocket Simulator allows the user to choose between two different engines. The F-1 rocket engine is a LOX-RP1 (kerosene) motor that was used on the Saturn V rocket that took men to the moon. The second engine choice is the RD-180, which is a more recent LOX-RP1 rocket engine that is used to power the Atlas 5 rocket. Specifications for the two rocket engines are shown in Table 11-3.[3, 4, 5, 6]

Table 11-3. *Rocket Specifications for the F-1 and RD-180 Rocket Engines*

Quantity	F-1 Engine	RD-180 Engine
Sea level thrust (N)	$6.67e + 6$	$3.83e + 6$
Vacuum thrust (N)	$7.86e + 6$	$4.15e + 6$
Sea level I_{sp} (s)	260	311.3
Vacuum I_{sp}, (s)	306	337.8
Engine burn time, (s)	150	227
Engine dry mass, (kg)	8371	5480
Propellant burn rate, (kg/s)	2616	1254

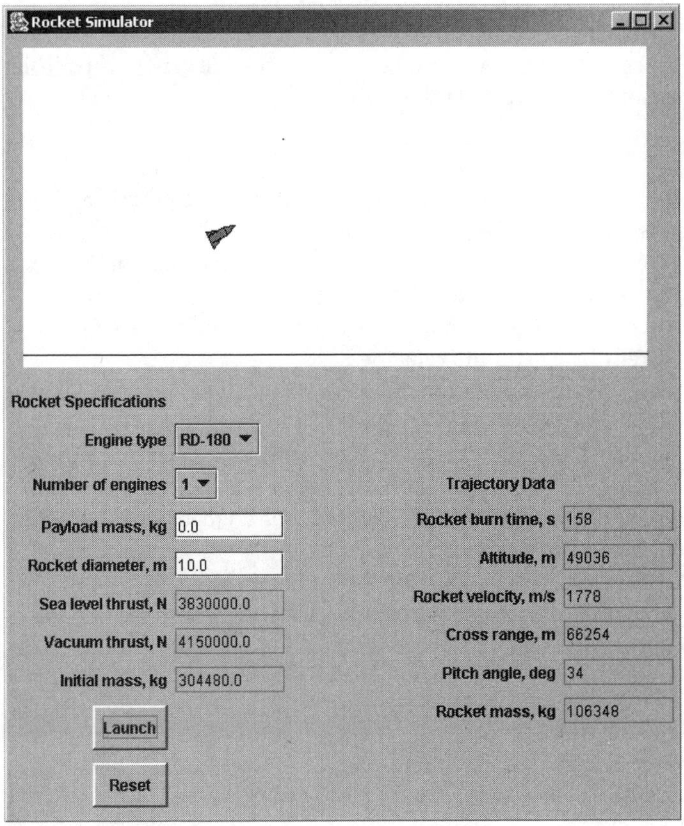

Figure 11-7. *A typical Rocket Simulator screen shot*

As with the Flight Simulator in Chapter 10, several simplifications and assumptions are made in the design of the Rocket Simulator:

- The effect of pitch angle is included in the model, but the rocket is constrained to move in the x-z plane. There is no y-directional component to the forces or accelerations.

- The rocket thrust varies from sea level to vacuum thrust values according to Equation (11.12).

- Altitude effects are modeled using the U.S. Standard Atmosphere 1976 model.

- The rocket pitches over at a constant rate. The pitch angle begins at 90 degrees, meaning that the rocket launches vertically, and decreases until it is 10 degrees at the end of the rocket burn time. In real life, the change in pitch angle for a rocket would probably vary over the course of the flight.

- The drag coefficient of the rocket is assumed to be a constant 0.5. Drag has a relatively small effect on the trajectory of the rocket, so assuming a constant value is probably reasonable.

- There is no wind in the simulation.

- The lift force acting on the rocket is assumed to be zero. Lift force will generally be insignificant for rockets during the ascent part of their flight.

- The effect of centripetal acceleration is ignored.

Two classes are required to create the Rocket Simulator—one to model the rocket and another to create the GUI. A class named SimpleRocket will be used to model a single-stage rocket. You might think that we could write the SimpleRocket class as a subclass of the SimpleProjectile or DragProjectile classes developed in Chapter 5, but there is a problem with that approach. The projectile classes are set up to solve six ODEs, three to solve for the locations of the projectile and three to solve for the velocities.

When modeling rockets, however, the mass of the rocket will be changing as well. To account for the case that mass flow rate might not be constant (if the rocket engine could be throttled, for instance), two additional ODEs will be solved to determine the mass flow rate and mass of the rocket as a function of time. The pitch angle of the rocket will change over the course of its trajectory. Two more ODEs will be added to compute the change of pitch angle, bringing the total number of ODEs to be solved to 10.

Because the SimpleRocket class can't be easily written as a subclass of SimpleProjectile, it will be written as a subclass of the ODE class. The SimpleRocket class declares a number of fields to store the values of quantities that characterize the rocket. A USatm76 object is declared that will compute the atmospheric pressure, temperature, and density needed to compute the thrust of the rocket.

```
public class SimpleRocket extends ODE
{
  //  Fields that define the rocket
  private int numberOfEngines;
  private double seaLevelThrustPerEngine;
  private double vacuumThrustPerEngine;
  private double rocketDiameter;
  private double cd;
  private double initialMass;
  private double burnTime;
  private USatm76 air;
```

The SimpleRocket constructor calls the ODE constructor, and then loads initial values for the location, velocity, mass, and pitch angle into the arrays needed by the ODE solver. The fields declared in the SimpleRocket class are assigned initial values based on the arguments passed to the constructor.

```
public SimpleRocket(double x0, double y0, double z0, double vx0,
                    double vy0, double vz0, double time,
                    double initialMass, double massFlowRate,
            int numberOfEngines, double seaLevelThrustPerEngine,
            double vacuumThrustPerEngine, double rocketDiameter,
            double cd, double theta, double omega, double burnTime) {
```

```
// Call the ODE class constructor.
super(10);

// Load the initial values into the s field
// and q array from the ODE class.
setS(time);
setQ(vx0,0);
setQ(x0, 1);
setQ(vy0,2);
setQ(y0, 3);
setQ(vz0,4);
setQ(z0, 5);
setQ(massFlowRate,6);
setQ(initialMass, 7);
setQ(omega, 8);  // d(theta)/dt in radians/s
setQ(theta, 9);  // pitch angle in radians

// Initialize the values of the fields declared
// in the SimpleRocket class.
this.numberOfEngines = numberOfEngines;
this.seaLevelThrustPerEngine = seaLevelThrustPerEngine;
this.vacuumThrustPerEngine = vacuumThrustPerEngine;
this.rocketDiameter = rocketDiameter;
this.cd = cd;
this.initialMass = initialMass;
this.burnTime = burnTime;

// Initialize the atmosphere model.
air = new USatm76(z0);
}
```

The usual assortment of get/set methods are declared to return or change the values of the location and velocity of the rocket and to return or change the values of the fields declared in the SimpleRocket class. Not all of the get/set methods are shown here.

```
// These methods return the value of the fields.
public double getVx() {
  return getQ(0);
}

public double getVy() {
  return getQ(2);
}

// Other get/set methods not shown ...
```

The SimpleRocket class declares a getRightHandSide method to compute the right-hand sides of the 10 ODEs that define the equations of motion for the rocket. The first part of the method proceeds as all of the other versions do, namely that intermediate values of the dependent variables are computed and some convenience variables are declared.

```
public double[] getRightHandSide(double s, double q[],
                                 double deltaQ[], double ds,
                                 double qScale) {
  double dQ[] = new double[10];
  double newQ[] = new double[10];

  //  Compute the intermediate values of the
  //  location and velocity components.
  for(int i=0; i<10; ++i) {
    newQ[i] = q[i] + qScale*deltaQ[i];
  }

  //  Assign convenenience variables to the intermediate
  //  values of the locations and velocities.
  double vx = newQ[0];
  double vy = newQ[2];
  double vz = newQ[4];
  double vtotal = Math.sqrt(vx*vx + vy*vy + vz*vz);
  double x = newQ[1];
  double y = newQ[3];
  double z = newQ[5];
  double massFlowRate = newQ[6];
  double mass = newQ[7];
  double omega = newQ[8];
  double theta = newQ[9];
```

The USatm76 object is used to compute the pressure and density at the current altitude.

```
  //  Update the values of pressure, density, and
  //  temperature based on the current altitude.
  air.updateConditions(z);
  double pressure = air.getPressure();
  double density = air.getDensity();
```

The thrust force for the rocket is determined according to Equation (11.12). The total thrust generated by the rocket is equal to the thrust generated by each engine multiplied by the number of engines.

```
  //  Compute the thrust per engine and total thrust.
  double pressureRatio = pressure/101325.0;
  double thrustPerEngine = vacuumThrustPerEngine -
    (vacuumThrustPerEngine - seaLevelThrustPerEngine)*pressureRatio;
  double thrust = numberOfEngines*thrustPerEngine;
```

The drag force is computed based on the frontal area of the rocket and Equation (11.14).

```
//  Compute the drag force based on the frontal area
//  of the rocket.
double area = 0.25*Math.PI*rocketDiameter*rocketDiameter;
double drag = 0.5*cd*density*vtotal*vtotal*area;
```

The gravitational acceleration will decrease as the rocket gets further and further away from the surface of the earth. The gravitational acceleration is calculated using Equation (11.13).

```
//  Compute the gravitational acceleration
//   as a function of altitude.
double re = 6356766.0;   // Radius of the earth in meters.
double g = 9.80665*re*re/Math.pow(re+z,2.0);
```

As was stated in the assumptions, the lift force is assumed to be zero.

```
//  For this simulation, lift will be assumed to be zero.
double lift = 0.0;
```

Once the thrust, drag, gravity, and lift forces have been determined, these forces are rotated into x- and z-components according to the sine and cosine of the pitch angle as shown in Equations (11.1) and (11.2).

```
//  Compute the force components in the x- and z-directions.
//  The rocket will be assumed to be traveling in the x-z plane.
double Fx = (thrust - drag)*Math.cos(theta) - lift*Math.sin(theta);
double Fz = (thrust - drag)*Math.sin(theta) + lift*Math.cos(theta) -
            mass*g;
```

The final thing the getRightHandSide method does is to load the appropriate terms into the right-hand sides of the ten ODEs. The mass flow rate and rate of change of pitch angle are assumed to be constant in this simulation.

```
//  Load the right-hand sides of the ODEs.
dQ[0] = ds*(Fx/mass);
dQ[1] = ds*vx;
dQ[2] = 0.0;           //  y-component of accleration = 0
dQ[3] = 0.0;
dQ[4] = ds*(Fz/mass);
dQ[5] = ds*vz;
dQ[6] = 0.0;           //  Mass flow rate is constant
dQ[7] = -ds*(massFlowRate*numberOfEngines);
dQ[8] = 0.0;           //  d(theta)/dt is constant
dQ[9] = ds*omega;

   return dQ;
 }
}
```

The GUI for the Rocket Simulator is defined in a class named RocketSimulator. The class is quite long and complicated, and only one aspect of it will be discussed here. The full RocketSimulator class code listing can be downloaded from the Apress website. When the Launch button is pressed, a `Timer` object begins to call the `actionPerformed` method every 0.1 seconds to update the location, velocity, mass, and pitch angle of the rocket. The first thing the method does is to get input data for the payload mass, rocket diameter, and number of engines from the GUI components.

```
// Get some initial quantities from the text fields.
double payloadMass = Double.parseDouble(payloadTextField.getText());
double rocketDiameter =
        Double.parseDouble(diameterTextField.getText());

// Determine number of engines and engine type.
String numEngineString = (String)numEngineComboBox.getSelectedItem();
int numEngines = Integer.parseInt(numEngineString);
```

There are two choices for engine type—F1 and RD-180. The values for thrust, mass flow rate, engine mass, and burn time are set according to which engine has been selected.

```
double seaLevelThrustPerEngine;
double vacuumThrustPerEngine;
double massFlowRate;
double engineMass;
double burnTime;
String engineSelection = (String)engineTypeComboBox.getSelectedItem();
if ( engineSelection.equals("F1") ) {
  seaLevelThrustPerEngine = 6.67e+6;
  vacuumThrustPerEngine = 7.86e+6;
  massFlowRate = 2616.0;
  engineMass = 8371.0;
  burnTime = 150.0;
}
else {
  // RD-180 data
  seaLevelThrustPerEngine = 3.83e+6;
  vacuumThrustPerEngine = 4.15e+6;
  engineMass = 5480.0;
  massFlowRate = 1254.0;
  burnTime = 227.0;
}
```

The propellant mass that will be used by each engine is determined by multiplying the mass flow rate and burn time. The structural mass of the rocket is estimated by a very simple relation based on the number of engines. The initial mass of the rocket is computed as the sum of the engine, propellant, structural, and payload masses. Keep in mind this is a highly simplified model of initial rocket mass.

```
//  Calculate propellant mass per engine.
double propellantMass = massFlowRate*burnTime;

//  Estimate rocket structural mass;
double structureMass = 20000.0 + numEngines*4000.0;

//  Compute initial mass of rocket.
double initialMass = numEngines*(engineMass + propellantMass) +
                     payloadMass + structureMass;
```

Initial values are set for the drag coefficient and the pitch angle. The rate of change of pitch angle is set such that at the end of the engine burn time the pitch angle of the rocket will be 10 degrees.

```
//  Set values for drag coefficient and pitch angle.
//  The pitch angle is in radians.
double cd = 0.5;
double theta = 0.5*Math.PI;

//  Set the change in pitch angle in rad/s so that at the end
//  of the burn time the rocket will be at a pitch angle of 10 deg.
double omega = -80*Math.PI/(180.0*burnTime);
```

When all of the input parameters have been determined, a SimpleRocket object is created. The start method is called on a Timer object to start the simulation.

```
//  Create a SimpleRocket object.
rocket = new SimpleRocket(0.0, 0.0, 0.0, 0.0, 0.0, 0.0, 0.0,
            initialMass, massFlowRate, numEngines,
            seaLevelThrustPerEngine, vacuumThrustPerEngine,
            rocketDiameter, cd, theta, omega, burnTime);

//  Launch the rocket using a Timer object.
gameTimer.start();
}
```

When you play around with the Rocket Simulator, you will notice that the rocket lifts off very slowly and then gains speed as it continues to ascend. Figure 11-8 displays typical velocity and altitude profiles of a rocket as a function of time. At liftoff the rocket propellant tanks are full, so the mass of the rocket is at its greatest. The acceleration of the rocket is at a minimum, and the velocity increases gradually. As the rocket continues its ascent, propellant is continually being burned, so the mass of the rocket is decreasing. As the altitude increases, the thrust generated by the engines increases because the atmospheric pressure is decreasing. The combination of increasing thrust and decreasing mass causes the acceleration of the rocket to increase. The slope of the velocity profile becomes steeper and steeper throughout the ascent.

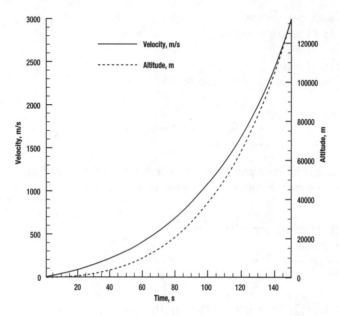

Figure 11-8. *Velocity profile for vertical ascent simulation*

The profiles shown in Figure 11-8 are for a rocket traveling vertically throughout its ascent. To achieve orbit, a rocket has to gradually pitch itself over so at the end of its ascent its velocity vector is horizontal or nearly horizontal relative to the earth. In the next section, we'll discuss a little bit about orbits and some other related topics.

Orbits

An object that is traveling in a curved path around a planet is said to be in **orbit** about the planet. An object, whether natural or man-made, that is in orbit around a planet is known as a **satellite**. One of the main functions of large-scale rockets is to put satellites into orbit around the earth. The subject of orbital mechanics can become fairly complicated, so this section will only provide a brief introduction.

In order to achieve orbit, a satellite must counteract the gravitational pull of the earth. In Chapter 3, you learned that the gravitational force, F_G, on an object due to the earth is proportional to the mass of the earth, m_e, the mass of the object, m_1, and the square of the distance, r, between the center of the two bodies.

$$F_G = 6.67e-11\frac{m_e m_1}{r^2} = 3.985e+14\frac{m_1}{r^2} \qquad (11.15)$$

Gravitational force pulls the satellite towards the center of the earth. Balancing this force is the centripetal force caused by the motion of the satellite as it travels in orbit around the planet. The centripetal force is equal to the mass of the satellite multiplied by the square of the velocity divided by the instantaneous radius of curvature of the flight path of the satellite.

$$F_c = \frac{mv^2}{r} \tag{11.16}$$

For a circle, the instantaneous radius of curvature, r, is simply the radius of the circle. For a more complicated shape such as an ellipse, the radius of curvature will vary depending on where on the ellipse the radius of curvature is being evaluated.

Circular Orbits

The easiest type of orbit to analyze is a circular orbit. The instantaneous radius of curvature of the flight path is constant and is equal to the radius of the orbit. The velocity required to maintain a circular orbit, v_c, can be found from Equations (11.15) and (11.16).

$$v_c = \sqrt{6.67e-11\frac{m_e}{r}} = \sqrt{\frac{3.985e+14}{r}} \tag{11.17}$$

As an example, the velocity required to maintain a 300 km circular orbit around the earth is 7737 m/s, where $r = (6356.8 + 300)$ km. Notice that the mass of the satellite does not affect the velocity necessary to maintain a circular orbit.

Other Types of Orbits

A circle is not the only possible orbital shape. Orbits can also be in the shape of an ellipse, a parabola, or a hyperbola. Most satellite orbits are circular or elliptical. There are some other general ways to classify orbits. A **geosynchronous** orbit is one that is synchronized with the rotation of the earth. A satellite in this type of orbit will pass over the same point on the surface at the same time (or several times) per day.

A satellite placed in a **polar** orbit passes within 20° of Earth's poles. This type of orbit allows observation of every point on the earth's surface and is commonly used for spy and weather satellites. A **geostationary** orbit is a circular orbit that allows the satellite to travel at the same rate as the rotation of the earth. TV broadcast satellites typically use geostationary orbits.

Escape Velocity

A satellite orbits a planet when the centripetal force generated by its motion around the planet balances the gravitational pull of the planet. A planetary probe or lunar landing mission has to break free of Earth's gravitational pull altogether. For a satellite to break free from the gravitational pull of a planet, the kinetic energy of the satellite must be equal to the work performed on the satellite by the gravitational pull of the planet.

$$\frac{1}{2}m_1v^2 = 6.67e-11\frac{m_e m_1}{r} \tag{11.18}$$

The velocity at which the kinetic energy equals the gravitational work is called the **escape velocity**, v_{esc}, and is a function of the mass of the planet and the distance the satellite is from the center of the planet. For Earth, the escape velocity is the following:.

$$v_{esc} = \sqrt{6.67e-11\frac{2m_e}{r}} = \sqrt{\frac{7.97e+14}{r}} \tag{11.19}$$

Comparing Equations (11.17) and (11.19), we see that the escape velocity is equal to the circular orbit velocity times the square root of 2. The escape velocity for an object in a 300 km orbit around the earth is 10,942 m/s. As was the case with the circular orbit velocity, the mass of the object has no effect on the escape velocity.

Using the Earth's Rotation

We have seen that fairly high velocities are required to maintain an orbit around the earth. Fortunately for rocket designers, the earth itself helps things out a bit. As you probably know, the earth rotates about its north-south axis. The rotational velocity at the surface of the earth is a function of the distance from the north-south axis of the earth. The maximum rotational velocity occurs at the equator and is equal to about 460 m/s.

The centripetal force experienced by a rocket traveling around the earth is relative to the center of the earth. If the rocket travels along the equator in the direction of Earth's rotation (east), it gets a "free" 460 m/s that it can use to achieve an orbit. Maximizing the available rotational velocity is the reason that most launch facilities are located as close to the equator as possible.

Payload to Orbit

Many rockets are used as delivery trucks to outer space. Their job is to lift a satellite or other payload and place it into orbit. The rocket has to generate enough thrust and maintain it long enough to overcome gravity and drag forces and lift the payload to the required altitude at the required orbital velocity.

The amount of payload that a single-stage rocket can lift into orbit can be estimated using the rocket equation. If drag forces are ignored, the ratio of final mass, m_f to initial mass, m_0, is proportional to the ratio of the final velocity, v_f the burn time, t, and the effective exhaust velocity, v_e.

$$\frac{m_f}{m_0} = e^{-\frac{v_f + gt}{v_e}} \tag{11.20}$$

The ratio of the final rocket mass to its initial mass is called the **mass ratio**. The final mass of the rocket includes all structural elements of the rocket as well as any payload the rocket is carrying.

The problem for single-stage rockets is that an unrealistically low mass ratio is often required to achieve orbital velocities. For example, let's look at a rocket powered by a single F-1 rocket engine. The vacuum exhaust velocity of the F-1 engine is about 3000 m/s. The burn time is 150 s. Let's assume that the rocket is supposed to reach the 300 km circular orbit velocity of 7737 m/s. Under these conditions, the mass ratio is equal to the following:

$$\frac{m_f}{m_0} = e^{-\frac{7737 + 9.8*150}{3000}} = 0.0465 \tag{11.21}$$

If the original mass of the rocket was $1.0e + 6$ kg, the final mass of the rocket can only be 46500 kg. This value is probably less than the minimum structural mass of the rocket, meaning that the rocket can't possibly reach a 300 km circular orbit.

Single-stage rockets have a difficult time reaching Earth's orbit. The solution to this problem is what is known as a **multistage** rocket.

Multistage Rockets

A multistage rocket is two or more rockets, called **stages**, that are piggybacked on top of one another to create a single launch system. The Saturn V rocket, shown in Figure 11-9, consists of three stages that are stacked one on top of the other. The advantage of using a multistage rocket is that the velocity gains from each stage are cumulative. One stage fires its engines, resulting in a given final velocity after the engine burn. When the next stage fires its engines, it starts (approximately) from the final velocity of the previous stage.

Figure 11-9. *The three-stage Saturn V rocket (Photo courtesy of NASA)*

As an example of the advantages of multistaging, let's analyze the three stages of the Saturn 5 rocket using the rocket equation. For this approximate analysis, we'll assume that the rocket is ascending vertically and that gravitational acceleration is constant. We'll ignore drag effects and use the vacuum thrust effective exhaust velocity in the computations. To calculate the change in velocity from each stage, we'll make use of the "delta-V" form of the rocket equation.

$$\Delta v = v - v_0 = v_e \ln\left(\frac{m_0}{m_f}\right) - gt \tag{11.22}$$

Typical stage data for the Saturn 5 is shown in Table 11-4.[4, 5] The initial and final masses for each stage include any higher stages that are part of the stack. In other words, the stage 1 masses include the mass of the second and third stages that sit on top of stage 1. When a stage has finished firing its engine, it separates from the stack, and the structural weight of the stage is no longer included in the rocket mass estimation. Stage 3 of the Saturn 5 normally performs two engine burns, but we'll use the total burn time here in our calculations.

Table 11-4. *Stage Data for the Saturn 5 Rocket*

Quantity	Stage 1	Stage 2	Stage 3
Initial mass (*kg*)	2.85e + 6	5.93e + 5	1.19e + 5
Final mass (*kg*)	8.85e + 5	1.54e + 5	1.54e + 4
Isp (*s*)	304	418	418
Exhaust velocity, (*m/s*)	2980	4096	4096
Burn time, (*s*)	150	359	480

The change in velocity for each stage can be computed from Equation (11.22).

$$\Delta v_1 = 2980 \ln \left(\frac{2.85e+6}{8.85e+5} \right) - 150 * 9.8 = 2015 \ \frac{m}{s} \tag{11.23a}$$

$$\Delta v_2 = 4096 \ln \left(\frac{5.93e+5}{1.54e+5} \right) - 359 * 9.8 = 2004 \ \frac{m}{s} \tag{11.23b}$$

$$\Delta v_3 = 4096 \ln \left(\frac{1.19e+5}{1.54e+4} \right) - 480 * 9.8 = 3671 \ \frac{m}{s} \tag{11.23c}$$

The total change in velocity for the rocket is the sum of the velocity changes for each stage.

$$\Delta v_{total} = \Delta v_1 + \Delta v_2 + \Delta v_3 = 7957.7 \ \frac{m}{s} \tag{11.24}$$

Let's compare the multistage Δv result to the value that would be obtained if the first stage of the Saturn 5 were flown by itself. In this situation, the initial mass of Stage 1 would be 2.18e + 6 *kg* and the final mass would be 2.13e + 5 *kg*. If the engines were fired for 150 seconds, the change in velocity according to the rocket equation would be the following:

$$\Delta v_1 = 2980 \ln \left(\frac{2.18e+6}{2.13e+5} \right) - 150 * 9.81 = 5461 \ \frac{m}{s} \tag{11.25}$$

The advantages of staging are pretty clear. In this example, going with a multistage rocket increased the potential Δv of the rocket by over 40%.

Incorporating a multistage rocket into a rocket simulation is pretty straightforward. When a stage finishes its burn time, it is separated from the rest of the stack. The mass of the rocket would be adjusted for structural weight of the stage that was jettisoned. There will typically be a several-second delay between stage separation and when the engines of the next stage will ignite. The general equations for thrust, drag, and gravity that we developed in this chapter are equally applicable to multistage rockets.

Missiles

Now that we have learned the basics of modeling the physics of rockets, let's spend a little time exploring the physics of missiles. The word "missile" has several definitions, but in this chapter a missile is defined simply as a rocket that is used for military purposes. Missiles can be large or small. Intercontinential ballistic missiles (ICBMs) can be as large as the rockets that are used to put satellites into orbit. Anti-aircraft or antitank missiles are relatively small, highly maneuverable rockets.

Missiles are often characterized by what they are launched from and where they end up. An **air-to-air missile** is fired from an airplane or helicopter and is meant to shoot down another airplane or helicopter. A **surface-to-air missile** is fired from the ground and aimed at a target that is in the air. A **surface-to-surface missile** is launched from the ground at a ground target. An **air-to-surface** missile is fired from air at a target on the ground. Figure 11-10 displays a picture of a Sidewinder air-to-air missile.

Figure 11-10. *The Sidewinder air-to-air missile (Photo courtesy of the U.S. Air Force)*

No matter what their purpose, missiles are in essence rockets and are governed by the same mathematical equations we derived for rockets earlier in this chapter. The only additional information needed to the position and velocity of a missile is the geometric and engine performance data specific to the missile.

Missile Guidance

Another difference between a missile and a rocket used to lift a satellite into orbit is that the missile is trying to hit something. Once a missile is released and its engines have fired, it needs a way to track its target. The part of the missile that tracks a target is called the **guidance system**. There are several guidance system technologies in use today. An **infrared**, or heat-seeking, guidance system homes in on the infrared energy (heat) generated by the target. Some missiles have a **laser seeking** guidance system whereby the missile homes in on a laser spot that is projected onto the target. **Radar tracking** guidance systems use radar signals to home in on their target.

Quite a bit of research has been performed on developing sophisticated guidance systems, but an equal amount of research has also gone into finding ways to confuse missile guidance systems so they lose sight of their target. Some targets may try to electronically jam a radar guidance system. Small metal strips, called **chaff**, can be thrown into the air to confuse radar guidance as well. High-temperature flares can be released by an airplane, causing a heat-seeking missile to lock on to the flares instead of the airplane. If you are developing a sophisticated missile simulation, you probably will want to include guidance system countermeasures as part of the simulation.

To accomplish their objective, missiles have to be highly maneuverable. Most missiles have control fins that can be rotated to change the direction of travel. The direction of the rocket nozzle exhaust can be adjusted using what is called a thrust vector control system to change the course of the missile as well.

Missile Specifications

In order to model a missile in a game simulation, the technical specifications of the missile must be obtained. Fortunately, there are a lot of resources online, in books, or in technical papers where missile specification data can be obtained. Unfortunately, some of the information, such as the thrust generated by the missile, can be classified information. Sometimes the missing information can be guessed at if other information about the missile is known. For example, if the maximum velocity of the missile is known and an estimate can be made of the drag coefficient, the thrust generated by the engine at the maximum velocity can be estimated by computing the drag force at the maximum velocity condition.

As an example of what missile specifications look like, Table 11-5 lists geometric and performance specifications for two missiles, the AIM9 Sidewinder and the AGM-114 Hellfire.[7] The Sidewinder is an older air-to-air missile, whereas the Hellfire is an air-fired antitank missile. Both missiles use a solid-propellant rocket motor. Because of their simplicity, solid-propellant rocket engines are used to power most small-scale military missiles. The thrust for the Sidewinder missile was unavailable from the publicly accessible sources, but could be estimated from the maximum velocity data.

Table 11-5. *Sidewinder and Hellfire Missile Specifications*

Quantity	AIM9 Sidewinder	AGM-114 Hellfire
Missile type	Air-to-air	Air-to-surface
Purpose	Anti-aircraft missile	Antitank missile
Guidance system	Infrared	Laser seeking
Length (m)	2.87	1.63
Diameter (m)	0.13	0.178
Mass (kg)	85.5	45.5
Engine type	Solid-propellant	Solid-propellant
Engine thrust (N)	Classified	2220–2670
Maximum velocity (m/s)	850	420

Tidbit The Sidewinder, first introduced in 1956, is a bargain in the world of military missiles. The unit cost of each missile is only $84,000.

Summary

In this chapter, you learned about the physics of rockets. We saw a little bit about how rockets were first invented and about the development of rocket technology through the years. We created a basic force diagram of a rocket in flight. We saw that in many ways modeling rockets is similar to modeling airplanes. Both problems involve evaluating lift, drag, thrust, and gravity forces. There are some new wrinkles when it comes to modeling rockets. For example, altitude effects can be important when computing the thrust, drag, and gravity forces on a rocket. Another unique feature of rockets compared to the other objects modeled in this book is that the mass of the rocket is continually changing during its flight.

Some of the other things you learned in this chapter include the following:

- How to compute rocket engine thrust based on mass flow rate and exhaust velocity

- What the specific impulse is and how it can be used to characterize rocket engines

- How the gravitational acceleration decreases with increasing altitude

- How to compute atmospheric pressure, density, and temperature as a function of altitude using the U.S. Standard Atmosphere 1976 model

- How to use the rocket equation to estimate the velocity of a rocket based on the exhaust velocity and the initial and final masses of the rocket

- How to compute circular orbit and escape velocities for a satellite

- How multistage rockets can piggyback on top of each other to increase the performance of a rocket

- An introduction to rocket-powered missiles including the different ways a missile can find its target

References

1. Specific Impulse of Various Types of Rocket Engines, www.marsacademy.com/propul/propul3.htm.

2. Space and Tech Space Database, www.spaceandtech.com/spacedata/engines/engines.shtml.

3. *Encyclopedia Astronautica*, www.astronautix.com/engines/f1.htm.

4. *Wikipedia Encyclopedia*, http://en.wikipedia.org.

5. The Apollo Saturn Reference page, www.apollosaturn.com/asnr/p9-13.htm.

6. Pratt and Whitney Space Products, www.pratt-whitney.com/prod_space_rd180.asp.

7. Federation of American Scientists Military Analysis Network, www.fas.org/man/dod-101/sys/missile/index.html.

CHAPTER 12

■ ■ ■

The Physics of Solids

For the most part in this book, we have been studying the external physics of various objects—how they fly through the air, drive across land, float over water. The main emphasis in the earlier chapters has been in modeling the external forces of thrust, drag, lift, gravity, and friction. In this chapter, we will explore some internal physics of objects you may use in your game simulations. For example, rather than discuss what happens to a projectile that is flying towards a target, we will look at what happens to the target once the projectile strikes it.

Many topics could be characterized under the title "physics of solids." In this chapter, we will explore two subjects that have application to game programming scenarios. The first subject we will cover is ballistic impacts—what happens to a target when a projectile or other object slams into it. The second topic we will discuss is how heat energy is conducted through solid objects. The applications to game programming for heat conduction might include determining how long before a gas tank exposed to a flame would explode or calculating how long it would take a laser to burn through the hull of a spaceship.

Specific points that will be covered in this chapter include the following:

- What happens to a projectile and target during a ballistic impact
- The concepts of energy and work and how they relate to a ballistic impact
- Ways to model the penetration of steel armor
- Modeling arrow penetrations
- Momentum and blunt trauma due to ballistic impact
- The physics of body wounds
- How Fourier's law relates heat energy transfer to a temperature gradient
- The heat conduction equation
- Methods to solve the heat conduction equation using the error function

Ballistic Impacts

A ballistic impact occurs when a projectile strikes another object at high speed. When this happens, basically three things can happen: the projectile can bounce off of the object, it can partially penetrate the object, or it can pass completely through the object. Which of these three possibilities will occur depends on the mass, composition, and velocity of the projectile and target. An arrow shot at a tank will bounce off the tank's armor. The same arrow shot at a wooden shield might penetrate part or all the way through the shield.

In this section, we'll start by talking about the general physical processes that can occur during a ballistic impact. We'll discuss energy and momentum issues. Then we'll see some details about some specific types of armor commonly found in game simulations. Finally, we talk a little bit about what happens when a bullet or arrow passes through the body of a person or animal.

What Happens During a Ballistic Impact

A lot of things can happen when a projectile strikes a target at high velocity. For example, let's consider a bullet that strikes a thick, immovable metal plate. When the bullet strikes the metal plate, the collision generates a force that acts on the bullet and on the area of the plate that the bullet impacts. The nose of the bullet will be compressed, and the bullet may experience a change in its shape due to inelastic (that is, permanent) deformation. Depending on the material properties and velocity, the shock caused by the impact may cause the bullet to fragment into two or more pieces.

The part of the plate that is struck by the bullet will be compressed towards the center of the plate. The metal in the impact zone will stretch. If the energy of the bullet is large enough, the plate will fracture, allowing the bullet to penetrate the metal plate. The bullet may even pass completely through the metal plate and continue its trajectory on the other side. Even if the bullet does not penetrate the armor, it can still damage the armor, weakening the resistance of the armor to future ballistic impacts.

Energy Considerations

Ballistic impacts can be analyzed in terms of the overall energy of the projectile and target. You learned in Chapter 3 that the overall energy of a system must be conserved. Consider a ballistic impact of a projectile striking and embedding itself into an immovable target. Just before the projectile impacts the target, it has a kinetic energy equal to one half the mass of the projectile, m_p, multiplied by its velocity, v_p, squared.

$$E = \frac{1}{2} m_p v_p^{\,2}$$

(12.1)

If the projectile penetrates partway into the target and comes to a stop, its kinetic energy is now zero. We know that energy must be conserved, so where did the preimpact kinetic energy go? Part of the energy would go into the inelastic deformation of the bullet and target. Friction between the projectile and target as the projectile was moving through the target would generate heat. A portion of the kinetic energy would also be expended as work performed by the bullet when it was penetrating the target. The amount of work performed is equal to the average force the bullet exerts on the target multiplied by the distance of penetration.

$$W = F_{ave} \Delta x$$

(12.2)

Whether or not a projectile passes through a target depends on whether the projectile has enough initial kinetic energy to push its way through the target. The amount of penetration, if it occurs at all, is a function of the material properties of the projectile, the shape of the projectile, the impact angle of the projectile, the thickness of the target, and the material properties of the target.

Creating a detailed model of projectile penetration into a target would be very complicated and not appropriate for game programming applications. For some situations, such as a shell hitting a steel plate, there are fairly simply mathematical formulas that can estimate whether a projectile will penetrate a target. In other situations, there may be experimental data that you can apply.

Let's take a look at a few specific ballistic impact situations in more detail, starting with a projectile impacting steel armor.

Steel Armor

Whether it's ships, tanks, or knights in shining armor, iron or steel has been a favorite armor material for thousands of years. For just as many years, people have developed weapons to penetrate iron or steel armor. When developing a game simulation in which the combatants are wearing armor, the simulation must determine whether a projectile that strikes the armor will penetrate the armor.

In the 1930s at the U.S. Naval Proving Ground, Dr. L. Thompson developed a relation known as the Thompson "F-Formula" all-purpose armor penetration formula[1] that predicted the armor thickness required to prevent a projectile from penetrating a steel plate. The equation was presented as a ratio between the plate thickness and the diameter of the projectile.

$$\frac{t}{d} = 0.0623 \frac{mv^2}{d^3 F^2} \cos^2 \theta \tag{12.3}$$

The armor thickness, t, and the projectile diameter, d, are in units of m. The mass of the projectile, m, is in kg, and the angle of impact, θ, is in degrees. The angle of impact is zero for a head-on impact in which the projectile strike is perpendicular to the steel plate.

The coefficient F is a measure of the penetration resistance of the armor. Harder, more difficult to penetrate armor will have a higher F value. Based on tests conducted at the U.S. Naval Proving Ground, an equation was developed to compute the "standard" value of F based on impacts between chromium-nickel-steel armor and standard navy armor piercing shells.

$$F = 1.8288 \left(\frac{t}{d} - 0.45 \right) \left(\theta^2 + 2000 \right) + 12192 \tag{12.4}$$

The value for the F coefficient given by Equation (12.4) is based on a "standard" projectile striking "standard" steel armor. One way to model a different type of steel armor that was more or less resistant to penetration than "standard" steel would be to multiply the results from standard F equation by a scale factor.

The original equation was expressed in terms of the ratio of the armor thickness to the projectile diameter, but it is also possible to rearrange the Thompson formula so that it is in terms of the minimum projectile kinetic energy, E_k, necessary to penetrate the armor.

$$E_k = \frac{1}{2} mv^2 = 8.025 \frac{td^2 F^2}{\cos^2 \theta} \tag{12.5}$$

The right-hand side of Equation (12.5) tells us which factors influence steel armor penetration. The thickness of the armor and the resistance of the armor to penetration increase (obviously) the kinetic energy of the projectile required to penetrate the armor. The diameter of the projectile also has an effect in that a thicker projectile requires more kinetic energy to penetrate a given thickness of armor than a thinner projectile. The greater the angle of impact, the more kinetic energy is required.

The Thompson "F-Formula" all-purpose armor penetration formula was originally designed to model the ballistic impacts and penetrations of naval armor, but it works fairly well for bullet impacts as well. As an example, let's use Equation (12.5) to compute the necessary kinetic energy to penetrate a 0.01 m steel plate with a 9 mm bullet. We'll assume the impact is head-on and use Equation (12.4) to compute the F coefficient value.

$$F = 1.8288\left(\frac{0.01}{0.009} - 0.45\right)(2000) + 12192 = 14610 \tag{12.6}$$

The kinetic energy required to penetrate the steel plate is computed from Equation (12.5).

$$\frac{1}{2}mv^2 = 8.025*0.01*0.009^2*14610^2 = 1387.5 \text{ J} \tag{12.7}$$

A high-velocity 9 mm bullet has a mass of 0.0082 kg and a muzzle velocity of about 440 m/s. The corresponding kinetic energy of the bullet is 794 J, which is less than the kinetic energy required to penetrate the plate, so the steel plate will stop the 9 mm bullet.

A projectile that doesn't penetrate steel armor can still damage it. Armor is susceptible to flaking or chipping (also called **spalling**) and fracturing. If any of these things happens, it weakens the ability of the armor to resist future ballistic impacts.

Body Armor

Armor was used to protect soldiers for thousands of years, but it was largely abandoned from military use in the eighteenth, nineteenth, and early twentieth centuries. During World War I, there were English and American officers who considered it an act of cowardice to wear anything that would protect oneself during combat. In more modern times, people have come to their senses, and it is now standard practice for soldiers and police officers to wear body armor when in a combat situation.

Rather than the metal armor that was worn in ancient times, modern body armor is generally constructed from Kevlar or a similar type of carbon composite material, which is strong yet significantly lighter than metal. The National Institute of Justice (NIJ) conducts tests of various types of police and personal body armor.[2] The armor is classified according to the types of bullets that the armor will stop. The armor is tested against both soft-tipped (typically exposed lead) bullets and hard-tipped (lead covered with a metal jacket) bullets.

The NIJ body armor classification standards are summarized in Table 12-1. The NIJ reference documents present the results in terms of types of bullets that a particular body armor class can stop, but these have been converted into kinetic energy values in Table 12-1. The kinetic energy values represent the maximum bullet kinetic energy that the body armor can stop. For example, a bullet with a kinetic energy value of 750 J would penetrate Type IIA body armor but would be stopped by Type II body armor.

Table 12-1. *NIJ Body Armor Classification Standards*

Classification	Max Kinetic Energy (J)
Type I	302
Type IIA	569
Type II	930
Type IIIA	1483
Type III	3371
Type IV	4078

The NIJ body armor tests were conducted by shooting bullets at body armor at a distance of about 3 m. The types of bullets tested and their mass and reference velocities are shown in Table 12-2. The abbreviation FMJ stands for "full metal jacket" and indicates a bullet consisting of a lead core covered with a copper-zinc alloy jacket. The abbreviation RN indicates a bullet with a round nose. A jacketed soft point (JSP) bullet, also known as a semijacketed bullet, consists of a lead core surrounded except at the tip with a metal covering. A jacketed hollow point (JHP) bullet is similar to a JSP bullet except a hollow cavity or hole exists at the nose. The last two bullets in the table, the ones with the highest kinetic energy values, are military bullets.

The velocities listed in Table 12-2 were measured 2 m away from the muzzle of the gun barrel. At that distance, it is a reasonable approximation to assume the measured velocity was equal to the muzzle velocity of the bullet. The measured velocities had an approximate error of plus or minus 9 m/s and are representative values for the particular bullet type. Different brands of the same type of bullet might have higher or lower velocities than the values shown in Table 12-2. Three different types of 9 mm bullets were tested, having approximately the same mass but different reference velocities.

Table 12-2. *Specifications of the Bullets Used in the NIJ Body Armor Tests*

Bullet	Mass (*kg*)	Reference Velocity (*m/s*)	Kinetic Energy (J)
.22 caliber Long Rifle RN	0.0026	329	141
.38 ACP FMJ RN	0.0062	322	321
9 *mm* FMJ RN	0.008	341	465
9 *mm* FMJ RN	0.008	367	539
0.40 S&W FMJ	0.0117	322	607
9 *mm* FMJ RN high velocity	0.0082	436	779
.357 Magnum JSP	0.0102	436	969
.44 Magnum JHP	0.0156	436	1483
7.62 *mm* NATO FMJ	0.0096	838	3371
.30 caliber M2 armor piercing	0.0108	869	4078

To model the effects of body armor penetration in your game simulations, you could equip your soldiers, law enforcement officers, or whomever with one of the types of body armor listed in Table 12-1. When a bullet strikes the person wearing the body armor, compute the kinetic energy of the bullet at impact. If the kinetic energy is greater than the value listed in Table 12-1, the bullet can be considered to have penetrated the body armor.

You will need to consider some other things when modeling body armor. For example, the armor generally only protects the torso of the wearer, and the person wearing the body armor could still be wounded if hit in the arms, legs, or face. Even if the body armor stops the bullet, the wearer may still be wounded by the blunt trauma caused by the impact. We'll discuss blunt trauma a bit later in the "Body Wounds" section when we talk about the momentum transfer caused by a ballistic impact.

Animal Skin Penetration

In some game simulations, hunting games for instance, the targets won't be wearing steel armor but will depend only on their hides for protection. There are also game situations in which the projectiles won't be bullets but will be arrows instead. Table 12-3 shows the approximate kinetic energy required of an arrow in order to penetrate the hide and cause a mortal wound to a whitetail deer and to larger game such as elk and moose. A typical hunting arrow with a mass of 0.034 kg that strikes its target at 61 m/s has a kinetic energy at impact of 63.3 J. According to Table 12-3, this arrow would kill a deer but would be unable to kill a larger animal such as a moose.

Table 12-3. *Arrow Penetration Data for Various Targets*

Projectile	Target	Required Kinetic Energy (J)
Hunting arrow	Whitetail deer	61
Hunting arrow	Larger game (elk, moose, etc.)	75

With some consideration, it's possible to extend the data shown in Table 12-3 to human targets as well. A villager wearing a leather shirt might have a similar penetration resistance as the hide of a whitetail deer. It is known that an arrow shot from an English longbow could penetrate chain mail armor at a range of 100 m. If the longbow arrow weighed 0.06 kg and struck the target at a representative velocity of 55 m/s, this would imply a kinetic energy at impact of about 90 J.

Momentum

We have discussed how the kinetic energy of a projectile determines whether a projectile will penetrate a target. There is another factor to consider when evaluating the damage caused by a ballistic impact—that of the momentum transfer caused by the impact. We saw in Chapter 6 that a force is required to change the momentum of the object.

$$F = \frac{d(mv)}{dt}$$

(12.8)

When the projectile strikes the target, whether it bounces off the target or penetrates the target, the momentum of the projectile changes because the target exerts a force on the bullet and the bullet exerts an equal and opposite force on the target. This force, also known as **blunt trauma**, can significantly damage a person wearing body armor even if the armor itself stops the bullet. When programming a combat simulation, you might consider adding blunt trauma to the damage calculation, making it some function of the projectile momentum at impact. If you use damage meters in your shoot-em-up game, the damage level should increase for every hit whether or not the projectile penetrates the armor of the target.

Force due to momentum change is also apparent when the bullet or other projectile is fired. When the exploding charge propels the bullet forward, the momentum of the bullet changes, indicating that a force is being applied to the bullet. An equal and opposite force is applied to the gun. This force is the recoil that occurs when the gun is fired. The recoil force is proportional to the momentum imparted to the bullet, which is why a heavier bullet such as the 44 Magnum will have greater recoil force than a lighter bullet such as a 9 *mm*. In fact, two separate recoil events take place. The first recoil occurs when the bullet starts to move down the muzzle, and a second recoil happens when the bullet leaves the muzzle into the surrounding air.

The impact force of a bullet is often ridiculously overstated in movies and games where a gunshot victim will be thrown backwards through a plate glass window or some such thing. Because drag forces will slow the bullet down during its flight, the impact force at the target will always be less than the initial recoil force. In your game programming simulations, if the recoil doesn't knock the shooter over, the impact shouldn't knock the victim over.

Body Wounds

In game simulations where participants are being wounded by guns, arrows, or other projectiles, you may want to model or display the wounds that the projectiles will cause. This section will provide a brief discussion of what happens when a bullet passes through a person's body. The intent is to provide you with the proper scenarios when you are creating the graphics to go with shoot-em-up games.

■**Caution** Just as a warning, some of the material in this section will be a bit graphic. If you don't want to add these kinds of effects to your games, you might be better off skipping down to "Heat Conduction."

As a bullet passes through a human body, it transfers some of its kinetic energy to the surrounding tissue, causing the tissue to move away perpendicularly from the path of the bullet. The tissue movement causes a temporary cavity that can be significantly larger in diameter than the diameter of the bullet. For low-velocity bullets, such as most handgun bullets, the kinetic energy transfer is small enough so that only a small temporary cavity is produced. Most of the damage caused by a low-velocity bullet is along the direct path of the bullet.

The situation is quite different and rather disturbing for high-velocity bullets such as the 7.62 *mm* NATO FMJ. When a high-velocity bullet enters the body, injured tissue is ejected out of the entrance wound in what is called a "tail splash." A large amount of kinetic energy is transferred to the surrounding tissue as the bullet passes through, causing a large temporary cavity inside the body. The expanding walls of the temporary cavity can cause very high local pressures to occur. When a bullet exits an object, such as the tomato shown in Figure 12-1, damaged tissue is ejected out of the exit hole behind the bullet.

Figure 12-1. *Damage caused by a high-velocity bullet (Photo courtesy of Prof. Andrew Davidhazy, Rochester Institute of Technology)*

The situation is more spectacular (and more disturbing) when a high-velocity bullet passes through a person's head. Because the skull is solid bone, there is no way to relieve the high pressures caused by the bullet passing through the head. If the pressure rises to a high enough level, the head will literally explode. So having a person get thrown backwards when he is shot is not realistic, but having his head explode when he is shot in the head actually is realistic.

Wounds caused by arrows are less dramatic than those caused by bullets because the impact velocity is so much lower. Arrows do most of their damage by slicing through arteries and internal organs. Victims of arrow wounds generally bleed to death. Arrows won't cause "tail splash," tissue ejection, or head explosion effects, so don't include them as part of your arrow game simulation.

Heat Conduction

So far in this book, the discussions on energy have covered primarily kinetic or potential energy. There are other forms that energy can take, and one of these other forms is thermal or heat energy. Thermal energy is related to temperature and will flow from a high-temperature region to a low-temperature region, similar to the way electricity flows through a wire. There are several ways that heat energy can be transferred. Heat transfer between a solid and a moving fluid, such as air blowing over a hot surface, is known as **convective** heat transfer. If the heat is transferred due to electromagnetic waves emanating from an object, it is known as **radiative** heat transfer. Heat transfer through a solid object is known as heat **conduction.**

Modeling heat conduction can be an important element of a game simulation. For example, the game may need to model how long it takes a laser to melt its way through the outer skin of a spaceship or how long it will take for the gas tank of a car that is on fire to explode. The physics of heat conduction is a rather involved subject, and this section will only provide an introduction to it, but it will give you the basic information you need to add heat conduction effects to your games.

Fourier's Law

In general, heat conduction will occur in all three directions, but that general case is too complicated for most game programming applications. The mathematics can be considerably simplified
if the heat conduction is assumed to be one-dimensional, acting only in the direction normal
to the surface of the object. For the analysis presented in this section, we will assume that heat
conduction occurs in the x-direction. According to a relation known as **Fourier's law**, the rate
of heat conduction at any point in the object is proportional to the temperature gradient at
that point.

$$q_x = -\kappa \frac{dT}{dx} \qquad (12.9)$$

The quantity q_x is the heat energy transfer rate (energy per unit time) per unit area.
In the SI system of units, q_x has units of W/m^2, where the W stands for Watts. The **thermal
conductivity**, κ, is a material property that measures how well a material conducts heat. It has
SI units of $W/m\text{-}K$. A material with a higher thermal conductivity will have a higher energy
transfer rate than will a material with a lower thermal conductivity. Materials with low thermal
conductivities are called **insulating materials**, because they do a poor job of conducting heat.

Table 12-4 lists thermal conductivity and density values for some common solid materials.
The thermal conductivity and density of metals are affected somewhat by temperature. The
values shown in Table 12-4 are for a temperature of 293 K (or 20°C). The density shown for
wood is a representative value as different types of wood will have different densities.

Table 12-4. *Typical Thermal Conductivity Values for Various Materials*

Material	Thermal Conductivity ($W/m\text{-}K$)	Density (kg/m^3)
Water	0.6	1000
Glass	0.9	2600
Wood	0.4	780
Concrete	1.3	2200
Aluminum	237	2700
Copper	390	8960
Iron	80	7000
Stainless steel	16	7900
Plastic insulation	0.03	50

Fourier's law assumes a steady-state situation in which the temperature profile through
the object is a function of distance but is constant over time. This situation will not always be
the case. For example, consider a metal rod that is kept at room temperature. If a lit match is
held next to one end of the rod, heat will flow into the rod, and the temperature profile through
the rod will change over time.

The Heat Conduction Equation

To model a **transient,** or time-varying, heat conduction problem, a heat energy equation that has a time derivative term must be developed. In order to come up with this equation, a heat energy balance is evaluated for the system. As shown in Figure 12-2, the heat energy that enters or leaves a section of material of width Δx is given by Fourier's law. The temperature derivative at the exit plane is equal to the derivative at the inflow plane plus the second derivative (the derivative of the derivative) of temperature with respect to x times Δx.

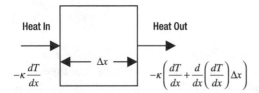

Heat In

$-\kappa \dfrac{dT}{dx}$

Δx

Heat Out

$-\kappa \left(\dfrac{dT}{dx} + \dfrac{d}{dx}\left(\dfrac{dT}{dx} \right) \Delta x \right)$

Figure 12-2. *A heat conduction energy balance*

Assuming that the object is not generating its own heat, the heat energy accumulation in the object over time is equal to the heat energy coming in minus the heat energy that is leaving the object.

$$c_p \rho \Delta x \frac{\partial T}{\partial t} = -\kappa \frac{\partial T}{\partial x} + \kappa \left(\frac{\partial T}{\partial x} + \frac{\partial^2 T}{\partial x^2} \Delta x \right) \tag{12.10}$$

The quantity ρ is the density of the material. The **specific heat capacity,** c_p, is a material property that represents the amount of heat energy required to raise a unit mass of a material by one degree in temperature. It has units of *J/kg-K*. The quantity, $\rho \Delta x$, is the mass-per-unit area of a slice of material of thickness Δx. Equation (12.10) can be cleaned up somewhat by removing terms that cancel each other out. What remains is an equation that relates the time rate of change of temperature at a given point to the second derivative of temperature with respect to x at the point.

$$c_p \rho \frac{\partial T}{\partial t} = \kappa \frac{\partial^2 T}{\partial x^2} \tag{12.11}$$

Equation (12.11) is known as the **1-D heat conduction equation**. If the object were generating heat internally (a nuclear reactor, for example), the energy generation term would be added to the right-hand side of the equation. Oftentimes the material properties are grouped together in a modified version of the 1-D heat conduction equation.

$$\frac{\partial T}{\partial t} = K \frac{\partial^2 T}{\partial x^2} \tag{12.12}$$

The **thermal diffusivity**, K, has units of m^2/s and is equal to the ratio of the thermal conductivity divided by the specific heat capacity and density.

$$K = \frac{\kappa}{c_p \rho} \tag{12.13}$$

The thermal diffusivity can be thought of as a measure of the ability of a material to transfer heat by conduction. Values of thermal diffusivity for various materials are shown in Table 12-5. As before, the values shown in the table are for a temperature of 293 K. There are order of magnitude differences of thermal diffusivity for different materials. Those with high diffusivities are good conductors, and those with low diffusivities are good insulators.

Table 12-5. *Thermal Diffusivity Values*

Material	Thermal Diffusivity (m^2/s)
Water	1.4e – 7
Glass	4.3e – 7
Wood	2.14e – 6
Concrete	6.6e – 7
Aluminum	9.975e – 5
Copper	1.116e – 4
Iron	2.545e – 5
Stainless steel	4.50e – 6
Plastic insulation	3.0e – 7

Solving the Heat Conduction Equation

The 1-D heat conduction equation allows us to compute the temperature profile through a solid object as a function of time. All we have to do now is to solve the equation. The heat conduction equation is a partial differential equation, or PDE, in that there is both a time derivative and a spatial derivative in the equation. If you remember when differential equations were discussed in Chapter 2, the text did not cover how to solve PDEs because it was a difficult topic that was beyond the scope of this book. But now we are faced with having to solve one.

All is not lost, because fortunately the 1-D heat conduction equation is simple enough that there is an analytical solution to it. It involves a bit of mathematical trickery in performing what is called a change of variables to make the PDE look like an ODE. To accomplish this conversion, a variable u is declared that is a function of both x and t.

$$u = \frac{x}{\sqrt{t}} \tag{12.14}$$

The 1-D heat conduction equation can be written in terms of the variable u as a second-order ODE.

$$-\frac{u}{2}\frac{dT}{du} = K\frac{d^2T}{du^2}$$ (12.15)

Without going into all of the details, the solution to Equation (12.15) is an integral equation in terms of u and the thermal diffusivity, K.

$$T(x,t) = A\int_0^{u_2} e^{-\frac{u^2}{4K}}\,du + B$$ (12.16)

The quantities A and B are constants that are determined according to the boundary conditions that are applied to the system. We'll talk about boundary conditions a bit more later on in the section. At first glance, it doesn't seem as if we have made any progress, because we still have to solve a nasty-looking integral. Fortunately for us, we can make use of a similarly nasty-looking but well-known integral known as the **error function**.

$$erf(x) = \frac{2}{\sqrt{\pi}}\int_0^x e^{-x^2}\,dx$$ (12.17)

The error function is important in this case because it can be used to solve the integral expression shown in Equation (12.16). With a little rearranging, Equation (12.16) can be expressed in terms of the error function, erf.

$$T(x,t) = A\sqrt{\pi K}\,erf\left(\frac{u}{2\sqrt{K}}\right) + B = A\sqrt{\pi K}\,erf\left(\frac{x}{2\sqrt{Kt}}\right) + B$$ (12.18)

The error function itself has been calculated and tabulated since the mid-1800s. It can be approximated by a series equation.

$$erf(x) = \frac{2}{\sqrt{\pi}}\left(x + \sum_{n=1}^{\infty}\frac{(-1)^n x^{2n+1}}{(2n+1)n!}\right)$$ (12.19)

The error function can be obtained by computing a certain number of the terms from Equation (12.19), although higher values of x (1.5–2.0) will require the evaluation of at least eight terms in the series. As an alternative, the error function could be tabulated for incremental values of x, and you could use a table lookup method to find the value for a given x.

The error function profile is shown in Figure 12-3. The curve has an exponential-type shape. At values of x above 2.0, the value of the error function is very close to 1.

The only thing left to do is to determine the constants A and B. These will depend on what boundary conditions are applied to the system. If you recall from Chapter 2, oftentimes there will be an infinite number of possible solutions to a differential equation. In order to "pin down" the solution to the one that we want, the conditions need to be specified at one or both ends of the object being analyzed.

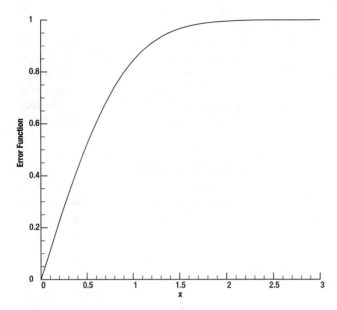

Figure 12-3. *The error function profile*

For the 1-D head conduction equation, two boundary conditions are required. As an example, let's assume we want to solve the 1-D heat conduction equation over a metal rod. One possible boundary condition would be to maintain a constant temperature, T_1, at the end of the rod where $x = 0$. If $x = 0$, then the argument to the error function in Equation (12.18) is zero, meaning that the value of the error function itself is zero. The first term in Equation (12.18) disappears, and the constant B is equal to T_1.

$$T(0,t) = T_1 = B \qquad (12.20)$$

Another boundary condition can be obtained from the initial condition of the metal rod. At time $t = 0$, the argument to the error function in Equation (12.18) is infinity, which means that the value of the error function is 1. If the entire rod initially has a constant temperature T_0, then Equation (12.18) reduces to the following:

$$T(x,0) = T_0 = A\sqrt{\pi K} + B \qquad (12.21)$$

If the boundary conditions shown in Equations (12.20) and (12.21) are used together, an expression can be found for the A constant.

$$A\sqrt{\pi K} = T_0 - T_1 \qquad (12.22)$$

Many other boundary condition combinations are possible depending on the situation that is being modeled. The temperature at both ends of a rod might be specified. The temperature derivative with respect to x might be specified at one or both ends. The temperature might be held constant at some intermediate location along the length of the rod.

The Gas Tank Simulator

Let's use the 1-D heat conduction equation to simulate how long it will take a gas tank to explode when exposed to a flame. A typical screen shot of the Gas Tank Simulator is shown in Figure 12-4. At the top of the GUI is a display window showing a not-too-bright soldier aiming a flamethrower at an aluminum or concrete gas tank. At the bottom left-hand corner of the GUI are text fields that allow the user to set the flame temperature, tank material, and tank thickness. At the right-hand side of the GUI are text fields that display the elapsed time for the simulation and the temperatures at the inner and outer walls of the gas tank.

When the Start button is pressed, the soldier fires his flamethrower at the gas tank. The heat from the flame conducts into the gas tank wall. The ignition temperature of gasoline[3] is about 550 K. When the inner wall temperature reaches this value, the gas tank will explode. In real life, the heat conduction from the flame would be three dimensional, but in this simulation the 1-D heat conduction equation will be used to compute the temperature through the gas tank wall as a function of time.

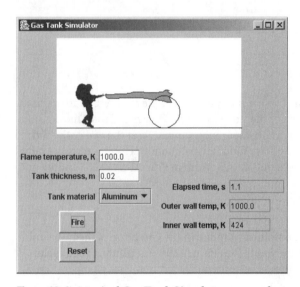

Figure 12-4. *A typical Gas Tank Simulator screen shot*

The temperature at any location inside the gas tank wall at any time can be determined from Equation (12.18). The A and B constants in that equation can be calculated based on the boundary conditions. The gas tank will initially have a temperature of $T_0 = 300\ K$ throughout its thickness. When the flamethrower is lit, the temperature at the outer wall of the gas tank will be maintained at the flame temperature. Based on these boundary conditions, the values of the constants A and B can be obtained from Equations (12.20) and (12.22).

$$B = T_1 = 1000 \tag{12.23}$$

$$A\sqrt{\pi K} = T_0 - T_1 = 300 - 1000 = -700 \tag{12.24}$$

If the boundary conditions are incorporated into Equation (12.18), the equation for the temperature at any point in the gas tank wall at any time is equal to the following:

$$T(x,t) = T_1 + (T_0 - T_1) erf\left(\frac{x}{2\sqrt{Kt}}\right)$$
(12.25)

To solve the heat conduction problem, we will write two classes. The first, called GasTank, represents (as you probably guessed) a gas tank. In this simple example, the GasTank class only declares four fields that contain values of the thickness of the tank wall, thermal diffusivity, initial temperature, and boundary temperature at the outer wall of the tank.

```java
public class GasTank
{
  private double thickness;
  private double diffusivity;
  private double initialT;
  private double boundaryT;

  public GasTank(double thickness, double diffusivity,
                 double initialT, double boundaryT) {
    this.thickness = thickness;
    this.diffusivity = diffusivity;
    this.initialT = initialT;
    this.boundaryT = boundaryT;
  }
```

Even though they aren't used in this example, it's good practice to declare a series of get/set methods to access or change the values of the fields declared in the class.

```java
  // These methods return the field values.
  public double getThickness() {
    return thickness;
  }

  public double getDiffusivity() {
    return diffusivity;
  }

  public double getInitialT() {
    return initialT;
  }

  public double getBoundaryT() {
    return boundaryT;
  }

  // These methods change the value of the fields.
  public void setBoundaryT(double value) {
    boundaryT = value;
    return;
  }
```

The GasTank class declares two other methods. The first is the getErrorFunction method that returns a value of the error function. The method uses a table lookup procedure to compute the error function value. The table lookup method is considerably faster than if the error function were computed according to Equation (12.19). If the argument to the error function is greater than 2.0, the error function value is set to 1.0. Otherwise, the error function value is found by interpolating between known values of the error function. The method is declared to be private, so it can only be used by the GasTank class. If we wanted to reuse this method for other applications, it could have been written as a public static method instead.

```
//  This method computes and returns the value of
//  the error function using a table lookup method.
private double getErrorFunction(double s) {
    double erf[] = {0.0, 0.1125, 0.2227, 0.3286, 0.4284,
                    0.5205, 0.6039, 0.6778, 0.7421, 0.7969,
                    0.8427, 0.8802, 0.9103, 0.9340, 0.9523,
                    0.9661, 0.9764, 0.9838, 0.9891, 0.9928,
                    0.9953};
    int j;
    double value;

    //  If the argument is greater than 2.0, set the
    //  error function value to 1. Otherwise, find the
    //  value using the data in the erf[] array.
    if ( s >= 2.0 ) {
      value = 1.0;
    }
    else {
      j = (int)(s*10.0);
      value = erf[j] + (s*10.0 - j)*(erf[j+1] - erf[j]);
    }

    return value;
}
```

The final method declared in the class is named getTemperature, and it computes and returns the temperature in the gas tank at any time and any location through the thickness of the tank based on Equation (12.25).

```
//  This method computes the value of the temperature
//  for any given x and time value.
public double getTemperature(double x, double time) {
    double temperature;
    double grp;
    double erf;
```

```
grp = 0.5*x/Math.sqrt(diffusivity*time);
erf = getErrorFunction(grp);
temperature = boundaryT + (initialT-boundaryT)*erf;

return temperature;
}
```

The GUI elements of the Gas Tank Simulator are implemented in the GasTankSimulator class. The class is a bit different than the GUI classes previously presented in this book, so we'll spend a little time talking about it. The first part of the class is similar to the others. A number of GUI components are created to accept user input and display the results. A GasTank object is declared that will represent the gas tank. A Timer object is used to control the execution of the game. When the Start button is pressed, the actionPerformed method declared in the GasTankSimulator method is called. The first thing the method does is to extract the user inputs for the tank thickness, tank material, and flame temperature from the text fields.

```
public void actionPerformed(ActionEvent event) {

  // Get some initial quantities from the text fields.
  double flameTemp = Double.parseDouble(flameTempTextField.getText());
  double thickness = Double.parseDouble(thicknessTextField.getText());
```

The value for diffusivity is set to the value for aluminum and the initial temperature of the tank is set to be 300 K. A GasTank object is created based on the input quantities.

```
  // Set the initial temperature.
  double initialT = 300.0;

  // Set the diffusivity according to the material selected.
  double diffusivity;
  String material = (String)materialComboBox.getSelectedItem();
  if ( material.equals("Aluminum") ) {
    diffusivity = 9.975e-5;
  }
  else {
    diffusivity = 6.6e-7;    // concrete
  }

  // Create a GasTank object.
  tank = new GasTank(thickness, diffusivity, initialT, flameTemp);
```

The value shown in the outer wall temperature text field is set to the flame temperature, the GUI display is updated, and the start method is called on the Timer object to start the simulation.

```
  // Set the display for the outer wall temperature text field.
  outerTempTextField.setText(""+flameTemp);
```

```
    //  Update the display.
    updateDisplay();

    //  Fire the flamethrower using a Timer object.
    gameTimer.start();
}
```

The GasTankSimulator class declares an inner class named GameUpdater. The Timer is set up to call the actionPerformed method declared in the GameUpdater class every 0.1 seconds to update the temperature distribution inside the gas tank. Because there is a closed-form solution to the 1-D heat conduction equation, there is no need to use an ODE solver in this simulation. The time value is incremented, and then the inner wall temperature of the tank at this time is determined by calling the getTemperature method on the GasTank object.

```
class GameUpdater implements ActionListener {
    public void actionPerformed(ActionEvent event) {

        //  Compute the new inner wall temperature.
        double timeIncrement = 0.1;
        time = time + timeIncrement;
        innerWallTemp = tank.getTemperature(tank.getThickness(),time);
```

The display is updated with the new time and inner wall temperature values. If the inner wall temperature exceeds the ignition temperature of gasoline, the simulation stops.

```
        //  Update the display.
        updateDisplay();

        //  Update the output data textfields.
        timeTextField.setText(""+(float)time);
        innerTempTextField.setText(""+(int)innerWallTemp);

        //  If the inner wall temperature exceeds the ignition
        //  temperature of gasoline, stop the simulation.
        if ( innerWallTemp > 550.0 ) {
            gameTimer.stop();
        }


    }
}
```

Play around with different flame temperatures and tank thicknesses and see how the variations affect the time it takes the gas tank to explode. You will notice that initially the inner wall temperature remains at 300 K. After a short time, the rate of change of inner wall temperature increases fairly rapidly before tapering off again. The user has two options for tank material. Aluminum is a good conductor with a thermal diffusivity of $9.975e-5$ m^2/s. Concrete, on the other hand, is a fairly good insulator and has a much lower thermal diffusivity value of $6.6e-7$ m^2/s. If you select a concrete gas tank, you will notice that it takes significantly longer for the inner tank temperature to begin to rise than it does with an aluminum tank.

Figure 12-5 shows the time variation of inner wall temperature for the case of an aluminum gas tank where the outer wall temperature is 1000 K and the tank thickness is 0.025 m. The inner wall temperature remains at 300 K for 0.3 seconds. As heat conducts through the tank wall, the inner wall temperature begins to rise quite steeply. For this case, the ignition temperature of gasoline of 550 K is reached after 3.7 seconds.

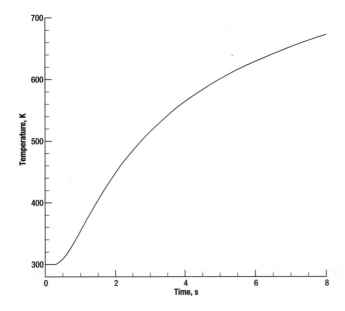

Figure 12-5. *Time-varying temperature profiles at the inner wall of an aluminum gas tank. Tank thickness = 0.025 m. Outer wall temperature = 1000 K.*

Summary

In this chapter, we took a departure from modeling external forces and explored some internal physics of solid objects. In particular, we studied what happens to an object when it is struck by a projectile and how heat energy is conducted through objects. At the end of this chapter, you should have the basic information you need to model armor penetrations and heat energy conduction in your game programs.

Specific topics that were covered in this chapter include the following:

- The complex processes involved in ballistic impact including inelastic deformation, fracturing, and other forms of energy transfer

- How the Thompson "F Formula" relation can be used to estimate whether a projectile penetrates steel armor

- The NIJ body armor classifications and the kinetic energy and bullet types that can penetrate a given type of body armor

- What happens when a bullet enters a human body and the differences between the effects of high-velocity and low-velocity bullet wounds

- How Fourier's law relates the heat energy flowing through an object to the temperature gradient inside the object

- The material properties of thermal conductivity and thermal diffusivity as measurements of the ability to conduct heat energy

- How the heat conduction equation can be used to model time-varying temperature profiles

- How the heat conduction equation can be solved using the mathematical integral relation known as the error function

References

1. N. Okun, "Major Historical Naval Armor Penetration Formulae," www.battlefield.ru/guns/defin_1.html.

2. National Institute of Justice Body Armor Standards and Testing, www.ojp.usdoj.gov/nij/sciencetech/body_armor.htm.

3. S. Christopher, "The Ignition Temperature of Gasoline," http://hypertextbook.com/facts/2003/ShaniChristopher.shtml.

CHAPTER 13

■ ■ ■

Explosions

We've already seen in this book how to model projectiles as they fly through the air and how to model the ballistic impact of a projectile with another object. Things don't always just fly through the air in game simulations. Sometimes they also blow up. The physics of explosions is very complex—you can literally get a PhD in the subject. As with some of the other topics covered in this book, we'll limit our treatment of the subject to what game programmers need to know to create realistic simulations.

It turns out that the term "explosion" has no fixed definition and is applied to some very different situations. Generally speaking, an explosion, as it is defined in this chapter, is a sudden release of energy that generates light, heat, noise, and/or a blast wave. Explosions don't always have to be caused by the rapid combustion of a solid or liquid material. When a meteor or comet strikes the earth, the impact will cause an explosion. In this chapter, the discussion will be limited to the subject of chemical and nuclear explosions.

A chemical explosion is caused by the energy released from a rapid chemical reaction. The chemical reaction may occur spontaneously (which is usually bad), or it can be initiated by an ignition source such as a flame or an electrical charge. A nuclear explosion is caused by the energy release due to nuclear fission or fusion. With fission, a heavy element such as uranium is split into two smaller elements. With fusion, a light element such as hydrogen is fused together into a heavier element.

Some of the topics this chapter will cover include the following:

- Some basic explosion terminology

- The processes that take place during an explosion

- An introduction to some commonly used explosives

- How to compute blast damage from an explosion

- Fragmentation devices

- Nuclear explosions

Let's begin our exploration of the world of explosions with some explosion terminology.

Some Explosion Terminology

Before we burrow into the physics of explosions, it's helpful to spend a little time defining some explosion terminology.

- **Autoignition temperature**: The temperature at which an explosive will explode without an external ignition source. As an example, the autoignition temperature of kerosene is $463\ K$ ($374\ {}^\circ F$).

- **Blast wave**: A region of high pressure that expands radially away from the point of explosion.

- **Flash point**: The minimum temperature at which the gas above a liquid fuel will ignite in the presence of a flame source. The flash point temperature is lower than the autoignition temperature.

- **Heat of explosion**: The theoretical amount of energy that is released during an explosion. Under the SI system of units, heat of explosion will be in units of J/kg.

- **Overpressure**: The difference between the pressure inside the blast wave and the ambient air pressure.

Explosion Basics

An explosion as defined in this chapter is a sudden release of energy. The energy released might be the result of a chemical reaction, nuclear fission, or some other process. Explosions happen in very short time durations, typically in thousandths of a second (milliseconds). Gas generated by the explosion expands rapidly in every direction from the **point of explosion**. The rapidly expanding gas pushes into the stationary gas in front of it, causing a region of high pressure known as a **blast wave**. The blast wave expands outwards at a very high velocity, oftentimes greater than the speed of sound. The blast wave loses energy quickly as its distance increases from the point of explosion. The difference between the blast wave pressure and the ambient air pressure is called the **overpressure** of the blast wave.

Because the blast wave expands outwards so rapidly, behind the blast wave is a region of low air pressure. This low-pressure region "sucks" the air along with it, causing a wind that initially follows the blast wave. As the blast wave continues outward, the relative pressure in front of and behind the blast wave changes such that the direction of the wind can reverse direction, and for a time it can blow in towards the point of explosion.

Explosions can also produce light, noise, and heat. Depending on the type of explosive, there may also be a fireball associated with the explosion. Most of the damage by an explosion to people, vehicles, and structures, however, is done by the overpressure in the blast wave. Recall from Chapter 3 that the force exerted by a pressure is equal to the pressure multiplied by the surface area on which the force acts. A blast wave with a relatively small overpressure (small compared to the atmospheric pressure) can exert a crushingly large force on an object it slams into.

When modeling the effects of a blast wave, as shown in Figure 13-1, keep in mind that the force vector from the explosion acts radially from the point of explosion. If the explosion is at the same level as an object such as a truck, the truck will not be thrown into the air but will be pushed sideways. Only if the truck was above the point of explosion could it be thrown into the air.

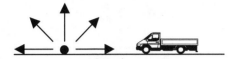

Figure 13-1. *Force due to overpressure will push the truck sideways.*

Explosive Types

There are many, many substances that will explode, and people are always coming up with new ones for good or evil purposes. This section will introduce some of the more commonly used explosive materials that you may want to incorporate into your game simulations.

Gunpowder

Gunpowder, originally known as black powder, is probably the oldest man-made explosive material. Gunpowder is made from a mixture of charcoal, sulfur, and potassium nitrate (also called saltpeter). It was first invented by the Chinese, and there are reports of its usage dating back to the 9th century A.D. Throughout its history, gunpowder has been used to propel projectiles and to fuel rockets. Gunpowder is also used as a blasting agent for mining applications.

Nitroglycerine

An Italian named Ascanio Sobrero invented nitroglycerine in 1846 as a more powerful explosive for mining and tunneling operations. He quickly realized that it was really dangerous stuff and abandoned further research. In 1863, a Swede named Immanuel Nobel and his son Alfred built a plant to manufacture nitroglycerine. The process involved mixing a substance called glycerol with a mixture of nitric and sulfuric acid. Nitroglycerine is more powerful than gunpowder, but it is also prone to accidental detonation. There were many accidents in the early development phase, including one in 1864 that demolished the Nobel factory.

Dynamite

Nitroglycerine, while a very powerful explosive, is quite unstable in its liquid state. In particular it is quite sensitive to shock. If you banged a vial of nitro against something, it could explode. In 1875, Alfred Nobel, having taken over the family business, discovered a way to make nitro-glycerine more stable. He mixed nitroglycerine with a silica-based soil, forming a soft paste. Nobel rolled the paste into a cylinder shape, wrapped paper around it, and called the result dynamite.

Dynamite is much more stable than liquid nitroglycerine and is insensitive to friction, shock, and heat. A stick of dynamite can be placed in fire, where it will burn without exploding (don't try this at home). In fact, detonating a stick of dynamite requires a **blasting cap** or other detonation device.

■Tidbit Alfred Nobel was bothered by the fact that the dynamite he invented was being used for death and destruction (well, duh!). When he died in 1896, his will provided for the establishment of the Nobel Prize in various scientific disciplines for peace and the betterment of all people.

TNT

Trinitrotoluene, better known as TNT, is a pale yellow crystalline explosive that is used as a standard against which other explosives are compared. TNT is not as powerful as other types of explosives, but it has many positive attributes that make it a widely used explosive. For one thing, TNT is quite stable. Unlike substances such as nitroglycerin, TNT will not detonate due to friction, blows, or jarring. It can get wet and still maintain its potency. TNT can be stored for many years, gradually becoming less stable over time. TNT melts at a fairly low temperature, 354 K. It can be melted and poured into a mold, meaning that TNT can take whatever shape is desired.

TNT was invented in 1863 by a German chemist named Joseph Wilbrand. It was actually not used as an explosive for many years because it is relatively hard to detonate. The German army poured molten TNT into artillery shells and used them to great effect during World War I. German TNT-filled shells were designed to detonate only after they had penetrated enemy armor, whereas British shells, which used a less-stable explosion named lyddite, exploded when they first struck the German armor, doing significantly less damage.

As we shall see later in this chapter, TNT is an important explosive in part because there is a lot of experimental data on the blast damage caused by a TNT explosion. To make use of this data, other explosives are often characterized by an equivalent mass of TNT. One kg of TNT releases $2.175e + 6$ J/kg of energy when it explodes. Other explosive materials are typically characterized by comparing them to the explosive energy of TNT. For example, ammonium nitrate releases 0.1–0.2 times the energy of TNT.

Ammonium Nitrate

Ammonium nitrate, or AN, is created by the reaction of ammonia gas with liquid nitric acid. The resulting ammonium nitrate solution can be stored in either a liquid or solid state. Ammonium nitrate is commonly used in fertilizers. When mixed with a substance such as fuel oil, ammonium nitrate can become a potent explosive. The infamous bombing of the Alfred P. Murrah Federal Building in Oklahoma City, Oklahoma, in 1995 was carried out with a car bomb made from a mixture of ammonium nitrate and a highly volatile racecar fuel known as nitromethane.

C4

C4, which is shorthand for Composition C-4, is part of a family of explosives known as **plastic explosives**. C4 is a composition of an explosive known as RDX, also called cyclonite, and some other binding ingredients. C4 is off-white in color and has the consistency of soft clay. It can be worked into whatever shape is desired. C4 is more powerful than TNT and quite stable. Supposedly, a bullet can be shot into a stick of C4 without causing it to detonate. To explode a stick of C4 requires a detonator. C4 is commonly used by military organizations and is widely used by terrorists and other bad guys as well.

Certain explosives such as C4 and TNT are stable enough that they need a detonator in order to explode. A detonator is a smaller explosive charge that is used to initiate the explosion of a larger explosive. Typical detonator explosive materials include mercury fulminate and diazodinitrophenol, also known as DDNP. The detonator charge is typically set off either electrically, where the detonator is attached to wires that are connected to a battery, or electronically.

Blast Damage

An explosion is a rapid release of energy. The energy of the explosion can be converted to light, heat, sound, and a **blast wave**. A blast wave is a region of highly compressed air or other gas that travels radially outwards from the point of explosion. The blast wave moves very quickly—well over 1000 km/hr. Behind the shock wave is a region of low pressure. Air rushes into this low-pressure region, causing a wind effect. The wind caused by an explosion can actually change direction. Initially the wind will be in the direction of the advancing shock wave. As the shock wave progresses, the wind can reverse direction depending on the relative pressures in front of and behind the shock.

The high pressures that exist in the blast wave are the primary cause of damage to buildings and other structures from an explosion. When a strong blast wave hits a building, the windows and possibly the exterior walls may be pushed inwards and break. Once the shock wave enters the interior of the building, it will press both upwards on the ceiling and possibly also downwards on the floors. The floors themselves may collapse because they have a large surface area for the pressure to act upon and are generally not designed to withstand the forces exerted by the blast wave. When modeling the effects that explosions have upon buildings, you should keep in mind this sequence of events.

The damage done to a structure is a function of the overpressure that exists in the shock wave. If you recall from Chapter 3, the force exerted on an object due to a pressure is equal to the pressure multiplied by the area on which the pressure acts. Table 13-1 shows the magnitude of overpressures, in N/m^2, that are typically required to cause certain types of structural damage.[1, 2] Keep in mind when looking at Table 13-1 that atmospheric pressure at sea level is 101,325 N/m^2.

Table 13-1. *Building and Structural Damage Levels Due to Blast Wave Overpressures*

Overpressure (N/m^2)	Damage Type
1000–1500	Window breakage
4000–5000	Minor structural damage to homes
10,000	Serious structural damage to homes
40,000	Collapse of wood-framed building
70,000	Probable destruction of all buildings

Any people inside a building subjected to a blast wave will suffer injuries in proportion to the damage done to the building. Shattered windows can cause lacerations to people behind them.

A wall or ceiling collapse will cause more serious injuries to anyone in the way of the falling debris. If a building collapses, most of the people inside the building will be killed.

Even if they are not struck by flying debris or crushed under a collapsing building, people can still be wounded by the effects of a blast wave. Without going into too many gory details, the most serious nondebris injuries caused by explosions involve the lungs, ears, eyeballs, and skull. As with structural damage, the severity of wounds to people from a blast wave is proportional to the strength of the blast wave. Table 13-2 lists typical overpressures required to cause certain types of injuries.[1, 3]

Table 13-2. *Personal Injury Levels Due to Blast Wave Overpressures*

Overpressure (N/m^2)	Injury Type
7000–14,000	Knocks a person over
35,000	Ruptured eardrums
100,000	Damaged lungs
240,000	Possibly fatal
340,000	50% fatalities
450,000	99% fatalities

It's interesting when comparing the values in Tables 13-1 and 13-2 that people are actually tougher than buildings when it comes to resisting blast wave overpressures. An overpressure of $40,000\ N/m^2$ will collapse a wood-framed building but will "only" knock down and rupture the eardrums of a person standing next to the building. Unless a person is standing fairly close to the point of explosion, the explosion itself won't kill him. Of course, shrapnel or other flying debris caused by the explosion might kill the person, a collapsing building may fall on him, and so on.

TNT Explosion Model

To compute the damage caused by a blast wave requires the estimation of the overpressures generated by the explosion. Earlier in this chapter you learned that TNT is a standard explosive against which other explosive types are compared. One reason that TNT is a standard is that a lot of experimental data is available on the overpressures that are generated by the explosion of a certain amount of TNT. Based on the experimental data, the **TNT explosion model** was derived, which determines the overpressures generated by a TNT explosion.

The overpressure level of a TNT explosion blast wave is a function of the distance from the point of explosion and the amount of TNT that is used. The TNT experimental data showed that TNT overpressure levels could be characterized by a **scaled distance**, Z, that is the ratio of the distance from the point of explosion divided by the cube root of the mass of TNT.

$$Z = \frac{d}{\sqrt[3]{m}} \qquad \frac{m}{kg^{1/3}}$$

(13.1)

The TNT explosion model states that an object will experience the same overpressure from different explosions if the object is at the same scaled distance from the explosions. For example, a person standing 10 m away from a 1000 kg TNT explosion will experience the same overpressure, and therefore the same blast damage, as he would if he were standing 1 m away from a 1 kg TNT explosion because the scaled distances for both situations are the same.

The overpressure for a given scaled distance, Z, can be estimated from Equation (13.2). The quantity p_0 is the overpressure value and p_a is the atmospheric pressure, which has a sea-level value of 101,325 N/m^2. There are three separate square root factors on the bottom of the right-hand side of Equation (13.2).

$$\frac{p_0}{p_a} = \frac{808\left[1+\left(\dfrac{Z}{4.5}\right)^2\right]}{\sqrt{1+\left(\dfrac{Z}{0.048}\right)^2}\ \sqrt{1+\left(\dfrac{Z}{0.32}\right)^2}\ \sqrt{1+\left(\dfrac{Z}{1.35}\right)^2}} \tag{13.2}$$

Figure 13-2 displays the overpressure as a function of scaled distance for a TNT explosion. In comparing the results of Figure 13-2 with the damage values from Tables 13-1 and 13-2, window breakage will occur when the scaled distance, Z, is equal to approximately 70. A wood-frame building will collapse at a scaled distance of about 4.2. A person will be knocked over at a scaled distance of about 10 and will be killed with a 99% probability if the scaled distance is 1.4.

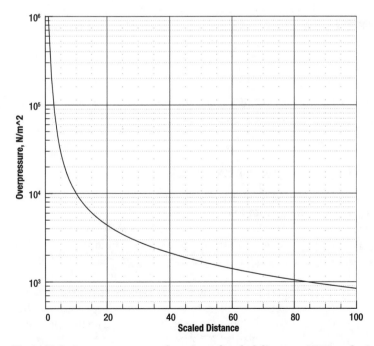

Figure 13-2. *Overpressure as a function of scaled distance, TNT explosion*

To summarize, the estimate of the damage to a structure or person from a blast of TNT is a three-step process:

CHAPTER 13 ■ EXPLOSIONS

1. Compute the scaled distance based on the distance from the target to the point of explosion and the amount of TNT that is exploding using Equation (13.1).

2. Use the scaled distance value to calculate the overpressure for the shock wave from Equation (13.2).

3. Use the computed overpressure value to estimate the damage inflicted on the structure or person from the information in Tables 13-1 and 13-2.

Example: Computing the Blast Damage for a Soldier Standing by a Window

Let's go through the process of a TNT blast damage calculation. A 5 *kg* charge of TNT is detonated 8 *m* from a soldier who is standing next to a wood-framed building with glass windows. What will happen to the soldier and building when the TNT explodes? The first step in the process is to determine the scaled distance for the explosion based on Equation (13.1)

$$Z = \frac{8}{\sqrt[3]{5}} = 4.68 \tag{13.3}$$

Using the scaled distance value in Equation (13.3), the overpressure experienced by the soldier and building can be determined from Equation (13.2).

$$p_0 = 101325 \frac{808\left(1 + \left(\frac{4.68}{4.5}\right)^2\right)}{\sqrt{1 + \left(\frac{4.68}{0.048}\right)^2} \sqrt{1 + \left(\frac{4.68}{0.32}\right)^2} \sqrt{1 + \left(\frac{4.68}{1.35}\right)^2}} = 33046 \ N/m^2 \tag{13.4}$$

Based on Tables 13-1 and 13-2, the soldier will be knocked down and his eardrums will be close to rupturing. The windows of the building will shatter and the building will suffer significant structural damage but probably won't collapse entirely.

Blast Damage from Other Types of Explosives

The TNT explosion model, as the name would suggest, is designed to compute the overpressures due to a TNT explosion. But how would one compute the overpressure from other types of explosives? As you might guess, many different models have been developed over the years to compute overpressure for other types of explosives. One of the simplest and most widely used models, and the one we will discuss in this chapter, is called the **TNT equivalence model**.

The TNT equivalence model is based on converting the explosive being considered to an equivalent mass of TNT by equating the energy released by the two explosives. The **equivalent mass** of a given explosive, $m_{equiv,TNT}$, is equal to the mass of the explosive, m_{ex}, multiplied by its specific combustion energy, ΔH_{ex}, and an efficiency factor, η, and divided by the specific combustion energy of TNT, ΔH_{TNT}.

$$m_{equiv,TNT} = \frac{m_{ex} \Delta H_{ex} \eta}{\Delta H_{TNT}} \tag{13.5}$$

The efficiency factor accounts for the fact that for many explosives only some fraction of the total specific combustion energy is converted into explosive energy.

Once the equivalent TNT mass for the given explosive is computed, the scaled distance and overpressure for the explosion can be determined from Equations (13.1) and (13.2) just as was done when TNT was the explosive. Sometimes the specific combustion energies and efficiency factor are combined into a single TNT equivalence factor, η_{equiv}.

$$\eta_{equiv} = \frac{\Delta H_{ex}\eta}{\Delta H_{TNT}} \tag{13.6}$$

Using Equation (13.6), the equivalent TNT mass for a given explosive can be written in terms of the mass of the explosive and its TNT equivalence factor.

$$m_{equiv,TNT} = m_{ex}\eta_{equiv} \tag{13.7}$$

Table 13-3 shows the equivalence factors for a number of different explosives.[2, 4, 5] TNT is the standard, of course, so its TNT equivalence factor is 1. C4 is 18% more powerful than TNT. Ammonium nitrate in its pure form is a fairly weak explosive. When combined with fuel oil, however, it gains an explosive power nearly equal to TNT.

Table 13-3. *Explosive-Specific Combustion Energies and Equivalence Factors*

Explosive	TNT Equivalence factor
TNT	1.0
C4	1.18
Ammonium nitrate	0.1–0.2
Ammonium nitrate with fuel oil	0.8
Natural gas	0.16

Other Explosion Models

As you might guess, the TNT equivalency model is not the only one available to model the effects of explosions. Other explosion models include the TNO, Multi-Energy, and Baker-Strehlow models. Details of these alternative explosion models won't be discussed in this chapter, but more details about these models can be found in the document "A Comparison of Vapor Cloud Explosion Models" (see the "References" section at the end of this chapter for details). The alternative models are available to use as options if the TNT equivalency model doesn't work for your particular game application.

TNT Equivalence of Bombs

It was mentioned before that TNT is used as a standard explosive against which other explosives are compared. The damage caused by a explosion can be enhanced if the explosive material is encased in another object. Terrorists frequently use car, briefcase, or pipe bombs to devastating effects. Typical TNT equivalence values in *kg* for various types of bombs[1] are shown in Table 13-4.

Table 13-4. *TNT Equivalence of Various Bomb Types*

Bomb Type	TNT Equivalent Explosive Mass (*kg*)
Car bomb	225–1800
Briefcase bomb	20–25
Pipe bomb	2

In addition to damage caused by the explosion itself, one of the main reasons to encase explosive material inside an object is to cause metal fragments to fly outward from the point of explosion. We'll discuss the effects of fragmentation next.

Fragmentation Devices

A fragmentation device consists of an explosive material that is encased in a shell typically made out of metal. A hand grenade is an example of a small fragmentation device. When the charge inside a fragmentation device explodes, the pressure quickly builds up inside the casing, causing it to burst. Fragments of the casing fly out in all directions like thousands of irregularly shaped bullets. Fragmentation weapons generally have a greater lethal range than standard explosive devices because the energy of the fragments dissipates more slowly than the energy of a blast wave.

The fragments from a fragmentation device are projectiles. The damage they inflict on impact and the distance they will travel are functions of their initial kinetic energy. The theoretical initial velocity of the fragments is a function of the nature of the explosive charge and the configuration of the fragmentation device.

$$v^2 = 2\Delta E \frac{m_c / m_e}{1 + K\left(m_c / m_e\right)} \tag{13.8}$$

In Equation (13.8), the quantity ΔE is the heat of explosion of the explosive charge. For TNT, the value would be $2.175e + 6\,J/kg$. The quantities m_e and m_c are the mass of the explosive charge and the mass of the fragmenting casing, respectively. The ratio m_c / m_e is also known as the **charge-to-metal** ratio. The quantity K is a geometrical constant. Values for K are shown in Table 13-5. Fragmentation devices are usually approximated by one of the three shapes shown in Table 13-5. A land mine, for example, would be modeled as a flat plate, a bomb as a cylinder, and a hand grenade as a sphere.

Table 13-5. *Fragmentation Device Geometrical Constants*

Shape	K
Flat plate	1/3
Cylinder	1/2
Sphere	3/5

As an example, let's use Equation (13.8) to compute the initial velocity of the fragments from an M-61 hand grenade. The M-61 uses 0.185 kg of an explosive material known as Comp-B for its explosive charge. Comp-B has a heat of explosion of $4.04e + 6 \ J/kg$. The mass of the metal casing is 0.210 kg. Using the spherical constant shown in Table 13-5, the initial velocity of the fragments is as follows:

$$v^2 = 2*4.04e+6\frac{0.185/0.21}{1+0.6\left(0.185/0.21\right)} = 4.656e+6 \quad \frac{m^2}{s^2} \tag{13.9}$$

$$v = 2158\frac{m}{s} \tag{13.10}$$

Once the initial velocity of the fragments is known, they can be treated like any other projectile. The forces of aerodynamic drag and gravity will slow down the fragments and cause them to eventually hit the ground. If a fragment hits an object, the penetration through the object can be modeled according to the relations that were discussed in Chapter 12.

To determine whether a fragment hits a target, several assumptions can be made. The blast wave can be assumed to be spherical. The distribution of fragments can be assumed to be spherical as well. The surface area of a sphere is proportional to the square of the sphere radius.

$$A = 4\pi r^2 \tag{13.11}$$

If the fragments are evenly distributed around the sphere, the number of fragments per unit area, n, is equal to the total number of fragments, N, divided by the surface area of the sphere.

$$n = \frac{N}{4\pi r^2} \tag{13.12}$$

Equation (13.12) can be used to determine the number of fragments that will strike a given target. Once the distance from the target to the point of explosion is determined, the number of fragments per unit area can be determined from Equation (13.12). Multiplying this value by the frontal area of the target gives the number of fragments that strike the target. This approach works best if the target is relatively close to the fragmentation device. Gravity will pull the fragments towards the earth, and this effect will become more pronounced the longer the fragments have been flying.

Nuclear Explosions

Unlike chemical explosions that are caused by chemical reactions and the sudden release of chemical energy, a nuclear explosion is caused by the splitting or forced combination of atoms. Nuclear explosions can be extremely powerful. The blast wave can damage structures and people miles away from the point of explosion. The winds following the blast wave can have speeds of several hundred km/hr. It is the combination of the blast wave and the wind effects that cause most of the damage from a nuclear explosion. Nuclear explosions also generate size-able amounts of harmful radiation.

Nuclear weapons, or nukes, can be designed to explode in the atmosphere, on the ground, under the ground, or underwater. A nuke that is exploded on the ground or underwater throws a lot of dirt, water, and other debris into the air into a mushroom-shaped cloud. A typical mushroom cloud is shown in Figure 13-3.

Figure 13-3. *A typical nuclear explosion mushroom cloud (Photo courtesy of U.S. Department of Energy)*

Nuclear weapons are almost always characterized in terms of the equivalent amount of TNT. When a reference is made to a nuclear weapon with a yield of 1 megaton, this means a weapon with an explosive energy equal to one million tons of TNT. For game programming purposes, the TNT equivalence equations developed earlier in this chapter can be applied to nuclear explosions as well.

Nuclear explosions generate a significant amount of heat. Approximately 35% of the energy released from a nuclear explosion is converted to thermal energy. The fireball from a 10-kiloton nuclear weapon can be 300 m in diameter. The thermal radiation from a 10-kiloton nuclear weapon can cause second-degree burns, called flash burns, on exposed skin at a distance of 2.4 km from the point of explosion. A 10-megaton bomb, 1000 times more powerful than the 10 kiloton bomb, can cause second-degree burns up to 32 km away.

Summary

In this chapter, you learned a little bit about how to model explosions. Starting with some basic terminology and concepts, we explored different types of explosives and how to model the damage from an explosion. Some of the specific things covered in this chapter include the following:

- The force vector due to an explosion and how to properly model it

- How TNT is used as a standard explosive and how other explosives compare to TNT

- How blast damage can be estimated using the TNT explosion model

- That the TNT explosion model can be applied to other explosive types using the concept of an equivalent mass of TNT

- How to compute the initial velocity of fragments from the explosion of a fragmentation device and how to estimate the number of fragments that will hit a target

- An introduction to the special features of a nuclear explosion

References

1. "Primer to Design Safe School Projects in Case of Terrorist Attacks," Federal Emergency Management Agency publication 428, www.fema.gov/pdf/fima/428/fema428.pdf.

2. R. J. A. Kersten and Mak, W. A., "Explosion Hazards of Ammonium Nitrate, How to Assess the Risks?" International Symposium on Safety in the Manufacture, Storage, Use, Transport, and Disposal of Hazardous Materials, March 2004.

3. "A Comparison of Vapor Cloud Explosion Models," *The Quest Quarterly*, Vol. 4, No. 1, Spring 1999, www.questconsult.com/99-spring.pdf.

4. G. F. Kinney and Graham, K. J., *Explosive Shocks in Air, Second Edition*, Springer-Verlag, New York, 1985.

5. Ribbands Explosives, www.ribbands.co.uk/prdpages/C4.htm.

6. Federation of American Scientists, "Introduction to Naval Weapons Engineering," www.fas.org/man/dod-101/navy/docs/es310/warheads/Warheads.htm.

CHAPTER 14

■■■

Lasers

Lasers, highly focused beams of energy, have been a standard in movies and games for many years. The word "laser" is an acronym that stands for Light Amplification by Stimulated Emission of Radiation. Don't worry what "Stimulated Emission" means right now. We'll go over that later in this chapter. One of the reasons that lasers can be powerful is that they concentrate light or other types of radiation into a narrow, concentrated beam. A laser beam can burn through the skin of an airplane, disable electronic devices, blind enemy soldiers, and lots of other things besides.

In this chapter, we'll talk about the theory of lasers, different types of lasers, and how you can incorporate them into your games. Specific topics covered in this chapter include the following:

- A brief history of lasers

- An introduction to atoms

- How lasers work

- Types of lasers

- Military lasers

- Computing laser damage

- Creating your own laser systems

- Laser visual effects

Let's start our discussion with a brief history of how lasers came to be.

A Brief History of the Laser

Although he never built one, Albert Einstein can be considered the father of the laser because in 1917 he came up with the theoretical framework that made the development of the laser possible. Einstein and an Indian physicist named S. N. Bose came up with the idea that light could be described as discrete particles called **photons**, and that these photons behaved in a certain way that made stimulated emission, the "S" and "E" in laser, possible.

Tidbit While Einstein is best known for his theories of relativity, he did not win the Nobel Prize for that work because it was considered too speculative at the time (the fact that Einstein was a complete unknown when he came up with relativity probably didn't help either). Einstein won the Nobel Prize in physics in 1922 for explaining a concept called the photoelectric effect.

In 1954, Charles Townes and other researchers at Columbia University used Einstein's theoretical groundwork to develop a device that generated a focused, concentrated beam of microwave energy. He called it a **maser**, which stood for Microwave Amplification by Stimulated Emission of Radiation. Critics ridiculed his device as an expensive waste of time, but Townes got the last laugh when he won the 1964 Nobel Prize in physics for his work on microwave lasers.

In 1958, Townes and another researcher named Arthur Schawlow wrote a paper on how the maser concept could be extended to create a machine that would generate a focused, concentrated beam of visible light, and the idea of the laser was born. Similar to the Space Race, Townes's and Schawlow's work set off a laser race to see who could build the first working laser. Theodore Maiman at Hughes Research Laboratories won the race in 1960 by creating a laser out of a synthetic ruby crystal that generated a red beam of light. Later that year, an Iranian physicist named Ali Javan invented the first gas laser.

Laser development has continued ever since 1960, and there are now many types of lasers and countless uses for them. Lasers are also cool things to add to your space battle or futuristic combat games. Now that you know a little bit about the history of lasers, let's turn our attention to a brief discussion of how lasers work. Before we can do that, however, we need to back up and talk a little bit about atoms.

An Introduction to Atoms

As you probably know, everything around you—your computer, yourself, your front lawn—is made up of tiny particles called **atoms**. As depicted in Figure 14-1, an atom is itself made up of particles called **protons** and **neutrons** that are clustered together in what is called the **nucleus** of the atom. The nucleus is surrounded by a cloud of particles called **electrons** that travel about the nucleus in different orbits.

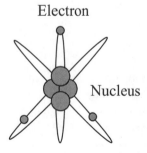

Figure 14-1. *A schematic of a typical atom*

Electrons have a negative electric charge. Protons have a positive electric charge. Because of the charge difference, there is an electrostatic force that pulls the electrons towards the nucleus. Balancing the electrostatic force is the centripetal force of the electrons as they travel around the nucleus. The radius of the electron orbit is determined by the energy stored by the electron, also known as the **energy level** of the electron. The orbits of electrons at lower energy levels will be closer to the nucleus. This description is a fairly simplified view of the structure of an atom, but it is useful to make the connection between electron energy levels and the corresponding electron orbit.

When an atom absorbs energy, whether it's from heat, light, electricity, or some other energy source, some of the electrons in lower energy states will transition into higher energy states and will acquire new orbits further away from the nucleus. These higher energy levels are known as **excited energy states**. It turns out that electrons can't be at just any old energy level. Instead, electrons can only exist at discrete energy levels. Another way to think about this situation is that electrons can only travel in certain discrete orbits around the nucleus.

As an example, Figure 14-2 shows the energy levels available to the electrons in a hydrogen atom. In Figure 14-2 the electron energy levels are represented as a column of horizontal lines. Electron energy levels are usually expressed in terms of electron volts, or eV, which is a very small amount of energy. One eV is equal to $1.602e-19\ J$. The lowest energy state is referred to as the **ground state**. The excited energy levels are expressed relative to the ground state.

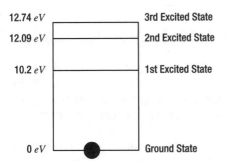

Figure 14-2. *Energy levels for hydrogen atom electrons*

Atomic hydrogen has three excited energy states. If a hydrogen atom absorbs 10.2 eV of energy, as shown in Figure 14-3, then one of its electrons can transition from the ground energy state to the first excited energy state. If the atom absorbed 12.09 eV, then an electron could transition from the ground state to the second excited energy state. Electrons can also move from one excited energy state to a higher one.

Just as electrons can transition from a lower energy state to a higher energy state, they can go the other way as well. In fact, excited electrons will naturally tend to return to lower energy states. In order for an electron to move to a lower energy state, it must release some of its energy as a **photon**—a particle of light. The amount of energy released, and the energy of the resulting photon, is equal to the energy difference between the two states. In Figure 14-4, a hydrogen atom electron is transitioning from the first excited state to the ground state. In order to do this, the electron emits a photon with an energy level of 10.2 eV.

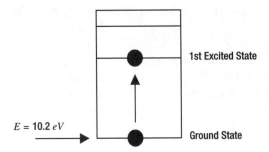

Figure 14-3. *When an atom absorbs energy, one of its electrons can move to a higher energy state.*

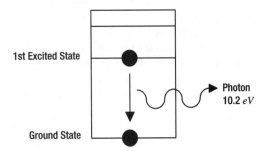

Figure 14-4. *When an electron transitions to a lower energy state, it emits a photon.*

Other energy level transitions would be possible with the hydrogen atom. If an electron transitioned from the third excited energy state to the second, a photon would be released with an energy level of 0.65 *eV*. You have seen the effect of electron energy level transitions many times. An incandescent light bulb works because the atoms in the metal filament are transitioning energy states and giving off photons.

Photons move about at the speed of light. The motion of a photon follows a wavelike pattern. As shown in Figure 14-5, every photon will have a **wavelength** associated with it that is the distance between successive peaks of the wave pattern of the photon.

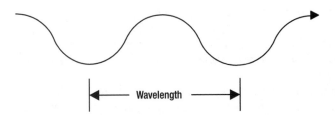

Figure 14-5. *Every photon will have a wavelength.*

The wavelength, λ, of a photon is related to the amount of energy, E, the photon is given when it is generated.

$$E = \frac{hc}{\lambda} \tag{14.1}$$

In Equation (14.1), c is the speed of light with a value of 3.0e + 8 *m/s* and h is the Planck constant, which has a value of 6.626e − 34 *J-s*. Let's use Equation (14.1) to determine the wavelength of a photon emitted by a hydrogen atom electron transitioning from the first excited state to the ground state. The energy of the photon is equal to the difference in energies between the two energy levels.

$$E = 10.2\,eV = 1.634e - 18\,J \tag{14.2}$$

The wavelength of the photon can now be determined from Equation (14.1).

$$\lambda = \frac{6.626e - 34 * 3.0e + 8}{1.634e - 18} = 1.216e - 7 \; m \tag{14.3}$$

Wavelengths are usually expressed in terms of nanometers, or *nm*, where 1 *nm* = 1.0e − 9 *m*. In the preceding example, the photon would have a wavelength of 121.6 *nm*.

Getting back to photon emission, the light given off by a "normal" object such as a flashlight is somewhat chaotic. The atoms of the filament of the flashlight bulb are transitioning from various excited energy states to various other states, producing photons of different energy levels and wavelengths. The flashlight emits light in all directions, and the strength of the light dissipates very quickly. The key element of a laser is its ability to "organize" the emitted photons into what is known as **coherent** light.

How Lasers Work

A laser is a device that controls the way photons are released from excited atoms. There are many different types of lasers, but the basic process is similar between them. Every laser will have some material, which can be gaseous, liquid, or solid, that serves as the lasing medium. Energy is added to the lasing medium in a process known as **pumping** the laser. Laser pumping is typically done with intense flashes of light or electrical discharges. The energy added to the lasing medium causes a large number of electrons inside the lasing medium to reach one of the excited energy states. When the electrons transition back to the ground energy state, they release the energy as a photon with a certain wavelength. Every photon that is created due to a transition from the same excited energy state will have the same wavelength.

Now we come to the "stimulated emission" part of lasers. When a photon caused by a transition from an excited energy state strikes another atom with an electron at the same energy state, as shown in Figure 14-6, the photon won't be absorbed by the atom but instead will cause or stimulate the atom to emit a photon that is identical to the first. The second photon will have the same energy and wavelength as the first photon and will travel in exactly the same direction. If one of the two photons strikes another atom at the same excited energy state, a third identical photon is created, and the process can continue over and over again.

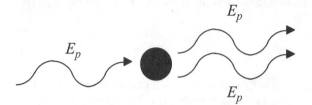

Figure 14-6. *Inside a laser, photon emissions can stimulate additional photon emissions.*

The energy of the emitted photons will depend on the difference in energy between the upper and lower energy states that the electron transitions. The energy levels themselves will depend on the material that makes up the lasing medium. Different lasing mediums will generate photons of different energy levels and wavelengths.

To generate a laser beam, two mirrors are placed on either end of the lasing medium. The laser is then pumped to create a large number of atoms in one of the excited energy states. When the atoms begin to transition from their excited state, the photons bounce back and forth between the mirrors, causing more and more of the atoms in the same excited state to transition and generate photons. One of the mirrors is only partially reflective, allowing some of the laser light to pass through.

Figure 14-7 shows a typical helium-neon laser. The laser is pumped using an electrical discharge inside the brightly glowing tube. The laser beam is the thin beam emanating from the left end of the device. Normally the laser beam itself would not be visible unless there were dust, mist, or some other particles in the air to reflect the light.

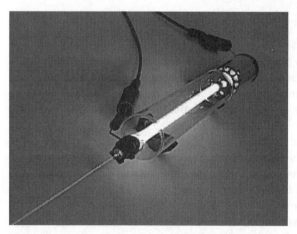

Figure 14-7. *A typical helium-neon laser (Photo courtesy of Meredith Instruments, www.mi-lasers.com)*

The light generated by a laser is very different from normal light. For one thing, laser light is monochromatic (one color) because the photons are emitted by atoms at the same energy state and therefore have the same wavelength. Rather than the chaotic light produced by a flashlight, laser light is coherent, meaning that the photons travel together in a narrow beam. Laser light is very directional and dissipates slowly. A laser beam can illuminate an object many miles away. Another characteristic of lasers is that many of them generate other forms of radiation than visible light, including **microwave** and **infrared** radiation.

Types of Lasers

A laser requires a lasing medium in which atoms can be excited to a higher energy state. Many different substances meet this requirement, and there are therefore lots of different types of lasers. As discussed, the lasing medium can be gaseous, liquid, or solid. In this section, we will see some general types of lasers and discuss some of the applications for each one.

Lasers are also characterized by the wavelength of the radiation that they emit. Some lasers will generate visible light and others will generate invisible forms of radiation such as microwave or infrared radiation. The range of possible laser wavelengths is part of what is known as the **electromagnetic spectrum** that divides all of the possible wavelengths into different regions. Table 14-1 displays the wavelength for the types of radiation that lasers can emit.

Table 14-1. *Laser Radiation Wavelengths*

Radiation Type	Wavelength (*nm*)
Ultraviolet	$1 - 400$
Visible light	$400 - 700$
Infrared	$700 - 1.0e + 5$
Microwave	$1.0e + 5 - 1.0e + 8$

Gas Lasers

Gas lasers use a tube filled with gas as the lasing medium. Typical gases used in gas lasers are helium, helium and neon, and carbon dioxide (CO_2). CO_2 lasers emit light in the infrared and microwave part of the electromagnetic spectrum. Infrared radiation is essentially heat, and powerful CO_2 lasers can melt through steel. Another type of gas laser known as an **excimer laser** uses a mixture of a volatile gas such as chlorine or fluorine with an inert gas such as argon, krypton, or xenon. Table 14-2 shows the wavelength and type of radiation emitted by various types of gas lasers.[1, 2]

Table 14-2. *Gas Laser Radiation Types*

Lasing Gas	Wavelength (*nm*)	Radiation Type
Argon-fluoride	193	Ultraviolet
Krypton-fluoride	248	Ultraviolet
Nitrogen	337	Ultraviolet
Argon	488 – 514	Blue or green light
Helium neon	543 – 633	Green or red light
Carbon dioxide	10,600	Infrared
Carbon monoxide	5000	Infrared
Oxygen-iodine	1315	Infrared

Typical uses for gas lasers include industrial drilling and cutting applications. Because of their potential to generate high power output levels, many lasers used for military applications are gas lasers.

Dye Lasers

Dye lasers use an organic dye in a liquid solution as the lasing material. Depending on the dye used, dye lasers can emit light over a broad range of wavelengths. An example of a dye laser is a Rhodamine 6G dye laser that can emit light in the wavelength range of 570–650 nanometers, which corresponds to green, yellow, or orange light.

Solid-State Lasers

Solid-state lasers employ a solid material as the lasing material. The solid material is generally a solid rod or slab of crystal imbedded with a small amount of an impurity, called doping, to facilitate the lasing action. The world's first working laser consisted of a synthetic ruby crystal that had been augmented, or **doped**, with chromium ions. The ruby laser was pumped with a xenon-filled flashtube similar to a camera flash bulb. A ruby solid-state laser emits red light with a wavelength of 694 nanometers. Another common solid-state laser is the neodymium-Yag laser that emits an infrared beam with a wavelength of 1064 nanometers.

Semiconductor Lasers

Semiconductor lasers, also called diode lasers, are electronic devices that are generally small and have low power requirements. Semiconductor lasers are used in laser printers, CD players, and DVD players. Diode lasers typically emit a red beam with a wavelength ranging from 630–680 nanometers.

Pulsed and Continuous Wave Lasers

Another fundamental distinction between lasers is whether the beam they produce is continuous or is generated as a series of short pulses. A pulse laser generates a beam for very short periods of time, usually tiny fractions of a second. The peak power, energy divided by pulse duration, generated by pulse lasers can be very high, but the average power, energy delivered per second, is usually quite low because the pulse times are small. Pulse lasers are used for such applications as nuclear or plasma (high-temperature gas) research.

Continuous wave or CW lasers generate a steady beam of light or other radiation for periods of time that generally exceed one second. A laser pointer is a typical example of a low-power CW laser. CW lasers generally have lower peak power than pulse lasers but have a relatively high average power. There is a wide range of uses for CW lasers from surgical operations to home electronics to research facilities. Military lasers, those used to shoot down missiles and airplanes or intended to strike ground targets, are typically CW lasers.

Military Lasers

Unless you are creating a "research laboratory" simulation, most of the time when you include lasers in your game simulations they will be used in combat situations. Lasers used in combat, generally classified as **military lasers** or **high-energy lasers** (HEL), aren't in the realm of science fiction. There have been military research programs for decades in many different countries to develop viable military lasers that will shoot down airplanes or missiles, disable sensors and electronic devices, burn through metal, and blind or kill people.

Military lasers are generally CW lasers. The damage done by a laser is proportional to the energy delivered to the target, and CW lasers generate a higher average power level than do pulse lasers. Existing or proposed military lasers are also very large and are generally housed inside an orbiting satellite, on board an aircraft or ship, or inside a ground facility. Currently, no high-energy lasers exist that are small enough or light enough to be carried by a person, partly because of the enormous power requirements of these weapons. Another big issue with powerful military lasers is that they generate an enormous amount of heat when they operate, and this heat must be dissipated somehow to allow continued operation of the laser.

There are a large number of previous or existing military laser programs. In the next subsections, we'll discuss details of three military laser research programs to give you a flavor of the military laser systems that are in the planning phase today. None of these systems have been successfully built, although all three of them have undergone development testing, and full or half-scale prototypes for the first two are anticipated within a few years.

ABL

The Airborne Laser, or ABL, is designed to be carried aboard an aircraft such as a Boeing 747. Its mission is to destroy intercontinental ballistic missiles (ICBMs) during the ascent portion of their flight.[3] The ABL uses a chemical oxygen-iodine (COIL) gas laser for the destructive laser beam and several smaller lasers for targeting and acquisition. The ABL system takes up most of the interior space inside the 747 aircraft. The laser beam is sent through a pipe to the forward part of the airplane where it is aimed towards its target using very fast, lightweight steering mirrors.

The average power of the laser will be in the 1 megawatt (*MW*) range. A megawatt is equal to 1.0*e* + 6 *W*. Complete technical details for the ABL system are unavailable to the public, but some of the ABL specifications are shown in Table 14-3. The system mass is for the laser alone and (obviously) does not include the mass of the airplane.

Table 14-3. *ABL Specifications*

Quantity	Value
Laser type	Oxygen-iodine chemical gas
Wavelength	1315 nanometers (infrared)
Average power	1 *MW*
Range	200–400 *km*
Beam diameter at target	0.38 *m*
System mass	8200 *kg*

SBL

The Space Based Laser, or SBL, is a U.S. Air Force project to develop a space-based high-energy laser system capable of shooting down ICBMs during their flight.[4] The SBL system is quite large. It is housed inside a 40 *m* long satellite with a diameter of 4.57 *m*. The laser beam is focused using an 8.0 *m* diameter mirror.

The SBL uses a deuterium-fluoride chemical gas laser that emits infrared radiation. The average power of the laser varies between 5 and 10 *MW* with an impressive effective range of 4000 *km*. A half-scale test model of the SBL is scheduled for testing in 2010. Some of the vital statistics for the SBL are shown in Table 14-4.

Table 14-4. *SBL Specifications*

Quantity	Value
Laser type	Deuterium-fluoride chemical gas
Wavelength	2700 nanometers (infrared)
Average power	5–10 *MW*
Range	4000 *km*
Beam diameter at target	0.3–1.0 *m*
Beam duration	10 *s*
System mass	35,000 *kg*

HELEX

The goal of the High Energy Laser Experimental (HELEX) program being studied in Germany is to develop a multimegawatt laser-based missile and antiaircraft defense system.[5] The HELEX system uses a CO_2 laser that is mounted on top of a tracked armored vehicle such as a Leopard 2 tank. The HELEX laser beam is directed to its target by way of a system of mirrors and an adjustable scaffolding. The vehicle is designed to carry enough fuel to fire 40–50 laser shots.

Some of the technical specifications for the HELEX air defense system are shown in Table 14-5. The HELEX system has a much shorter effective range than either the ABL or SBL systems, and is the least exotic of the three systems presented in this section. The CO_2 for the laser is created by burning two common compounds—benzene and nitrous oxide.

Table 14-5. *HELEX Specifications*

Quantity	Value
Laser type	CO_2 chemical gas
Wavelength	9350 or 10,600 nanometers (infrared)
Average power	2–3 *MW*
Range	5–10 *km*
System mass	18,000–36,000 *kg* (including vehicle mass)

Laser Damage

Now that we have talked at some length about the theory of lasers and discussed details of some current or proposed laser systems, it's time to talk about ways to estimate the damage caused by military lasers. Military lasers are used primarily to burn through things and to disable electronic devices. In both instances, the damage inflicted on the target is a function of the amount of laser energy that is absorbed by the target. The absorbed energy is equal to some fraction of the power density of the beam, I, multiplied by the duration of the contact of the beam with the target, t.

$$E = \alpha I t \tag{14.4}$$

In Equation (14.4), the α term is an absorption factor to account for the fact that the target won't absorb all of the energy in the laser beam. The nominal beam energy will be decreased due to transmission losses in the optical system and the atmosphere. Part of the laser energy that strikes the target will be reflected off of the target surface. The amount of reflection is a function of the target material, the surface finish of the target, and the wavelength of the laser beam.

Highly reflective materials, as you might expect, reduce the absorption factor. The absorption factor for a ruby laser beam with a wavelength of 694 nanometers is 0.11 for aluminum, 0.35 for light-colored human skin, and 0.2 for white paint. Higher-wavelength laser beams tend to have higher absorption factors. The absorption factor for a CO_2 laser beam with a wavelength of 10,600 nanometers is 0.95 for light-colored human skin.

The power density, I, is typically expressed in units of W/cm^2 and is equal to the power of the laser beam, P, in W divided by the area of the beam, A, that strikes the target. The absorbed energy can be expressed in terms of the beam power and area.

$$E = \alpha \frac{Pt}{A}$$ (14.5)

The energy absorbed by the target in Equations (14.4) and (14.5) is really the energy absorbed per unit area and typically has units of J/cm^2. The use of cm rather than m in these expressions is a standard convention. In looking at Equation (14.5), you might wonder, since there is a time factor in the equation, whether any laser could meet the required energy density if it was focused on the target for a long enough time. The problem with this line of thinking is that the energy applied to the target by the laser will dissipate fairly quickly. It will radiate back into the air, be conducted throughout the target material, or be removed by convection. In order to melt through a material, the energy from the laser must be absorbed in a short enough period of time to overwhelm the dissipative mechanisms. So a 1 MW laser applied for 0.1 seconds is not the same as a 1 W laser applied for 100,000 seconds.

There are a lot of ways that a military laser can damage a target, and you can have some "fun" when modeling the effects. A laser beam could melt through a fuel tank, causing it to explode. It could similarly cause bombs or other munitions stored on board a tank, airplane, or helicopter to explode. The beam could blind the pilot of an aircraft or disable the plane's electronic systems, causing the aircraft to career off into a hillside. A laser could conceivably cause a soldier's uniform to catch on fire. These are just some of the examples of what a laser could do in a combat situation, but there are many more possibilities that you can build into your simulations.

Because the energy absorbed by a target is influenced by several variables (laser wavelength, surface material, surface finish), determining the amount of energy required to disable or destroy a given target is really a case-by-case situation. However, Table 14-6 provides some general energy-level damage guidelines that you can use in your game simulations.[6] The energy level required to penetrate the steel armor of a tank would be considerably in excess of 10,000 J/cm^2, and there are no lasers in operation today that can meet that energy delivery requirement.

Table 14-6. *Laser Beam Damage Energy Levels*

Damage Type	Required Energy Level, (J/cm^2)
Damage eye cornea.	1
Disable optical sensors.	10
Burn exposed skin.	15
Penetrate airplane metal skin.	700
Shoot down airplane or helicopter.	5000–10,000
Destroy missile.	10,000

Let's go through the process of determining how long it will take the Space Based Laser to destroy an enemy missile. The average power of the laser will be assumed to be 7.5 *MW*, and the diameter of the beam when it strikes the target will be assumed to be 70 *cm*. If the energy density required to destroy the missile is 10000 *J*/*cm*² and the absorption factor of the laser is assumed to be 0.75, the beam duration time to destroy the missile can be calculated from a rearranged version of Equation (14.5).

$$t = \frac{EA}{\alpha P} = \frac{10000 * \pi (35)^2}{0.75 * 7.5e + 6} = 6.84 \ s \qquad (14.6)$$

There are some other issues to keep in mind when modeling a laser attack upon a target. Because the energy absorbed by a target due to a laser beam is a function of the power of the beam multiplied by the duration of the beam, the beam must be held fixed on a particular spot on the target for the required amount of time. If the target is moving, the laser will have to track and adjust to the movement of the target during its flight.

Unlike projectiles, laser beams are not affected by gravity, aerodynamic drag, or wind. A laser beam will travel in a straight line from laser to target. The diameter of the beam will increase very slowly, but the effect is so gradual that you can usually ignore it for game programming purposes. The only other thing that will affect a beam as it travels from laser to target is whether it travels through dust, smoke, mist, or fog, in which case some of the light will be reflected away and the beam will lose some of its power.

Laser Simulation

Let's use the results from the previous section to create a simple laser air-defense simulation. A typical screen shot for the Laser Simulation is shown in Figure 14-8. The laser is housed in a square block on the ground. The user has the ability to specify the beam power, beam radius, and absorption coefficient of the target. The mouse controls the target point of the beam. If the mouse is clicked or if the cursor is dragged across the display window, the target point of the laser is moved to that point. The Start button starts the airplane flying across the screen and the Reset button redraws the GUI.

The airplane is destroyed if the user can keep the laser beam in contact with the airplane until the plane absorbs 10,000 *J*/*cm*² worth of energy. The time required for this energy absorption level is determined by Equation (14.6). The simulation is implemented in a class called LaserSimulator. The entire code listing won't be discussed, but we will talk about the three methods that are used to control the action.

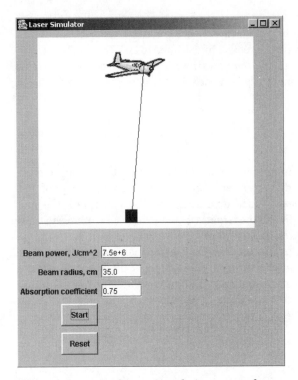

Figure 14-8. *A typical Laser Simulation screen shot*

When the Start button is clicked, the actionPerformed method declared in the LaserSimulator class is called. The process followed by this version of the method is similar to that of the other sample games presented in this book. Values for the laser beam power, radius, and absorption coefficient of the airplane are extracted from the text inside the text fields. The time required for the plane to absorb 10,000 J/cm^2 is computed from Equation 14-6. The start method is called on a Timer object to start the airplane moving across the screen.

```
// The actionPerformed() method is called when
// the Start button is pressed.
public void actionPerformed(ActionEvent event) {

  // Get some initial quantities from the text fields.
  double power = Double.parseDouble(powerTextField.getText());
  double radius = Double.parseDouble(radiusTextField.getText());
  double absorption = Double.parseDouble(absorptionTextField.getText());

  // Determine the beam area.
  double area = Math.PI*radius*radius;

  // Compute beam contact time required to destroy airplane.
  explosionTime = 10000.0*area/(absorption*power);
```

```
  // Start the airplane using a Timer object.
  gameTimer.start();
}
```

The target point of the laser is stored in two fields named laserX and laserZ. Clicking or dragging the mouse to a new location on the screen changes the value of the laserX and laserZ fields. When the mouse is clicked or dragged, either the mouseClicked or mouseDragged method is called.

```
  // These methods are used to update the position of the
  // laser.
  public void mouseDragged(MouseEvent me) {
    laserX = me.getX();
    laserZ = me.getY();
  }

  public void mouseClicked(MouseEvent me) {
    laserX = me.getX();
    laserZ = me.getY();
  }
```

The LaserSimulator class declares an inner class named GameUpdater. Inside this class is an actionPerformed method that the Timer calls every 0.1 seconds. The first thing the method does is to determine whether the laser is in contact with the airplane. If it is, then the value of the elapsedTime field is incremented. If the laser loses contact with the airplane, the elapsedTime field is reset to zero.

```
  // This ActionListener is called by the Timer.
  class GameUpdater implements ActionListener {
    public void actionPerformed(ActionEvent event) {

      // Set the time increment.
      double timeIncrement = 0.1;

      // If the laser is hitting the airplane, increment
      // the elapsedTime variable. If not, set the elapsedTime
      // variable to zero.
      if ( laserX > airplaneX && laserX < airplaneX + airplaneIconWidth &&
           laserZ > 10 && laserZ < 10 + airplaneIconHeight ) {
        elapsedTime = elapsedTime + timeIncrement;
      }
      else {
        elapsedTime = 0.0;
      }
```

The airplane moves horizontally across the screen at a constant speed of 20 *pixels/s*. The new location of the airplane is determined and the GUI display is updated.

```
// The airplane cartoon moves across the screen at a
// constant velocity of 20 pixels/second.
airplaneX = airplaneX + 20.0*timeIncrement;

// Update the display.
updateDisplay();
```

If the elapsed time that the laser has been in contact with the airplane exceeds the time required to absorb 10,000 *J/cm²*, then the airplane explodes. The simulation stops and, as shown in Figure 14-9, an explosion cartoon is shown on the screen.

```
// If the time that the laser has been on the airplane is
// greater than the necessary time to destroy the airplane,
// stop the simulation.
if ( elapsedTime > explosionTime ) {
  gameTimer.stop();
}
```

Figure 14-9. *The laser has destroyed the airplane.*

Creating Your Own Laser Systems

Up to this point in this chapter, we have been discussing the performance and characteristics of laser systems that are either in existence today or are projected to be built in the next few years. But you as a game programmer don't have to be restricted by what is possible at this point and time. Like all other technology, laser technology will improve dramatically in the coming years. There is no reason to think that at some point in the future backpack-sized 1 *MW* combat lasers won't be available, and there is no reason why you can't place such a device into one of your game simulations.

The key issues with "personal" military lasers are how to generate the required power and how to keep them cool enough so they don't cook the person carrying it. As long as you can come up with a reasonably plausible technology explanation to accomplish those two objectives, your futuristic laser systems should pass the "realism" test. Then again, you may say "to heck with realism" and arm your soldiers with 10 megawatt CO_2 laser rifles. In any case, if you do decide to create your own laser systems, you can still use Equations (14.5) and (14.6) to estimate the damage caused by them.

Laser Visual Effects

The last topic this chapter will cover is how to show laser beams in your game simulations. This may come as a shock to you, but Hollywood takes some liberties when depicting laser beams. A laser beam is never visible in the vacuum of space, so the stirring battle scenes in movies like *Star Wars* would not look that way in real life. The laser beam would be apparent only if it caused the surface of a spaceship, starfighter, or whatever to glow from the buildup of heat.

A laser beam is generally not visible when it travels through air either and usually can only be seen if it passes through dust, smoke, mist, or fog. Very high-intensity laser beams can be visible in clear air due to effects known as **Rayleigh scattering** or **Raman scattering**. Most high-energy military lasers emit infrared radiation rather than visible light, so you wouldn't be able to see those types of laser beams under normal circumstances. Another thing to keep in mind is that laser beams travel at the speed of light. You will never see the beam traveling from point A to point B. Instead, to a human observer the beam will traverse the distance from laser to target instantaneously.

Now, of course, it is a lot more fun and interesting in games if the laser beams are visible, so this may be an instance when you want to ignore the proper physics to achieve a desired visual effect. If the setting for your game is the surface of a dusty planet and/or if the combatants are using extremely powerful lasers, you can probably show the laser beams with a clear conscience. Even if your game is set in the emptiness of outer space, your users would probably forgive you if you showed the laser beams.

Summary

In this chapter, we looked briefly at the world of lasers. Starting with a little historical background, we discussed the structure of atoms and how particles of light called photons are generated. We saw that under the right circumstances a laser beam can be generated where all the photons have the same wavelength and are traveling in the same direction. We discussed the different types of lasers including military lasers that can destroy missiles and airplanes.

Some of the other things this chapter covered include the following:

- How a photon can strike an atom and stimulate the emission of an identical photon traveling in the same direction.

- How lasers can be created from many different substances—gases, liquids, and solids.

- The power, range, weight, and other specifications of land-, air-, and space-based military laser systems.

- How laser damage is assessed based on the total energy absorbed by the target. The absorption is a factor of the laser power, the area of the beam, an absorption factor, and the duration of the beam.

- That laser beams are not visible in space and usually aren't visible in air either, but you may choose to ignore this fact to make your laser-based games more fun to watch.

References

1. C. R. Nave, "Laser Types," http://hyperphysics.phy-astr.gsu.edu/hbase/optmod/lastyp.html#c1.

2. M. Weschler, "How Lasers Work," http://science.howstuffworks.com/laser8.htm.

3. "ABL YAL 1A Airborne Laser," www.airforce-technology.com/projects/abl/.

4. "Space Based Laser," www.fas.org/spp/starwars/program/sbl.htm.

5. "Laser Weapon Technology," www.ifa.au.dk/~balling/alp/starwars.pdf.

6. B. Anderberg and Wolbarsht, M., *Laser Weapons: The Dawn of a New Military Age*, Plenum Press, 1992.

CHAPTER 15

■ ■ ■

Probabilistic and Monte Carlo Simulations

As you probably know, there is a lot of randomness in the world. If a golfer hits a golf ball ten times, chances are it will wind up in ten different locations when it comes to rest. At the same time, there is often some structure to the randomness. While the temperature on any given day will vary, the average maximum daily temperature for a given time of year will probably remain more or less the same.

The field of probability attempts to mathematically model the likelihood that random events will occur in order to predict the behavior of a larger system. This chapter will provide an introduction to the world of probability and how to incorporate it into your game programs. Probability techniques will allow you to build structured randomness into your games. Rather than having a flight of arrows all travel along the same trajectory, which would be boring and fake-looking, probability techniques can give the arrows a range of initial velocities and flight angles for a much more realistic appearance. Probability techniques can be used to vary the speeds of snowmobiles in a snowmobile game, how far golf balls are hit in a golf game, and many other things besides.

This chapter will be more mathematically oriented than most of the previous ones, but the concepts discussed here can be (and are) used to model physical phenomena. After studying the basics of the mathematical expressions that model probability, we will look at Monte Carlo simulations, which use probability theory and random number generation to model complex systems by modeling the behavior of the individual subcomponents that make up the system. For example, the movement of traffic through a busy intersection might be simulated by modeling the movements of the individual cars, trucks, and motorcycles.

This chapter will only scratch the surface of Monte Carlo and probabilistic simulations. A lot of people have spent a lot of time over the years developing very sophisticated and complicated probabilistic techniques that are beyond the scope of this book, but this chapter will introduce you to the subject and show how probability concepts can be applied to game programming simulations by modeling the charge of a company of soldiers. Specific topics covered in this chapter include the following:

- How to generate random numbers to use in your game simulations

- Probability functions and how they can be used to incorporate "structured randomness" into a game simulation

- The Gaussian distribution—the most commonly used probability function

- Other probability functions

- Monte Carlo simulations and how they can be used to simulate the behavior of large systems

- How Monte Carlo simulations can be used to simulate crowd behavior

- Using Monte Carlo techniques to compute mathematical functions

Let's start the discussion with a brief overview of random number generation.

Random Number Generation

One thing that most Monte Carlo and probabilistic simulations (and many other game programming applications as well) need is a way to generate random numbers. Fortunately, every modern programming language provides a way to generate them. The examples in this book are written in Java, so we will discuss a little bit how the Java language supports random number generation. Most other languages use a similar approach to generating random numbers.

Java actually provides several ways to generate random numbers. The most versatile approach, and the one used for the examples in this chapter, makes use of the Random class from the java.util package. The Random class can provide the random numbers as integer, floating-point, or byte numbers. The range over which the random numbers are generated can also be specified.

Like most programming languages, random numbers generated by the Random class aren't truly random. Instead, the Random class uses what is called a **linear congruential algorithm** to generate a sequence of "pseudo" random numbers. Don't worry about the details of the linear congruential algorithm; the important point is that the sequence of numbers generated by the algorithm is deterministic, meaning that if the sequence is entered at the same starting point, known as the **seed**, the subsequent series of numbers in the sequence will be the same.

The key to getting a different sequence of random numbers every time is to provide the Random object with a different starting point, or seed, every time it is used. The Java language provides for this feature automatically. When a Random object is created using the default constructor:

```
Random randomObject = new Random();
```

the resulting Random object is given a seed equal to the number of milliseconds that have elapsed since January 1, 1970 (no kidding!). As long as the Random objects are created at different times, they will have different seeds and will generate different sequences of random numbers.

Let's write a short program that demonstrates the Random class in action. The class is called RandomDemo, and its code listing is shown next. The nextDouble method is called on the Random object to return a double precision floating-point number between 0 and 1.

```
import java.util.Random;

public class RandomDemo
{
  public static void main(String args[]) {
```

```
// Create a Random object to generate random
// numbers. The object is seeded with the time
// in milliseconds since Jan 1, 1970.
Random random = new Random();

double x;

// Retrieve 8 floating-point random numbers
// between 0 and 1.
for(int j=0; j<8; ++j) {
  x = random.nextDouble();
  System.out.println("x = "+x);
  }
 }
}
```

Here is a typical output when the RandomDemo code is executed. Because the Random object will have a different seed each time the program is run, the output from the code will be different each time as well.

```
x = 0.12166301656769563
x = 0.7040696650721638
x = 0.6330423734744145
x = 0.7314827972956403
x = 0.299262216506065
x = 0.8277476660869888
x = 0.02470816980699342
x = 0.9898129649660115
```

To see that the random numbers generated by the Random class aren't truly random, change the line that creates the Random object so that the seed is set to a fixed value.

```
Random random = new Random(1234);
```

When this modification is made, the Random object will always use the same starting point, and the same sequence of "random" numbers is returned every time the code is run.

Probability Functions

A **probability function**, also referred to as a **probability distribution function**, is simply a mathematical expression or geometrical curve that models the probability of an event occurring within certain dimensions. Probability functions are used in scientific modeling all the time. The energy state of an individual air molecule in a volume of air is characterized using a probability function. There are many cases in game programming where probability functions could be used as well. For example, a probability function might be used to model the speed of the opponent snowmobiles in a snowmobile race game.

Usually a probability function is defined by a mathematical equation. In some situations there is an equal likelihood of all possible outcomes. For example, when a die is rolled there is an equal chance that any of the six sides will be face up. In this case, the probability function is a straight line.

$$f(x) = 0.166667 \tag{15.1}$$

What Equation (15.1) says is that there is an equal probability, $f(x)$, of any of the six possible die rolls and that the probability of any particular value being rolled is equal to 1/6. There are a lot of times when you will not want to assign an equal likelihood to all possible outcomes. If you were designing a poker simulation, for example, and the computer player started with a pair of jacks, you might want to have the computer raise 60% of the time, check 30% of the time, and fold 10% of the time. If a flight of arrows from a group of bowmen were being simulated, it might be desirable to give the arrows different initial velocities and flight angles. In these situations, a nonlinear probability function is used.

Figure 15-1 shows a typical nonlinear probability function. The vertical axis displays the probability that a given value of x will occur. For the purposes of this discussion, what x represents is irrelevant. The probability function in Figure 15-1 is symmetric, but symmetry is not required and some probability functions are asymmetric. The peak of the probability function is called the **mean**. It is the most likely value of the quantity x. In Figure 15-1, there is a 40% chance that x will have the mean value of 10.

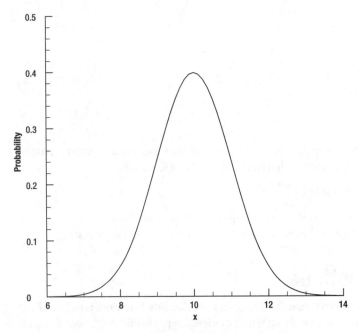

Figure 15-1. *A typical probability function*

In looking at Figure 15-1, it is clear that some values of x are more likely than others. It is much more likely, for example, that x will have a value between 9 and 11 than it is for x to have a value greater than 12. The width of the profile is defined by a quantity called the **standard deviation**, which we will discuss in more detail a little later in the chapter.

There are some other important plots that can be generated based on a given probability function. For example, the **cumulative distribution function** is the integral (the area under the curve) of the probability function. The cumulative distribution function indicates the probability that a variable value will be less than or equal to a given value. The cumulative distribution function corresponding to Figure 15-1 is shown in Figure 15-2. The probability at $x = 11$ is 0.841, meaning that based on the probability function shown in Figure 15-1 there is an 84.1% chance the value of x will be less than or equal to 11. The cumulative probability of the mean value is always 0.5. In this example, the mean value is 10, and that is the value in Figure 15-2 at which the cumulative probability is 0.5.

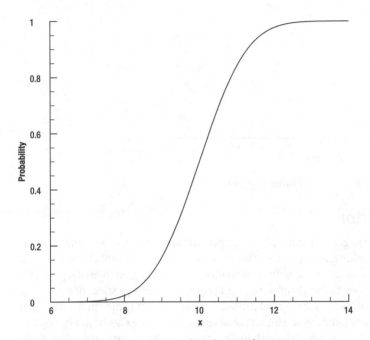

Figure 15-2. *A typical cumulative distribution function*

Here is a typical game programming probability question: in a horse racing simulation where the speed of the horses is given by a probability distribution function, what will be the speed of a randomly selected horse? The probability or cumulative distribution functions won't provide the answer to this type of question. To obtain information of this nature, we need to look at the **inverse cumulative distribution function**, also known as the **percent point function** or PPF. The inverse cumulative distribution function for the curve shown in Figure 15-2 is shown in Figure 15-3. The probability is now on the horizontal axis, and the corresponding value of x, now the dependent variable, is on the vertical axis.

Here is the process for how to use the inverse cumulative distribution function to solve the horse speed problem mentioned previously. Assume that Figure 15-3 represents the inverse cumulative distribution function for the speed of a horse in *m/s*. A random number generator can be used to produce a number between 0 and 1, representing a probability value. The speed of a randomly selected horse can be found from the probability value and the curve shown in Figure 15-3.

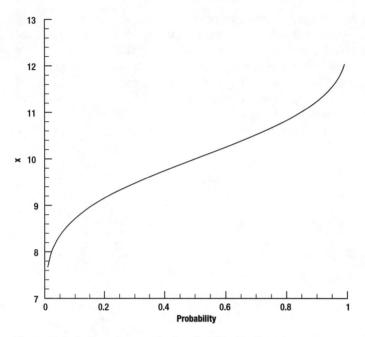

Figure 15-3. *An inverse cumulative distribution function*

Gaussian Distribution

Now that we've learned some general concepts about probability functions, let's learn about some specific types of probability functions. One of the most commonly used probability functions is the **Gaussian** or normal distribution. Gaussian distributions are widely used to model physical effects for subjects ranging from the height of women in Europe to the energy states of molecules.

The Gaussian distribution is a symmetrical probability function. It is the "Bell curve" that your teachers have been threatening you with all these years. The curve shown in Figure 15-1 is a Gaussian distribution. It is a symmetric probability function. The curve to the left of the mean value has the same shape as the curve to the right of the mean value. The Gaussian distribution function is called a normal distribution because the area under the probability function curve is equal to 1. An exponential mathematical equation characterizes the Gaussian distribution.

$$f(x) = \frac{1}{\sqrt{2\pi\sigma^2}} e^{-\frac{(x-\mu)^2}{2\sigma^2}} \qquad (15.2)$$

The quantity μ is the mean value of the function. As described in the previous section, it is the peak of the probability function curve. The quantity $f(x)$ is the probability for a given value of x. The quantity σ is called the **standard deviation** and is a measure of the narrowness or thickness of the profile. As shown in Figure 15-4, a lower standard deviation, $\sigma = 0.5$ for example, results in a narrower profile, meaning that most of the variable values will be close to the mean value. A larger standard deviation indicates a wider profile, which means there is a greater range of likely values.

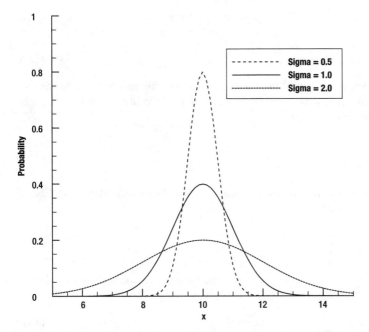

Figure 15-4. *The effect of standard deviation on the Gaussian distribution curve*

For the Gaussian and any other normal distributions, the standard deviation also indicates how close a value is likely to be to the mean value of the curve. If values are selected randomly according to the inverse cumulative distribution function, 68% of them will lie within a distance of one standard deviation from the mean value. Looking at the $\sigma = 0.5$ curve from Figure 15-4, 68% of randomly selected values will be between $x = 9.5$ and $x = 10.5$.

The distance relations extend further out as well. About 95% of randomly selected values will lie within two standard deviations from the mean and 99.7% will lie within three standard deviations. The 68-95-99.7 rule only applies to normal probability functions.

To obtain the cumulative and inverse cumulative distribution functions for the Gaussian distribution requires the integration of Equation (15.2). Unfortunately, there isn't a closed-form solution to that problem. Several approximate relations have been developed over the years to compute the inverse cumulative distribution function for the Gaussian distribution. Abramowitz and Stegun[1] presented a relation that expresses the inverse cumulative distribution function as the ratio of two algebraic equations.

$$x = -t + \frac{2.515517 + 0.802853t + 0.010328t^2}{1 + 1.432788t + 0.189269t^2 + 0.001308t^3} \tag{15.3}$$

The quantity t is a function of the probability, p, which has a value between 0 and 1.

$$t = \sqrt{\ln\left(\frac{1}{p^2}\right)} \tag{15.4}$$

Equations (15.3) and (15.4) were used to generate the curve shown in Figure 15-3. Equation (15.3) assumes that the mean value is 0 and that the standard deviation is 1.

An x-value computed from Equation (15.3) can be converted to another μ and σ value using the following equation:

$$x' = \mu + \sigma x \tag{15.5}$$

For example, let's say we want to compute the x value for a Gaussian distribution with a mean value of 10 and a standard deviation of 2 when the probability value, p, is 0.4. The t value can be found according to Equation (15.4).

$$t = \sqrt{\ln\left(\frac{1}{0.4^2}\right)} = 1.354 \tag{15.6}$$

The x value for a Gaussian distribution with a mean value of 0 and a standard deviation of 1 can be computed from Equation (15.3).

$$x = -t + \frac{2.515517 + 0.802853t + 0.010328t^2}{1 + 1.432788t + 0.189269t^2 + 0.001308t^3} = -0.253 \tag{15.7}$$

The value of x for a Gaussian distribution with a mean value of 10 and standard deviation of 2 can be determined from Equation (15.5).

$$x' = \mu + \sigma x = 10 + 2*(-0.253) = 9.494 \tag{15.8}$$

Other Probability Functions

There are many other possible probability functions besides the Gaussian distribution, and a few of them will be briefly introduced in this section. The Gaussian distribution function is symmetric, but there may be times when you will want to use an asymmetric distribution function. For example, in a horse racing game, you may want it to be more likely that a horse's speed will be less than the mean value than the probability that it will be greater than the mean value.

Some of the other standard distribution functions that are used in science and physics include the **Poisson** and **exponential** distribution functions. Details on these functions can be found in the document "Distributions."[2] As a game programmer you don't even have to be limited by the "standard" distribution functions. Almost any function that is continuous between values of 0 and 1 can serve as the inverse cumulative distribution function for your simulations.

Monte Carlo Simulations

So far in this chapter, you have learned about random number generators and probability functions. These tools are the building blocks in creating probabilistic simulations known as **Monte Carlo** simulations. The fundamental idea behind Monte Carlo simulations is that the behavior of an overall system is equal to the behavior of the objects that comprise the system. A Monte Carlo approach would simulate an anthill by modeling the behavior of the individual ants inside the anthill. The behavior of the individual subcomponents of a system (for example, the ants) in a Monte Carlo simulation is governed by a probability function. While the Monte Carlo technique is numerical and statistical in nature, it can be used to model physical phenomena. Some of the physical processes Monte Carlo simulations are used to model include nuclear reactions, stellar evolution, and low-density airflow over spacecraft reentering the earth's atmosphere.

■**Tidbit** The term "Monte Carlo" was introduced by one of the pioneers of probabilistic methods, Stanislaw Marcin Ulam, in honor of his uncle, who was a gambler at the Monte Carlo casino.

Monte Carlo simulations are fairly recent; formal Monte Carlo simulations were first performed in the 1940s, but the theoretical background for the Monte Carlo technique evolved from earlier research. Nineteenth century scientists tried to estimate the value of functions by throwing darts at a picture of the function curve. In the early twentieth century, statisticians in British universities were working with experimental sampling methods that had some similarities to Monte Carlo.

The real driving force in the development of Monte Carlo methods occurred during World War II when research was being performed to develop the atomic bomb. Scientists realized that probabilistic techniques could be used to simulate neutron diffusion. Before long, Monte Carlo methods were being applied to solve complex equations in nuclear physics, and scientists soon discovered many other subjects to which Monte Carlo methods could be applied.

Monte Carlo methods can be used in game programming situations as a way of applying "orderly" randomness to a system of objects. The behavior of an individual object is random in that there will be more than one state the object can be in, and there is no way of knowing what that state will be at any given time. While the behavior of any given object is random, it is also orderly in that some states are more likely than others according to the nature of the probability function.

For example, let's say you were modeling the flight of arrows released from a company of bowmen. It would be pretty boring if the arrows all flew in exactly the same trajectory and landed on exactly the same spot. Using a probability function and a random number generator, the arrows can be given a distribution of initial velocities and flight angles. This process would give a much more realistic look to the flight of arrows.

The basic elements of a Monte Carlo simulation are system subcomponents, probability functions, and random numbers. A probability function is used to assign behaviors to the system subcomponents. The subcomponents might be air molecules, ants, or anything else for that matter. The probability values to apply to the probability function are normally obtained from a random number generator. The overall behavior of the system can be found by summing up, or integrating, the behavior of the subcomponents.

The concept of a Monte Carlo simulation may seem rather confusing to you, so let's go over a couple of simple applications for the Monte Carlo technique.

Using Monte Carlo Methods to Simulate Crowd Behavior

One good use of Monte Carlo methods in game programming situations is to simulate the behavior of a group of independent objects. The individual objects (people, cows, cars, etc.) can have characteristics (speed, weight, height, etc.) whose values are assigned based on a probability function. When the simulation begins, random numbers are generated, and these random numbers are used to model the behavior of the individual objects. The objects act independently of each other, but their behavior will tend to follow the trends defined by the probability function.

As an example, let's write a simple Monte Carlo simulation to model an army of soldiers charging across the field. The simplest approach to use in this situation is to have all of the soldiers move at the same speed, but this is not a very satisfying solution. In real life, unless the army is highly disciplined, the individual soldiers would move at different rates of speed. Some soldiers would simply run faster than others, and there might be some less-brave soldiers who slow down to let their comrades reach the enemy first.

A more elegant solution is to use a probability function to assign speeds to individual soldiers. A mean value can be assigned, say 5 *m/s*, and the actual speeds assigned to the soldiers will be some random distribution about the mean value. This approach results in a more realistic look for the charging soldiers.

We will implement the Monte Carlo approach to the speed of a group of charging soldiers in a game called the Soldier Game. The GUI display for the Soldier Game is shown in Figure 15-5. In a more sophisticated game, the soldiers might be displayed using realistic 3-D renderings, but here they are represented by + signs. Initially, the soldiers are lined up in two rows waiting for the order to charge. The GUI has text fields in which the user can specify the mean and standard deviation of the probability function curve. A Start button sets the soldiers in motion and a Reset button stops the simulation and returns the soldiers to their starting positions.

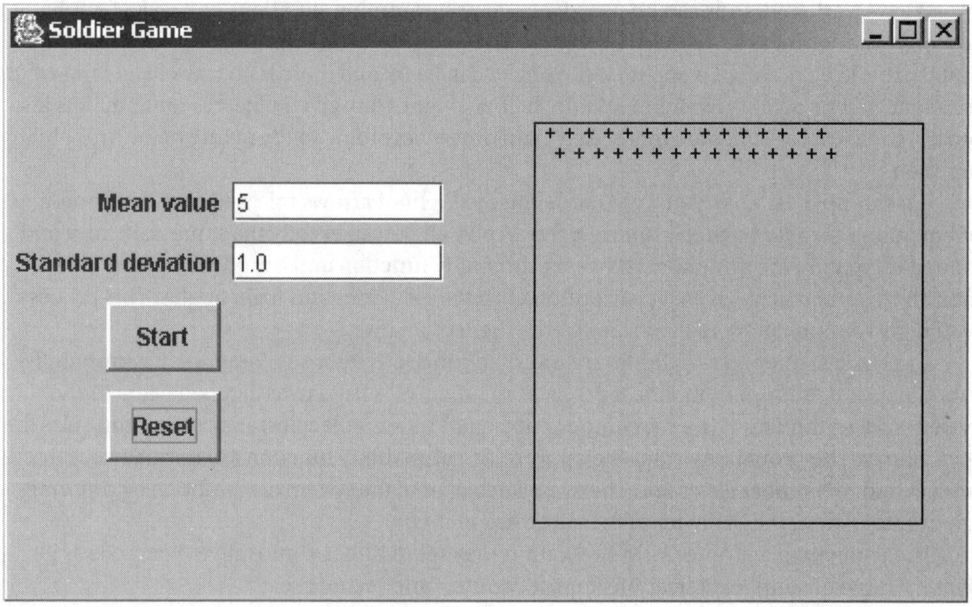

Figure 15-5. *The Soldier Game GUI display*

When the Start button is pressed, the soldiers begin to charge down the display. The rate at which an individual soldier will run at any given point in time will be determined using a Gaussian distribution function and a random number generator. Figure 15-6 shows a typical display partway through the charge. The line is no longer straight because the soldiers are acting independently and have different speeds.

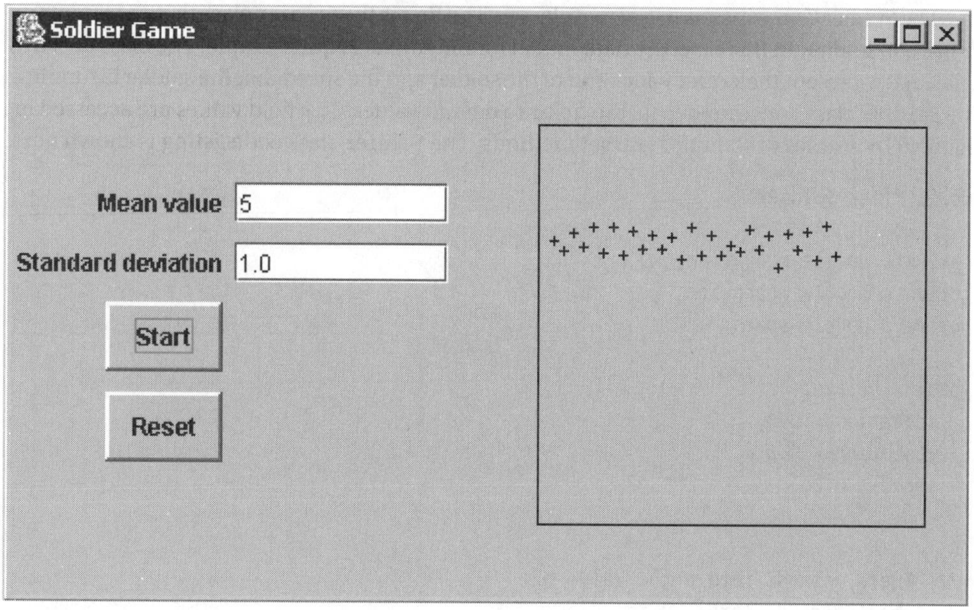

Figure 15-6. *The soldiers charge at different speeds.*

As the simulation progresses, the soldiers continue to charge and, as shown in Figure 15-7, the separation between them becomes more and more random. The speed of any individual soldier at any given time is determined according to the probability distribution function, so it is possible that the group of soldiers might bunch back up again during their charge.

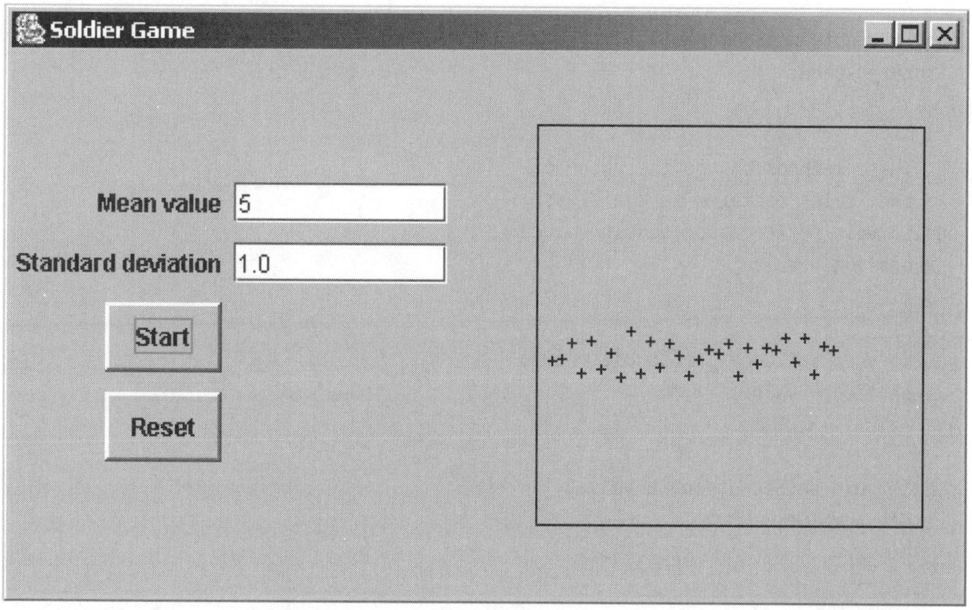

Figure 15-7. *As the charge progresses, the location of the soldiers becomes more and more random.*

The Soldier Game makes use of two classes. The first is the Soldier class that represents an individual soldier. In this case, the data model for the soldier is quite simple. The class declares fields that represent the x- and y-location of the soldier and the speed that the soldier is running. The Soldier class constructor sets the fields to default values. The field values are accessed or changed by a series of standard get/set methods. The Soldier class code listing is shown next.

```java
public class Soldier
{
  private double xLocation;
  private double yLocation;
  private double speed;

  public Soldier() {
    xLocation = 0.0;
    yLocation = 0.0;
    speed = 0.0;
  }

  //  These methods return the value of
  //  the fields declared in the class.
  public double getXLocation() {
    return xLocation;
  }

  public double getYLocation() {
    return yLocation;
  }

  public double getSpeed() {
    return speed;
  }

  //  These methods change the value of
  //  the fields declared in the class.
  public void setXLocation(double value) {
    xLocation = value;
  }

  public void setYLocation(double value) {
    yLocation = value;
  }

  public void setSpeed(double value) {
    speed = value;
  }

}
```

The GUI for the Soldier Game is defined in the SoldierGame class. As with the other GUI classes in this book, we won't go over every detail of the SoldierGame class but instead focus on the Monte Carlo aspects of the code. The complete SoldierGame class code listing can be downloaded from the Apress website.

The first thing the SoldierGame class does is to declare the fields used by the class. Besides the fields corresponding to the GUI components, the class also declares an array of Soldier objects. As was the case with some of the other game examples, a Timer object is used to slow the action down.

```
import javax.swing.*;
import java.awt.*;
import javax.swing.border.BevelBorder;
import java.awt.event.*;
import java.util.Random;
import javax.swing.Timer;

public class SoldierGame extends JFrame implements ActionListener
{
  //  Other field declarations not shown

  private Soldier soldier[];
  private SoldierUpdater soldierUpdater;
  private Timer soldierTimer;
```

The SoldierGame constructor initializes the GUI and Timer components used by the game. Thirty soldiers are simulated in this game. The constructor initializes the 30 individual Soldier objects by setting their initial x- and y-locations and speed. The soldiers are initially arranged in two rows at the top of the square display area.

```
public SoldierGame() {
    //  Create an array of 30 soldiers and set their
    //  x- and y-locations.
    soldier = new Soldier[30];

    for(int j=0; j<15; ++j) {
      soldier[j] = new Soldier();
      soldier[j].setXLocation(15.0 + j*10.0);
      soldier[j].setYLocation(10.0);
      soldier[j].setSpeed(10.0);

      soldier[j+15] = new Soldier();
      soldier[j+15].setXLocation(20.0 + j*10.0);
      soldier[j+15].setYLocation(20.0);
      soldier[j+15].setSpeed(10.0);
    }

    //  GUI and Timer component initialization not shown.
```

The Start button is associated with an event listener (the SoldierGame class itself). When the Start button is pressed, the actionPerformed method is called. This method calls the start method on the Timer object that was declared in the class.

```
// The actionPerformed() method is called when
// the Start button is pressed.
public void actionPerformed(ActionEvent event) {
   // Start the soldiers moving using a Timer object
   // to slow down the action.
   soldierTimer.start();
}
```

The SoldierGame class declares an inner class named GameUpdater that declares its own actionPerformed method. The Timer object is set up to call this actionPerformed method every 1 second. It is this method that computes the speed of each soldier and updates his position on the screen. The first thing the method does is to obtain the values of the mean and standard deviation from the text field components. It then creates a Random object to generate the random numbers needed by the method.

```
public void actionPerformed(ActionEvent event) {
     // Extract sample size number from text.field.
     double mean = Double.parseDouble(meanTextField.getText());
     double sigma = Double.parseDouble(sigmaTextField.getText());

     // Create a Random object to generate random
     // numbers. The object is seeded with the time
     // in milliseconds from Jan 1, 1970.
     Random random = new Random();
```

The actionPerformed method then updates the speed for each of the 30 soldier objects. The Random object is used to obtain a random number between 0 and 1. This number is treated as a probability and is used to obtain a speed according to Equation (15.3). The distribution of speeds will follow the Gaussian probability function.

```
     // Update the speed of each soldier based on a
     // Gaussian distribution and then update the
     // position of each soldier based on the new speed.
     double x;
     double grp1;
     double grp2;
     double speed;
     double t;
     double newY;
     double dt = 1.0;
     for(int j=0; j<30; ++j) {
        // Generate a random number between 0 and 1.
        x = random.nextDouble();
```

```
//  Find the speed corresponding to the random
//  number using the Gaussian distribution with a
//  mean value of 0 and a standard deviation of 1.
t = Math.sqrt( Math.log(1.0/(x*x)) );
grp1 = 2.515517 + 0.802853*t + 0.010328*t*t;
grp2 = 1.0 + 1.432788*t + 0.189269*t*t +
       0.001308*t*t*t;
speed = -t + grp1/grp2;
```

Equation (15.3) assumes that the mean value is equal to 0 and the standard deviation is equal to 1. The computed speed is corrected to the user-specified mean and standard deviation values using Equation (15.4). The setSpeed method is then called to update the value of the speed field in each Soldier object. Because the speeds are determined randomly using the Gaussian probability function, each Soldier object will have a different speed value.

```
//  Shift the converted speed to the proper
//  mean and standard deviation value.
speed = mean + speed*sigma;

//  Update the value of the speed field for
//  each Soldier object.
soldier[j].setSpeed(speed);
```

The soldiers are constrained to only move vertically, so the y-location of each Soldier object is updated based on the previous y-location and the speed of the Soldier object. The time step, *dt*, is set to be equal to 1 second. Once the y-locations have been updated, the GUI display is updated to show the new positions of each Soldier object.

```
//  Update the y-location of each soldier.
//  If they reach the bottom of the panel, they stop.
newY = soldier[j].getYLocation() + dt*soldier[j].getSpeed();
if ( newY > drawingPanel.getHeight() - 1 ) {
  newY = drawingPanel.getHeight() - 1;
}

soldier[j].setYLocation(newY);
}

//  Update the display.
updateDisplay();
```

As with some of the other example games in this book, when you first run the Soldier Game, you may have to press the Reset button to get the GUI properly rendered. Press the Start button and see what happens. The individual soldiers will move down the screen independently. Try changing the value of the standard deviation and see what happens. Increasing the standard deviation will increase the range of speeds that the soldiers are likely to have, resulting in a more chaotic charge. Lowering the standard deviation value essentially instills more discipline in the army in that soldiers will tend to run at more or less the same speed.

The graphics in the Soldier Game are primitive, but the probabilistic simulation of the physics of a group of charging soldiers is real. The soldiers are acting independently of each other, but the behavior of the group (for example, the speed of the group) will be more or less equal to the specified mean speed, and the distribution of speeds within the group of soldiers will follow the Gaussian probability function. Of course, modeling crowd movement is not the only way to use Monte Carlo techniques in your game simulations. There are many other applications, from weather prediction to combat resolution, in which you will want some "structured" randomness.

Using Monte Carlo Methods to Estimate Functions

Another thing Monte Carlo methods can be used for is to estimate the values of complex functions, and historically that was one of the motivations behind the development of Monte Carlo techniques. To show an example of how it is done, let's use the Monte Carlo method to compute the value of π. Consider a circle drawn inside a box as shown in Figure 15-8. The box is a square with a width and height equal to 1 (the units don't matter in this example). The circle has a radius equal to 0.5 and the origin of the circle is at x-y coordinates of (0.5, 0.5).

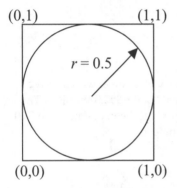

Figure 15-8. *To compute the value of π, start with a circle inside a box.*

Let's say that a series of random number pairs are generated with values between 0 and 1. These pairs correspond to x-y coordinates inside the box and/or sphere. The random numbers are generated such that there is an equal probability of any number, in other words that the probability distribution is a horizontal line. Every generated x-y point will lie inside the box, but only some fraction of the points will lie inside the circle. The ratio of the number of points inside the circle, n_{circle}, to the total number of sample points, n_{total}, is equal to the ratio of the area of the circle to the area of the box.

$$\frac{n_{circle}}{n_{total}} = \frac{\pi r^2}{4r^2} \tag{15.9}$$

If π is treated as the unknown, Equation (15.9) can be rearranged to yield an expression in terms of π.

$$\pi = 4\frac{n_{circle}}{n_{total}} \tag{15.10}$$

Like all Monte Carlo simulations, the accuracy of π as computed by Equation (15.10) increases with an increasing number of sample points. And because Monte Carlo simulations are probabilistic, a different answer will be obtained every time the simulation is run. The difference between subsequent simulations should decrease with increasing sample size.

Let's write a simple code that will use a Monte Carlo simulation to estimate π according to Equation (15.10). The GUI for the PiEstimator class is shown in Figure 15-9. It has two text field components—one allows the user to input the sample size to be used, and the other displays the computed value of π. There is a Start button that starts the simulation, and a Reset button that clears the display. On the right-hand side of the GUI is a panel that shows the circle and the square and where the sample points lie.

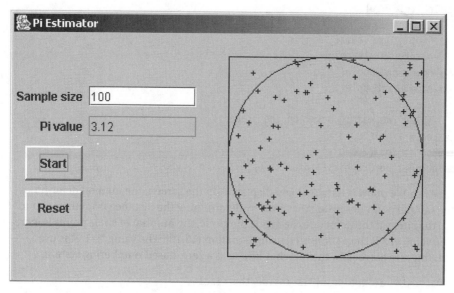

Figure 15-9. *A typical screen shot when the PiEstimator program is run*

We won't go over the entire PiEstimator class code listing, but we will discuss the actionPerformed method that is called when the Start button is pressed. The first thing the method does is to extract the sample size value from the text field. It then creates a Random object that will generate the random x-y coordinate points. The Random object is "seeded" by default with the current time in milliseconds. The seed will be different every time the method is called so the random number sequence will be different.

```
// The actionPerformed() method is called when
// the Start button is pressed.
public void actionPerformed(ActionEvent event) {
  // Extract sample size number from text field
  int sampleSize = Integer.parseInt(sampleSizeTextField.getText());

  // Create a Random object to generate random
  // numbers. The object is seeded with the current
  // time.
  Random random = new Random();
```

The `actionPerformed` method then creates the sample points using random numbers generated by the `Random` object. The location of the sample points is displayed in the panel on the right-hand side of the GUI display.

```
// Create the sample points. Generate
// two random numbers representing a data point.
// See if the data point is inside the circle area
// or not.
double x;
double y;
double distance;
int numInCircle = 0;
double piValue = 0.0;
for(int j=0; j<sampleSize; ++j) {
  // Generate an x-y point.
  x = random.nextDouble();
  y = random.nextDouble();

  // Display the sample point on the screen.
  int xLoc = (int)(200.0*x);
  int yLoc = (int)(200.0*y);
  drawingPanel.getGraphics().drawString("+", xLoc, yLoc);
```

Once the sample point is obtained and displayed on the screen, the method determines whether the sample point lies inside the circle by determining the distance from the point to the origin of the circle. If the point does lie inside the circle, the number of circle points is incremented. The value of π is then computed using Equation (15.10). The value "j+1.0" is used when computing π to correct for the fact that Java uses a zero-based numbering system.

```
// Determine if the point is inside the circle
// by computing the distance from the point to
// the center of the circle. If the distance is
// less than 1, the point is inside.
distance = Math.sqrt((x-0.5)*(x-0.5) + (y-0.5)*(y-0.5));
if ( distance <= 0.5 ) {
  ++numInCircle;
}

// Update the value of pi.
piValue = 4.0*numInCircle/(j+1.0);
piValueTextField.setText(""+(float)piValue);
  }
}
```

Play around with the `PiEstimator` program. Start by setting the sample size to a low value like 10. You'll notice that the results aren't all that accurate and that they vary quite a bit from run to run. Increase the sample size to 100 and then 1000 and see what happens to the accuracy and variability of the results. Try a really big sample size like 29987 and see what happens.

In effect what the `PiEstimator` class is doing is computing the area of the circle. Monte Carlo methods aren't limited to circles. They can be used to compute the area under (that is, integrate) any function. The `PiEstimator` class represents a simplistic Monte Carlo simulation in that the probability function was linear. The same technique could just as easily been applied with a nonlinear (Gaussian, exponential, etc.) probability function.

Summary

In this chapter we took a brief foray into the world of probability and how it can be applied to game programming. We discussed how probability can be used to determine the likelihood of random events. We looked at probability functions, cumulative distribution functions, and inverse cumulative distribution functions. We discussed a commonly known probability distribution function known as the Gaussian distribution and briefly touched on some other probability functions.

Some of the specific things we saw in this chapter include the following:

- How the mean and standard deviation define the peak and width of a probability function curve

- How the inverse cumulative distribution function can be used to assign values to variables based on a probability function curve

- How Monte Carlo techniques can be used to simulate crowd behavior by allowing each component of the crowd to act independently

- How Monte Carlo methods can estimate complex mathematical functions such as evaluating the value of π

References

1. M. Abramowitz and Stegun, I., *Handbook of Mathematical Functions*, Dover Publications, 1974.

2. Bourke, P., "Distributions," `http://astronomy.swin.edu.au/~pbourke/analysis/distributions/`.

INDEX

forums.apress.com